The AMERICAN'S CREED

I BELIEVE IN THE UNITED STATES OF
AMERICA AS A GOVERNMENT OF THE
PEOPLE, BY THE PEOPLE, FOR THE
PEOPLE; WHOSE JUST POWERS ARE
DERIVED FROM THE CONSENT OF THE
GOVERNED; A DEMOCRACY IN A REPUB-
LIC; A SOVEREIGN NATION OF MANY
SOVEREIGN STATES; A PERFECT UNION,
ONE AND INSEPARABLE; ESTABLISHED
UPON THOSE PRINCIPLES OF FREEDOM,
EQUALITY, JUSTICE AND HUMANITY FOR
WHICH AMERICAN PATRIOTS SACRIFICED
THEIR LIVES AND FORTUNES.

I THEREFORE BELIEVE IT IS MY DUTY
TO MY COUNTRY TO LOVE IT; TO SUPPORT
ITS CONSTITUTION; TO OBEY ITS LAWS;
TO RESPECT ITS FLAG; AND TO DEFEND
IT AGAINST ALL ENEMIES. — (AUTHOR-
IZED VERSION.)

ISMS

A Review of Alien Isms, Revolutionary Communism
and their Active Sympathizers in the United States

(Second Edition)

Compiled by the
National Americanism Commission of The American Legion
National Headquarters, Indianapolis, Indiana

1937

FOREWORD

THE Eighteenth Annual National Convention of The American Legion, held in Cleveland, Ohio, September 22 to 25, 1936, mandated what was, without a doubt, the most intensive drive to rid America of un-American propaganda ever undertaken by any organization. Realizing that sinister forces are expending greater effort than ever before to wreck the nation; and, voicing the sentiments of millions of our people, The American Legion has stated emphatically that all destructive alien "isms" must be driven from this nation.

In carrying out the mandates of the National Conventions, your National Americanism Commission has placed under way a number of educational projects, all of which are designed for the purpose of combating the menace of destructive alien "isms" and for the teaching of sound Americanism. The sustained effort of The American Legion as expressed in the mandates of its several National Conventions and formulated into constructive endeavor by its National Americanism Commission is without doubt the most effective program ever undertaken by any organization to rid America of un-American "isms."

It is believed, however, that the greatest need at this particular time is the enlightenment of all of our people to the menace of Communism. American citizens must be informed of the many ways in which the Communistic movement bores from within. They must know of the many subsidiary and co-operating organizations and of their activities. That is the purpose of this book.

It is vitally important to keep in mind at all times the fact that The American Legion is not a law enforcement body. Our mission is an educational one. It is to acquaint the public with the growth of subversive activities, and to recommend the legal cure; to show the public that Communism is attempting to undermine our government; that it is reaching into the schools, the churches, agriculture, and, in fact, into every phase of American life.

The compilation of this publication was placed under way during the year Frank N. Belgrano, Jr., served as National Commander of The American Legion and Ray Murphy served as Chairman of the National Americanism Commission. This revised edition comes in the continuance of the battle which Harry W. Colmery, as our National Commander for the year 1936-1937 is waging. It is hoped that in this more permanent cover in which a large part of this edition will be bound, this volume may find profitable employment in the libraries of our high schools, colleges and communities of the Nation. Frank N. Belgrano was indeed militant and outspoken in his fight against un-American activities. Ray Murphy, during his year as Americanism Chairman and during his administration as National Commander, was equally as militant and as outspoken in his battle against these agents of destruction. It was these three outstanding Legionnaires along with Stephen F. Chadwick, National Americanism Chairman for 1936 and 1937, who inspired the office of the National Americanism Commission with the determination to complete this book so that all Americans might know something of the "boring from within" tactics used by the advocates of "isms" in America, and because of that knowledge, join with The American Legion in the battle to crush, for all time to come, every destructive alien "ism" in this our beloved Nation.

> H. L. CHAILLAUX,
> Director.
>
> C. M. WILSON,
> Assistant Director,
> National Americanism Commission.

Even though this book is actually a history of un-American activities in the United States, we do not charge all individuals whose names are listed herein with membership in the Communist Party or with membership in Nazi or Fascist groups. Yet, their affiliations and sympathies are very closely defined in each case and are set forth to further show the boring from within tactics.

This book does not represent the opinion of a few Legionnaires. The readers will note that more than seventy-five per cent of the evidence produced here is either excerpts from United States Government reports of investigating committees or taken from material prepared by the Communist Party or its affiliated or sympathetic groups.

In publishing this Book the National Americanism Commission urges all who may read it to keep three fundamental facts clearly in mind. It is important to the success of our campaign against Communism and other alien "isms" that Legionnaires especially should do so.

They are:

1. Remember, no Legionnaire and no citizen has the privilege of police authority. Our policy must be one of waging a campaign of education by disclosing the truth as we find it. We must not take the law into our own hands. To do so would be equivalent to descending to the level of Communists.

2. The right of all nations to maintain their present form of government can not be denied. Our interest as Legionnaires and American citizens begins and ends with the attempts of those governments to force their principles upon America.

3. As an organization we do not oppose progress in government. The Constitution of the United States, our basic law, provides the orderly, American way for such progress. It reserves to the citizens the right to change that basic law as they, in their conscience and judgment, decide may be necessary. That traditional American principle must not be denied. The American Legion demands only that we shall proceed and progress in an orderly way, every member reserving to himself the inalienable right to support or oppose changes as he sees fit. *Political motives are neither intended nor implied in this expose.*

THE EDITORS.

FREEDOM OF SPEECH

The following is a pronouncement on the subject of freedom of the press by the Supreme Court of the United States in Milwaukee Publishing Company v. Burleson, 255 U. S. 407:

"Freedom of the press may protect criticism and agitation for modification or repeal of laws, but it does not extend to protection of him who counsels and encourages the violation of the law as it exists. The Constitution was adopted to preserve our government, not to serve as a protecting screen for those who, while claiming its privileges, seek to destroy it."

ANOTHER PRONOUNCEMENT

"652—Benjamin Gitlow, Plff. in Err.,

People of the State of New York.

"69 Law Ed. Oct. Term, 1924—U. S. 266-268.

"(Argued April 12, 1923. Restored to docket for reargument May 7, 1923. Reargued November 23, 1923. Decided June 8, 1925.)

"Anarchy—advocating overthrow of government—lawfulness.

"1. The advocacy for the purpose of bringing about the destruction of organized parliamentary government, of mass industrial revolts usurping the functions of municipal government, political mass strikes directed against the parliamentary state, and revolutionary mass action for its final destruction, necessarily implies the use of force and violence, and in its essential nature is inherently unlawful in a constitutional government of law and order.

"Constitutional Law—freedom of speech—scope.

"3. The freedom of speech and of the press, which is secured by the Constitution, does not confer an absolute right to speak or publish, without responsibility, whatever one may choose, or an unrestricted and unbridled license that gives immunity for every possible use of language, and prevents the punishment of those who abuse this freedom.

"Constitutional Law—punishment of abuse of freedom of speech.

"4. A state may punish those who abuse the constitutional freedom of speech by utterances inimical to the public welfare, tending to corrupt public morals, incite to crime, or disturb the public peace.

"Constitutional Law — punishing utterances endangering foundations of government.

"5. A state may punish utterances endangering the foundations of organized government, and threatening its overthrow by unlawful means.

"Courts—power over police statutes.

"7. The state is primarily the judge of regulations required in the interest of public safety and welfare, and its police statutes may only be declared unconstitutional where they are arbitrary or unreasonable attempts to exercise authority vested in the state in the public interest."

"That utterances inciting to the overthrow of organized government by unlawful means present a sufficient danger of substantive evil to bring their punishment within the range of legislative discretion is clear. Such utterances, by their very nature, involve danger to the public peace and to the security of the state. They threaten breaches of the peace and ultimate revolution. And the immediate danger is none the less real and substantial because the effect of a given utterance cannot be accurately foreseen. The state cannot reasonably be required to measure the danger from every such utterance in the nice balance of a jeweler's scale. A single revolutionary spark may kindle a fire that, smoldering for a time, may burst into a sweeping and destructive conflagration. It cannot be said that the state is acting arbitrarily or unreasonably when, in the exercise of its judgment as to the measures necessary to protect the public peace and safety, it seeks to extinguish the spark without waiting until it has enkindled the flame or blazed into the conflagration. It cannot reasonably be required to defer the adoption of measures for its own peace and safety until the revolutionary utterances lead to actual disturbances of the public peace or imminent and immediate danger of its own destruction; but it may, in the exercise of its judgment, suppress the threatened danger in its incipiency."

NATIONAL AMERICANISM COMMISSION

STEPHEN F. CHADWICK, *Chairman*
W. D. SCHWARTZ, JR., *Vice-Chairman*

To Serve Until November 1, 1937
Stephen F. Chadwick, Washington
Winthrop P. Robinson, New York
Harvey G. Wood, Florida
Joe Rabinovich, North Dakota
W. D. Schwartz, Jr., South Carolina

To Serve Until November 1, 1938
Clinton Brome, Nebraska
C. Richard Allen, New Jersey
Jeremiah J. Twomey, Massachusetts
Dan Sowers, Kentucky
Charles Ladden, Connecticut

To Serve Until November 1, 1939
Frank Estabrook, Idaho
James F. O'Neil, New Hampshire
Frank T. Sullivan, Kansas
Leslie P. Kefgen, Michigan
Arthur F. Lamey, Montana

MANDATES OF THE EIGHTEENTH ANNUAL NATIONAL CONVENTION AS THEY AFFECT THE CURBING OF UN-AMERICAN ACTIVITIES

AMERICANISM PROGRAM

"WHEREAS, It is very necessary that The American Legion develop a strong program of public service so that:

"1. Its members may feel that there is something definite for them to do.

"2. The general public may develop favorable attitudes toward Legion activities.

"And since the Americanism Program seems to offer a very wide scope of possible activities; therefore, be it

"Resolved, That Americanism be continued as the major program of The American Legion for the year 1936-37."

COMMUNISTIC YOUTH MOVEMENT

"Whereas, A loyal and patriotic citizenship is necessary to the preservation of the nation; therefore, be it

"Resolved, That The American Legion vigorously oppose the Communistic Youth Movement, especially as expressed in the Summer Camps for children, and the formation of like clubs in our schools and colleges."

COMMUNISM

"Whereas, The combat of Communism should be a major activity of The American Legion; therefore, be it

"Resolved, That The American Legion shall actively combat Communism, and in order to carry it out, the National Commander shall instruct and order all Posts in the organization to vigilantly combat Communism and all other organizations whose purposes are to undermine, sap, overthrow or otherwise destroy the principles of American Government.

"And to appoint committees to actively carry out the purposes of this resolution."

CO-OPERATION AGAINST COMMUNISTS

"Resolved, That we recommend and offer our co-operation to all those organizations in the United States who are now waging an active fight against Communism and other subversive movements."

FASCISM, HITLERISM, ETC.

"Resolved, That The American Legion continue its active opposition to the advocacy in America of Nazism, Fascism, Communism, or any other isms that are contrary to the fundamental principles of democracy, as established under the Constitution of the United States of America."

RECOGNITION OF SOVIET RUSSIA

"Whereas, The American Legion has heretofore opposed the recognition of the Union of Socialist Soviet Republics for the reason it was feared such recognition would be inimical to the best interests of this country, and

---

WHAT THE AMERICAN LEGION STANDS FOR

(Taken from the Preamble to the Constitution of
The American Legion)

"FOR GOD AND COUNTRY"

"TO UPHOLD AND DEFEND THE CONSTITUTION OF THE UNITED STATES
OF AMERICA"

"TO MAINTAIN LAW AND ORDER"

"TO PROMOTE PEACE AND GOODWILL ON EARTH"

"TO SAFEGUARD AND TRANSMIT TO POSTERITY THE PRINCIPLES OF
JUSTICE, FREEDOM AND DEMOCRACY"

"TO INCULCATE A SENSE OF INDIVIDUAL OBLIGATION TO COMMUNITY,
STATE AND NATION"

"Whereas, Prior to recognition of said government by the United States, promises were duly and solemnly made by the Soviet Government that Communist propaganda and activities emanating from Russia, directly or indirectly, would forthwith cease, and

"Whereas, Such activities have not ceased, but have on the contrary greatly increased; therefore, be it

"Resolved, That we urge the immediate rescission of recognition of the U. S. S. R. by the United States of America."

SUBVERSIVE DOCTRINES

"RESOLVED, That the President of the United States of America and the Attorney-General thereof be and each of them is hereby urged to use the full power of the Department of Justice and every other governmental agency to investigate the methods employed by and the activities of those who are now engaged in propagating and disseminating subversive doctrines and to prosecute and punish those responsible in all cases warranted by the evidence, including as a part of such punishment the prompt deportation of all aliens convicted."

ISMS

"We recommend that each Post be encouraged and urged to make a study of the book called 'Isms,' published by the National Americanism Commission."

FINGER PRINTING

"We recommend the universal application of the finger printing system for identification of all persons in the United States. We further recommend the finger printing of all persons upon entry to the United States."

WHAT COMMUNISM STANDS FOR

(Taken from report 2290, U. S. House of Representatives)

"HATRED OF GOD AND ALL FORMS OF RELIGION"

"DESTRUCTION OF PRIVATE PROPERTY, AND INHERITANCE"

"PROMOTION OF CLASS HATRED"

"REVOLUTIONARY PROPAGANDA THROUGH THE COMMUNIST INTERNATIONAL, STIRRING UP COMMUNIST ACTIVITIES IN FOREIGN COUNTRIES IN ORDER TO CAUSE STRIKES, RIOTS, SABOTAGE, BLOODSHED, AND CIVIL WAR"

"DESTRUCTION OF ALL FORMS OF REPRESENTATIVE OR DEMOCRATIC GOVERNMENTS, INCLUDING CIVIL LIBERTIES, SUCH AS FREEDOM OF SPEECH, OF THE PRESS, OF ASSEMBLY, AND TRIAL BY JURY"

"THE ULTIMATE AND FINAL OBJECTIVE IS BY MEANS OF WORLD REVOLUTION TO ESTABLISH THE DICTATORSHIP OF THE SO-CALLED PROLETARIAT INTO ONE WORLD UNION OF SOVIET SOCIALIST REPUBLICS WITH THE CAPITOL AT MOSCOW"

NATURALIZATION REQUIREMENTS

"We rededicate ourselves to the high duty of citizenship as defined by our United States Supreme Court in the Schwimmer and other United States Supreme Court decisions wherein it is held that 'It is a duty of citizenship by force of arms when necessary to defend the country against all enemies,' and we abhor any consideration being given, particularly from any official of our government, to those aliens seeking United States citizenship concerning wherein there is any doubt about their willingness to bear arms in defense of the United States of America against all enemies.

"And we direct the officers of The American Legion to call to the attention of Congress any sanctions departing from this principle."

ALIENS

"We Recommend:

"1. The deportation of any alien who has been convicted of violation of any narcotic law of any State, Territory, insular possession, or the District of Columbia.

"2. The deportation of any alien who has been convicted in the United States within five years of the institution of deportation proceedings against him of a crime involving moral turpitude or a felony.

"3. The deportation of any alien who has knowingly encouraged, induced, assisted, or aided anyone to enter or try to enter the United States in violation of law.

"4. That all persons entering the United States illegally shall upon apprehension be immediately deported.

"5. That our border patrol of the Immigration Service be increased to the point that efficient service will reduce illegal alien entry.

"6. That designated persons holding supervisory positions in the Immigration and Naturalization service be given power to issue warrants of arrest for persons believed to be subject to deportation.

"7. The deportation of any alien who has been engaged in espionage for a foreign government.

"8. That the present quota for immigrants from those countries granted quotas be reduced by ninety (90) per cent.

"9. The deportation of all aliens who are anarchists or Communists, or aliens who are affiliated with any organization associated directly or indirectly with the Third Internationale.

"10. The administration of all alien and immigration laws enacted by Congress strictly according to the provisions of said laws. We recognize, however, the possibility of meritorious exceptions arising and the necessity of judicial interpretation of appeals from strict enforcement of the foregoing deportation provisions, and therefore recommend the power to exempt from deportation be vested in the Judges of the respective United States District Courts before whom all such appeals should be heard.

"11. Legislation providing that the ability to read English as well as to speak English be made a prerequisite to naturalization.

"12. That Congress appropriate sufficient funds to carry out the purposes of this resolution."

The program called for by the foregoing resolutions of The American Legion is one in which not only Legion members but every real American can participate. If the objectives set forth are to be reached all must co-operate. Every American should urge your representative or senator to support legislation to cure the disease of Communism in the United States.

Many people in our country believe that Communism is just another form of public hysteria and ridicule all attempts to combat it. The facts outlined in the pages of this book, however, will disprove this typical American attitude. Just a part of the story can be told in the short space of this book, but that part is accurate fact.

COMMUNISM COSTLY TO FREEDOM, *says Educator*

In an AP dispatch as of February 1, 1937, Dr. David Kinley, President Emeritus of the University of Illinois, characterized Communism today as "economically unsound, religiously atheistic, socially destructive, ethically indefensible and morally debasing." Dr. Kinley said he never had seen a Socialistic or Communistic plan which did not involve "deprivation of freedom."

LIST OF MOSCOW'S "INTERNATIONALS" AND THEIR AMERICAN SUBORDINATE BRANCHES[1]

The Moscow Third International

Communist International
Workers International Relief
Sovkino
Friends of the Soviet Union
(Profitern) Red International of Labor Unions
League Against Imperialism
Red Pioneers
Young Communist International
Peasants' International
Educational Workers League
Labor Sports International
International Red Aid
Intourist
Society for Cultural Relations Between Russia and Foreign Countries
International Union of Revolutionary Writers

Moscow's Agent in the United States

Communist Party of the U. S. A.
Workers International Relief
Amkino
Friends of the Soviet Union
Trade Union Unity League (21 principal Revolutionary Unions)
Anti-Imperialist League
Young Pioneers of America
Young Communist League of America
United Farmers League
Educational Workers League
Labor Sports Union (Hundreds of Workers Athletic Clubs)
International Labor Defense (10 or more sections; 200 or more branches)
Intourist (World Tourist)
American Society for Cultural Relations with Russia
Workers Cultural Federation (1,000 or more clubs and cultural organizations)
John Reed Clubs

You have seen the publicity in your local communities of one or more of the above listed groups, but it was easier for you to negligently proceed with your reading than to check the activity of that peculiarly named group, who were sponsoring a meeting in your home town. It is because of that spirit of utter indifference that Communism with all of its interwoven and interlocking branches has grown to the danger point in the United States.

-----

[1]Reference Wm. H. Green report on Communism.

HISTORY OF THE COMMUNIST PARTY

COMMUNISM

THE MOST recent Congressional investigation of the activities of the Communist Party and its affiliated organizations in the United States was made during the first session of the 74th Congress, by a committee of the House of Representatives, with Congressman John W. McCormick, of Massachusetts, as Chairman. Report No. 153 submitted to the Congress of the United States on February 15, 1935, is indeed educational and most interesting to any student of revolutionary radicalism. We submit for your study the following extended excerpt from that report.

"The resolution creating this committee was broad in its general terms instructing it to examine into all 'subversive activities.' Such an examination included an investigation into Communistic activities.

"This committee confined its investigation to that period of time following the thorough inquiry made by the special committee, of which our colleague, Mr. Fish of New York was Chairman. The inquiry made by Mr. Fish's committee was profound and comprehensive. In making its recommendations, this committee also gave consideration to the report made by the special committee above referred to.

"This committee took the testimony of several prominent Communist leaders.

"In December, 1934, it held a series of public hearings at Washington, D. C., at which representatives from various organizations and agencies that have recently been investigating Communism presented statements of their findings accompanied by one or more recommendations.

"The Communist Party of the United States is not a national political party concerned primarily and legitimately with conditions in this country. Neither does it operate on American principles for the maintenance and improvement of the form of government established by the organic law of the land.

"The nature and extent of organized Communist activity in the United States have been established by testimony and the objectives of such activities clearly defined. Both from documentary evidence submitted to the committee and from the frank admission of Communist leaders (cf. Browder and Ford, New York hearing, July 12, 1934) these objectives include:

"1. The overthrow by force and violence of the republican form of government guaranteed by article IV, section 4, of the Federal Constitution.

"2. The substitution of a soviet form of government based on class domination to be achieved by abolition of elected representatives both to the legislative and executive branches, as provided by article I, by the several sections of article II of the same Constitution and by the fourteenth amendment.

"3. The confiscation of private property by governmental decree, without the due process of law and compensation guaranteed by the fifth amendment.

"4. Restriction of the rights of religious freedom, of speech, and of the press as guaranteed by the first amendment.

"These specific purposes by Communist admission are to be achieved not by peaceful exercise of the ballot under constitutional right, but by revolutionary upheavals, by fomenting class hatred, by incitement to class warfare and by other illegal, as well as by legal, methods. The tactics and specific stages to be followed for the accomplishment of this end are set forth in circumstantial detail in the official program of the American Communist Party adopted at the convention held at Cleveland on April 2 to 8, 1934.

"The 'manifesto' and the 'resolutions' incite to civil war by requiring one class 'to take power' by direct revolutionary process and then assume dictatorship over the country in the manner followed by the Communists in the Union of Soviet Socialist Republics which is frequently mentioned as a guiding example.

"In pursuance of the revolutionary way to power, the program instructs members of the party to obtain a foothold in the Army and the Navy and develop 'revolutionary mass organizations in the decisive war industries and in the harbors.' The trade unions should be undermined and utilized as recruiting grounds for revolutionary workers. How faithfully these particular injunctions have been executed was demonstrated by Navy officers appearing before the committee and by officials of the American Federation of Labor.

"The American Communist Party is affiliated with the Third International, which was created by officials of the Soviet Government and is still housed in Moscow with governmental approval and co-operation. This affiliation is not one of general sympathy or broad uniformity of purpose and program; it is of a definitely organic character involving specific jurisdiction on the part of the governing body over the Communist Party of the United States.

"The executive secretary of the Communist Party of the United States testified to this committee that his party was 'a section of the Communist International'; that it participates in all the gatherings which decide the policies of the Communist International and sends delegates to the various conferences in Moscow. This admission is confirmed by the records available.

"Because it constitutes a virtual plea of guilty to charges that have been made against the Communist Party of America, we submit in full the testimony of Earl Browder, general secretary of that party. This testimony was corroborated by James W. Ford, a member of the executive committee of that party.

"TESTIMONY OF EARL BROWDER

"(The witness was duly affirmed.)

"The Chairman: Please give your name and address.

"Mr. Browder: Earl Browder, 35 East Twelfth Street. (N. Y.)

"The Chairman: Mr. Browder, will you state, please, your official position with the Communist Party in America?

"Mr. Browder: I am executive secretary of the central committee.

"The Chairman: Is there a central committee?

"Mr. Browder: There is a central committee.

"The Chairman: How many does that committee comprise?

"Mr. Browder: Twenty-nine members and six alternates.

"The Chairman: That central committee determines the policy of the party?

"Mr. Browder: Yes.

"The Chairman: And its affiliates in the United States?

"Mr. Browder: Between conventions.

"The Chairman: Between conventions. And the committee is elected at conventions?

"Mr. Browder: Yes.

"The Chairman: The convention is composed of delegates of the various organizations and affiliates throughout the United States?

"Mr. Browder: The convention is composed of delegates elected by districts at district conventions. District conventions are composed of delegates on a broader basis.

"The Chairman: And the National Communist Party—is that the name?

"Mr. Browder: The Communist Party of the United States.

"The Chairman: The Communist Party of the United States is affiliated with the Third International?

"Mr. Browder: It is a section of the Communist International.

"The Chairman: Is it in contact with the Third International?

"Mr. Browder: Yes.

"The Chairman: Constantly?

"Mr. Browder: I cannot say constantly.

"The Chairman: I mean, there is that contact?

"Mr. Browder: At intervals, yes.

"The Chairman: There is that contact between them?

"Mr. Browder: The American Party as a section of this Communist International participates in all of the gatherings which decide the policies of the Communist International.

"The Chairman: And send delegates to the Third International and their various meetings?

"Mr. Browder: Yes.

"The Chairman: In other words, it is an affiliate? Would you call it a regional party of the Third International? I would rather you would put it in your own language.

"Mr. Browder: To give an exact idea, you cannot draw a strict parallel with other party organizations, inasmuch as it is a world party; a world party.

"The Chairman: But the Third International is the central body?

"Mr. Browder: Yes.

"The Chairman: In April, 1934, was there a convention in Cleveland in the United States?

"Mr. Browder: That is correct.

"The Chairman: At that convention were certain resolutions adopted?

"Mr. Browder: That is correct.

"The Chairman: Have you copies of the resolutions, Mr. Browder?

"Mr. Browder: I have. This pamphlet contains all of the decisions; that is, the manifesto of the convention, the resolution on the present situation, and the tasks of the Communist Party, the lessons of economic struggles and tasks of the Communists in the trade unions, and a resolution on the winning of the working-class youth. These were the decisions of the Cleveland convention.

"The Chairman: On what page will we find the resolution that was adopted as a result of the passage of a similar resolution by the Third International in December, 1933?

"Mr. Browder: Pages 35 and 36 of this pamphlet.

"The Chairman: That is the only one we are really concerned with now. This here is on pages 35 and 36 in the pamphlet?

"Mr. Browder: Yes.

"The Chairman: That resolution was adopted in the convention?

"Mr. Browder: Yes.

"The Chairman: Is it identically the same resolution that was adopted at the Third International?

"Mr. Browder: The resolution of the Third International is not in its entirety reproduced here.

"The Chairman: Is not in what?

"Mr. Browder: In its entirety reproduced, but reference is made to the thesis of the thirteenth plenum of the Communist International, and this resolution declares that this fully applies also to the United States.

"The Chairman: Was this resolution adopted as a result of the action of the thirteenth plenum of the Third International?

"Mr Browder: No; I would not say that.

"The Chairman: In part?

"Mr. Browder: I would not say that.

"The Chairman: Well, in part was it adopted as a result of it?

"Mr. Browder: Well, I would say that it is fully in harmony with it and expresses its approval.

"The Chairman: Of the action of the Third International?

"Mr. Browder: Of the action of the thirteenth plenum.

"The Chairman: Were instructions received from the Third International with reference to the adoption of the resolution which they adopted in December, 1933?

"Mr. Browder: No instructions; no.

"The Chairman: You knew of a resolution being adopted in the Third International in December, 1933, did you not?

"Mr. Browder: Yes; this resolution was published by us in our official journal, the Communist, for February, 1934.

"The Chairman: On what page, Mr. Browder?

"Mr. Browder: It begins with page 131 of this issue and continues to page 144.

"The Chairman: May we have this?

"Mr. Browder: Yes.

"The Chairman: I introduce this as an exhibit, entitled, 'The Way Out,' and that part of it which is pages 35 and 36, I believe.

"Mr. Browder: Yes.

"The Chairman: And this book entitled 'The Communist,' and so much as relates to the pages which Mr. Browder has referred to.

(The documents were marked 'Exhibits 1 and 2').

"The Chairman: Both of these pamphlets will now be made a part of this record and will be marked 'Exhibits Nos. 27 and 28' of these hearings.

(The two pamphlets were marked 'The Way Out, Exhibit No. 27' and 'The Communist, Exhibit No. 28.')

"The Chairman: In January, did the executive committee of the Communist Party of the United States adopt a similar resolution to that which was adopted at the Cleveland convention?

"Mr. Browder: In January the central committee met and expressed its agreement with the resolutions adopted by the Communist International.

"The Chairman: So, in chronological order, what happened was in December, the thirteenth session of the Third International—

"Mr. Browder: That is right.

"The Chairman: Adopted a resolution, of which you were made cognizant?

"Mr. Browder: Yes.

"The Chairman: And of which movement the party in the United States was made cognizant?

"Mr. Browder: Yes.

"The Chairman: The executive committee in January, 1934, adopted a resolution based along the same lines?

"Mr. Browder: Declaring its agreement with it.

"The Chairman: Declaring its agreement with it?

"Mr. Browder: With the contents of that document.

"The Chairman: That action in January, is it fair to assume that that action in January was the result of the action of the thirteenth session of the Third International in the preceding month?

"Mr. Browder: I think it would be more correct to say that it was a result of the fact that the leadership of the party in the United States was in agreement with the action that was taken.

"The Chairman: I want you to put it your own way. I want you to put it in the way that it occurred, but one followed the other?

"Mr. Browder: One followed the other.

"The Chairman: And the action at the convention at Cleveland in April was also a follow-up of the action of the Third International and the agreement of the leaders in the United States thereto?

"Mr. Browder: I think your formulation will perhaps narrow the understanding of the Cleveland convention too much.

"The Chairman: I am talking only so far as this particular resolution is concerned, but will you explain that? The action of the executive committee was in between conventions?

"Mr. Browder: Yes.

"The Chairman: Of course, that matter came up, I assume, in the regular convention?

"Mr. Browder: Yes.

"The Chairman: The regular convention confirmed the action of the executive committee?

"Mr. Browder: That is correct.

"The Chairman: Have you official minutes as to those actions?

"Mr. Browder: The official minutes are the documents contained in the pamphlet which I gave you, plus the official publication of the reports made to the convention. This would include in addition to the—

"The Chairman: We are concerned only with that limited part, that part to which I have confined my questions, the resolution, and those are copies of the special actions taken by the Third International in the case of the resolution printed in The Communist and of the convention in the case of the resolution adopted there, printed in the pamphlet entitled 'The Way Out.'

"Mr. Browder: Yes; that is substantially correct.

"Perhaps I should add that if you want the complete record of the convention you should add to that the two additional pamphlets, the report to the convention on behalf of the central executive committee, the general report, and the special report on the Negro question.

"The Chairman: May we have these?

"Mr. Browder: Yes.

"The Chairman: Thank you.

"Mr. Dickstein: This central executive committee is located where?

"Mr. Browder: The members of the committee are in various places.

"Mr. Dickstein: But the central executive committee, this one?

"Mr. Browder: The seat of the central executive is in New York City.

"Mr. Dickstein: In New York City?

"Mr. Browder: Yes, sir.

"Mr. Dickstein: And that body represents almost all communities wherein your party exists in the United States?

"Mr. Browder: Yes.

"Mr. Dickstein: And when you talk about the report on the Negro question, what do you mean by that? What kind of a report is that?

"Mr. Browder: It is a discussion of the problems involved in the struggle for liberation of the Negroes from their special oppression in the United States.

"The Chairman: We do not want to go into any philosophy.

"Mr. Dickstein: That is all.

"The Chairman: Could you furnish or have furnished a list of the organizations in the United States which comprise the Communist group in the country?

"Mr. Browder: You will find a complete report of it in the report to the eighth convention.

"The Chairman: I see; thank you. I do not know of any other questions. Do you, Senator?

"Mr. Hardwick: I want to ask him one or two questions.

"This thirteenth plenum of the International was adopted at Moscow, was it not?

"Mr. Browder: That is right.

"Mr. Hardwick: When?

"Mr. Browder: In December of 1933.

"Mr. Hardwick: The New York committee, the central executive committee, I think you called it—is that right?

"Mr. Browder: That is right; central committee.

"Mr. Hardwick: Approved that resolution when?

"Mr. Browder: In January.

"Mr. Hardwick: In just about a month?

"Mr. Browder: About a month.

"Mr. Hardwick: Were you present when the resolution was approved?

"Mr. Browder: I was.

"Mr. Hardwick: How many members of the committee were present?

"Mr. Browder: I could not answer offhand. I would say—

"Mr. Hardwick: Well, I mean substantially. I do not care about whether you give it exactly or not.

"Mr. Browder: A substantial majority of the members of the committee.

"Mr. Hardwick: A substantial majority. Was there any fight over the adoption of the resolution?

"Mr. Browder: There was no difference of opinion.

"Mr. Hardwick: No difference of opinion. After which you had your national convention at Cleveland I believe, did you not?

"Mr. Browder: That is correct.

"Mr. Hardwick: When was that?

"Mr. Browder: In April.

"Mr. Hardwick: April, 1934?

"Mr. Browder: 1934.

"Mr. Hardwick: Were you there?

"Mr. Browder: I was there.

"Mr. Hardwick: Did that convention adopt a resolution approving this thirteenth plenum of the International?

"Mr. Browder: The resolution adopted in Cleveland substantially approves that resolution.

"Mr. Hardwick: All right. Were there many people at that convention?

"Mr. Browder: There were a considerable number. I can tell you the exact number of delegates, if you wish, by referring to the record.

"Mr. Hardwick: Yes; I would like to have it.

"Mr. Browder. There were 233 regularly elected voting delegates.

"The Chairman: Were there any alternates?

"Mr. Browder: There were some 237 additional nonvoting delegates.

"Mr. Hardwick: Something like—

Mr. Browder: Four hundred and seventy, to be exact.

"Mr. Hardwick: Did that convention endorse this thirteenth plenum in practical unanimity?

"Mr. Browder: Yes; complete unanimity.

"Mr. Hardwick: You have already indicated to the chairman where those things will all be found in the record?

"Mr. Browder: Yes.

"Mr. Hardwick: That is all.

"Mr. Dickstein: How many members do these 470 delegates represent?

"Mr. Browder: The regular voting delegates represent the dues-paying membership of the party.

"Mr. Hardwick: How many members?

"Mr. Browder: Which at that time was approximately 24,500.

"Mr. Hardwick: In the United States?

"Mr. Browder: Yes.

"Mr. Hardwick: That is all.

"Mr. Browder: The other delegates represented various nonparty organizations.

"Mr. Hardwick: That is, the 237?

"Mr. Browder: Yes; the 237.

"Mr. Hardwick: How much did they represent?

"Mr. Browder: The total number of the membership of which I could not state with any exactitude. It would run into some few hundred thousands.

"Mr. Hardwick: They are members of the Communist Party, too; the delegates or the alternates that represented in that convention?

"Mr. Browder: Not all; not all.

"Mr. Hardwick: They were representing the same principle as the 233 delegates? I mean the basic principle of communism?

"Mr. Browder: Certainly. Their presence at the convention is itself an indication that they support the general policies but they are not organizationally—

"Mr. Hardwick: Communists?

"Mr. Browder: Not all of them.

"Mr. Hardwick: I mean affiliated.

"Mr. Browder: Some of them are; some are not.

"The Chairman: Mr. Browder, when you say that there is an agreement, the fact that one succeeded the other, is it not fair to assume that in part the action of the thirteenth session of the Third International was a contributing factor, at least, to the adoption of these resolutions by the national committee at the convention?

"Mr. Browder: Certainly. There is a distinct political continuity throughout all these actions.

"The Chairman: I think it is fair to make this statement, so there will be no misunderstanding, Mr. Browder and Mr. Ford were called into executive session because they had to leave on important business, with the understanding that at the proper time, when the committee saw fit, his evidence could be made public. I want to make that statement so that there will be no misunderstanding at the public hearing, if and when the evidence is made public, to the fact that they are absent. It is with a distinct understanding with the members of the committee in this respect.

"Mr. Browder: I would like to make a request that if any of the questions involved in these statements are matters of controversy or become the basis for any conclusions of the committee, that we be permitted to give further evidence with regard to them.

"Mr. Hardwick: Let me say this, Mr. Chairman: It does not seem that is necessarily involved. We just want to show by you and Mr. Ford, too, if you think it is necessary, although I do not think it is necessary to swear Mr. Ford, that your committee in New York, your executive committee, passed a resolution endorsing this thirteenth plenum, and that your convention in Cleveland did the same thing. Those are just bare facts.

"Mr. Browder: Matters of public knowledge and record.

"Mr. Hardwick: Yes. They have been printed in the newspapers, but we thought we had better get some direct evidence.

"The Chairman: I can assure you gentlemen that the Chair will try to see that eminent fairness is extended to every person appearing before the committee, either in executive or public hearing. The committee is just asking questions on a very narrow field; and if there is any extension beyond that field, the committee will naturally see that the rights of every person are protected.

"You are executive secretary, as I understand it?

"Mr. Browder: General secretary.

"The Chairman: You have charge of all the records?

"Mr. Browder: I have charge of the national office.

"The Chairman: The national office?

"Mr. Browder: And I am an executive of the central committee.

"The Chairman: If later the committee desires, would you co-operate in every way possible with the examination of the records and the accounts?

"Mr. Browder: Yes.

"The Chairman: Thank you."

"TESTIMONY OF JAMES W. FORD

"(The witness was duly affirmed.)

"The Chairman: You live where, Mr. Ford?

"Mr. Ford: 27 West One Hundred and Fifteenth Street. (N. Y.)

"The Chairman: Are you an official in the Communist Party of the United States?

"Mr. Ford: I am an organizer of the Harlem section of the Communist Party, and a member of the centrtal committee.

"The Chairman: You have heard Mr. Browder's testimony?

"Mr. Ford: Yes.

"The Chairman: Do you agree with the testimony which he has given as to the adoption of the resolutions?

"Mr. Ford: Yes; the testimony.

"The Chairman: You agree in other respects about the continuity of the happening of the adoption of those resolutions?

"Mr. Ford: Yes.

"The Chairman: That they are all official actions of the thirteenth session of the Third International and of the executive committee and of the convention at Cleveland?

"Mr. Ford: That is as Mr. Browder has said, the continuity of the thirteenth plenum of the Third International.

"The Chairman: Yes; and that one followed the other?

"Mr. Ford: Yes.

"The Chairman: And that they are all official acts?

"Mr. Ford: Yes; in our convention.

"The Chairman: Are there any questions you want to ask Mr. Ford now?

"Mr. Hardwick: No.

"(Witness excused.)

"This relationship and responsibility was further demonstrated by the Communist Party itself in its central organ, the Daily Worker, on January 6, 1934. That publication reproduced on that occasion a telegram of congratulation and approval of Communist activities in the United States, signed by the presidium of the executive committee of the Communist International, received by the Radio Corporation of America and delivered from its branch office at 28 East Seventeenth Street, New York City. The text reads as follows:

"Daily Worker,
   "New York.

"Warmest fraternal greetings to the Daily Worker on its tenth anniversary. The Daily Worker has been the only American newspaper that has vigorously and boldly defended the interest of the workers and farmers, combating the treachery of the Socialists and trade-union bureaucrats, uncompromisingly fighting against white chauvinism and all forms of oppression of Negroes, as well as fighting decisively against imperialist war.

"The presidium of the executive committee of the Communist International welcomes the efforts of the Daily Worker to become a real collective agitator and organizer of the workers' struggle for the interests of the working masses, establishing close contacts with the masses in the factories, broadening its network of workers' correspondence, and securing a large number of workers in the task of supporting the paper and increasing its circulation, thus becoming the standard bearer in the struggle of the great masses of the American working class.

(Signed) PRESIDIUM E. C. C. I.

"Some of the instructions from Moscow which have had the approval of the Communist Party in this country are:

"1. In carrying out these tasks the Communists must utilize all legal possibilities to develop mass work and to link up legal and illegal work.

"2. There is no way out . . . other than the one shown by the October Revolution . . . confiscation of banks, of the factories, mines, transport, houses . . . stocks of goods . . . lands, . . . etc., etc.

"3. The plenum of the executive committee of the Communist International obliges all sections . . . for the revolutionary preparation . . . for the impending decision . . . battles for power."

THE FOUNDATION OF THE COMMUNIST INTERNATIONAL[1]

The compilers believe that it is vitally important that the reader, if he is to help in combatting the Communist menace, have some knowledge of the foundation of the Communist International. Therefore, the following is reprinted from the leaflet entitled "The Foundation of the Communist International," written by V. I. Lenin:

"In March of this year, 1919, there took place an international congress of Communists in Moscow. This Congress founded the Third, Communist International, the union of the workers of the whole world striving to establish Soviet power in all countries. The First International, founded by Marx, existed from 1864 to 1872. The Second International existed from 1889 to 1914, until the War." P. 3.

"Throughout the world the Union of Communists is growing. In a number of countries Soviet power has already been victorious. It will not be long before we see the victory of Communism throughout the world, the foundation of the World Federal Republic of Soviets." P. 3.

"The foundation of the Third, Communist International is the forerunner of the International Republic of Soviets, of the International victory of Communism." P. 25. Published in Pravda, March 6, 1919.

"Today, when the word 'Soviet' has become understood by all, the victory of the Communist revolution is certain. The comrades who are present in this hall saw how the first Soviet Republic was formed. They now see how the Third, Communist International has been formed. They will all see how the World Federal Republic of Soviets will be formed." P. 47.

"CONSTITUTION AND RULES OF THE COMMUNIST INTERNATIONAL

In order that the reader may have first-hand information of the constitution and rules of the Communist International, of which the Communist Party in the U. S. A. is a part, the following is reprinted from the pamphlet entitled "The Program of the Communist International":

"1. The Communist International—the International Workers' Association— is a union of Communist Parties in various countries; it is a World Communist Party. As the leader and organizer of the world revolutionary movement of the proletariat and the upholder of the principles and aims of Communism, the Communist International strives to win over the majority of the working class and the broad strata of the propertyless peasantry, fights for the establishment of the world dictatorship of the proletariat, for the establishment of the World Union of Socialist Soviet Republics, for the complete abolition of classes and for the achievement of Socialism —the first stage of Communist society.

"2. Each of the various Parties affiliated to the Communist International is called the Communist Party of .... (name of country), (Section of the Communist International). In any given country there can be only one Communist Party affiliated to the Communist International and representing its Section in that country.

"3. Membership in the Communist Party and in the Communist Interna-

---

[1]The above excerpts are exact quotations from the Communist publication, The Foundation of the Communist International, by V. I. Lenin.

tional is open to all those who accept the program and rules of the given Communist Party and of the Communist International, who join one of the basic units of a Party, actively work in it, abide by all the decisions of the Party and of the Communist International, and regularly pay Party dues.

"5. The Communist International and its Sections are built up on the basis of democratic centralism . . . (c) decisions of Superior Party committees to be obligatory for subordinate committees, strict Party discipline and prompt execution of the decisions of the Communist International, of its leading committees and of the leading Party centres.

"Party questions may be discussed by the members of the Party and by Party organizations until such time as a decision is taken upon them by the competent Party committees. After a decision has been taken by the Congress of the Communist International, by the Congress of the respective Sections, or by leading committees of the Comintern, and of its various Sections, these decisions must be unreservedly carried out even if a Section of the Party membership or of the local Party organizations are in disagreement with it. . . .

"6. In all non-Party workers' and peasants' mass organizations and in their leading committees (trade unions, co-operative societies, sport organizations, ex-service men's organizations, and at their congresses and conferences) and also on municipal bodies and in parliament, even if there are only two Party members in such organizations and bodies, Communist fractions must be formed for the purpose of strengthening the Party's influence and for carrying out its policy in these organizations and bodies.

"13. The decisions of the [1]E. C. C. I. are obligatory for all the Sections of the Communist International and must be promptly carried out. . . .

"14. The Central Committees of the various Sections of the Communist International are responsible to their respective Party Congresses and to the E. C. C. I. The latter has the right to annul or amend decisions of Party Congresses and of Central Committees of Parties and also to make decisions which are obligatory for them.

"15. The E. C. C. I. has the right to expel from the Communist International, entire Sections, groups and individual members who violate the program and rules of the Communist International or the decisions of the World Congress and of the E. C. C. I. . . .

"16. The programs of the various Sections of the Communist International must be endorsed by the E. C. C. I. . . .

"17. The leading organs of the press of the various Sections of the Communist International must publish all the decisions and official documents of the E. C. C. I. These decisions must, as far as possible, be published also in the other organs of the Party press. . . .[2]

"19. The E. C. C. I. elects a presidium responsible to the E. C. C. I., which acts as the permanent body carrying out all the business of the E. C. C. I. in the interval between the meetings of the latter. . . .

[1]E. C. C. I. is abbreviation for Executive Committee Communist International.

[2]This policy is carried out by the Communist Party in the U. S. A. by their official organ, The Daily Worker.

"21. The Sections must carry out the instructions of the permanent bureaus of the E. C. C. I. . . .

"22. The E. C. C. I. and its Presidium have the right to send their representatives to the various Sections of the Communist International. Such representatives receive their instructions from the E. C. C. I. or from its Presidium, and are responsible to them for their activities. . . . Representatives of the E. C. C. I. must carry out their commission in close contact with the Central Committee of the Section to which they are sent. They may, however, speak in opposition to the Central Committee of the given Section, at Congresses and Conferences of that Section, if the line of the Central Committee in question diverges from the instructions of the E. C. C. I. . . .

"The E. C. C. I. and its Presidium also have the right to send instructors to the various Sections of the Communist International. . . .

"23. Meetings of the E. C. C. I. must take place not less than once every six months. . . .

"24. Meetings of the Presidium[3] of the E. C. C. I. must take place not less than once a fortnight. . . .

"25. The Presidium elects the Political Secretariat, which is empowered to take decisions, and which also prepares questions for the meetings of the E. C. C. I. and of its Presidium, and acts as their executant body.

"28. The International Control Commission investigates matters concerning the unity of the Sections affiliated to the Communist International and also matters connected with the Communist conduct of individual members of the various Sections. . . . Audits the accounts of the Communist International. . . .

"30. Resignation from office by individual members or groups of members of Central Committees of the various Sections are regarded as disruptive of the Communist movement. Leading posts in the Party do not belong to the occupant of that post, but to the Communist International as a whole. Elected members of the Central leading bodies of the various Sections may resign before their time of office expires, only with the consent of the E. C. C. I. Resignations accepted by the Central Committees of Sections without the consent of the E. C. C. I. are invalid.

"31. The Sections affiliated to the Communist International must maintain close organizational and informational contact with each other, arrange for mutual representation at each other's conferences and congresses, and with the consent of the E. C. C. I., exchange leading comrades. . . .

"33. The Sections of the Comintern must regularly pay affiliation dues to the E.C.C.I.; the amount of such dues to be determined by the E.C.C.I. See page 29.

"35. The International League of Communist Youth (Communist Youth International) is a Section of the Communist International with full rights and is subordinate to the E. C. C. I.

"36. The Communist Parties must be prepared for transition to illegal conditions. The E. C. C. I. must render the Parties concerned assistance in their preparations for transition to illegal conditions.

[3]According to the "Daily Worker," members of the Presidium of the Communist International include: J. Stalin, Union of Soviet Socialist Republics; Bela Kun, Hungary; Fritz Hecker, Germany.

"37. Individual members of Sections of the Communist International may pass from one country to another only with the consent of the Central Committee of the Section of which they are members.

"Communists changing their domicile must join the Section in the country of their new domicile. Communists leaving their country without the consent of the Central Committee of their Section, must not be accepted into other Sections of the Communist International."

The Formation of the Communistic Party in the U. S. A.

In accordance with information contained on page eight of report 2290 U. S. House of Representatives, a call was issued for the organization of communist parties throughout the world and their adhesion to the Communist International immediately after the creation of the Communist International at Moscow in March, 1919. A call for a national convention for the purpose of organizing a Communist Party in America, mailed out of Chicago, Illinois, was issued July 7, 1919, over the signatures of the following individuals: Dennis E. Batt, D. Elbaum, O. C. Johnson, John Keracher, S. Kopnagel, I. Stilson, Alexander Stoklitsky.

The call to this meeting read as follows and is quoted from Volume I, Part I, of Revolutionary Radicalism, better known as the Lusk Report, page 739.

" 'Call for a National Convention for the Purpose of Organizing a Communist Party in America

" 'In this, the most momentous period of the world's history, capitalism is tottering to its ruin. The proletariat is straining at the chains which bind it. A revolutionary spirit is spreading throughout the world. The workers are rising to answer the clarion call of the Third International.

" 'Only one Socialism is possible in this crisis. A Socialism based upon understanding. A Socialism that will express in action the needs of the proletariat. The time has passed for temporizing and hesitating. We must act. The Communist call of the Third International, the echo of the Communist Manifesto of 1848, must be answered.

" 'The National Executive Committee of the Socialist Party of America has evidenced by its expulsion of nearly half of the membership that they will not hesitate at wrecking the organization in order to maintain control. A deadlock has been precipitated in the ranks of revolutionary Socialism by the wholesale expulsion or suspension of the membership comprising the Socialist Party of Michigan, locals and branches throughout the country, together with seven Language Federations. This has created a condition in our movement that makes it manifestly impossible to longer delay the calling of a convention to organize a new party. Those who realize that the capturing of the Socialist Party as such is but an empty victory will not hesitate to respond to this call and leave the 'Right' and 'Center' to sink together with their 'revolutionary' leaders.

" 'The majority of the delegates to the Left Wing Conference in New York meekly neglected to sever their connections with the reactionary National Executive Committee. Rendered impotent by the conflicting emotions and lack of understanding present they continued to mark time as Centrists in the wake of the

Right. Their policy is one of endeavor to capture the old party machinery and the stagnant elements who have been struggling for a false unity and who are only ready to abandon the ship when it sinks beneath the waves of reaction.

" 'This condition confronting the minority delegates representing the following organizations—Socialist Party of Michigan; Left Wing State Convention of Minnesota; Locals, Buffalo; Chicago; Union Local, N. J.; Cudahy, Wis.; Rochester, N. Y.; Rockford, Ill.; Kenosha, Wis.; New York; Providence; Nanticoke, Pa.; Milwaukee, Wis.; Boston, Mass.; Polish, Lettish, Russian, Jewish, Lithuanian, Esthonian Federations—at the Left Wing Conference has been met by this call for the organization of a Communist Party in America.

" 'No other course is possible, therefore, we, the minority delegates at the Left Wing Conference, call a convention to meet in the city of Chicago on September 1, 1919, for the purpose of organizing a Communist Party in America.

" 'This party will be founded upon the following principles:

" '1. The present is the period of the dissolution and collapse of the whole capitalist world system; which will mean the complete collapse of world culture, if capitalism with its unsolvable contradictions is not replaced by Communism.

" '2. The problem of the proletariat consists in organizing and training itself for the conquest of the powers of the state. This conquest of power means the replacement of the state machinery of the bourgeoisie with a new proletarian machinery of government.

" '3. This new proletarian state must embody the dictatorship of the proletariat, both industrial and agricultural, this dictatorship constituting the instrument for the taking over of property used for exploiting the workers, and for the reorganization of society on a communist basis.

" 'Not the fraudulent bourgeois democracy—the hypocritical form of the rule of the finance-oligarchy, with its purely formal equality—but proletarian democracy based on the possibility of actual realization of freedom for the working masses; not capitalist bureaucracy, but organs of administrations which have been created by the masses themselves, with the real participation of these masses in the government of the country and in the activity of the communistic structure —this should be the type of the proletarian state. The workers' councils and similar organizations represent its concrete form.

" '4. The dictatorship of the proletariat shall carry out the abolition of private property in the means of production and distribution, by transfer to the proletarian state under Socialist administration of the working class; nationalization of the great business enterprises and financial trust.

" '5. The present world situation demands the closest relation between the revolutionary proletariat of all countries.

" '6. The fundamental means of the struggle for power is the mass action of the proletariat, a gathering together and concentration of all its energies; whereas methods such as the revolutionary use of burgeois parliamentarism are only of subsidiary significance.

" 'In those countries in which the historical development has furnished the opportunity, the working class has utilized the regime of political democracy for its organization against capitalism. In all countries where the conditions for a workers' revolution are not yet ripe, the same process will go on.

" 'But within the process the workers must never lose sight of the true character of bourgeois democracy. If the finance-oligarchy considers it advantageous to veil its deeds of violence behind parliamentary votes, then the capitalist power has at its command in order to gain its ends, all the traditions and attainments of former centuries of upper class rule, demagogism, persecution, slander, bribery, calumny and terror. To demand of the proletariat that it shall be content to yield itself to the artificial rules devised by its mortal enemy, but not observed by the enemy, is to make a mockery of the proletarian struggle for power—a struggle which depends primarily on the development of separate organs of the working-class power.

" '7. The old Socialist International has broken into three main groups: (a) Those frankly social patriots who since 1914 have supported their bourgeoisie and transformed these elements of the working class which they control into hangmen of the international revolution.

" '(b) The 'Center,' representing the elements which are constantly wavering and incapable of following a definite plan of action, and which are at times positively traitorous; and

" '(c) The Communists.

" 'As regards the social patriots, who everywhere in the critical moment oppose the proletarian revolution with force of arms, a merciless fight is absolutely necessary. As regards the 'Center,' our tactics must be to separate the revolutionary elements by pitilessly criticizing the leaders. Absolute separation from the organization of the 'Center' is necessary.

" 'It is necessary to rally the groups and proletarian organizations who, though not as yet in the wake of revolutionary trend of the Communist movement, nevertheless have manifested and developed a tendency leading in that direction.

" 'Socialist criticism has sufficiently stigmatized the bourgeois world order. The task of the International Communist Party is now to overthrow this order and to erect in its place the structure of the Socialist world order. Under the Communist banner, the emblem under which the first great victories have already been won; in the war against imperialistic barbarity, against the privileged classes, against the bourgeois state and bourgeois property, against all forms of social and national oppression—we call upon the proletarians of all lands to unite!' "

CONDITIONS OF ADMISSION INTO THE COMMUNIST INTERNATIONAL

Taken from "The Twenty-One Conditions of Admission to the Communist International," by O. Piatnitsky.

"1. The daily propaganda and agitation must bear a truly Communist character and correspond to the program and all the decisions of the Third International. All the organs of the press that are in the hands of the Party must be edited by reliable Communists who have proved their loyalty to the cause of the proletarian revolution. The dictatorship of the proletariat should not be spoken of simply as a current hackneyed formula; it should be advocated in such a way that its necessity should be apparent to every rank-and-file working man and woman, each soldier and peasant and should emanate from the facts of everyday life systematically recorded by our press day after day.

"The periodical and non-periodical press and all Party publishing organizations must be wholly subordinate to the Central Committee of the Party, irrespective as to whether the Party as a whole, at the given moment, is legal or illegal. That publishing organizations, abusing their autonomy, should pursue a policy that does not completely correspond to the policy of the Party, cannot be tolerated.

"In the columns of the newspapers, at public meetings, in the trade unions, in the co-operative societies—wherever the adherents of the Third International gain access, they must systematically and mercilessly denounce not only the bourgeoisie, but also its assistants, the reformists of every shade.

"2. Every organization desiring to belong to the Communist International must steadily and systematically remove from all responsible posts in the Labor movement in the Party organization, editorial boards, trade unions, parliamentary fractions, co-operative societies, municipalities, etc., all reformists and followers of the 'Center,' and have them replaced by Communists even at the cost of replacing at the beginning, 'experienced' leaders by rank-and-file working-men.

"3. The class struggle in almost all the countries of Europe and America is entering the phase of civil war. Under such conditions the Communists can have no confidence in bourgeois law. They must everywhere create a parallel illegal apparatus, which at the decisive moment could assist the Party in performing its duty to the revolution. In all countries where, in consequence of martial law or exceptional laws, the Communists are unable to carry on all their work legally, a combination of legal and illegal work is absolutely necessary.

"4. The obligation to spread Communist ideas includes the particular necessity of persistent, systematic propaganda in the army. Wherever such propaganda is forbidden by exceptional laws, it must be carried on illegally. The abandonment of such work would be equivalent to the betrayal of revolutionary duty and is incompatible with membership in the Third International.

"5. It is necessary to carry on systematic and steady agitation in the rural districts. The working class cannot consolidate its victory without the backing of at least part of the agricultural laborers and the poorest peasants, and without having neutralized, by its policy, a part of the rest of the rural population. Communist work in the rural districts is acquiring a predominant importance during the present period. It should be carried on in the main, by revolutionary Communist workers of both city and country only, who have connections with the rural districts. To refuse to do this work or to transfer such work to untrustworthy half-reformists is equal to renouncing the proletarian revolution.

"6. Every party that desires to belong to the Third International must expose, not only open social patriotism, but also the falsity and hypocrisy of social-pacifism; it must systematically demonstrate to the workers that without the revolutionary overthrow of capitalism, no international arbitration courts, no disarmament, no 'democratic' reorganization of the League of Nations will save mankind from new imperialist wars.

"7. The Parties desiring to belong to the Communist International must recognize the necessity of a complete and absolute rupture with reformism and the policy of the 'Center,' and they must carry on propaganda in favor of this rupture among the broadest circles of the party membership. Otherwise a consistent Communist policy is impossible.

"The Communist International unconditionally and peremptorily demands that this split be brought about with the least delay. The Communist International cannot reconcile itself to the fact that such avowed reformists, as Turatti, Kautsky, Hilferding, Hillquit, Longuet, MacDonald, Modigliani, and others should be entitled to consider themselves members of the Third International. This would make the Third International resemble, to a considerable degree, the late Second International.

"8. On the question of the colonies and oppressed nationalities an especially distinct and clear line must be taken by the parties in those countries where the bourgeoisie possesses colonies or oppresses other nations. Every party desirous of belonging to the Third International must ruthlessly denounce the methods of 'their own' imperialists in the colonies, supporting, not in words, but in deeds, every independence movement in the colonies. It should demand the expulsion of their own imperialists from such colonies, and cultivate among the workers of their own country a truly fraternal attitude towards the toiling population of the colonies and oppressed nationalities, and carry on systematic agitation in its own army against every kind of oppression of the colonial population.

"9. Every party that desires to belong to the Communist International must carry on systematic and persistent Communist work in the trade unions, in workers' and industrial councils, in the co-operative societies, and in other mass organizations. Within these organization, it is necessary to create Communist groups, which by means of practical and stubborn work must win over the trade unions, etc., for the cause of Communism. These cells should constantly denounce the treachery of the social-patriots and the vacillations of the 'Center,' at every step. These Communist groups should be completely subordinate to the Party as a whole.

"10. Every party that belongs to the Communist International must carry on a stubborn struggle against the Amsterdam 'International' of yellow trade unions. It must give all the support in its power to the incipient international alliance of the Red trade unions affiliated to the Communist International.

"11. The parties desiring to belong to the Third International must overhaul the membership of their parliamentary fractions, eliminate all unreliable elements from them, to control these fractions, not only verbally but in reality, to subordinate them to the Central Committee of the Party, and demand from every Communist member of parliament that he devote his entire activities to the interests of really revolutionary propaganda agitation.

"12. Parties belonging to the Communist International must be built up on the principle of democratic centralism. At the present time of acute civil war, the Communist Party will only be able fully to do its duty when it is organized in the most centralized manner, if it has iron discipline, bordering on military discipline, and if the Party center is a powerful, authoritative organ with wide powers, possessing the general trust of the party membership.

"13. The Communist parties of those countries where the Communists' activity is legal shall make periodical cleanings (re-registration) of the members of the Party organizations, so as to systematically cleanse the party from the petty-bourgeois elements who inevitably attach themselves to it.

"14. Every party that desires to belong to the Communist International must give every possible support to the Soviet Republics in their struggle against all counter-revolutionary forces. The Communist parties should carry on a precise and definite propaganda to induce the workers to refuse to transport munitions of war intended for enemies of the Soviet Republics, carry on legal or illegal propaganda among the troops, which are sent to crush the workers' republics, etc.

"15. The parties which up to the present have retained their old Social-Democratic programs must in the shortest possible time overhaul these programs and draw up a new Communist program in conformity with the special conditions of their respective countries and in accordance with resolutions of the Communist International. As a rule, the program of every party that belong to the Communist International must be ratified by the next Congress of the Communist International or by the Executive Committee. In the event of the Executive Committee of the Communist International failing to ratify the program of a particular party, that party has the right to appeal to the Congress of the Communist International.

"16. All decisions of the Congresses of the Communist International, as well as the decisions of its Executive Committee, are binding on all parties affiliated to the Communist International. The Communist International, operating in the midst of most acute civil war, must have a far more centralized form of organization than that of the second International. At the same time, the Communist International and its Executive Committee must, of course, in all their activities, take into consideration the diversity of the conditions under which the various parties have to work and fight, and should issue universally binding decisions only on questions on which the passing of such decisions is possible.

"17. In connection with all this, all parties desiring to join the Communist International must change their names. Every party that desires to join the Communist International must bear the name: Communist Party of such-and-such country (Section of the Third, Communist International). This question as to name is not merely a formal one, but a political one of great importance. The Communist International has declared a decisive war against the entire bourgeois world and all the yellow, Social-Democratic parties. Every rank-and-file worker must clearly understand the difference between the Communist Parties and the old official 'Social-Democratic' or 'Socialist' parties which have betrayed the cause of the working class.

"18. All the leading Party organs of the press in all countries must publish all the chief documents of the Executive Committee of the Communist International.

"19. All parties belonging to the Communist International, or having made an application to join it, must, in the shortest possible period, but not later than four months after the Second Congress of the Communist International, call special Party congresses, for the purpose of discussing these obligations. In this connection, the Central Committees must take measures to enable all the local organizations to become acquainted with the decisions of the Second Congress of the Communist International.

"20. The parties that would now like to join the Third International but which have not yet radically changed their former tactics, must, before joining, take steps to ensure that their Central Committees and all most important central bodies of the respective parties, shall be composed, to the extent of at least two-thirds, of such comrades as even prior to the Second Congress of the Communist International have openly and definitely declared for joining the Third International. Exceptions may be made with approval of the Executive Committee of the Third International. The Executive Committee of the Communist the representatives of the 'Center' mentioned in point 7.

"21. Members of the Party who reject the conditions of theses of the Communist International, on principle, must be expelled from the party.

"This applies also to the delegates to the special Party Congresses."

PLAN OF DISTRICT ORGANIZATION COMMUNIST PARTY U. S. A.

The Central Committee, Communist Party, U. S. A., Section Communist International:

Earl R. Browder, General Secretary Communist Party, U. S. A.; Robert Minor, see P. 1 D.W. 4/19/35, Communist Candidate for mayor of New York City, 1934; Clarence Hathaway, Editor Official Communist Organ, "Daily Worker," New York; Max Bedacht, Delegate to Communist International, General Secy. International Workers' Order; Wm. K. Gebert, Organizer, District No. 8, Chicago, Illinois; Morris Childs, International Labor Defense. National Director Agit-Prop (Agitation-Propaganda): Alexander Bittelman, a charter member of the Communist Party, U. S. A.

The United States and its territories were sub-divided into 32 geographical districts, outlined as follows, with these reported organizers:

1. Boston, district headquarters (territories included in the district, Massachusetts, Rhode Island, Maine, Vermont and New Hampshire); Phil Frankfeld, district organizer, Boston, see P. 1 D.W., 11/6/35; William Burke, Communist leader, New Bedford, Massachusetts, see P. 4, D.W., 11/6/35; Dewitt W. Parker, Springfield, Mass., organizer, P. 4, D.W., 8/6/36; Edward Peters, state organizer of Maine, P. 3, D.W., 9/8/36; Jack Wilgus, Barre, Vermont, section organizer, P. 4, D.W., 3/12/36.

2. New York City, district headquarters (territories included in the district, New York City and Yonkers—Israel Amter, district organizer for Communist Party of New York (Pg. 1, D.W., 4/22/35); James W. Ford, negro Communist is organizer of the Harlem section, (Pg. 1, D.W., 3/21/35); Frank Hillman, district organizational secretary for New Jersey, (Pg. 2, D.W., 5/2/35); H. Sazer, district organizer in New Jersey, (Pg. 3, D.W., 5/7/35); R. Otis, Rochester, N. Y., is Communist Party organizer for that section, (Pg. 3, D.W., 4/3/35); Harry Wallace, organizer in section three of New York, (Pg. 1, D.W., 4/18/35;

Max Steinberg, organizational secretary of Communist Party, New York District (Pg. 5, D.W., 8/9/35); Bernard Burton, section organizer, Ellenville, N. Y. (Pg. 3, D.W., 10/12/35); Alex Bittleman, district organizer, New York, (Pg. 2, D.W., 11/22/35); James Ashford, section organizer, New York City, and John Little, district organizer, New York City (Pg. 1, D.W., 11/13/35); Harry Winitsky, Secretary, New York District (P. 2, D.W., 1/18/36); Sam Abbott, Elmira, New York, section organizer (P. 2, D.W., 5/3/35); Bernard Burton, Ellenville, New York, section organizer (P. 3, D.W., 10/12/35); Pete Cacchione, Brooklyn, New York, organizer (P. 4, D.W., 9/12/36); Charles Krumbein, State Secretary of New York (P. 3, D.W., 10/30/36); Max Steinberg, Organizational Secretary, New York (P. 1, D.W., 4/16/36); Harry Yaris, Bronx, New York, organizer (P. 4, D.W., 9/12/36).

3. Philadelphia, district headquarters (territories included in the district, Washington, D. C., Delaware, Eastern Pennsylvania, Maryland, Western New Jersey)—Alexander Mills, District organizer in Philadelphia, (Pg. 3, D.W., 5/11/35); Pat Toohey, district organizer, Philadelphia, (Pg. 3, D.W., 9/28/35); Pete Karpa, section organizer, Ambridge, Pennsylvania, (Pg. 3, D.W., 10/1/35); Joseph Dougher, Communist Party Secretary, Scranton, Pennsylvania, (Pg. 3, D.W., 10/23/35); Grace Hutchins, Communist Party member, (Pg. 1, D.W., 10/23/35); Tony Minerich, member Communist Party, Johnstown, Pennsylvania, (Pg. 3, D.W., 11/9/35); Robert E. Ray, Washington, D. C., section organizer, (Pg. 4, D.W., 1/24/36); A. G. Mills, Philadelphia, Pa., district organizer, (Pg. 3, D.W., 5/11/35); Pat Toohey, Philadelphia, Pa., district organizer, (Pg. 2, D.W., 10/11/35); John Dean, Reading, Pa., section organizer, (Pg. 1, D.W., 11/6/36); Ralph Glick, Philadelphia, Pa., district organizer, (Pg. 3, D.W., 4/9/36).

4. Buffalo, district headquarters, (territories included in the district, Northwestern New York State, Erie, Pennsylvania)—Henry Shepard reported organizer; Buffalo, New York, (Pg. 1, D.W., 9/3/35); A. Guss, Buffalo, New York, western New York district organizer, (P. 1, D.W., 10/29/36); R. Otis, Buffalo, New York, section organizer, (Pg. 2, D.W., 9/15/36); H. Shepard, Buffalo, New York, district organizer, (Pg. 1, D.W., 9/3/35).

5. Pittsburgh, district headquarters (territories included in the district, Western Pennsylvania)—Jack Johnstone, district organizer, Pittsburgh, (Pg. 2, D.W., 11/22/35); John Prini, Johnstown, Pa., section organizer, (Pg. 4, D.W., 1/24/36); Tom Myerscough, Pittsburgh, Pa., section organizer, (Pg. 9, D.W., 1/19/35); Pete Karpa, Beaver Valley, Pa., section organizer, (Pg. 4, D.W., 1/24/36); Ben Careathers, Pittsburgh, Pa., section organizer, (Pg. 4, D.W., 3/13/36).

6. Cleveland, district headquarters (territory included in the district, Ohio) —I. O. Ford was Communist candidate for Governor in Ohio. John Williamson, district organizer, (Pg. 2, D.W., 5/8/35) Ohio, chairman, first session Communist Party, U. S. A. Convention, April, 1934. Communist Party headquarters at Youngstown, Ohio, is 334 E. Federal Street. James Keller is section organizer of the Communist Party, Akron, (Pg. 4, D.W., 11/20/35); John Steuben, section

organizer of Communist Party, Youngstown, Ohio, (Pg. 2, D.W., 11/7/35); Phil Bart, section organizer, Ohio, (Pg. 5, D.W., 4/24/36); Louis Block, Cleveland, Ohio, section organizer, (Pg. 4, D.W., 1/24/36); Carl Evans, Columbus, Ohio, section organizer, (Pg. 4, D.W., 1/24/36); James Keller, Akron, Ohio, section organizer, (Pg. 2, D.W., 5/9/36); John Meldon, section organizer, Ohio, (Pg. 1, D.W., 6/4/35); Andrew R. Onda, Cleveland, Ohio, section organizer, (Pg. 3, D.W., 9/14/36); Frank Rogers, Cleveland, Ohio, section organizer, (Pg. 4, D.W., 1/24/36); John Steuben, Youngstown, Ohio, section organizer, (Pg. 4, D.W., 1/11/36); Peter Vzara, Cleveland, Ohio, section organizer, (Pg. 4, D.W., 1/24/36); John Williamson, Cleveland, Ohio, organizer, (Pg. 4, D.W., 4/16/36).

7. Detroit, district headquarters (territories included in the district, Lower Michigan)—Wm. W. Weinstone, district organizer, (Pg. 1, D.W., 5/21/35) Michigan District; Nat Ganly, Communist Party organizer, Detroit, (Pg. 3, D.W., 11/6/35); Lawrence Emery, section organizer, Detroit, (Pg. 1, D.W., 9/9/35); Francis Walker, organizational secretary, Detroit, (Pg. 1, D.W., 9/11/35); Edward Williams, Detroit, Michigan, section organizer, (Pg. 3, D.W., 2/1/36); Francis Walker, Detroit, Michigan, organizational secretary, (Pg. 1, D.W., 9/11/35); George Kristalski, Detroit, Michigan, section organizer, (Pg. 1, D.W., 1/9/36); Lawrence Emery, Detroit, Michigan, section organizer, (Pg. 4, D.W., 3/14/36; James Allan, Michigan, section organizer, (Pg. 4, D.W., 8/18/36).

8. Chicago, district headquarters (territories included in the district, Illinois and Lower Wisconsin)—Wm. K. Gebert, district organizer, and member central committee Communist Party U. S. A. Candidates on Communist ticket: Karl Lochner, candidate for Mayor of Chicago, 1935. M. Childs, district organizer for Communist Party in Chicago District; K. Erlich is section organizer in Chicago, (Pg. 8, D.W., 4/6/35); David Poindexter, member Communist Party, Chicago, (Pg. 3, D.W., 11/7/35); Bob Brown, Communist Party organizer, Gary, Indiana, (Pg. 5, D.W., 10/26/35); S. Simonsen, Chicago, Ill., section organizer, (Pr. 4, D.W., 3/10/36; Beatrice Shields, Agitprop director Chicago Communist District No. 8, (Pg. 3, D.W., 4/16/36); William K. Gebert, Chicago, Ill., district organizer, (Pg. 3, D.W., 2/1/35); Morris Child, Chicago, Ill., district organizer, (Pg. 4, D.W., 6/11/36); Gene Dennis, Milwaukee, Wisconsin, State Secretary, (Pg. 2, D.W., 6/30/36); Harold Hartley, Milwaukee, Wisconsin, section organizer, (Pg. 4, D. W., 1/24/36); John Sekat, Wisconsin organizer, (Pg. 3, D.W., 8/10/35).

9. Minneapolis, District headquarters (territories included in the district, Minnesota and part of Wisconsin); Unemployed Council, 212 Hennepin Ave.; Communist Party District headquarters is now located at Room 2, 321 Hennepin Avenue, Minneapolis, (Pg. 3, D.W., 4/20/35). Alfred Tiala, district organizer Minneapolis, Minnesota, (Pg. 1, D.W., 10/22/35). Alfred Tiala, district organizer in Minnesota, (Pg. 3, D.W., 3/3/35); Nat Ross, Minneapolis, Minn., district organizer, (Pg. 4, D.W., 2/6/36).

10. Omaha, Nebraska (territories included in the district, Nebraska, Texas and New Mexico)—Ray Wycoff, "Daily Worker" agent, East St. Louis. "Bud" Reynolds is Communist Party organizer, Omaha, Nebraska, (Pg. 5, D.W., 9/30/35); William Simons, Omaha, Nebraska, district organizer, (Pg. 3, D.W.,

4/22/36); H. Schroeter, Omaha, Nebraska, section organizer, (Pg. 4, D.W., 2/26/36); Juan Ochoa, Gallup, New Mexico, acting section organizer, (Pg. 1, W.W., 4/11/35); Max Salzman, Topeka, Kansas, organizer, (Pg. 1, D.W., 9/3/36).

11. Bismarck, North Dakota, district headquarters (territories included in the district, North Dakota)—Alfred Knutson was at one time reported district organizer in North Dakota now in Montana.

12. Seattle, Washington, district headquarters (territories included in the district, Washington and Oregon)—Emil Linden of the Fishermen and Cannery Workers' Industrial Union, Louis Olson, reported section organizer, Portland; J. Rapport, district organizer, Seattle, (Pg. 2, D.W., 11/22/35); Harold Brockway, section organizer, Seattle, Washington, (Pg. 3, D.W., 3/9/35); H. G. Huff, Aberdeen, Wash., section organizer, (Pg. 4, D.W., 3/18/36); Edward Denny, Seattle, Wash., section organizer, (Pg. 4, D.W., 2/27/36).

13. San Francisco, district headquarters, 37 Grove Street (territories included in the district, California, Nevada and Arizona). Louise Todd is section organizer at Los Angeles, (Pg. 3, D.W., 5/1/35 and Pg. 1, W.W., 4/25/35); Stanley Hancock, section organizer of Communist Party at San Diego, Calif. (Pg. 1, W.W., 4/29/35). Pat Callahan, section organizer for Communist Party of Arizona at Tucson. (Pg. 1, W.W., 8/30/34); Bill Schneiderman, district organizer, San Francisco, California, (Pg. 1, W.W., 10/28/35); Robert Minor, Member Communist Party, (Pg. 3, D.W., 10/25/35); O. B. Powell, Stockton, Calif., section organizer, W.W., 10/11/34); Charles McLaughlan, Santa Ana, Calif., organizer, (Pg. 4, D.W., 10/22/35); Peter J. Garrison, San Francisco, Calif., district educational director, (Pg. 1, W.W., 9/23/35); Jack Johnstone, member Central Committee of California, (Pg. 2, D.W., 6/27/36).

14. Newark, New Jersey, district headquarters (territory included in the district, New Jersey)—Rebecca Grecht, reported district organizer; Morris M. Brown was Communist Party candidate for Governor in New Jersey; Jack Rose, reported Newark section organizer; H. Sazer, district organizer New Jersey, (Pg. 5, D.W., 5/7/35); Frank Hillman, New Jersey, district organizational secretary, (Pg. 3, D.W., 5/6/35); Fred Gray, Trenton, New Jersey, section organizer, (Pg. 3, D.W., 2/1/36); Lena Davis, Newark, New Jersey, district organizer, (Pg. 2, D.W., 6/25/36); Jay Anyan, Paterson, New Jersey, organizer, (D.W., 1/19/35).

15. New Haven, Connecticut, district headquarters (territory included in the district, Connecticut)—Candidates for office have been active. DeWitt Parker, section organizer of Communist Party, New Haven, Connecticut; Michael Russo, Communist Party organizer, Bridgeport, Connecticut, (Pg. 4, D.W., 10/24/35); L. Marra, section organizer, New London, Connecticut, (Pg. 3, D.W., 11/13/35); Sam Krieger, Danbury, Connecticut, section organizer, (Pg. 2, D.W., 5/3/35); I. Wofsy, Secretary of Connecticut, (Pg. 3, D.W., 9/24/36); Michael Russo, organizer, Bridgeport, Connecticut, (Pg. 4, D.W., 10/24/35); L. Marra, New London, Connecticut, section organizer, (Pg. 4, D.W., 2/25/36).

16. Charlotte, North Carolina, district headquarters (territories included in the district, North Carolina, South Carolina)—Paul Crouch, reported district organizer (he was dishonorably discharged from the United States Army in 1925,

after being convicted for violation of a territorial law forbidding secret organizations of a revolutionary character and also for violation of the 96th and 62nd articles of war dealing with conduct prejudicial to military discipline and disrespect for the President of the United States). Angelo Herndon, negro Communist out on bail furnished by I. L. D.. Communist activities in the textile industry and among the negro population have been notorious.

17. Birmingham, Alabama, district headquarters, with address P. O. Box 1813, Birmingham, (territories included in the district, Alabama, Tennessee, Georgia and Mississippi)—Jim Mallory, Editor, "Southern Worker," Birmingham, Alabama. The Scottsboro, Alabama case has received international support of revolutionists. R. F. Hall, Atlanta, Georgia, district secretary, (Pg. 3, D.W., 9/19/36); Jack Barton, Birmingham, Alabama, (Pg. 5, D.W., 11/16/36).

18. Madison, Wisconsin, district headquarters (territories included in the district, balance of Wisconsin—part not included in two previous districts)—Gene Dennis, district organizer of Communist Party, Milwaukee, (Pg. 2, D.W., 11/22/35).

19. Denver, Colorado, district headquarters (territories included in the district, Colorado, Utah and Wyoming)—John Harvey, reported district organizer; Gene Gordon, reported section organizer, Denver; Cliff Irwin, Denver, Colorado, section organizer, (Pg. 4, D.W., 2/18/36); James Allander, Denver, Colorado, district organizer, (Pg. 4, D.W., 3/5/36).

20. Texas with sections organized at Port Arthur and Houston.

21. St. Louis is headquarters for the activity out of western Illinois, eastern Missouri and Arkansas. Alfred Wagenknecht, Communist Party leader at St. Louis (P. 3, D.W., 11/14/35); Jack Shaw, Communist Party organizer, Kansas City, Mo. (Pg. 3, D.W., 9/30/35); Ralph Shaw, section organizer southern Illinois, (Pg. 3, D.W., 2/1/36).

22. West Virginia has now been made into a special district because of the many efforts of the party organizers to foment strikes in the coal industry of that state.

23. Kentucky. Norman Link, Communist Party member in Kentucky and D. L. West, Communist Party organizer in the same state, are also members of the United Mine Workers of America. (Pg. 5, D.W., 11/1/35). Louisville is headquarters for Kentucky District No. 23.

24. Louisiana with address at P. O. Box 465, New Orleans, La. W. G. Binkley, New Orleans, La., district organizer, (Pg. 3, D.W., 10/13/36).

25. Florida with headquarters in Jacksonville and Tampa. Jack Strong, organizer, Florida, (Pg. 3, D.W., 10/28/36).

26. South Dakota with headquarters reported to be at 223 E. 8th St., Sioux Falls, S. D. and another reported to be at Aberdeen, S. D.

27. Upper Michigan.

28. Indiana has just recently been designated as District No. 28, with headquarters in the Wimmer Building, 66 West New York Street, Indianapolis. Charles Stadfeld, Indianapolis, Ind., state chairman, (Pg. 1, D.W., 8/3/36); Andrew

Remes, Indianapolis, Ind., district organizer, (Pg. 4, D.W., 5/30/36); Miles Blansett, Terre Haute, Ind., section organizer, (Pg. 3, D.W., 9/12/35).

29. Richmond, Va., district headquarters with territory taking in all of the state. Donald Burke is section organizer, (Pg. 2, D.W., 10/8/36); Jim Porter, Norfolk, Va., section organizer, (Pg. 4, D.W., 1/13/36).

30. Montana is a new Communist Party district. Most of activity is reported to be directed from Butte. Charles E. Taylor is a party leader, (Pg. 3, D.W., 5/9/35).

31. Oklahoma now comprises District No. 31, with district headquarters in Oklahoma City, Okla.

32. Iowa was designated as District No. 32 in early September, 1936, with headquarters at Des Moines. Jim Porter was an early district organizer, (Pg. 3, D.W., 9/8/36).

Changes are constantly being made in Communist Districts in the United States.

"NEW PARTY DUES PAYMENTS

(From Party Organizer)

"The Ninth National Convention of the Party decided to reduce dues payments. This decision is being put into effect beginning with January, 1937. Instead of weekly dues payments, we will have monthly payments. The International Solidarity payments have also been changed from once a month to once every four months.

"The following contains necessary information for every Party member regarding dues, initiations, assessments, the International Solidarity payments, attendance and activity:

"MEMBERSHIP

"*Initiation*

"The initiation fee of each applicant for membership is 50 cents if his weekly wage is over $10.00. For those whose earnings are less than $10.00 a week, or who are on relief, or housewives, the initiation fee is 10 cents. This amount is receipted for by an initiation stamp furnished by the Central Committee. Fifty per cent of the sale of the initiation stamp goes to the National Office and 50 per cent to the District Office. There is no extra charge to the new member for the membership book.

"DUES

"Each member pays dues monthly, based on the month's earnings. The dues are receipted for by dues stamps issued by the Central Committee. Dues stamps are issued in the following categories:

"All members earning up to $10 a week ($40 a month) pay 10 cents a month.

"All housewives pay 10 cents a month.

"All earning between $11 and $25 a week (up to $100 a month) pay 50 cents a month.

"All earning between $26 and $40 a week (up to $160 a month) pay $1.00 a month.

Communist Party of the U. S. A.
(Section of the Communist International)

Membership Book No.

for

Name ....

Date Admitted to Communist Party..............

Entered Revolutionary Movement...............

District *13* ....City ....

Section *La* ...Shop or Street Nucleus.........

Signature of Member (in ink)................

This Book was issued on.......................

(date)

Sam Darcy

Signature of District Organizer
and Party Seal

No Party Membership Book Valid Unless It Has
Party Seal Stamped On

Issued by the Central Committee, C.P.U.S.A.

NOTE: Photostat of first page of Communist Party Membership Book loaned us by a California member of CP. District Organizer Sam Darcy was an unsuccessful candidate for Governor of California at the November, 1934, elections.

"Members receiving over $40 a week (or over $160 a month) wages pay in addition to the regular dues, additional dues at the rate of 50 cents for each $10.00 (or fraction).

"The dues are proportioned as follows:

"Twenty-five per cent to the units.

"Twenty per cent to the sections.

"Twenty per cent to the districts.

"Twenty-five per cent to the center.

"Ten per cent to the center for a special national trade union fund.

"Members who are two months in arrears in payment of dues cease to be members of the Party in good standing. Members who are four months in arrears are stricken from the Party rolls.

"ASSESSMENTS

"All local or district assessments or collections are prohibited except by special permission of the Central Committee. Special assessments may be levied by the National Convention or the Central Committee. No member is considered in good standing unless he purchases such special assessment stamps.

"INTERNATIONAL SOLIDARITY

"This is a special fund, contributed to by every member, as an act of our international solidarity with the Communist Parties of other countries that need our financial aid. Every member is to pay every four months an amount equal to one month's dues, based on the average of the previous four months dues.

"ATTENDANCE AND ACTIVITY

"The rules of the Party provide that Party members attend the meetings of their Party organization regularly, participate in its activities, pay their dues regularly, and carry out the decisions of the Party." P. 12-13.

COMMUNIST PARTY ON THE BALLOT

In December, 1921, the Workers' Party of the United States was formed as a camouflage for the Communist Party. In 1925, the official name was changed to Workers' Communist Party of America. At the March, 1928, convention, the Communists came out in the open boldly as the Communist Party of the United States of America, and made their first fight to become a legalized political party, and to go on the ballot as such. The following review will give you a history of the growth of the Communist Party on the ballot from 1928 to 1936. You will particularly note that in fifteen states the Communist Party was not on the ballot in the November election of 1936. There were more than 75,000 signers of the petition for a place on the ballot in Illinois, but enough were ruled illegal to prevent their appearing on the state-wide ballot. This 1934 vote does not include the county and local, or even the Congress votes, but merely the highest communist vote cast for a candidate on a state-wide ticket.

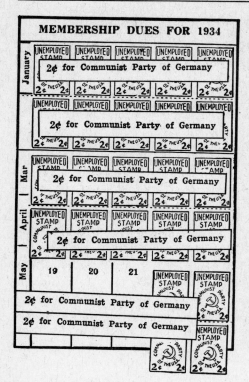

MEMBERSHIP DUES FOR 1934					
July	27	28	29	30	21
August	32	33	34	35	
September	36	37	38	39	
October	40	41	42	43	44
November	45	46	47	48	
December	49	50	51	52	

NOTE: Photostat of dues pages of Communist Membership Book shown on previous page. It is interesting to note that two cents of every ten cents dues for 1934, indicated by red stamp across each line, went to the cause of the CP in Germany.

Sam Darcy, former Communist Party district organizer at San Francisco, Calif., attended the Seventh Congress of Communist International at Moscow last July and August. He is under indictment in San Francisco and has not yet returned to the United States, at least under his own name.

The records in the office of the National Americanism Commission are very complete, with reference to the criminal history of many of the Communist leaders in the U. S. One of the highest Communist Party officials, one of the heads of the American Civil Liberties Union, and one of the founders of the Federated Press served federal prison terms for refusal to defend this country during the world war.

COMMUNIST PARTY STANDS FOR VIOLENCE

If you will turn to page 16, you will find the decision of a committee of Congress pointing to the error of calling the Communist Party a legal political party in the United States.

The Communist Party leaders, when under fire for their proposed programs of violence, disclaim that they stand for force and violence. However, all the written propaganda of the Party recommends action by force. The reproduced leaflet on page 45 shows the method used to incite hatred and action if possible. While denying that they seek to overthrow our government by force and violence, they claim that it must be overthrown and that the change to a Soviet America cannot be made without force.

We have, by permitting the Communist Party a place on the ballot, legalized their revolutionary acts against the United States government. They have been able to force the radio stations to give them free time on the air. These broadcasts would not be dangerous if they boldly told of their true stand for a dictatorship of the so-called proletariat, through which the citizens of the country would be denied all freedoms now enjoyed. But instead, when on the air, they paint a beautiful picture of this country operating under Communism, not well supported by fact as conditions exist in Russia today.

	1928	1930	1934	1936
Alabama			270	678
Arizona			12,321	
Arkansas				446
California			100,820	10,877
Colorado	675	924	1,290	1,039
Connecticut	730	1,523	1,283	1,225
Delaware			69	51
Florida				
Georgia				
Idaho				
Illinois	3,851	3,118		
Indiana			6,609	1,183
Iowa	328	1,471	1,457	1,373
Kansas				
Kentucky			38	204
Louisiana				
Maine			422	257
Maryland	636	1,432	1,792	915
Massachusetts	2,464	8,730	14,013	11,691
Michigan	2,881	3,988	5,734	3,384
Minnesota	4,853	14,719	5,791	2,574
Mississippi				
Missouri			418	417
Montana			975	385
Nebraska				
Nevada				
New Hampshire			244	193
New Jersey	1,257	1,700	2,874	1,639
New Mexico			134	43
New York	10,876	19,539	55,664	67,336
North Carolina				11
North Dakota	936	5,754	1,979	540
Ohio			15,854	7,373
Oklahoma				
Oregon			1,475	
Pennsylvania	4,720	8,950	6,170	5,190
Rhode Island				481
South Carolina				
South Dakota	232	3,974	2,568	
Tennessee	111	3,392		319
Texas	209	282	325	253
Utah			1,207	280
Vermont			177	905
Virginia			431	8,907
Washington			3,470	1,939
West Virginia			94	
Wisconsin	1,528	3,155	2,454	2,197
Wyoming			195	91
	36,287	82,651	248,617	134,396

SMASH EFFORTS TO ILLEGALIZE YOUR PARTY
The COMMUNIST PARTY

To All Workers and Friends:

Eight or ten men and women face Grand Jury indictments for perjury! These men and women were circulators of the petition of the Communist Party to participate in the August Primary elections; the petition which received the signatures of over 31,000 registered voters in California. In spite of thousands of these signatures being disqualified for various technical reasons, or no reason at all, Frank C. Jordan, Secretary of State, certified 15,200 of the signatures, officially placing the Communist Party on the ballot.

At the instigation of the Chamber of Commerce, the Industrial Association, the "Red Squad" under Capt. John J. O'Meara, a "probing" of the petitions was started, with one aim in view: TO TAKE THE COMMUNIST PARTY OFF THE BALLOT! Vigilante raids, arrests, jail sentences, have failed to silence the Communist Party, which daily carries on its task of leading the struggles of workers for better conditions and for their democratic rights. So the campaign of intimidation continues. But instead of limiting this campaign to the members and sympathizers of the Communist Party, it is being broadened to include every last worker who indicated his support to our Party by signing the petition; it is being broadened, by indicting workers for perjury, rather than arresting them only on vagrancy.

ANSWER THIS CAMPAIGN WITH YOUR PROTEST—PILE UP A HUGE COMMUNIST VOTE!

We call on all workers—citizens of San Francisco—to support the Communist Party in its struggle against capitalist terror! The boss class is against our Party:

Because the Communists in the striking unions were the most active, and the entire membership supported the maritime strike; *because* they exposed the sell-out tactics of the Greens, Vanderleurs, Caseys, Ryans, Kidwells, in the General Strike; *because* they exposed the manifestations of fascism in California, Governor Merriam's sending armed troops against the strikers, the scab-herding of the Industrial Association, the anti-Communist activities of the City administration, the Chamber of Commerce, the American Legion, the vigilante mob raids on private homes and halls.

Because the Communists fight for higher wages, *because* we demand the right of workers to organize into trade unions and political parties of their own choosing, to strike and picket without police and National Guard interference, the right to free speech and assemblage.

Because the Communists struggle for Unemployment Insurance, for relief to the farmers.

Because the Communist Party is leading the workers toward the establishment of a Socialist society in the United States—the establishment of a WORKERS' AND FARMERS' GOVERNMENT!

WHAT YOU CAN DO!

SEND A LETTER, TELEGRAM OR PHONE CALL OF PROTEST TO MAYOR ROSSI, REGISTRAR COLLINS, CAPTAIN JOHN J. O'MEARA, JUDGE WALTER PERRY JOHNSON OF THE SUPERIOR COURT, DEMANDING THE DROPPING OF THE RIDICULOUS CHARGES OF PERJURY AGAINST THE CIRCULATORS OF OUR PETITIONS!

READ AND SUBSCRIBE TO THE "WESTERN WORKER," OFFICIAL ORGAN OF THE COMMUNIST PARTY! Write for a free sample to 37 Grove street, San Francisco, Calif.

PASS THIS LEAFLET ON TO YOUR FELLOW WORKERS!

ANSWER THE REIGN OF TERROR BY JOINING THE COMMUNIST PARTY!

VOTE FOR BETTER LIVING CONDITIONS, FOR YOUR DEMOCRATIC RIGHTS, AND AGAINST FASCISM AND WAR BY VOTING COMMUNIST!

SAM DARCY for Governor.
PETTIS PERRY for Lieut. Governor.
HAROLD ASHE for Secretary of State.
ARCHIE BROWN for Treasurer.
ANITA WHITNEY for Comptroller.
LEO GALLAGHER — Non-Partisan Candidate, Associate Justice, Supreme Court

COMMUNIST PARTY OF U. S. A.
California District,
37 Grove Street, San Francisco, Calif.

VOTE COMMUNIST!

—Printing Donated by Union Labor—

NOTE: Photostat of handbill scattered by Communist Party in opposition to legislation sponsored by The American Legion and other American groups to bar the alien un-American Communist Party from the ballot in the United States.

"THE ACCOMPLISHMENTS AND SHORTCOMINGS OF THE COMMUNIST PARTY ELECTION CAMPAIGN

(Statement by Earl Browder.)

"At the Ninth Convention of our Party in June, in charting our course for the elections, we established that, first, the Republican Party represented nationally the point of concentration of the most reactionary forces in America, moving toward fascism and war. The task was to defeat this threat at all costs. Secondly, Roosevelt, heading the Democratic Party, stood for a middle-of-the-road course. The support of the organized labor and progressive movement went to Roosevelt, as the practical alternative to aggressive reaction. Our tasks became to teach this progressive and labor movement not to rely upon Roosevelt, to secure independent political organization and action, to win all possible concessions from Roosevelt while using this campaign to prepare its future complete independence in a Farmer-Labor Party.

"Some comrades are still influenced by the idea that the Party vote is the only correct measure of our achievements. To the degree that they are influenced by this idea they are somewhat pessimistic because our vote did not show any great jump forward. These comrades look upon our refusal to go into head-on collision with the progressive labor movement, in sharp competition for votes, like Norman Thomas did, as a sacrifice necessary to assure that Landon would not be elected. Therefore, they ask us why we did not change our position in the last days before election, when it was becoming clear that Roosevelt would be elected. They wonder why we did not swing over to the Thomas tactic of grabbing the utmost possible votes for ourselves at the last minute (even though this failed so signally to win votes for Thomas).

"To pose such a question reveals a shallow understanding of our whole strategy and a wrong evaluation of our accomplishments. Let us throw light on this question from another angle. Suppose that our proposals last summer for a National Farmer Labor Party had been adopted by the progressive movement. Then we would have withdrawn our national ticket entirely. But we would have made an equally energetic campaign without getting any separate Communist Party vote at all as a result. Would our doubting comrades will have kept their eyes fixed on the C.P. vote, this time zero, and feared that we had disappeared entirely from the political scene? Of course not. Clearly, it would have been recognized as a much greater victory. However, the urgent need for a united front, which everyone felt was realized in another and less satisfactory way under such circumstances that we could not fight against it—the united front of the labor and progressive forces around Roosevelt.

"We foresaw, before the campaign opened, that our separate vote would register only our irreducible minimum and not our maximum influence. This was inherent in the situation and our strategy. There is nothing to weep about. We do not have to explain away our vote by special local circumstances or special weaknesses on our part. Weaknesses there were aplenty in our compaign but they must not be sought in this question of the relation of our influence and our vote. There is no direct relation between them at all. Not to understand this is to have a very

INDIVIDUAL REGISTRATION BLANK

(This part of the registration blank should be filled out by the Unit Secretary in advance.)

(Answer every question. Write with ink or indelible pencil. Print the name)

Unit No........................... Section No........................... District No....... .... Date...........................
(State if shop nucleus)

Old Membership Book No........................... New Membership Book No........................... *(To be filled by District)*

Party name...........................

Date joined Party:........................... Date of birth........................... Male......... Female.........
(Month—Year)

Place of birth........................... Nationality........................... Negro or White...........
(City—State—County)

Employed or unemployed........................... Trade...........................

(This part of the registration blank should be filled out together with the member.)

If employed, state kind of factory—number of workers employed...........................

....

What union exists in your place of employment........................... With how many members...........

Trade union affiliation: (1) A. F. of L........................... Since when...........................

(2) T. U. U. L........................... Since when...........................

(3) Indep. Union........................... Since when...........................

If unemployed—since when........................... Which unemployed org. do you belong to...........................
What other mass org. are you a member of (ILD—FSU—IWO—Language org.—Other reformist or reactionary fraternal organizations)...........................

Function in the Party (unit, section, district, center)...........................

If full time functionary, state where (Party, mass org.) and since when...........................

....

Do you read the *Daily Worker* regularly?........................... *Party Organizer*........................... *The Communist*...........................

Party schooling received: Workers School........................... Study circle........................... Section school...........................

District Training School........................... National Training School...........................

Have you ever server in the Army—Navy........................... When........................... Where...........................

Are you in the National Guard...........................

NOTE: Photostat of latest registration blank for members of the CP. This record is very complete, thus making it easy to find the right classification in which to place the member.

narrow understanding of the whole strategy of the people's front, which is not a mere election tactic but a strategy for a whole period.

"Where our strategy was realized in its most satisfactory form—as in Minnesota, we had no state ticket at all, but were among the most effective campaigners for the Farmer-Labor ticket. Does that mean that we were weakened in that state? On the contrary, we made the greatest advance of Communist influence among the masses, precisely there. Equally significant were our advances in Wisconsin, which again can in no wise be measured by our separate vote. Even in the very unsatisfactory American Labor Party in New York, with its crude organization from the top alone, there were greater advances of our influence than would have accompanied a situation where the American Labor Party was absent, even though that had meant a higher Communist Party vote. We made greater advances with the lower vote in New York with the American Labor Party in the field than we could have made with a higher vote and the American Labor Party not in existence.

"Then, too, we should point out one possible development which was not realized but which might have occurred if the progressive leaders had taken only a part of our advice. Suppose these leaders and their organizations had adopted our proposal for a National Farmer-Labor Party convention, including the Socialists and the Communists. Suppose that this convention had come together and formed a national Farmer-Labor Party with all of us in it, and then decided to place Roosevelt at the head of the ticket nationally, like the American Labor Party did in New York, but followed it up with state Farmer-Labor Party tickets wherever possible. Under such circumstances would the Socialist Party and the Communist Party have accepted the discipline of such a broad national united front of all progressives? Would we have refrained from putting forward our own independent tickets and supported the Farmer-Labor Party ticket even with Roosevelt at the head? I venture to say that under such conditions we would almost surely have done so. The united peoples' front and the cause of Socialism as well would have been advanced much more than by what actually happened in the election campaign.

"One of the greatest accomplishments of our party in this campaign was that it began to learn how, even with small forces, to find its road in the midst of the most complicated political situation—we drove in the center of a national political storm toward a definite goal, without ever losing sight of it, and without allowing our forces to be broken up, dispersed or demoralized, but rather gaining strength and clarity out of it all. This ability is the hall-mark of Bolshevism and to the degree that our Party demonstrated this ability, we can say that we are in the process of becoming a real Bolshevik Party.

"Can any one, even our worst enemies, deny that the Communist Party played an important role in the campaign; that millions of people thought that what the Communist Party had to say was of serious importance, that millions were influenced in their thinking and their actions by the Communist Party? No one can deny this undisputed fact. Can any one say that we lost our heads at any moment, that we hesitated, or doubted at any point, that our strategical or tactical line was ever blurred or unclear or had to be changed? It is possible to differ with us but it is not possible to say that. Everyone recognized that the Communist Party was an exceptionally effective striking force precisely because of its conviction and clarity, its drive and unity. That is another of the hall-marks of Bolshevism.

"Can anyone deny that in this campaign the Communist Party broke through and smashed the legend of our enemies that our party is something foreign, imported from abroad, not organically a part of the American political scene Nor one can deny that we thoroughly established our Party as an American Party, that our slogan—"Communism is 20th Century Americanism"—registered deeply with the American people. This was a great achievement. This is also a sign of Bolshevism."

Pages 3 and 4, Daily Worker, December 14, 1936.

Program of the Communist International
(Excerpts from Communist Publication Titled Above)

"The ultimate aim of the Communist International is to replace world capitalist economy by a world system of Communism. . . . After abolishing private ownership in the means of production and converting them into social property, the world system of Communism will replace the elemental forces of the world market." P. 30.

"The Soviet State completely disarms the burgeoisie and concentrates all arms in the hands of the proletariat; it is the armed proletarian State. The armed forces under the Soviet State are organized on a class basis, which corresponds to the general structure of the proletarian dictatorship, and guarantees the role of leadership to the industrial proletariat. This organization, while maintaining revolutionary discipline, ensures to the warriors of the Red Army and Navy close and constant contacts with the masses of the toilers, participation in the administration of the country and in the work of building up Socialism." P. 39.

Communism calls for, "The confiscation and proletarian nationalization of all large landed estates in town and country (private, church, monastery and other lands) and the transference of State and municipal landed property including forests, minerals, lakes, rivers, etc., to the Soviets with subsequent nationalization of the whole of the land. . . . The amount of land to be so transferred to be determined by economic expediency as well as by the degree of necessity to neutralize the peasantry and to win them over to the side of the proletariat; this amount must necessarily vary according to the different circumstances." P. 41.

"The Proletarian nationalization of private banks (the entire gold reserve, all securities, deposits, etc., to be transferred to the proletarian State); the proletarian State to take over State, municipal, etc., banks. . . . The Nationalization of wholesale trade and large retail trading enterprises (warehouses, elevators, stores, stocks of goods, etc.) and their transfer to the organ of the Soviet State. . . . The monopoly of foreign trade. The repudiation of State debts to foreign and home capitalists." P. 42-43. This they have done with the United States in spite of recognition.

"The confiscation of big house property. The transfer of confiscated houses to the administration of the local Soviets. Workers to be removed to bourgeois residential districts. . . . The nationalization of printing plants. The monopoly of newspaper and book-publishing. The nationalization of big cinema enterprises, theatres, etc." P. 44-45.

"At the same time the proletarian State, while granting liberty of worship and abolishing the privileged position of the formerly dominant religion, carries on anti-religious propaganda with all the means at its command and reconstructs the whole of its educational work on the basis of scientific materialism." P. 55.

The Communist International considers the following to be its most important tasks in the balance of the world; "To overthrow the rule of foreign imperialism, of the feudal rulers and of the landlord bureaucracy. To establish the democratic dictatorship of the proletariat and the peasantry on a Soviet basis. Complete national independence and national unification. Annulment of State debts. The confiscation of landlord, church and monastery lands. The organization of revolutionary workers' and peasants' armies." P. 59.

"The International Communist discipline must find expression in the subordination of the partial and local interests of the movement to its general and lasting interests and in the strict fulfillment, by all members, of the decisions passed by the leading bodies of the Communist International." P. 86-87.

" 'The Communists disdain to conceal their views and aims. They openly declare that their aims can be attained only by the forcible overthrow of all the existing social conditions. Let the ruling class tremble at a Communist revolution. The proletarians have nothing to lose but their chains. They have a world to win.' " P. 87.

WHY COMMUNISM?

By N. J. OLGIN

(Excerpts from Communist Publication Titled Above)

"The overthrow of the State power, and with it, of the capitalist system, grows out of the everyday struggles of the workers. One is historically inseparable from the other." "The clearer the class-consciousness of the workers, the more steeled they are in fighting, the better the revolutionary leadership they have developed in the course of years, the greater the number of friends they have allied with themselves from among the other oppressed classes, the more capable are they to deal the final blow." P. 75-76.

"It is not necessary that this final blow, i. e., the revolution, should come in connection with an imperialist war, although this is most likely. Capitalism will seek to prevent a revolution by plunging the country into war." P. 76.

Here is how a general uprising should begin: "Workers stop work, many of them seize arms by attacking arsenals." "Street fights become frequent. Under the leadership of the Communist Party, the workers organize Revolutionary Committees to be in command of the uprising. There are battles in the principal cities." "Army units begin to join the revolutionary fighters; there is fraternization between the workers and the soldiers, the workers and the marines. The movement among the soldiers and marines spreads." "The police as a rule continue fighting, but they are soon silenced and made to flee by the united revolutionary forces of workers and soldiers. The revolution is victorious." P. 76-77.

"It has been done more than once." "A Workers' revolution was accomplished

WHY COMMUNISM ?

PLAIN TALKS ON VITAL PROBLEMS

By

M. J. OLGIN

●

Price 10 cents

NOTE: Photostat of front page of Communist leaflet from which preceding excerpts were taken. The author of the above leaflet, which is a strong supporter of revolutionary action, is also the editor of "Freiheits", a Jewish Communist Newspaper.

in Russia in November, 1917." "A Workers' revolution took place in Germany in 1918, in Hungary and Bavaria in 1919, in China in 1927, in Spain in 1932." "In Russia the revolution has survived first of all because the workers had a strong, well organized Bolshevik (Communist) Party that headed their fight. The defeat of the other revolutions does not argue against the eventuality of revolution. In fact, revolutions are inevitable." P. 77.

"The Soviet government will have to expropriate the expropriators by force." "The Soviet State will have to crush these with an iron hand. The former exploiters will be given no quarter." "This means that the Soviet State must be ruthless; it must destroy the counter-revolutionary forces—the quicker the better for the workers and for the future of mankind. This is why the Soviet state is named Dictatorship of the Proletariat." "It uses force and violence against that class." "And it does away with exploitation and oppression forever. This is Communism." P. 82-83.

15 Years of the Communist International
(Excerpts from Communist Publication Titled Above)

"Fifteen years ago, on March 4, 1919, in Red Moscow, the First Congress, under Lenin's leadership, established the Communist International—the new International Workingmen's Association." P. 3.

"The Communist International openly declares that the dictatorship of the proletariat can be accomplished only by means of violence '. . . the violence of the bourgeoisie can only be suppressed by the stern violence of the proletariat.' " P. 9.

"The fifteen years of the Communist International have been fifteen years of uneven but constant development of the world proletarian revolution." P. 10.

"Having assumed power as a result of the workers' uprising, the German Social-Democratic Party betrayed the proletarian revolution." P. 11.

"The Path of October, the path of the dictatorship of the proletariat brought the Soviet Union to socialism. The path of bourgeois democracy brought Germany to fascism." P. 12.

"A mighty wave of the proletarian revolution led to the formation of the Hungarian Soviet Republic on March 21, 1919. Under the leadership of Communists the Hungarian Soviets disarmed the gendarmerie and the police, organized a Red Army . . . After existing about four and a half months, the Hungarian Soviet Republic was betrayed by Hungarian social-democracy and drowned in blood by the international counter-revolution. Not 'democracy' but fascism took the place of the Soviets. 'No Communist should forget the lessons of the Hungarian Soviet Republic.' " P. 15.

"The Bavarian Soviet Republic which arose on April 13, 1919, under Communist leadership, disarmed the bourgeoisie, armed the proletariat, proclaimed the nationalization of industry and the banks. But it, too, was crushed by the White Guards with the active co-operation of German social-democracy after having existed 18 days." P. 15-16.

"The Leninist national policy of the Communist International is an irreplaceable weapon in the struggle against fascism." P. 19.

"In Italy, too, the victory of the bourgeoisie, which was made certain by the social-democrats, ended not in a strengthened 'democracy' but in the triumph of fascism." P. 20.

". . . the slogan 'To the Masses,' was that this slogan was a program of struggle for all the sections of the Comintern for an entire historical period, a program of preparation for the second round of revolutions and wars.' " P. 22.

"The Communist Parties have thousands and tens of thousands of members each; their influence extends over hundreds of thousands and millions of workers and peasants, they have already scored their first successes in establishing the united front. There is not a single Communist Party whose influence has not grown among the masses since the beginning of the economic crisis. The Communists are the only leaders of the masses, the motor of every revolutionary struggle, and they are the first to receive the blows of the class enemy. Most of the Communist Parties have gained the necessary prerequisites for becoming real mass fighting parties of the proletariat in the near future." P. 37.

"The task of winning over the majority of the working class demands the transformation of the factory committees of the trade union oppositions, of the Committees of Unemployed, of the peasant committees, and especially the transformation of the big enterprises, into strongholds of the Communist Parties." P. 39.

The following quotation from Moscow News, issue of October 7, 1936, shows the method used by the Communist Party in the U. S. S. R. to purge its ranks of undesirable party members. It also gives the definite proof that liberties are granted only to those who adhere to the decisions of the dictators in power in Russia.

Party Reopens Ranks to New Membership

"Instructions on reopening of the ranks of the Communist Party of the Soviet Union to candidates for membership, and resumption of the transfer of candidates on probation to full membership, beginning Nov. 1 of this year, were issued this week by the Central Committee of the Party to all of its organizations. This measure, following upon the completion of the exchange of Party documents, calls upon these organizations to benefit by the lessons learned during the verification and exchange of these papers.

"The instructions point out that many Party organizations have in the past systematically violated the Party constitution by admitting applicants in groups instead of passing personally upon each applicant. Other defects in the former procedure in connection with the handling of membership applications are also pointed out.

"In the admission of new members, Party organizations are instructed by the Central Committee to be guided by the following rules:

" 'Party organizations must enforce individual selection of the most advanced, the most developed, the best people of the country—primarily workers but also peasants and toiling intellectuals who have been tested on various sections of the struggle for Socialism.

" 'Admission of candidates and transfer of candidates to membership must be carried out individually and not collectively in every organization. Every applicant must write out his application personally in accordance with the prescribed form and submit recommendations and references from his place of work. The recommendations must be checked prior to consideration of the application. The same ruling applies to members of the Young Communist League.

" 'Applications must be considered at meetings of the primary Party organizations whose secretaries or organizers must themselves report on each applicant, who together with endorsers must be present at the meeting. Only after the decision of the primary organization is approved by the district committee will admission be regarded as valid.' "

SIGNIFICANCE OF DECISION

"The Party decision on the admission of new members is widely commented upon by the Soviet press, which points out that the decree came nearly four years after the Central Committee of the Party had closed the membership ranks in order to purge the Party of undesirable elements. Since the 1933 purge proved insufficient, however, the verification and exchange of all documents pertaining to Party membership was resorted to on Stalin's initiative. 'Pravda,' central organ of the Party, states that during the enforcement of these measures many well-disguised enemies were removed from its ranks and simultaneously large numbers of younger Communists began to take an active part in its work. Now that the exchange of documents has been completed, the Party ranks can be opened again.

" 'There is nothing nobler than the title of a member of the Party of Lenin-Stalin,' states 'Trud,' organ of the Central Council of Trade Unions. The newspaper points out that as a result of this decision of the Central Committee of the Party, the best of the non-Party Bolsheviks will have the opportunity to become members of the Party.

" 'The number of active non-Party Bolsheviks has grown tremendously in the country,' states 'Pravda.' 'Wherever Stakhanovism is busily working, there have grown up and been steeled talented organizers of Socialist economy, devoted to Communism, from among the non-Party workers, peasants and the toiling intelligentsia.'

" 'There can be no more noble task for each Young Communist League organization than to prepare active fighters for Communism,' declares 'Komsomolskaya Pravda,' newspaper of the Young Communist League, in commenting on the Party decision.' "

RECOGNITION OF RUSSIA

EVERY AGENCY of Communist support was centered upon the task of forcing the United States to recognize officially the government of the U. S. S. R. Thousands of prominent American men and women were invited to tour Russia where they were escorted by Soviet agents to model factories, schools and *unused churches*. American college and university professors as well as students were enrolled in Summer Schools, to lay the ground work for the teaching of Marxian-Socialism upon their return to the United States, while still others were drilled in the art of selling recognition from the lecture platform upon their return.

It has even been suggested that the U. S. S. R. subsidized a part of the expenses of such American agents of the Soviet propaganda system.

Revolutionary writers sold the glories of the new Godless Russia. Returned subsidized Americans lectured in church and in school and before clubs but never telling the true story of the great experiment through which the Russian working class had lost all freedom of speech, of press, of religion, and became super-slaves. Foreign agents were given travel admission to the United States to allure thoughtless Americans as well as support for recognition by the U. S.

The Friends of the Soviet Union, the American Civil Liberties Union, the International Labor Defense and at least a score of other supporting groups lectured, prepared petitions, traveled to far corners of the U. S., arranged public meetings of protest and demands, spoke over the radio and gained headlines in the press in the interest of recognition of the U. S. S. R.

The American Legion continued to say NO.

Finally all of these agents called the attention of our people to the millions of dollars in Soviet trade—told how our unemployed would all go to work in our factories, and on farms to supply the demands of the U. S. S. R. after recognition, to say nothing of the fact that they would buy all of our surplus if we loaned them the cash or gave them unlimited credit. No mention to be made of all former repudiations of war loans to Russia. They had long ago been *good enough* to say they would pay nothing of the old debt.

The Legion rightfully and emphatically continued to say NO.

The American Legion held mass meetings in almost every part of our country warning the public against recognition of such a Godless government. We pointed out the types of leaders now at the helm in the U.S.S.R.—bank robbers, plunderers, anarchists, rank revolutionist and criminals of every type. Were we going to place any faith in verbal or written words from representatives of such a government?

In spite of all such warnings our government accepted the word of the U.S.S.R. agent as you will find in the pages of this chapter. It is also clearly pointed out how all trust has been broken and the continued spread of revolutionary propaganda has gone forward.

A copy of a petition demanding recognition of the U. S. S. R. is reproduced on the following page to show the strength of Soviet support in the United States.

News Release

Release on
January 30, 1933

THE FELLOWSHIP OF RECONCILIATION
383 Bible House, New York, N. Y.
J. B. Matthews, Executive Secretary

EDUCATORS URGE RECOGNITION OF RUSSIA

Eight Hundred College Presidents and Professors Join in Request

Two hundred sixty-eight colleges in forty-five States and the District of Columbia were represented in the list of eight hundred college presidents and professors who addressed a petition to President-elect Roosevelt today urging the recognition of the Government of the Union of Socialist Soviet Republics.

From the headquarters of the Fellowship of Reconciliation, Professor Reinhold Niebuhr, national chairman of the organization, issued the following statement:

"This petition signed by eight hundred educators in favor of the recognition of Russia has been initiated by the Fellowship of Reconciliation because the Fellowship is interested in every political policy which makes for the peace of nations. The Fellowship believes that the failure of America to recognize the Soviet Government is one of the most serious hazards to peace in the present critical world-situation. It has contributed to the serious situation in the Orient and prevented adoption of policies which might have frustrated the imperialistic ventures of Japan. It will continue to breed dangers in international relations because it destroys relations with one of the most important and strategic nations in the present world-situation. The Fellowship hopes this petition will contribute to the rising tide of American sentiment in favor of recognition which will lead the administration and congress to act."

J. B. Matthews, executive secretary of the Fellowship, stated that signatures endorsing recognition of Russia were coming in daily.

The same 800 names of college Presidents and Professors who were on the staff of the 268 colleges in 45 states and the District of Columbia, mentioned in the news release from Fellowship of Reconciliation, are on file in the office of the National Americanism Commission, The American Legion, Indianapolis, Indiana.

TRADE RELATIONS WITH THE U. S. S. R.

Just prior to official recognition of the U. S. S. R. by the United States, the press of the nation carried stories telling in glowing terms the enormous amount of trade the United States would conduct with the U. S. S. R. in the event official recognition was granted. Communist organizations and sympathetic groups painted beautiful word pictures of United States manufacturers and commercial concerns of all kinds selling tremendous orders of goods to the U. S. S. R. None of these predictions have come true, as will be shown by the following report from the United States Tariff Commission, Washington, D. C.

The following table of exports and imports covering trade with the U. S. S. R. from 1932 to 1935 is self-explanatory.

	U. S. Exports to U. S. S. R.	U. S. Imports from U. S. S. R.
1932	$12,466,249	$ 9,128,795
1933	8,743,129	11,347,568
1934	14,866,515	11,915,331
1935	24,743,000	17,736,000

It is of particular interest to note that in 1935 we exported to Soviet Russia only 1.1 per cent of the United States exports to foreign countries and that nation stood twentieth on the list of those nations purchasing American goods.

The following additional table shows the amount purchased by the twenty leading buyers of American goods in 1935 and 1936. The percentage figure after the name of the country designates the percentage of our entire export business purchased by that government:

Our Best Buyers of American Goods

(* indicates countries making larger purchases from the United States in 1935 than in 1934)

1935	Value of U. S. Exports
1. United Kingdom (19.0%)*	$433,385,000
2. Canada (14.2%)*	323,191,000
3. Japan (8.9%)	203,260,000
4. France (5.1%)*	116,920,000
5. Germany (4.0%)	91,662,000
6. Italy (3.2%)*	72,450,000
7. Mexico (2.9%)*	65,576,000
8. Cuba (2.6%)*	60,153,000
9. Belgium (2.6%)*	58,208,000
10. Australia (2.5%)*	57,088,000
11. British South Africa (2.4%)*	53,625,000
12. Philippine Islands (2.3%)*	52,595,000
13. Argentina (2.2%)*	49,288,000
14. Netherlands (2.1%)	48,540,000
15. Brazil (1.9%)*	43,618,000
16. Spain (1.8%)*	41,341,000
17. Sweden (1.7%)*	38,214,000
18. China (1.7%)	38,156,000
19. British India (1.4%)*	31,452,000
20. Soviet Russia (1.1%)*	24,743,000

1936	Value of U. S. Exports
1. United Kingdom (17.1%)*	$295,978,000
2. Canada (16.0%)*	277,035,000
3. Japan (7.9%)*	137,109,000
4. France (4.9%)*	85,211,000
5. Germany (4.1%)*	70,840,000

6.	Mexico (3.2%)*	54,848,000
7.	British South Africa (2.9%)*	50,411,000
8.	Cuba (2.8%)*	48,819,000
9.	Australia (2.7%)*	46,550,000
10.	Philippine Islands (2.6%)*	44,417,000
11.	Italy (2.4%)	41,728,000
12.	Argentina (2.3%)*	39,976,000
13.	Belgium (2.3%)*	39,581,000
14.	Netherlands (2.1%)*	37,123,000
15.	Brazil (2.0%)*	34,843,000
16.	China (2.0%)*	34,363,000
17.	Sweden (1.6%)*	27,991,000
18.	Soviet Russia (1.6%)*	27,805,000
19.	Spain (1.2%)	21,280,000
20.	British India (1.2%)	19,932,000

RECOGNITION OF THE U. S. S. R. BY THE U. S. A.

On October 10, 1933, the President of the United States corresponded with the President of the All-Union Central Executive Committee of the Union of Soviet Socialist Republics in Moscow, with reference to the possibility of the U. S. S. R. sending to the United States a representative for the purpose of discussing terms that would lead to official recognition. Under date of October 17, Mikail Calinin, President of the All-Union Executive Committee of the U. S. S. R., replied to the President's letter accepting the President's proposal and advising that his government was sending to this country M. M. Litvinov, People's Commissar for Foreign Affairs of the U. S. S. R., for the purpose of discussing questions of interest to both nations. Upon the arrival in Washington, D. C., of M. M. Litvinov, a series of conferences took place between himself and the President of the United States of America. These conferences resulted in the following proposal being placed with the President of the United States on November 16, 1933. The letter of M. M. Litvinov to the President of the United States set forth the proposals reading as follows:

"Washington, November 16, 1933.

"My dear Mr. President:

"I have the honor to inform you that coincident with the establishment of diplomatic relations between our two Governments it will be the fixed policy of the Government of the Union of Soviet Socialist Republics:

"1. To respect scrupulously the indisputable right of the United States to order its own life within its own jurisdiction in its own way and to refrain from interfering in any manner in the internal affairs of the United States, its territories or possessions.

"2. To refrain, and to restrain all persons in government service and all organizations of the Government or under its direct or indirect control, including organizations in receipt of any financial assistance from it, from any act overt or covert liable in any way whatsoever to injure the tranquillity, prosperity, order, or security of the whole or any part of the United States, its territories or possessions, and, in particular, from any act tending to incite or encourage armed intervention, or any agitation or propaganda having as an aim, the violation of the territorial integrity of the United States, its territories or possessions, or the bringing about by force of a change in the political or social order of the whole or any part of the United States, its territories or possessions.

"3. Not to permit the formation or residence on its territory of any organization or group—and to prevent the activity on its territory of any organization or group, or of representatives or officials of any organization or group—which makes claim to be the Government of, or makes attempt upon the territorial integrity of, the United States, its territories or possessions; not to form, subsidize, support or permit on its territory military organizations or groups having the aim of armed struggle against the United States, its territories or possessions, and to prevent any recruiting on behalf of such organizations and groups.

"4. Not to permit the formation or residence on its territory of any organization or group—and to prevent the activity on its territory of any organization or group, or of representatives or officials of any organization or group—which has as an aim the overthrow or the preparation for the overthrow of, or the bringing about by force of a change in, the political or social order of the whole or any part of the United States, its territories or possessions.

"I am, my dear Mr. President,

"Very sincerely yours,

"MAXIM LITVINOFF,

"People's Commissar for Foreign Affairs,

"Union of Soviet Socialist Republics."

The President of the United States replied under date of November 16, 1933, as follows:

"THE WHITE HOUSE
"Washington, November 16, 1933.

"My dear Mr. Litvinov:

"I am glad to have received the assurance expressed in your note to me of this date that it will be the fixed policy of the Government of the Union of Soviet Socialist Republics:

"1. To respect scrupulously the indisputable right of the United States to order its own life within its own jurisdiction in its own way and to refrain from interfering in any manner in the internal affairs of the United States, its territories or possessions.

"2. To refrain, and to restrain all persons in government service and all organizations of the Government or under its direct or indirect control, including organizations in receipt of any financial assistance from it, from any act overt or covert liable in any way whatsoever to injure the tranquillity, prosperity, order, or security of the whole or any part of the United States, its territories or possessions, and, in particular, from any act tending to incite or encourage armed intervention, or any agitation or propaganda having as an aim, the violation of the territorial integrity of the United States, its territories or possessions, or the bringing about by force of a change in the political or social order of the whole or any part of the United States, its territories or possessions.

"3. Not to permit the formation or residence on its territory of any organization or group—and to prevent the activity on its territory of any organization or group, or of representatives or officials of any organization or group—which makes claim to be the Government of, or makes attempt upon the territorial integrity of, the United States, its territories or possessions; not to form, subsidize, support or permit on its territory military organizations or groups having the aim of armed struggle against the United States, its territories or possessions, and to prevent any recruiting on behalf of such organizations and groups.

"4. Not to permit the formation or residence on its territory of any organization or group—and to prevent the activity on its territory of any organization or group, or of representatives or officials of any organization or group—which has as an aim the overthrow or the preparation for the overthrow of, or the bringing about by force of a change in, the political or social order of the whole or any part of the United States, its territories or possessions.

"It will be the fixed policy of the Executive of the United States within the limits of the powers conferred by the Constitution and the laws of the United States to adhere reciprocally to the engagements above expressed.

"I am, my dear Mr. Litvinov,

"Very sincerely yours,

"FRANKLIN D. ROOSEVELT.

"Mr. Maxim M. Litvinov,

"People's Commissar for Foreign Affairs,

"Union of Soviet Socialist Republics."

The reader's attention is directed to the fact that the People's Commissar of Foreign Affairs of the U. S. S. R. pledged his government to prevent the activity on its territory of any organization or group or of representatives or officials of any organization or group which has as an aim the overthrow or the preparation for the overthrow of, or the bringing about by force of a change in the political or social order of the whole or any part of the United States, its territories or possessions. When a complete review of the activities of the Communist Party in America has been made, there can be no doubt in the reader's mind but that the pledge of the U. S. S. R. to the U. S. A. has been broken.

Proof of the stand repeatedly taken by The American Legion against the recognition of Soviet Russia, because of their failure to comply with their agreement with the President of the United States, and set forth in the following excerpts of speech of the Honorable George Holden Tinkham, Congressman from Massachusetts, in the House of Representatives, May 14, 1935, reproduced here.

"Among the pledges given on November 16, 1933, by Maxim Litvinoff on behalf of the Union of Soviet Socialist Republics to obtain United States recognition were the following:

"To refrain and to restrain all persons in Government service and all organizations of the Government or under its direct or indirect control, including organizations in receipt of any financial assistance from it, from any act overt or covert liable in any way whatsoever to injure the tranquillity, prosperity, order, or security of the whole or any part of the United States, its territories, or possessions, and, in particular, from any act tending to incite or encourage armed intervention, or any agitation or propaganda having as an aim the violation of the territorial integrity of the United States, its territories, or possessions, or the bringing about by force of a change in the political or social order of the whole or any part of the United States, its territories, or possessions.

"And—

"Not to permit the formation or residence on its territory of any organization or group—and to prevent the activity on its territory of any organization or group of or representatives or officials of any organization or group—which has as an aim the overthrow or the preparation for the overthrow of, or the bringing about by force of a change in, the political or social order of the whole or any part of the United States, its territories, or possessions.

"Actual and indisputable evidence of the repudiation of these pledges was first laid before the State Department by Mr. Matthew Woll, acting president of the National Civic Federation and vice president of the American Federation of Labor, in a letter dated February 7, 1934, supplemented by a written memorandum accompanied by supporting documents. Further evidence of the repudiation of the Litvinoff pledges was submitted to the House Committee Investigating Un-American Activities at its hearing in New York on July 12, 1934, and at its hearing in Washington on December 17, 1934. The committee received and now has in its possession original and undisputed documents which show beyond reasonable doubt that there is in this country an organized movement seeking to prepare itself to seize and to destroy this Government by the use of force and to substitute for it the Soviet form of government known as the 'dictatorship of the proletariat'; and that this movement is directed and controlled by the Communist International, a political organization which has been, and still is, located in Moscow within the territory of the Union of Soviet Socialist Republics and controlled by the Soviet Union.

"In a report which the Committee Investigating Un-American Activities made to the House of Representatives on February 15, 1935, there appears the following:

"In December, 1934, it (the House Committee Investigating Un-American Activities) held a series of public hearings at Washington, D. C., at which representatives from various organizations and agencies that have recently been investigating communism presented statements of their findings accompanied by one or more recommendations.

"The Communist Party of the United States is not a national political party concerned primarily and legitimately with conditions in this country. Neither does it operate on American principles for the maintenance and improvement of the form of government established by the organic law of the land.

"The nature and extent of organized Communist activity in the United States have been established by testimony and the objectives of such activities clearly defined. Both from documentary evidence submitted to the committee and from the frank admission of Communist leaders (cf. Browder and Ford, New York hearing, July 12, 1934) these objectives include:

"1. The overthrow by force and violence of the republican form of government guaranteed by article IV, section 4, of the Federal Constitution.

"2. The substitution of a soviet form of government, based on class domination to be achieved by abolition of elected representatives, both to the legislative and executive branches, as provided by article I, by the several sections of article II of the same Constitution, and by the fourteenth amendment.

"3. The confiscation of private property by governmental decree, without the due process of law and compensation guaranteed by the fifth amendment.

"4. Restriction of the rights of religious freedom, of speech, and of the press as guaranteed by the first amendment.

"These specific purposes by Communist admission are to be achieved not by peaceful exercise of the ballot under constitutional right, but by revolutionary upheavals, by fomenting class hatred, by incitement to class warfare, and by other illegal, as well as by legal, methods. The tactics and specific stages to be followed for the accomplishment of this end are set forth in circumstantial detail in the official program of the American Communist Party adopted at the convention held at Cleveland on April 2 to 8, 1934."

"The 'manifesto' and the 'resolutions' incite to civil war by requiring one class 'to take power' by direct revolutionary process and then assume dictatorship over the country in the manner followed by the Communists in the Union of Soviet Socialist Republics, which is frequently mentioned as a guiding example.

"In pursuance of the revolutionary way to power, the program instructs members of the party to obtain a foothold in the Army and Navy and develop 'revolutionary mass organizations in the decisive war industries and in the harbors.' The trade unions should be undermined and utilized as recruiting grounds for revolutionary workers. How faithfully these particular injunctions have been executed was demonstrated by Navy officers appearing before the committee and by officials of the American Federation of Labor.

"The American Communist Party is affiliated with the Third International, which was created by officials of the Soviet Government and is still housed in Moscow with governmental approval and co-operation. This affiliation is not one of general sympathy or broad uniformity of purpose and program; it is of a definitely organic character involving specific jurisdiction on the part of the governing body over the Communist Party of the United States.

"The executive secretary of the Communist Party of the United States testified to this committee that his party was 'a section of the Communist International'; that it participates in all the gatherings which decide the policies of the Communist International and sends delegates to the various conferences in Moscow. This admission is confirmed by the records available.

"Obviously, what I have said is not sufficiently full to give a complete picture of the extent of which these Communist activities are being carried on throughout the United States. They do show, however—

"First. That the Communist International, acting upon Russian territory and controlled by the Soviet Union, has, since the giving of the Litvinoff pledges, directed the Communist Party of the United States and the Young Communist League of America to use every available means to prepare for the forceful overthrow of our Government, by propaganda and the organization of revolutionary trade unions, leagues, committees, and groups, and for the substitution in its place of a soviet form of government to be affiliated with the Union of Soviet Socialist Republics.

"Third. That this action on the part of the Communist International is a complete repudiation of the Litvinoff pledges.

"Fourth. That the publication in the English language in the Union of Soviet Socialist Republics for use in the United States of books and pamphlets attacking our form of government and their shipment to this country also constitutes a complete repudiation of the Litvinoff pledges.

"The evidence discloses that there has been an organized Nation-wide, systematic and rapidly developing attempt to undermine the institutions of the United States and to overthrow its Government. An official committee of the House of Representatives has certified to the truth of this statement.

"This evidence discloses also that since the recognition by the United States of the Union of Soviet Socialist Republics there have been a great increase in communistic activities and an enhancement of the prestige of those in control of them.

"This undisputed evidence from Russian and American sources shows that the Union of Soviet Socialist Republics promotes these activities to undermine the institutions of the United States and to overthrow its Government in complete repudiation of the pledges which it gave to obtain United States recognition.

"Since the Russian Government has failed to respect the pledges upon which United States recognition was conditioned, diplomatic relations with the Soviet Union should be severed at once.

"Refusal of those in authority to sever diplomatic relations with the Soviet Union places a serious responsibility upon the Congress of the United States."

1935 REPORT OF SOVIET ACTIVITIES IN THE UNITED STATES

THE REPORT of Earl Browder, Secretary of the Communist Party, U. S. A., at the Seventh World Congress in Moscow, as taken from the Daily Worker of July 29, 1935. Browder was the Communist Party candidate for President of the United States in 1936.

"BROWDER TRACES COMMUNIST PARTY WORK IN REPORT AT SEVENTH WORLD CONGRESS

"*Stresses Anti-Fascist Work and Development Toward Labor Party*
"By Vern Smith
"(By Cable to the Daily Worker)

"MOSCOW, July 28.—Tracing the *historic growth to maturity of the Communist Party of the United States,* Earl Browder, the Party's General Secretary, declared in a 90-minute address at last night's session of the Seventh Congress of the Communist International that the *American Communist Party had fulfilled the chief tasks assigned to it at the Sixth World Congress in 1928.*

"The present situation in the United States is the race between Fascism and Communism for the leadership of the masses. *Our task,* Browder especially emphasized, is now *to rally* the disillusioned *masses* into an anti-fascist organization and *anti-capitalist political movement with the development of a workers' and farmers' labor party as the goal."*

"TELLS OF PARTY'S DEVELOPMENT

"Browder enumerated the great *tasks carried out by the American Communist* Party: It liquidated factionalism within the Party, emerging united by 1930. The *Party gained a three-fold increase in membership,* cadres were developed for mass work, a *30 per cent increase in the native-born* membership took place and the *growth of Negro composition of the Party rose* from *one hundred to 2,500.*

"He reported *500 shop units* and *4,000 members,* which is one-third of all employed Party members. He pointed out that *one-fourth of the membership lay in the basic industries,* with a *growing intrenchment in the trade unions.* The Party *initiated an unemployed organization* and *extended its work among the farmers,* the *Negro masses,* the *students,* and on the *cultural front."*

"EXAMPLES OF PARTY WORK

"Browder reported that the Party has issued slogans which the masses accept as their own; *unemployment insurance, which forced a temporary national relief program;* against war and fascism; for civil rights for the Negro people; against class collaboration, for the united front. He cited the *recent massing of forces and agitation for a labor party movement,* the growing influence with the Socialist Party members and with the followers of the Epic and similar movements. He gave examples of the experience of the Communist Party of the United States in overcoming sectarianism.

"*The Party played an important role in the great strike wave, in which* political objectives emerged from the economic struggle. He described as instances the *general strikes' collision with the state power, as in the San Francisco general strike and at present in Terre Haute. In strikes the Communist Party often wielded a decisive and leading influence.* The Party learned 'Not only *how to start strikes but how to end them with victory or partial victory.'* "

"Organization of Youth

"Turning to the vital question of *winning the American youth,* Browder reported how the Party had achieved successes after the Eighth National Convention. He described the successes of the Party and the *Young Communist League in transforming a youth movement* initiated by fascists into anti-fascist *fighting organizations* and *showed the successful activity of the Young Communist League among the memberships of religious and Y. M. C. A. groups.*

"Browder spoke in detail of the *great strides in Negro work,* centering around the *Scottsboro,* Herndon *and Negro rights struggle, citing Harlem.* He reported on the energetic activities of the *American League Against War and Fascism, the Friends of the Soviet Union* and their struggle against Father Coughlin and *Admiral Stirling.* He described the effective campaign of the Communist Party in unmasking the Harry Lang type, resulting in the masses of Socialist workers repudiating the anti-Soviet policy of Socialist leaders like Cahan. Browder gave the Congress a description of the factional struggle within the Socialist Party. A detailed report followed on the *Communist successes on the cultural* front, citing the American Writers' Congress, the *New Masses, etc.*"

"Cites Weakness in Farm Work

"While reporting on the *progress of agrarian work,* Browder stated that this field was the weakest in Communist Party work.

"He told of the *growth of the workers' and veterans' movement* at present in the fight for their bonus bill. He emphasized in all these *struggles the growing sentiment for the slogan of Soviet Power.* "We *have naturalized in America the slogan for Soviet power,*" he declared. *Following Lenin's advice in* 1918, *the Communist Party has appropriated the traditions of 1776.*

"Browder here reserved a section of his speech for the future order of business and turned to the collapse of the 'grandiose schemes of the N. R. A.,' pointing out that their collapse has resulted in a wavering uncertainty and confusion of the old political parties and in a threatened constitutional crisis."

"United Front First Step to Revolution
"Broadest Struggles Tasks of Communists—Must Show Masses Only Road to Their Liberation
"(Special to the Daily Worker)

"MOSCOW, July 28.—The opening report of Wilhelm Pieck at the Seventh Congress of the Communist International was delivered in the forenoon session, July 26. A comprehensive summary of Pieck's report in the name of the Executive Committee of the Comintern follows:

"The Sixth World Congress had the question of the future international development of economy.

"The Social-Democrats foresaw a period of perpetual prosperity. The right opportunists in the Communist International had the perspective of the further strengthening of capitalist stabilization. *At the Sixth Congress the initiative of Stalin foresaw the sharpening of all the contradictions of capitalism and the new revolutionary trend, shattering capitalist stabilization, and this was what happened.*

"*Shortly after the Sixth Congress began, unparalleled strikes took place in* many countries and the anti-imperialist movements in China and India grew in strength. Capitalist production continued strongly, but by means of rationalization and increased unemployment. Social-Democracy involved itself ever more with the capitalist state and with the industrial apparatus and ever more drove the economic struggle of the workers into the background."

"CLASS AGAINST CLASS

"*Out of this situation arose the Communist opposition tactics, 'class against* class,' against Socialist bourgeois policies. This Communist tactic in nowise contradicted the united front; however, in carrying it out, sectarian mistakes occurred. It was correct sharply to differentiate the Communist Party from the Social-Democratic Party, but it was also incorrect to isolate it from the Socialist workers.

"Without a loosening of the reformist trade union discipline, without an independent *Communist strike leadership*, the bourgeoisie could have carried out its wide plans of wage cuts even in periods of the greatest economic activity, and there would have been neither a Lodz strike nor the struggle in the Ruhr; many workers would have left the movement disgusted. However, some Communists did not understand how to crystallize their influence in the reformist unions and among the unorganized.

"It was correct for the *Red International of Labor Unions to struggle against the hegemony of the reformist leadership,* but the Strassbourg Conference resolutions in 1929 for independent leadership 'in spite of and against the reformist unions' was incorrect. It was correct to oppose the Brandler theory of 'compelling the Bonzes,' but it was incorrect to say that no influence could or should be brought to bear on the bureaucrats through the membership. While correctly fighting the mass expulsion policies of the bureaucrats, we still made mistakes in transforming the Red Union Opposition into new unions, and especially bad was the sectarianism in England, where the trade unionists were soaked in the old trade union traditions. Yet it is a fact that even during this period, before the crisis, the Communists were the principal leaders of strikes in several countries."

"THE WORLD CRISIS

"The crisis of 1929 brought unspeakable misery to millions of workers, farmers and members of the petty-bourgeoisie, and also increased the exploitation of the colonial peoples. A furious armaments race commences. Japan seizes Manchuria, Bolivia and Paraguay are at war, fascist dictatorship is set in Germany. These were accompanied by sharp class battles in Spain and China, the welling up of anti-imperialist and agrarian revolutionary struggles, the formation of Soviets, the establishment of the mighty Red Army of China and the peasant uprising in Indo-China.

"*The Twelfth Plenum of the E.C.C.I. could say in 1932 that the temporary stabilization of capitalism was ended and a new period of wars and revolutions was approaching. The Soviet Union showed the example. The tasks of the Communists lay in the organization of the masses for a struggle for any advantage,* however slight, and for carrying on the drive against fascism, against finance capital and *for proletarian dictatorship.* The tactical task was to prevent the placing of the burden of the crisis on the shoulders of the masses. The strategic center of the struggle was Germany. The Communists succeeded in mitigating the lot of large numbers of the unemployed through this struggle. Sabotage by Social-Democrats prevented the still further progress of the struggle."

"Growth of Political Struggles

"The Communists also, despite their hard struggle, failed to use all possible methods. While the Social-Democrats preached the doctrine that the crisis was abating, the workers were engaged in continuous struggles. However, there was a failure sufficiently to unite the actions of the workers and the unemployed.

"A whole series of political struggles flared up in Germany, the United States and Hungary; *there were farmers' strikes and veterans' marches in the United States,* the Spanish revolution, the strike at Invergordon of the British naval sailors, the mutiny of the Chilean fleet, the peasant uprising in the Polish Ukraine, the mutiny of the cruiser Seven Provinces. But these did not result in political mass struggle against the capitalist state, and there was also failure in the organization and co-ordination of forces. There were cases of brilliant organizational work but there was underestimation of the fact which *Stalin emphasized in 1925—that the average worker saw his safety in the trade unions, be they good or bad; in the United States for a long time Communists considered the American Federation of Labor as only a strike-breaking organization and saw only Green and such leaders and overlooked the average member.*"

"Underestimation of Fascism

"A great mistake was underestimation of the fascist danger, but on the other hand fascism was seen where it did not exist. There was the failure to win as allies to the proletariat the farmers and the petty bourgeoisie.

"The weaknesses of the working class were caused by the splitting and the treachery of Social-Democracy, which enabled the bourgeoisie to deceive the petty bourgeoisie and the peasantry and to use them in launching the fascist offensive. In order to avoid the fascist catastrophe in Germany there was needed a broad united front and the Red Front organization should have formed a united fighting organization with the Reichsbanner. They should have been able to force the Weimar government to disarm the fascist bands and tear up the Versailles Treaty.

"The majority of the workers did not do this, and instead blindly followed the Social-Democratic leaders, despite the Communists' warnings.

"The Communists alone were not able to ward off the catastrophe, although they mobilized all their strength in the struggle for the united front and sought at any cost to arrive at an agreement with the Socialist Party and the reformist trade unions. The Social-Democrats rejected every proposal, even on July 20, 1932, and on January 30, 1933, when *the Communists proposed a general strike.*"

"COMMUNISTS OPPOSE ADVENTURISM

"The Communists do not desire that trained revolutionists shall be sacrificed merely to show their heroism but instead that they shall organize new struggles and win new victories.

"In spite of the temporary retardation of the growth of the revolutionary movement, the workers of various countries have won big victories, as in China, Spain, the Soviet Five-Year Plan, and so forth. There was increased revolutionary strength and determination to fight for Soviet Power among the toilers of the whole world.

"Although the crisis changed to a depression, the bourgeoisie did not succeed in weakening the revolutionary world front. The victory of fascism does not bring in a long period of reaction, as the Social-Democrats predicted, but rather as Stalin said at the Seventeenth Congress of the Communist Party of the Soviet Union, 'The idea of storming the citadel of capitalism is ripening in the minds of the masses,' and it is spreading also among the broad masses of the Social-Democracy. The first expression of this was in the world united front for the Leipzig trial defendants, where Dimitroff's courageous defense of Communism played a great role, and in other significant struggles."

"UPRISINGS IN AUSTRIA AND SPAIN

"The Austrian and Spanish uprisings were not victorious, because the Social-Democrats there disregarded the lessons of the Russian Revolution and directed their policy before the uprisings towards the strengthening of the bourgeoisie instead of the proletariat. The Spanish Socialists in the government allowed the church to keep the land, gave the peasants no land, left the bourgeois state apparatus unaltered and did not fight for the disarming of the reactionary bands. The Austrian Social-Democrats surrendered one after another the victories previously won and allowed the fascists to pick the time of the struggle, never thinking of creating a fighting mass organization, but in Blanquist style turned the struggle over to the Schutzbund alone.

"We know that under the pressure of the masses the Social-Democratic leaders decided on a fight against the bourgeoisie. The Communists supported the struggle whole-heartedly. But precisely these struggles showed that the proletariat can not win under Social-Democratic leadership, and the revolutionary elements drew the correct conclusions when they went over to the Communists.

"The French proletariat in the face of the growth of fascism did not fall into the error of the theory of the lesser evil, but beat down the first great fascist attack. The election victories of the French Communists were the result of united front activity."

"UNITED FRONT ACHIEVEMENTS

"In England and America the Communists Parties strengthened the proletariat and increased their influence by correct united front tactics. Under pressure of the masses in Poland various Social-Democratic organizations formed a united front with Communists. On the initiative of the Communist Parties there was a welling up of political strikes and peasant movements, resulting in the further revolutionizing of the Social-Democratic masses and in the further building up of the united front.

"The united front movement takes many forms in various capitalist countries. Anti-working class Socialists in the government of Czechoslovakia and in the Scandinavian countries made the masses conscious that Social-Democratic ministers are no protection against fascism, war and the capitalist offensive. Especially important are the results of the united front in the fascist countries of Germany, Hungary, Italy and Poland.

"The united front is no simple uniting of two parties but indicates the turning of the masses from reformist to revolutionary policies, and is the *first step toward a strong revolutionary party of the proletariat.* Without a doubt the movement for a united revolutionary party will develop further as the victory of socialism in the Soviet Union destroys the basis of reformism."

"CHINESE SOVIET REVOLUTION

"An outstanding event is the Chinese revolution, which takes the Soviet form. The heroic struggle of the Red Army and the formation of Soviets resulted in a bettering of living conditions for the toilers, and is an example for all oppressed colonial peoples.

"The chief lesson of the Bolshevik revolution is that we Communists must ceaselessly work in the mass organizations, strengthening the Communist Parties and their unity with the masses, and strengthening the Communist International. If we do not carry out these tasks, then there is the danger of fascist dictatorships in more countries.

"In the period under discussion there was an important organizational and political strengthening of the Communist Parties, along with an increase in their mass influence. In the fight against opportunists and "left" sectarians the Communist Parties steeled themselves against opportunist influence and acquired the ability better to maneuver against the bourgeoisie and the reformists. Evidence of this is found in the heroic struggle of the Chinese Red Army, the world of the Communist Party of Germany, the clever tactics of the Communist Party of France, in the October battles in Spain, and so forth."

"MUST ACT TO WIN MASSES

"The Communist Parties must use these opportunities presented by the upswing of consciousness in the working masses in order to win them. Without fighting Social-Democracy it was impossible to fight against the bourgeoisie, because the prerequisite of this conflict is the winning of the Social-Democratic workers. The present situation demands increased criticism of those Social-Democratic

Parties and leaders who hold the masses back from struggle by strikebreaking tactics. *Our agitation and propaganda must be directed against the bourgeoisie,* especially against their most reactionary and *Fascist Parties*. The *exposure of the social-national demagogy* of the Fascists is the chief task of our agitation.

"The workers are for a united party, but often place the question too simply. A real united party can only come on the basis of a fundamental unity of program, strategy and tactics. The program and tactics of the Social-Democracy are bankrupt. *The program, strategy and tactics of the Comintern have stood every test.* Therefore we must struggle for the uniting of all revolutionary forces on the basis of our program, strategy and tactics and take the offensive against the reformists along the whole front.

"The sections of the Communist International in all countries have gained politically and numerically, yet organizational gains do not keep pace with the gains in influence. This is due in part to the sectarian attitude to the influx of Social-Democratic workers. The Austrian Party today consists two-thirds of comrades who a year ago were in the Social-Democratic Party. In the Congress delegation itself a considerable number are comrades who until the events of February, 1934, were functionaries in the Socialist Party. Precisely this Austrian Congress delegation is the best evidence of the downfall of reformism and the victory of our slogans."

"WORK AMONG WOMEN AND YOUTH

"Especially important is the work among women and youth work in the trade unions and other organizations. Here in recent times there *has been great improvement* in England, Hungary, Poland and the *United States*.

"We can have the greatest pride in the steadfastness of the German Communists under the most bestial terror, as well as in the fact that the Spanish and Austrian Communists not only manned the barricades but organized the united front after their defeat and laid the solid foundation for future victories."

"ACHIEVEMENTS IN FRANCE

"The glorious Chinese Communist Party stood during the period under discussion in the most advanced fighting positions. It has 300,000 members, a Red Army, a big Soviet area, but it has not won the majority of the toilers of Kuomintang China. As yet the organization of the proletarians in the industrial centers is one of its most urgent tasks.

"A tremendous event is the creation of the Communist Party of India.

"The greatest successes among all the parties in the imperialist countries were achieved by the Communist Party of France. It tripled its membership. It has become an important political factor in France throughout its successful carrying out of the united front.

"The Communist Party of England has increased its membership, achieved a united front with the Independent Labor Party but is still a small organization.

"The Communist Party of the United States has begun the rapid extension of its influence. It must itself still grow and consolidate its positions in the trade unions

more energetically for the *creation of a* broad *mass party of workers and farmers as a coalition of all organizations of* toilers *hostile to the bourgeoisie.*

"The Communist Party of Japan has organized the struggle against the Japanese plunder campaign in China in a Bolshevik manner. Prerequisite to further successes is the resolute extirpation of sectarian remnants, the resolute utilization of all legal possibilities of struggle."

"GROWTH OF PARTY IN POLAND

"The Communist Party of Poland overcame its drawn-out factional struggle, increased its membership three-fold, extended its political influence and led great mass movements. It must exploit every legal possibility to defend the last democratic rights to be able to lead the masses in the struggle for the overthrow of the Fascist dictatorship for a Soviet Poland.

"The Communist Party of Czechoslovakia led big mass movements, consolidated itself politically and organizationally and did good mass work. It must develop the united front movement broadly.

"*The Communist Party of the Soviet Union under the leadership of Stalin has achieved new world historical victories and is fighting for the establishment of a classless Socialist Society.* For us it is the great example of how one must fight and win.

"*In many countries the Communist Parties are already tremendous political factors,* in many countries have become the *decisive factors, in the labor movement.* This means that now there can be *no question either of foreign or domestic policy on which the Communists do not take a stand.* The Communists *must exploit every change in the policy of the bourgeoisie of their country, every antagonism within the ruling classes* for the repulse of reaction, Fascism and the war-mongers."

"ERA OF SOCIAL DEMOCRACY OVER

"The era of the Second International in the labor movement is at an end. A new rise, a new flourishing, or reformism is no longer possible. In some countries the Social-Democrats can perhaps still consolidate themselves, but we are experiencing a crisis of world reformism produced by the turn of the masses to revolution. The theories of the Second International are bankrupt, while the theory of the Comintern is confirmed by life. The crisis of Social-Democracy place before the Social-Democratic workers and all honest functionaries the question: What now?

"We propose to all members of the Social Democratic Parties and we propose to all Social-Democratic Parties the sole correct road: The marching together with the Communists in a united front struggle against Fascism and war and against capitalism for socialism. We propose the union of all revolutionary forces of the proletariat into a united revolutionary party on the tested theoretical foundations of the doctrines of Marx and Lenin.

"Before us Communists of the whole world stands the task of seeing to it, through the work of our own party, that every possibility is blocked for the bourgeoisie to demagogically deceive the masses disappointed in reformism. We must win the proletariat on the basis of the united front for revolution, for the struggle for Soviet power.

"[After the mid-day recess, Harry Politt of Great Britain, opened the evening session. Henri Barbusse appeared in the hall, was greeted with a burst of applause and took a seat in the Praesidium. Pieck continued his report:]"

"CAPITALISM DEEPLY SHAKEN

"The capitalist system is shaken to its foundations by the development of the general crisis of capitalism, by the *increasing revolutionization of the toilers,* and by the symptoms of political crisis in many countries.

"*The Soviet Union is exercising increasing influences on the development of the emancipation struggle of the world proletariat and oppressed peoples.* Here is an expression of the victory of Socialism in one country that leads to the victory of Socialism in the whole world. *From the victory of socialism we draw the certainty that our influence on the toiling masses of the whole world will grow tremendously fast.*

"But the capitalist system does not leave the stage of world history without a fight. It is weakened, but it has succeeded in getting out of the bottom of the trough of economic crisis. But despite the growth of war armaments it has not yet attained a pre-crisis level. In most countries there prevail evident tendencies to the further prolongation of the depression; the short-lived increase in production is unequal in various countries, and the industrial difficulties will most likely be accompanied by new onsets of the economic crisis."

"BELIEF IN CAPITALISM UNDERMINED

"The belief in capitalism is undermined among wide masses of people and the authority of the imperialists is weakened in the colonies. In a very tangible manner the situation shows the masses the contrast between capitalism and socialism. In this situation the indignation of the masses against the capitalist regime must grow rapidly and the struggle of the oppressed against their oppressors intensify quickly. The whole development of capitalism drives toward the maturing of the revolutionary crisis.

"The power of the bourgeoisie is tottering more and more because its reformist social basis is shaky and disappearing. Therefore it must, in more and more countries, out of necessity and not of its own free will, go over from parliamentary to Fascist methods for ensuring its rule. But *Fascist dictatorship intensifies the contradictions of capitalism,* exceptionally intensifies the war danger and at the same time *must produce an intensification of the anti-Fascist movement in all countries where the remnants of parliamentary democracy still remain.* Our slogan is the struggle against Fascism."

"WAR CAN BE AVOIDED

"*We are convinced that by a joint struggle of the proletariat in the capitalist countries and in the Soviet Union war can be avoided.* If this should not succeed, war will bring unspeakable misery to all the toilers. It will *lead to the open clash of all the contradictions* of the imperialist system and *bring the toilers of all coun-*

tries and whole peoples to the highest intensification of class struggles. The *task of the proletarians of the whole world will be to fight together with the Red Army against the bourgeoisie* for the *victory of the revolution,* for the *transformation of the imperialist war into a civil war. No social order falls by itself,* no matter how rotten it may be. *It must be overthrown.*

"It is *our task to organize the toiling masses rising against capitalism into a resolute revolutionary army of the proletariat* and to *lead the latter to the storming of capitalism.* Our World Congress must *mobilize the will of all proletarians* for the elimination of splits in the working class and for the *establishment of a wide united front of struggle against the capitalist* offensive of Fascism and war. It must show the proletariat the way to a *unified revolutionary party on the firm basis of Marxism-Leninism.* The demand of our Congress is the consolidation of the *Communist Parties* as the *leaders in the struggle for Soviet Power.*

"The world situation is extremely tense. Any day may place before us the *necessity of putting ourselves at the head* of the *movement of millions* for their emancipation. *We Communists show the masses* that the only way out is *the way of Soviet Power.* We enter the struggle for freedom, peace, bread, *Soviet Power and Socialism.* Our *main slogan* is the fight for *Soviet Power.* Our banner is the *banner of Marx, Engels, Lenin and Stalin.* The *leader* of the *world proletariat is Stalin.* Communists! *Weld the revolutionary class into a single army of millions.* (Prolonged applause.)"

All emphasis shown by italics in quoted sections of the foregoing chapter is by the editors and is emphasized for the purpose of calling the special attention of the reader to those sections of the quotations.

ACTION FOLLOWS "THEORY" TRAINING
"The Workers Must Arm Themselves with Revolutionary Theory

"We Communists are people of action. Ours is the problem of practical struggle against the offensive of capital, against fascism and the threat of imperialistic war, the struggle for the overthrow of capitalism. It is precisely this practical task that imposes upon the Communist cadres the obligation to equip themselves with revolutionary theory. For, as Stalin, that greatest master of revolutionary action, has taught us, theory gives those engaged in practical work the power of orientation, clarity of vision, assurance in work, confidence in the triumph of our cause.

"But real revolutionary theory is irreconcilably hostile to any emasculated theorizing, any futile toying with abstract definitions. Our theory is not a dogma, but a guide to action, Lenin used to say. It is such theory that our cadres need, and they need it as badly as they need their daily bread, as they need air, water.

"Revolutionary theory is the generalized, summarized experience of the revolutionary movement. Communists must carefully utilize in their countries not only the experience of the past but also the experience of the present struggle of other detachments of the international labor movement. However, correct utilization of experience does not by any means denote mechanical transposition of ready-made forms and methods of struggle from one set of conditions to another, from one country to another, as so often happens in our Parties. Bare imitation, simple copying of methods and forms of work, even of the Communist Party of the Soviet Union, in countries where capitalism is still supreme, may with the best of intentions result in harm rather than good, as has so often actually been the case. It is precisely from the experience of the Russian Bolsheviks that we must learn to apply effectually, to the specific conditions of life in each country, the single international line; in the struggle against capitalism we must learn pitilessly to cast aside, pillory and hold up to general ridicule all phrase-mongering, use of hackneyed formulas, pedantry and doctrinairism.

"It is necessary to learn, to learn always, at every step, in the course of the struggle, at liberty and in jail. To learn and to fight, to fight and to learn. We must be able to combine the great teaching of Marx, Engels, Lenin and Stalin with Stalin's firmness at work and in struggle, with Stalin's irreconcilability, on matters of principle, toward the class enemy and deviators from the Bolshevik line, with Stalin's fearlessness in face of difficulties, with Stalin's revolutionary realism."

From pages 48-49-50—"The United Front Against Fascism and War," by G. Dimitroff.

THEORY IN ACTION—WAR

Taken from "How the Soviet Union Helped Spain" by Harry Gannes.

"The guiding principle of the U. S. S. R. in defense of revolutionary Spain and its . . . government was expressed in the burning words of Joseph Stalin to the Central Committee of the Communist Party of Spain when the most fateful battle for Madrid was raging.

"On October 16, Comrade Stalin wired to Jose Diaz, Secretary of the Spanish Communist Party:

" 'The toilers of the Soviet Union only do their duty when they give all the aid within their power to the revolutionary masses of Spain.' " P. 5-6.

"Pravda, central organ of the Communist Party of the Soviet Union, spoke out:

" 'The working people of the world cannot remain indifferent and keep silent when the fate of the Spanish people is being decided and when the mercenaries of Franco are trying to annihilate the free people of Spain with bayonet, bullet, bomb and hunger.

" 'The brave Spanish people turn their eyes toward the Soviet Union. In our struggle for socialism the Spanish people find their strength, inspiration and energy.'

"For the first time in their history—during this bitter civil war with reaction trying to overthrow the legitimate government—Spain and the Soviet Union exchanged ambassadors. In both countries the envoys were greeted with joy and enthusiasm, with firm pledges of the closest ties and unbreakable co-operation." P. 15.

SOVIET MASSES ACT

"Meanwhile, the Soviet toilers were giving 'all the aid within their power to the revolutionary masses of Spain.'

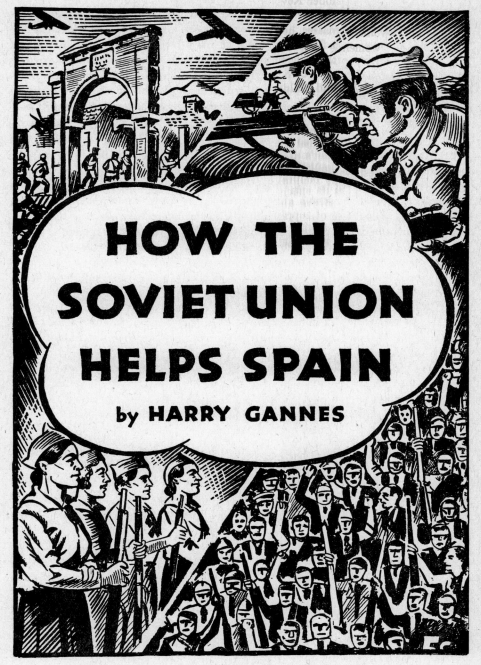

(Taken from—"How the Soviet Union Helps Spain," by Harry Gannes)

"Never since the October Revolution were the masses of Russia so thoroughly aroused, so aware of the danger to the Spanish people and to world peace.

"True, the Soviet masses held monster mass meetings in behalf of Spain. They collected huge sums. They did everything in their power to help Spain defeat fascism. By October 2, the toilers in the Soviet Union had collected $10,000,000 for Spain. The women of the U. S. S. R. had sent $2,000,000 in food and clothing for the Spanish women and children. A number of boatloads of food had been openly sent." P. 20.

"The Soviet Union never denied it sent thousands of tons of food, clothing and medical supplies. It denied that arms were sent.

"After the Soviet Union's dramatic and effective action in London, the world press reported that the Spanish government received new shipments of arms from many sources, undoubtedly facilitated by the Soviet Union's exposure of the action of the fascist powers and its encouragement of sources capable of supplying arms.

"The Soviet Union strove almost alone at first to end the non-intervention farce as the quickest way of supplying the greatest amount of arms to Spain.

"The position of the Soviet Union was perfectly grasped and enthusiastically greeted in Spain by every anti-fascist group." P. 37.

AFFILIATED AND/OR SYMPATHETIC GROUPS

IN STUDYING Communist activities in this country, one finds that there are hundreds of affiliated and sympathetic groups giving aid to a program having as its objective, the overthrow of the United States form of government. Practically all of these groups are fully aware of the objectives of Communism. In fairness, however, it must be said that certainly, some of our church leaders lending moral support to the Communist cause, must not be in possession of the full and complete facts concerning the objectives of these subversive groups, because the first of the Communist objectives is "hatred of God and all forms of religion." It is almost impossible to list in full all of these affiliated and sympathetic groups, because new ones are being formed daily and the names of old ones are being changed daily. The compilers of this publication, however, have only mentioned in this chapter those groups which are proven to be supporting the Communist cause, and this evidence is in the files of the National Americanism Commission of The American Legion.

While discussing sympathetic and affiliated groups it is interesting to note the following paragraph taken from "Political Education the Communist Party, International Publishers," "Today, in addition to candidates, the Party is organizing groups of sympathizers. This is all that active mass which has come very close to the Party, which stands on the threshold of the Party and acts under the direct leadership and according to the directive of the Party. Sympathizers are those who are the Communists of tomorrow."

THE AMERICAN FUND FOR PUBLIC SERVICE, INCORPORATED
(Better known as the Garland Fund)

There are three sources of information concerning the Garland Fund. The first is Report 2290, United States House of Representatives; second, the report of William Green, President of the American Federation of Labor to the United States Government, and third, the reports issued by The American Fund for Public Service, Incorporated, itself.

The following quotation is taken from Report 2290:

"The American Fund for Public Service (Inc.), located at 2 West Thirteenth Street, New York City, generally known as the Garland fund, has helped to keep alive the American Civil Liberties Union, International Labor Defense, the Communist legal defense committee headed by J. Louis Engdahl, the Workers' Communist School in New York City, and the Pioneer camps, as well as the Daily Worker and many other Communist and advanced Socialist and radical and ultra-radical organizations. This fund, in an original amount of about $900,000, was established in 1922 by a rich son of a Massachusetts industrialist and increased in amount, due to enhanced values of the stock—First National Bank of the City of New York—held by the fund, up to nearly $2,000,000."

The directors of the Garland fund are: Roger N. Baldwin, Robert W. Dunn, Morris L. Ernest, Lewis S. Gannett, Benjamin Gitlow, Clinton S. Golden, James Weldon Johnson, Freda Kirchwey, Clarina Michelson and Norman M. Thomas.

From President William Green's report, the following is taken:

"In April, 1923, the American Federation of Labor issued a statement calling public attention to the operations of the Garland Fund, citing the character of the work and those agencies which it helped and stating the methods which it had taken to discover these facts. Repeated re-examination of the situation has shown no reason to change anything said in that statement of 1923. The Workers' Education Bureau, an institution affiliated with the American Federation of Labor, had, for the specific purpose of securing an authentic statement of the policies of the Garland Foundation, and with the full knowledge of the American Federation of Labor, applied for financial assistance. The application was filed on February 25, 1923, and an answer was received on March 26, 1923. The trustees of the Garland Foundation, over the signature of Mr. Roger Baldwin, stated:

" 'At last we came to the consideration of workers' education at our meeting on March 21. In view of the report we had from Stuart Chase, the Board defined its policy in dealing with such applications in the following language:

" 'The American Fund for Public Service (Inc.) in its support of labor education, shall favor those organizations and institutions which instill into the workers the knowledge and the qualities which will fit them for carrying on the struggle for the emancipation of their class in every sphere.

" 'As it seems to us pretty clear that the work of the Workers' Education Bureau does not come within this definition, we came to the conclusion that we could not make the appropriation you request. We do not see our way clear to financing any enterprise except those definitely committed to a radical program of the character indicated in that resolution.'

"The American Federation of Labor said:

" 'It is thus made clear by Mr. Baldwin's letter that the American Fund for Public Service is interested in the promotion of "education" only when a revolutionary purpose is to be served.'

"Then, as during the intervening time, the board of trustees has been partly Communist and partly non-Communist, but always sufficiently Communist to throw the influence of the Garland wealth in that direction. Among the trustees during the latter years have been such well-known Communists as Robert W. Dunn, Benjamin Gitlow, Elizabeth Gurley Flynn and Freda Kirchwey. Institutions which have benefited by the Garland Fund are the Federated Press, whose Washington representative has been likewise the representative of the Soviet Telegraphic Agency; the pro-Communist 'Labor Action.' Brookwood College has likewise been a beneficiary to the extent of roughly $200,000.00. The Fur Workers' Union of New York City, which has been in constant turmoil because of Communist inroads and which the American Federation of Labor has been compelled to completely reorganize in order to destroy Communist control, was given $45,000.00. The struggle with Communism in this union continues to this day and there can be no doubt that a goodly portion of the trouble can be traced to the money given to the organization by the Garland Foundation when Communists in that union were in the ascendancy.

"One of the most ambitious projects of the trustees was the establishment of the 'Vanguard Press' in New York City, with a capital of $135,000.00. The 'Vanguard Press' has been assisted materially in other ways. The Garland Foundation has caused many studies to be made, the results of which have been published by the 'Vanguard Press,' along with a list of books literally filled with volumes helpful to the cause of revolution. The 'Studies of American Imperialism' was one of the studies thus conducted at a cost to the Fund of $35,000, while a series of 'Studies on Russia' cost $13,000. Such other institutions as the Committee on Militarism in Education, the League for Industrial Democracy, the American Civil Liberties Union, the International Labor Defense, the United Front Textile Committee, the Women's International League for Peace and Freedom, the Daily Worker and the New Masses have been beneficiaries. Practically all of these are operating at this time, continuing the spread of Communist propaganda and conducting subversive activities in whichever row is assigned to them by the Communist high command."

Following is a partial report of the loans and expenditures from the Garland Fund over a period of twelve years, as taken from their own records:

"TABLE OF GIFTS FOR TWELVE YEARS, 1922-1934
Including Cancelled Loans and Forfeited Bail

Periodicals and publications	$ 479,344
Workers' education	352,902
Research	141,767
Legal defense	135,821
Educational propaganda	83,905
Negro agencies	74,594
Education for children	59,262
Civil liberty	53,851
Strike relief and publicity	94,965
Workers' health	36,043
Legislative campaigns	18,865
Birth control	13,456
Trade union organization	15,170
Fund for aid to individuals doing creative work	10,000
Producers' and consumers' co-operatives	46,267
Co-operative farm	2,500
Student delegation to Russia	350
Agricultural reconstruction in Russia	18,097
Loan fund to radicals in need	5,000
Workers' summer camps	6,750
Total	$1,648,909"

It is not difficult to understand how the Communist Party can carry on such a widespread series of activities when you see some of the sources of its income. Strangely many leading persons in this country have unknowingly helped to finance the very destruction of their own business by such contributions to Communism should revolution from this source ever come in the United States.

"AMERICAN FUND FOR PUBLIC SERVICE
CHIEF ENTERPRISES AIDED DURING FOUR YEARS 1930-34

By Gifts

Brookwood Labor College, maintenance...$50,000

American Civil Liberties Union, national office and branches, for special
    campaigns and court cases..13,799

        Gifts $11,938

        Loans cancelled 1,861

National Association for the Advancement of Colored People, special liti-
    gation 8,082

Publication of studies on American imperialism........................... 4,204

League for Industrial Democracy, Chicago office, maintenance.......... 4,000

Federated Press, maintenance... 4,000

International Publishers, for particular publications......................... 3,194

        Gifts $2,500

        Loan cancelled 694

Mooney-Billings campaign 2,780

Southern Summer School for Women Workers in Industry............... 2,858

Joint Action Committee, Paterson Silk Workers............................ 2,000

By Cancellation of Loans

International Ladies' Garment Workers' Union, in settlement by part pay-
    ment of loan in 1926 strike.. 55,945

Associated Textiles, Inc., Minneapolis, uncollectible after securing judgment,
    on original loan of $50,000.. 40,767

International Labor Defense, national office and branches, forfeited bail and
    loans cancelled 37,239

Russian Reconstruction Farms, in settlement by part payment.................. 18,097

Unity House, I. L. G. W. U., in settlement by part payment of $25,000 loan.... 6,750

League for Mutual Aid, for use as revolving loan fund....................... 5,000

Independent Shoe Workers' Union, uncollectible (no longer functioning)........ 2,800

Il Martello Book Store, uncollectible (no longer functioning)......................... 2,500

GIFTS
Four Years—July 1, 1930, 1934

(Figures in brackets indicate year during which gifts were made.) (Those marked * are
loans and bail which were cancelled as gifts or uncollectible. Those marked ** are loans
which were made by the American Liberties Union out of a revolving loan fund and
cancelled as uncollectible.)

Total for four years..$270,299.09

Workers' Education—Total 53,708.70

Brookwood, Inc., Katonah, N. Y.—For operating expenses................... 50,000.00
        (1930-31—$15,000; 1931-32—$15,000;
          1932-33—$10,000; 1933-34—$10,000)

Seattle Labor College, Seattle, Wash.—For operating expenses (1930-31)   850.00

Southern Summer School for Women Workers in Industry—For operating expenses (1930-31)   2,858.70

Legal Defense—Total   41,020.29

American Indian Defense Committee, Washington, D. C.—Toward expenses of litigation in behalf of Pueblo Indian titles to lands (1930-31)   500.00

Eastman, Max, Croton-on-Hudson, N. Y.—Toward legal expenses in receivership for Russian film aided by Fund (1933-34)   100.00

International Labor Defense, New York City.
1. *Fund's claim to bail bonds in Michigan cases waived (1932-33)   1,879.37
2. *Balance due on various loans cancelled (1933-34)   447.00
3. **Various loans to national office and branches cancelled by American Civil Liberties Union (1933-34)   2,058.30
4. *Forfeited bail (1933-34)   28,747.03
    (In the Gastonia cases $18,247.03; Fred Beal, Pontiac, Mich., case $10,000; a North Carolina bond $500)
5. *Forfeited bail guaranteed by the Los Angeles branch (1933-34)   1,051.35

Tom Mooney and Warren K. Billings Campaign:
1. National Mooney-Billings Committee, New York City (1930-31)   1,500.00
2. Mooney Molders' Defense Committee, San Francisco (1930-31)   1,000.00
3. *Northern California Mooney-Billings Committee, loan of June 4, 1929, cancelled (1930-31)   250.00
4. **N. Y. Mooney-Billings Committee—Loan cancelled (1933-34)   30.00

Washington Conciliation Committee—Campaign on behalf of Centralia prisoners (1930-31—$300; 1931-32—$100)   400.00

Periodicals and Publications—Total   13,611.37

American Civil Liberties Union, New York City—For the publication of three pamphlets (1930-31)   542.00

Affiliated Summer Schools, New York City—Toward publication of Syllabus on unemployment (1931-32)   30.00

Federated Press, New York City—For operating expenses (1930-31)   4,000.00

Il Martello Book Store, New York City—Loan of October 28, 1925, cancelled as uncollectible (1933-34)   2,500.00

International Labor Defense, New York City—For publication of pamphlet (1930-31)   150.00

International Pamphlets, New York City—For publication of six pamphlets on economic and social problems (1930-31)   1,200.00

International Publishers, New York City—For publication of four books on economic and social problems (1930-31)   2,000.00
    *Balance on loan of March 29, 1926, cancelled (1930-31)   694.69

Series of Studies on Russia—Toward publication of 12 volumes
(1931-32) 150.00
Art Shields and Esther Lowell, Federated Press correspondents—For
research and writing on industrial conditions in the South and West
(1930-31) 500.00
Studies of American Imperialism—For publication and distribution of
two volumes (1931-34).. 1,844.68
Civil Liberties—Total 13,841.40
American Civil Liberties Union, New York City:
    1.   Campaign against injunctions in labor disputes (1930-31)........ 2,500.00
    2.   Salary and expenses of field organizers for local civil liberties
       campaigns (1931-33) 5,296.29
    3.   Emergency case fund, for legal defense cases (1930-31).......... 2,850.58
    4.   Philadelphia Civil Liberties Committee—Operating expenses
       (1930-31) 500.00
      **Loan cancelled (1933-34).. 250.00
    5. **Pittsburgh Branch—Loan cancelled (1930-31)........................... 400.00
    6. **Loan for Gastonia cases cancelled as uncollectible (1931-32).... 500.00
    7. **Loan for Philippine sedition cases cancelled (1933-34)............ 450.00
    8. **Balance in revolving fund contributed for future defense
       purposes (1933-34) 511.09
Revolutionary Age, New York City—Legal defense against action by
Post Office authorities (1930-31)... 583.44
Research—Total 4,360.99
Labor Research Association, New York City—For secretarial assistance
for Scott Nearing in connection with a series of books on economics
(1930-33) 2,000.00
Studies of American Imperialism—Under direction of a special commit-
tee; toward research for three studies... 2,360.99
Educational Propaganda—Total 4,313.49
Anti-Imperialist League, U. S. A.—For reorganization (1930-31)......... 313.49
League for Industrial Democracy, Chicago office—For operating ex-
penses (1930-31) 4,000.00
All Others—Total 139,442.85
*Associated Textiles, Inc., Minneapolis, Minn.—Balance of $50,000 loan
of April 28, 1926, written off after suit as uncollectible; $9,232.63
paid by receiver (1933-34)... 40,767.37
*Independent Shoe Workers' Union, New York City—Loans of June
12, 1930, and March 2, 1931, cancelled as uncollectible (1933-34) 2,800.00
Joint Action Committee, Paterson Silk Workers—For organizing cam-
paign (1931-32) 2,000.00
*League for Mutual Aid, New York City—Loan contributed to per-
manent loan fund (1933-34).. 5,000.00

National Association for the Advancement of Colored People, New
York City—For campaign for court cases for Negro rights
(1930-31—$6,000; 1931-32—$582.76; 1932-33—$1,500)............   8,082.76
*Russian Reconstruction Farms—Balance due on $21,015 loans of Jan.
7 and April 22, 1925, and $10,000 stock cancelled. ($12,918
repaid) (1933-34) 18,097.00
*International Ladies' Garment Workers' Union, New York City—
Part of $111,891.45 loan of September 30, 1928, cancelled in set-
tlement (1930-31) 55,945.72
*Unity House (International Ladies' Garment Workers' Center) Forest
Park, Pa.—Part of loan of October 28, 1925, cancelled in settle-
ment ($18,250 repaid 1933-34)..   6,750.00"

INTERNATIONAL WORKERS' ORDER

The International Workers' Order claims to be a fraternal sick and death benefit organization. It no doubt is, but, in carrying out its benefit program, we find a large percentage of the membership is either Communist or affiliated with Communist agencies. Financial assistance has on many occasions been provided for Communist Party programs and listed as given by the I. W. O.

Max Bedacht, who has long been an active Communist, is General Secretary of the International Workers' Order, with home office at 80 Fifth Avenue, New York City. Max Bedacht, according to government records, was director of the Communist Workers' School in New York City in 1930 and 1931.

According to the Sunday Worker, issue of January 17, 1937, the I. W. O. in its recent drive gained 29,864 new members, which brought the grand total membership, as of January 1, 1937, up to 127,332. This reported growth increase is, according to Daily Worker news stories, credited to the broad support given to strike and other labor disturbances.

Additional branch headquarters of the I. W. O. can be found at the following locations:

Chicago Office:
184 W. Washington Ave.
Chicago, Ill.

Philadelphia Office:
629 Chestnut Street
Philadelphia, Pa.

Boston Office:
5 Harrison Avenue
Boston, Mass.

Pittsburgh Office:
326 Fourth Ave., Room 31
Pittsburgh, Pa.

Detroit Office:
6432 Cass Avenue
Detroit, Mich.

Cleveland Office:
942 Prospect Avenue
Cleveland, Ohio

New Jersey Office:
40 Clinton St.
Newark, N. J.

"The Amtorg Trading Corporation[1]
(According to U. S. Report 2290)

"The Amtorg Trading Corporation was chartered under the laws of the State of New York. In May, 1924, it was organized by the consolidation of the Products Exchange Corporation and the Arcos-America (Inc.), both under Russian control. The capital stock was $1,000,000, but, with the profits added, the capital investment now is approximately $2,000,000. All of the stock of this corporation stands of record in the name of Peter A. Bogdanov, chairman of the board of directors of Amtorg, as trustee for the Bank of Foreign Trade of the Soviet Union. This bank is owned by the State Bank of Russia; and the State Bank of Russia is owned by the Soviet Government. Not a share of the stock of this corporation is owned by its directors and officials. Every official of the corporation, except one, is a citizen of Soviet Russia.

"Victor Nogine was in charge of Russian purchases in this country just prior to the incorporation of the Amtorg Trading Corporation. Nogine was a Russian Communist. He organized a great number of strikes. He died in Moscow in May, 1924. The first chairman of the board of directors of Amtorg was Isaiah J. Hoorgin, who was succeeded, respectively, as chairman of the board, by Alexis V. Prigarin, S. G. Bron, and Peter A. Bogdanov, the present chairman. All were Russian Communists.

"These several chairmen of the board of the Amtorg Trading Corporation, before coming to America, held high positions in the Soviet Government and in the Communist Party. They were all Communists before coming to the United States. They conform to communistic requirements and rules while here. They have the right to avow their Communism when they return home.

"The Amtorg Trading Corporation is owned by the Soviet Government. The Soviet Government is under the Communist dictatorship. Well-known and trusted Communists are the controlling officials of Amtorg. Practically all of the various lines of Russian trade in America are through or with Amtorg. Other Russian corporations function, but Amtorg is the parent, and its approval must be had on American trade. The All-Russian Textile Syndicate of New York has for its main function the purchasing of American cotton for shipment to the Soviet Union. The Amtorg Trading Corporation built up a credit, as its officials state, with American banks and business interests, amounting to $80,000,000. Financial journals now state that Soviet Russia owes American business interests $170,000,000.

"The Soviet Government engages in foreign trade through its agents. The Amtorg Trading Corporation is a Soviet Government agency and wholly owned by that Government. Its business is conducted largely on a credit basis, with only $2,000,000 invested capital, and the commerce to America from Russia is only about one-third of the amount of the purchases in the United States. From 60 to 65 per cent of its business must of necessity be on a credit basis. In case of failure of the Soviet Government, or the repudiation by that Government, Amtorg's ability to pay would be gone. It would be in hopeless bankruptcy. It could stand on no higher ground nor have a better position than its principal. The creditors

---

[1]Quoted from 2290.

of Amtorg would stand in exactly the same position as the creditors dealing directly with and having contractual relations with the Soviet Government.

"The committee hearings were begun in Washington, D. C., June 9, 1930. When Amtorg officials knew that it was to be investigated, a conference was called to outline the evidence to be offered this committee. Its high officials, including the chairman of the board, Mr. Bogdanoy; Vice-President John G. Ohsol, and its resident attorney, Mr. Michael, were present. The record discloses that it was the purpose to keep from this committee the evidence which might be damaging to Amtorg. A reading of the record will show that officials of that corporation were not frank and candid in answering questions, but were evasive, argumentative, and evidently sought to cover up rather than disclose the facts. In answering material questions, scarcely one of them was answered directly 'yes' or 'no.'

"They were unable to remember material facts or to remember important persons highly connected with the Amtorg organization. Some of these would have been important witnesses to your committee. Sixty-four employees left Amtorg from February 1, to July 15, 1930. Seven of these returned to Soviet Russia. In the same time 21 employees were transferred to other organizations. Your committee had its first hearing in New York City on July 15, 1930, at which time Amtorg had 23 employees on vacation.

"Amtorg has brought a large number of Russians to this country, claiming that they were connected with its business; 66 in 1926; 171 in 1927; 220 in 1928; 552 in 1929; and the first half of 1930, 525 not including families. Visa matters of Amtorg are handled through its attorneys, Simpson, Thacher, and Bartlett. When a Russian desires to come to the United States a telegram is sent to Amtorg, and Amtorg then writes Simpson, Thacher & Bartlett, and these attorneys inform the American Consul at Berlin that the man is all right. One witness states that no one could get a visa unless he has the approval of this firm of lawyers.

"The best inside view of Amtorg is given by Basil W. Delgass, who was three and a half years vice-president of Amtorg. He was born in Russia, was never a Communist, and he came to this country in 1926. Mr. Delgass resigned as vice-president of Amtorg July 23, 1930. He resigned of his own accord, although a month before he was advised to return to Russia. He is now under a death sentence in Russia, sentenced to be shot, and all of his property forfeited, he says, because he resigned from Amtorg and refused to return to Russia. With respect to the meeting of Amtorg officials, looking to the investigation by the Fish committee, Mr. Delgass says that statements were prepared which different officials should swear to, and, using Mr. Delgass's own language, 'I did not want to participate in perjury, as was done by Mr. Bogdanov and the others. All officials mentioned in the Whalen documents were in this meeting.' Delgass says there was a Communist organization in Amtorg, composed of the members who came from Moscow. A woman referred to as Comrade Liza, mentioned in the Whalen papers, was secretary of this organization. There was an American Communist organization in Amtorg. Bogdanov and the other officials denied knowing Comrade Liza, or that any such woman was in Amtorg. Mr. Delgass says everybody knew Comrade Liza. She was secretary of the Communist organization in Amtorg, and she looked after the behavior of the Communist employees of Amtorg, and when they did wrong she reprimanded them. In this meeting preparatory to giving evidence before the Fish Committee the witnesses were told to say that they did not know Comrade Liza, that they never knew a woman of that name. They were told to say there were no Communist activities whatsoever in Amtorg. On the question of how Soviet citizens came to Amtorg and became its officials, they were told to say that they drew no salaries from Amtorg, and that they worked for other organizations with which they were connected in Moscow. The facts were, they were in the employ of and received their salaries from Amtorg.

"The Soviet citizens employed by Amtorg were required to send their children to the senior and junior Communist cell, where lectures were given by different members of Amtorg, and they were in charge of one of the members of the Communist Party, employed by Amtorg. The witness sent his son and daughter to this school in conformity to the rules of Amtorg. This rule, however, did not apply to American citizens.

"Doctor Sheftel came to the United States, pretending to represent the Russian Department of Health, but instead he taught a Communist school and was in constant touch with Amtorg officials. He was in the meeting in which the evidence was outlined to be given to the Fish committee relating to Amtorg activities and the Whalen documents.

"The witness says that collections were handled by Amtorg for the Passaic strike conducted by the Communists. He says collections were taken for various causes. There was a regular 2 per cent deduction from the salaries of the Soviet citizens. This was for 'professional needs.' Further deductions were made for 'State loans.' These amounted to two months' salary each year. The witness paid $14 per month for three months for a 'special fund.' He filed two receipts of the Amtorg Trading Corporation—one for $67 and one for $56. The first recited, it was for: 'Mosamtorg special, $14; F State Bank Sub. a/c $28; F Coop House membership, $25.' The last subscription of $56 was for 'F Sub a/c State Bank.'

"Two other Russian Communists, Piatakoff and Ossinsky, were slated as officials of Amtorg, but their communistic records were such that visas were denied them. Bogdanov and Ziavkin are the highest officials of the Amtorg Trading Corporation. They may be called the representatives of agents of the Soviet Government, but when the relative connection and importance of Amtorg is considered they approach the dignity of officials of that government.

"Both the present chairman of the board and the business manager of Amtorg were not only Communists, but revolutionists. They now say they are not Communists.

"A man does not ordinarily cease to be a Communist, and become a non-Communist, simply by saying so. These high officials hold their present positions as political appointments. They represent the Russian Government controls, and they are dictated to by Communists. Only by word of mouth have they ceased to be Communists. They were called upon to renounce Communism that they might enter the United States. In every question relating to Communism, where evasion could be had, they have availed themselves of it, but there was one test—the oath. Both refused to take the oath. They remained loyal to the communistic basic principle—atheism—in a disbelief of and a hatred for the Supreme Being; they still adhere to the first principle of Communism.' "

The official publication of Amtorg Trading Corporation is "Economic Review of the Soviet Union," published monthly by Amtorg. The New York office of Amtorg is 261 Fifth Avenue, New York, the San Francisco office is at 260 California Street and the Head Office for the U. S. S. R. is Amtorg, Sovietskaya Plochchad L, Moscow. Ivan V. Boyeff is U. S. Chairman of the Board of Directors.

FRIENDS OF THE SOVIET UNION

The Friends of the Soviet Union is one of the more active groups aiding in the dissemination of Communist propaganda in America today. According to information contained in report 2290, all officials of this organization must be Communists. Corliss Lamont is National Secretary of the F. S. U., p. 3, D.W., 12/24/35. Elsie Trebst is the New England Organizer for the F. S. U., p. 2, D.W., 5/18/35.

The organization has for its purpose the raising of money to promote friendly relations with Russia, and continuously sponsors the showing of propaganda films depicting the merits of the Soviet system.

This organization took the initiative in the fight for official recognition of the U. S. S. R. by the United States government. It circulated petitions throughout the United States in an attempt to roll up at least one million signatures.

Another one of its major activities is the sponsoring of lectures for meetings in various cities throughout the country, which meetings, in the main, have been held in public school auditoriums. Within the past year it is noted that in the State of California, in the City of Los Angeles, action was taken by the school board to bar the use of American school rooms to these agents of foreign, un-American, subversive propaganda.

The official publication of the F. S. U. is Soviet Russia Today; published monthly at the same address given as headquarters for this group. It has units all over the United States and its headquarters is at 80 East Eleventh Street, New York City.

Friends of the Soviet Union in their January, 1935, meeting in Chicago announced Eugene Bechtold and Prof. Frederick L. Schuman, University of Chicago, as speakers at the mass-meeting memorializing the assassination of Kirov, of Moscow. February, 1935, they featured Scott Nearing, Communist ousted from the party for insubordination, and Anna Louise Strong, associate editor of the "Moscow News," then in the United States on a lecture tour. Vol. 9, No. 7, V., 2/13/35.

INTERNATIONAL LABOR DEFENSE

The International Labor Defense is the subordinate organization in the United States to the International Red Aid in the U. S. S. R. The official publicity organ for the I. L. D., is the Labor Defender, issued monthly at 80 East Eleventh Street, New York City. The I. L. D. was formed in 1925, according to the report 2290, as a Communist organization, to defend class war prisoners, and for the repeal of all sedition and criminal syndicalist laws. In this connection, it is interesting to note that the I. L. D., along with the A. C. L. U., led the fight in 1935 against the enactment of laws in the various states in the Union, which would have barred the Communist Party from the ballot; and another law, which would have compelled teachers in all educational institutions to take an oath of allegiance to the Constitution of the United States of America.

The program of the I. L. D., in brief, is as follows:

1. Defense of foreign-born workers, and against deportation.
2. Gives publicity to persecution of workers.
3. Fights for the right of workers to organize for self-defense.
4. Support to prisoners and to their families.

WHAT IS THE I. L. D.[1]
Excerpts from publication titled above.
"What To Do When Under Arrest."

"There are certain simple rules to remember in this connection:

1. Give no information to officers.
2. Plead not guilty and demand a jury trial.
3. Demand of the court that the I. L. D. defend you or insist on your right to self-defense.
4. Do not sign anything.
5. Telephone the I. L. D.

"But most of all, self-defense gives the worker the opportunity to throw aside every legal trick used by the prosecution." P. 11.

"The I. L. D. became a member of the only international working class defense organization, the International Red Aid. This organization has sections in 70 countries and a total membership of over 14,000,000." P. 16.

"The Soviet Russian section of this organization, the M. O. P. R., has several millions of members who are engaged in extensive relief activities for the victims of terror in capitalist countries." P. 16.

Anna Damon is acting National Secretary of the I. L. D. P. I., D.W., 4/2/35.

We list here a few International Labor Defense attorneys: Joe K. Grodsky, New York City; Leo Gallagher, San Francisco and Los Angeles; Grover Johnson, San Bernardino, California; David Levinson, Philadelphia, Pennsylvania (this is the same Levinson who participated in the Gallup, New Mexico, trouble in May, 1935); Maurice Sugar, Chicago and Detroit.

I. L. D. office in San Francisco is located at 1005 Market Street. I. L. D. headquarters at Denver, Colorado, is 1450 Lawrence Street.

---

[1]The above quotations from the pamphlet of the ILD show you the admitted connection of the ILD with the International Red Aid, the Soviet section being the M. O. P. R. This Communist defense group was formed in Chicago in 1925. It boasts of its part in the defense of—Debs, Joe Hill, Mooney, Billings, McNamara, Ettor, Giovanitti, Sacco and Vanzetti. A long list of Red defending attorneys are affiliated with the ILD. One of the most highly advertised defenders under the ILD is Leo Gallagher of California.

Fight the
Deportation
Racketeers

With the deepening of the economic crisis, the sharpening of the contradictions in the capitalist system, and the growing enlightenment of the working class, the rulers of imperialist countries are intensifying their efforts to intimidate or exterminate class-conscious workers

Especially are attacks being made upon workers of foreign origin

Prevent Deportation!

Don't tell anybody whether or not you are a citizen of this country.

In case of arrest don't tell when you arrived in this country or on what ship you arrived.

REFUSE to answer questions asked by any immigration inspectors.

Don't be fooled into answering questions asked by an immigration inspector who will tell you he wants to help you.

Don't give any information about parties or membership in parties.

Avoid giving your address to an officer. Your room may be searched.

DON'T CARRY MEMBERSHIP CARDS IN YOUR POCKETS that might be used to establish evidence.

Remember, you are *not compelled by law* to answer the questions asked by police or inspectors without the presence of an attorney.

Demand the presence of a lawyer from the INTERNATIONAL LABOR DEFENSE before you answer questions.

Notify in writing, telephone, or insist that the I. L. D. be notified as to where you are The I. L. D. will send an attorney to you

International Labor Defense
1179 Market Street
Telephone: UNderhill 3425

EDITOR'S NOTE: Photostat of International Labor Defense handbill which shows their fight against deportation of aliens subject to deportation.

David Bentall and Irving Krane are on the legal staff at Chicago. P. 3, D.W., 5/1/35. Edward Speigel is an I. L. D. attorney at Boston, Massachusetts. P. 3, D.W., 5/21/35. George Kaplan is an I. L. D. organizer at Gallup, New Mexico. P. 4, D.W., 5/11/35. Augustin Calvillo is active for the I. L. D. at Santa Fe, New Mexico. P. 1, D.W., 5/11/35.

AMERICAN CIVIL LIBERTIES UNION

One has but to read the daily press of America to find that the Communists have a staunch friend and supporter in the American Civil Liberties Union. In reviewing report No. 2290, it is found that the A. C. L. U. is reported closely affiliated with the Communist movement in the United States, and fully ninety per cent of its efforts are in behalf of Communists, radicals and aliens who have come into conflict with the law. Its headquarters are 100 Fifth Avenue, New York City. Its chairman is Harry F. Ward (Ward also heads up the American League Against War and Fascism, and is affiliated with the Methodist Federation for Social Service).

The photostatic copy of the A. C. L. U. letterhead will reveal the names also of the officials and the National Committee. When Roger N. Baldwin appeared before the Congressional Committee investigating Communism in the United States, he was asked by John Hamilton Fish, Jr., if his organization (the A. C. L. U.) upheld the right of a citizen or alien, it does not make any difference which, to advocate murder. Baldwin answered, "Yes." The chairman asked him, "Or assassination?" And Baldwin answered "Yes."

Roger Nash Baldwin, Director of the American Civil Liberties Union travels regularly in the United States to areas of conflict of workers' rights organizing meetings which he calls civil rights conferences. Although Mr. Baldwin has claimed that he is not a Communist, and has ofttimes attempted to rebuke those who tie the American Civil Liberties Union in with the Communist Party, we find the following quotation appearing on Page 7 of the Harvard College Class Book, of the Class of 1905, published in 1935:

" 'My chief aversion is the system of greed, private profit, privilege, and violence which makes up the control of the world today, and which has brought it to the tragic crisis of unprecedented hunger and unemployment. . . . I seek social ownership of property, the abolition of the propertied class and sole control by those who produce wealth. Communism is the goal."

The following list of Officers, National Committees, local committees and state chairmen of the American Civil Liberties Union are listed from the 1934 Annual Report entitled, "Liberty Under the New Deal," pages 58-61:

The report of the American Civil Liberties Union for the year 1935-36 is entitled "How Goes the Bill of Rights?" Listed below are a number of most interesting excerpts from this report which clearly tell the nature of the A. C. L. U.'s work in defense of programs closely related to the Communist activities in the United States, as well as the actual defense of Communists who have fallen into the hands of law enforcement agencies:

"Of the forces most active in attacking civil rights, the American Legion led the field—29 of the 89 correspondents so reporting. Nineteen gave Chambers of Commerce the lead." P. 9.

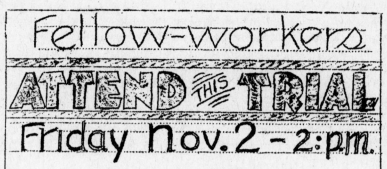

Fellow-workers

ATTEND THIS TRIAL

Friday Nov. 2 - 2:pm.

JUDGE WALTER PERRY JOHNSON'S COURT
City Hall
Fourth Floor

ELAINE BLACK   Secretary, International Labor Defense
HARRY JACKSON   Organizer, Marine Workers Industrial Union

have been convicted of "vagrancy", despite the fact that they
are functionaries of legal organizations of the working
class, giving full time in the service of the workers. These
cases are now being appealed to a higher court.

PACK THE COURTROOM.

MASS   SOLIDARITY   ALONE   WILL   FREE   THESE   WORKERS

Fight this drive of the ship owners, the Industrial Association and the police to smash militant workers' organizations!   Defend your rights as workers to organize, strike
and picket!!

JOIN AND BUILD THE INTERNATIONAL LABOR DEFENSE!!

Issued by the International Labor Defense
1005 Market Street, Room 410   San Francisco

NOTE: Photostat of leaflet used to prevent proper trial in court. It shows clearly the methods of procedure commonly used by the ILD.

"The forces fighting for civil liberties considerably strengthened their organization during the year. More local committees of the Union were active. The Union's membership increased by a quarter, both locally and nationally. Newspaper support of our campaigns was greater. Defense work was strengthened by the new policy of the Communist Party, which has encouraged the formation of united front defense committees to bring together diverse agencies in common and harmonious action. Rivalry and antagonism in defense work have practically ceased. The growing organization of the League Against War and Fascism all over the country has also reinforced the fight for civil liberty and given it a far wider popular appeal and support." P. 9.

"The Civil Liberties Union continues to mobilize all defenders of American democracy and to oppose any restrictions on freedom of agitation and propaganda, whatever their form." P. 10.

"The bill to punish advocacies of the 'overthrow of the government by force and violence,' known as the Kramer sedition bill, reported favorably in the House, was strongly opposed and did not come to vote." P. 14.

"Other repressive measures did not get far. The Post Office Department's bill to permit prosecutions for sending obscene or seditious matter through the mails at the place of receipt as well as the place of mailing did not even come to a hearing. The Union prepared and distributed widely a brief against the bill by attorneys Morris L. Ernst and Alexander Lindey." P. 14.

"The Union also supported bills sponsored by other agencies— . . . to make military training in land-grant colleges optional; to admit alien pacifists to citizenship; . . ." P. 15.

"In California the 1935 legislature enacted an amendment to a law concerning the use of public school buildings by citizens' associations, prohibiting their use by any organization 'advocating the overthrow of the government by force and violence.' The amendment was of course aimed at Communists, but grew out of a court test at San Diego in which the Board of Education had refused the American Civil Liberties Union permission to hold meetings in school buildings." P. 16.

"In New York the most damage to civil liberty was done by the passage in the closing hour of a joint resolution . . . for an investigation of 'subversive activities' in the public schools. An innocuous bill to require display of the American flag in school assembly rooms was passed, but bills requiring flag display in every school room and in all public assemblages of fifteen persons or more, . . . were defeated." P. 18.

"The Civil Liberties Union has offered to aid the International Labor Defense in combating the prosecutions, which will probably not go to trial until the case of Angelo Herndon in the Georgia court is finally disposed of. Eighteen more persons are held in Atlanta on the same charges, all connected with Communist or left-wing organizations.

"Of the cases from previous years in the courts, eight Communists convicted at Sacramento, Cal., stand out. While they are serving sentences, their cases are being appealed." P. 21.

"An extraordinary proceeding under the criminal anarchy law took place in New York City when the district attorney's office began investigating charges

Mass Protest Meeting

Wednesday, September 5, 8:00 P. M.

KNIGHTS OF RED BRANCH HALL, 1133 Mission Street

Workers and Friends of Labor: ADMISSION FREE

DEFEND VICTIMS OF THE VICIOUS CRIMINAL SYNDICALISM & VAGRANCY LAWS
FIGHT FOR YOUR RIGHTS OF FREE SPEECH, PRESS AND ASSEMBLY!
FIGHT AGAINST FASCIST TERROR!

The reign of terror by police and so-called vigilantes, paid hirelings of the Industrial Association, masquerading as upholders of the Constitution, is a threat against all organized labor and progressive people.

Fascism invariably starts with suppressing the most advanced section of the working class and then proceeds to smash all labor and liberal organizations. This is what happened under the bloody rule of Hitler in Germany and Mussolini in Italy. Therefore, the fight for workers' civil rights and the defense of all those whose rights have already been flagrantly violated must be the concern of all organized and unorganized workers and all progressive thinking people.

The INTERNATIONAL LABOR DEFENSE (ILD) is in the forefront of the struggle to defend all workers' rights! And is now defending the hundreds of workers arrested on framed charges (of "vagrancy, criminal syndicalism, disturbing the peace, etc.") because they participated in the recent general strike or hold political opinions contrary to the wishes of the reactionary groups—Chamber of Commerce, the Industrial Association, the Merchants' and Manufacturers' Associations and reactionaries among labor officials.

HEAR:

EMMA CUTLER, I. L. D. Organizer, out on bail pending habeus corpus proceedings in Imperial Valley.
LLOYD STROUD, seaman member of the M. W. I. U. and other hunger strikers.
ELAINE BLACK, Chairman.

Auspices INTERNATIONAL LABOR DEFENSE DISTRICT, No. 13, 1005 Market St., Room 410.

60

NOTE: Photostat copy of this leaflet distributed in San Francisco tells the story of action against legislation pending in many states.

against the Daily Worker, Communist publication. Vigorous protests from the Civil Liberties Union and others apparently caused the district attorney's office to desist.

"One old case from war days popped up when Joseph V. Stilson, convicted in Philadelphia under the espionage act for publishing anti-war material and who jumped bail, was arrested. He is serving an eighteen-month sentence in a Federal prison. The Civil Liberties Union has joined others in backing his application for pardon." P. 22.

"The new political prisoner during the year was Charles Krumbein, New York organizer for the Communist Party, who was sentenced for using a fraudulent passport abroad. While that of course is not in itself a political offense, the fact that he was sentenced to eighteen months with four years' probation, a severe sentence for such an offense, indicated political prejudice. Krumbein was paroled in May. The Civil Liberties Union joined in urging both pardon and parole." P. 23.

"Defense work for political prisoners has been greatly strengthened in the last year by the formation of united front committees representing diverse agencies, previously often in conflict over defense policies. The change in tactics was chiefly due to the new co-operative attitude of Communist-controlled agencies." P. 23.

"The Union is aiding in presenting to the Pennsylvania Board of Pardons the cases of three members of the Young Communist League convicted at McKeesport, Pa., in 1934 for inciting to riot in attempting to hold a meeting prohibited by the police.

"Four Communist demonstrators who had been convicted in Milwaukee in 1933 on a charge of riot growing out of an anti-Nazi demonstration against the German ambassador lost when their cases were appealed to the Supreme Court. They served sentences up to six months. The Civil Liberties Union and other agencies endeavored without success to get pardons from Governor LaFollette." P. 25.

"An unemployed leader in Racine, Wis., Sam Herman, a Communist, who had been prosecuted for criminal libel a year before when he charged that the police were implicated in his kidnapping, lost when he appealed to the Supreme Court of Wisconsin. His six months' sentence was cut by Governor Philip LaFollette to three months, but a pardon was denied." P. 26.

"Meetings and demonstrations conducted by the American League Against War and Fascism have run into a few difficulties in getting halls or public meeting places. The Board of Education of Spring Valley, N. J., revoked a permit granted the League for use of the high school for a meeting addressed by Major General Smedley D. Butler. The Board of Education of New Haven, Conn., has refused the use of high schools for meetings under Communist Party or left-wing auspices, including that of the League." P. 27.

"One incident was reported from Topeka, Kansas, in the spring of 1936 in which unsuccessful efforts were made to secure an investigation by the governor into the abduction and beating of one Max Salzman, an organizer for the Communist Party. No results were obtained, since identification of his assailants was impossible." P. 30.

"A local station in Fargo, N. D., WDAY, cancelled a program by Waldo

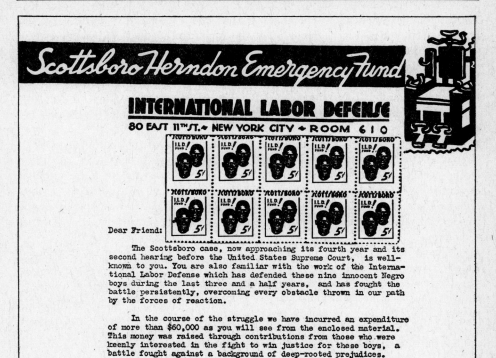

Scottsboro Herndon Emergency Fund

INTERNATIONAL LABOR DEFENSE

80 EAST 11TH ST. ✦ NEW YORK CITY ✦ ROOM 610

Dear Friend:

The Scottsboro case, now approaching its fourth year and its second hearing before the United States Supreme Court, is well-known to you. You are also familiar with the work of the International Labor Defense which has defended these nine innocent Negro boys during the last three and a half years, and has fought the battle persistently, overcoming every obstacle thrown in our path by the forces of reaction.

In the course of the struggle we have incurred an expenditure of more than $60,000 as you will see from the enclosed material. This money was raised through contributions from those who were keenly interested in the fight to win justice for these boys, a battle fought against a background of deep-rooted prejudices.

At this critical moment in the defense, we are desperately in need of an additional $6,000 to complete the necessary legal documents and to continue, what we are convinced is the basis of our past success in this and other cases, our campaign to arouse mass sentiment in defense of these boys.

Enclosed you will find $1.00 worth of stamps. We also ask you, as true friends of the Scottsboro Defense to return whatever stamps you do not sell—so that we can send them on to someone else. Won't you help us raise the defense fund by selling them among your friends? We appeal to you, to do whatever you can to help us continue in our work — to contribute as much as you will, but immediately, to the Scottsboro-Herndon Defense Fund

Very sincerely yours,

INTERNATIONAL LABOR DEFENSE

Anna Damon

Acting National Secretary

NOTE: Photostat of appeal of the International Labor Defense for money to aid in the defense of Angelo Herndon, admitted Communist labor agitator in Georgia.

McNutt of the American League Against War and Fascism after protests by the head of the Americanism Commission of the American Legion." P. 34.

"The drive of reactionary interests on all progressive forces, lumped together as Communist, has continued unabated. The Hearst press has led the attack, pushing the program of the American Legion, the Daughters of the American Revolution, the Chamber of Commerce of the United States, the Order of the Elks and a host of minor red-baiting agencies, profiting by the fears of the propertied classes.

"The chief efforts were directed to the passage of bills in Congress to strengthen the deportation laws against alien radicals, to penalize the 'advocacy of the overthrow of the government by force and violence' and to make criminal any utterance or publication which might induce soldiers or sailors to disobey orders. Their efforts failed to produce results, but they succeed in maintaining a widespread public opinion fearful or suspicious of any movement or person labeled 'Communist.'

"The Union, a favorite target of attack by these psuedo-patriots, distributed widely a pamphlet 'Who's un-American,' an answer to the false charges so frequently made, characterizing the philosophy and motives of this repressive propaganda. The Union has also undertaken a thorough investigation of the professional patriotic agencies, for use shortly in book form." P. 42.

"Outside Chicago, the Committee aided in establishing the right of the Communist Party to hold meetings in Hammond and Gary, Ind., in obtaining a private hall for a Lincoln memorial meeting conducted by the Communist Party in Springfield; and in preparing a test case of the Indiana law excluding radical parties from the ballot." P. 49.

"Attorneys were provided to members of the local American League Against War and Fascism arrested for demonstrating against a propaganda film, 'The Red Salute.' They were discharged. The Branch joined other groups in countering pressure upon the Board of Education to withdraw a permit to the local Communist Party for use of a high school auditorium for a Lincoln Memorial meeting." P. 50.

"For the first time this year the Committee undertook at the request of the Union's Board of Directors the handling of all legislative matters at Albany. Samuel Paul Puner of New York represented the Committee as lobbyist and legislative counsel." P. 63.

"The Committee opposed some thirty bills and endorsed twenty, of which we drafted five.

"Of the bills opposed, few were enacted. Only one was serious—the McNaboe resolution to investigate 'Communism' in the schools. One other was quite undesirable—granting contempt powers to magistrates. Among the most important of the bills successfully opposed were one barring from the ballot political parties advocating 'the overthrow of the government by force,' and the so-called anti-Nazi bill which would have made criminal any language stirring up 'race or religious hatred.' " P. 63.

"The Union (Northern California Branch) handled three deportation cases during the past year. Dominic Sallitto and Vincent Ferrero, alleged Oakland an-

AMERICAN CIVIL LIBERTIES UNION

31 UNION SQUARE WEST • NEW YORK CITY
TOmpkins Sq. 6-1330

HARRY F. WARD, *Chairman* • HELEN PHELPS STOKES, JAMES H. MAURER, BISHOP EDWARD L. PARSONS, *Vice-Chairmen* • B. W. HUEBSCH, *Treasurer* • ROGER N. BALDWIN, *Director* • ARTHUR GARFIELD HAYS, *Counsel* • MORRIS L. ERNST, *Counsel* • LUCILLE B. MILNER, *Secretary*

Oct. 20, 1936.

Mr. H. L. Chaillaux
The American Legion
Indianapolis, Ind.

Dear Mr. Chaillaux:

Three copies of our pamphlet "The American Legion and Civil Liberty", which you request in your letter of October 13th, were mailed you on October 17th. We shall be very glad to have your comments as soon as you have had a chance to go over this.

Sincerely yours,

Lucille B. Milner

Secretary

LBM:RW

Photostat of letter from headquarters of the A. C. L. U. (Report 2290 of the U. S. Congress on Communist activities states that this organization is more than 50 per cent in support of Communists who have come into conflict with the law.) Note the leaders of church and education serving on the National Committee—they probably have not read the government report.

archists, secured voluntary departure to Italy, but then removed their cases to New York City to take advantage of a favorable decision in that jurisdiction. Jack Warnick, one of the acquitted defendants in the Sacramento criminal syndicalism cases, was charged with membership in the Communist Party and illegal entry. His case was appealed to the Board of Review at Washington where it is being handled by the national office." P. 67.

"Another deportation case handled by the committee (Portland, Oregon) involved Chris, Anna and Alma Reinis, alleged Communists. Alma, the daughter, one year old when the family came to America, graduated from high school and the Oregon Normal School and taught in the public schools. When she appeared at the local immigration office to secure her second naturalization papers, she was charged with advocating prohibited doctrines, based on her activity in the Friends of the Soviet Union." P. 68.

"On October 1st last, A. L. Wirin, who had been our counsel for nearly a year, resigned to take a position with the National Labor Relations Board at Washington." P. 73.

"The number of members showed a gratifying increase during the year from 2,700 to 3,530. Most new members joined in response to appeals from old members and through circular letters to selected lists. Almost 400 members were obtained as a result of a national broadcast by Alexander Woollcott, in which he appealed for support of the Union's work. . . . The total number of members and supporters was therefore on January 31st, the close of our fiscal year, approximately 4,500 as gaianst a total of 3,700 the year previous." P. 77-78.

"The National Committee in control of the Union's policies now totals seventy-four. Five new members were added during the year—the Rt. Rev. Benjamin Brewster, Episcopal Bishop of Maine; Mrs. Margaret DeSilver of Brooklyn, N. Y., whose husband, Albert DeSilver, was one of the founders of the Union, and until his death its director; Sidney Howard of New York, playwright; Prof. Lloyd K. Garrison, Dean of the Law School, University of Wisconsin; and Bishop Edgar Blake of the Methodist Church, Detroit.

"The Board of Directors, meeting weekly in New York to carry on the Union's work, was increased by the election of William G. Fennell, attorney, Harold E. Fey, secretary of the Fellowship of Reconciliation and formerly the Union's representative in Manila, Sidney Howard and A. J. Isserman, Newark attorney and representative of the New Jersey Committee. Prof. William L. Nunn and Amos Pinchot resigned because of inability to attend meetings.

"The officers of the Union remain unchanged. So does the staff except for the addition of Charles E. Clift of Wilkes-Barre who has generously volunteered his services for full-time work as secretary of the New York City Committee and to handle research work and correspondence as well. Publicity work at the national office continues in charge of Clifton R. Read. The office was also aided greatly during the year in membership work by the volunteer services of A. H. Sakier.

"The Union continued close co-operation with all defense agencies throughout the country. Delegates or observers from the Union were sent to numerous conferences and conventions—the American Association for Labor Legislation, the Crime Conference called by Governor Lehman of New York, the American Academy of

Political and Social Science in Philadelphia, the Congress of the League Against War and Fascism at Cleveland, and the bienniel convention of the Young Women's Christian Association at Colorado Springs." P. 75.

OFFICERS

Dr. Harry F. Ward, Chairman; Helen Phelps Stokes, James H. Maurer and Rt. Rev. Edward L. Parsons, Vice-Chairmen; B. W. Huebsch, Treasurer; Roger N. Baldwin, Director; Lucille B. Milner, Secretary; Arthur Garfield Hays and Morris L. Ernst, Counsel.

BOARD OF DIRECTORS

Including the Officers, except the Vice-Chairmen, and Robert W. Dunn, William G. Fennell, Harold E. Fey, Osmond W. Fraenkel, Walter Frank, John Haynes Holmes, Quincy Howe, Sidney Howard, A. J. Isserman, Dorothy Kenyon, Corliss Lamont, Florina Lasker, Frank L. Palmer, W. Charles Poletti, Eliot D. Pratt, Elmer Rice, William B. Spofford, Norman Thomas, Mary Van Kleeck and Raymond L. Wise.

NATIONAL COMMITTEE

Hon. Charles F. Amidon, Hon. George W. Anderson, Dr. Harry Elmer Barnes, John Beardsley, Herbert S. Bigelow, Bishop Edgar Blake, Prof. Edwin M. Borchard, Bishop Benjamin Brewster, Heywood Broun, Prof. Richard C. Cabot, John S. Codman, Clarence Darrow, Margaret DeSilver, Prof. John Dewey, Dr. James H. Dillard, John Dos Passos, Robert W. Dunn, Sherwood Eddy, Elizabeth Glendower Evans, John F. Finerty, Elizabeth Gurley Flynn, Walter Frank, Prof. Felix Frankfurter, Dean Lloyd K. Garrison, Kate Crane Gartz, Norman Hapgood, Powers Hapgood, Rev. Hubert C. Herring, Rev. John Haynes Holmes, Charles H. Houston, Sidney Howard, Frederic C. Howe, Henry T. Hunt, Prof. James Weldon Johnson, Dr. George W. Kirchwey, Dr. John A. Lapp, Agnes Brown Leach, Dr. Henry R. Linville, Prof. Robert Morss Lovett, Mary E. McDowell, Anne Martin, Prof. Alexander Meiklejohn, Prof. Henry R. Mussey, A. J. Muste, Prof. Walter Nelles, Prof. William L. Nunn, Julia S. O'Connor Parker, William Pickens, Amos Pinchot, Jeanette Rankin, Prof. Edward A. Ross, Dean Elbert Russell, John Nevin Sayre, Rt. Rev. William Scarlett, Joseph Schlossberg, Prof. Wida D. Scudder, Rabbi Abba Hillel Silver, John F. Sinclair, Prof. Clarence R. Skinner, Norman Thomas, Edward D. Tittmann, Millie R. Trumbull, Oswald Garrison Villard, B. Charney Vladeck, George P. West, Peter Witt and L. Hollingsworth Wood.

LOCAL COMMITTEES
California

Northern California Branch, 434 Mills Bldg., San Francisco
    Dr. Charles A. Hogan, Chairman; Ernest Besig, Director
Santa Barbara Committee, 340 Channel Drive
    Dr. Oliver Hart Bronson, Chairman; Mrs. Thomas M. Dillingham and Mrs.
    E. F. Hammond, Secretaries
Southern California Branch, 624 American Bank Building, Los Angeles
    Dr. Edwin P. Ryland, Chairman; Clinton J. Taft, Director

Chicago Civil Liberties Committee, 160 N. LaSalle St.
    Jessie F. Binford, Chairman; Ira Latimer, Secretary
Iowa Civil Liberties Union, 1120 Capitol Theatre Bldg., Des Moines
    Prof. Edward S. Allen, Chairman; Carl Bogenrief, Secretary
Maryland Civil Liberties Committee, 513 Park Ave., Baltimore
    Dr. Arthur O. Lovejoy, Chairman; Elisabeth Gilman, Secretary

Massachusetts

Massachusetts Civil Liberties Committee, 20 Pemberton Square, Boston
    George E. Roewer, Chairman; A. Frank Reel, Secretary
Western Massachusetts Civil Liberties Committee, Amherst
    Prof. Colston E. Warne, Chairman

Michigan

Ann Arbor Civil Liberties Committee, 1403 Packard St.
    John Dawson, Chairman; Edith M. Bader, Secretary
Detroit Civil Liberties Committee, 401 W. Jefferson St.
    Rev. John H. Bollens, Chairman; Fannie Ziff, Secretary
New Jersey Civil Liberties Union, 24 Commerce St., Newark
    Rev. Archey D. Ball, Chairman; Rev. Jay Wright, Secretary

New York

New York City Civil Liberties Committee, 31 Union Square West
    Florina Lasker, Chairman; Charles Clift, Secretary
Erie County Civil Liberties Committee, 48 Irving Place, Buffalo
    Dean Julian Park, Chairman; Miss C. I. Claflin, Secretary
New Mexico Civil Liberties Committee, Box 1119, Santa Fe
    Michael Shepard, Chairman; Katharine Gay, Secretary

Ohio

Cincinnati Civil Liberties Committee, 147 Mason St.
    Dr. George A. Hedger, Chairman; Mary D. Brite, Secretary
Cleveland Civil Liberties Committee, 1013 Society for Savings Bldg.
    Rev. John Sommerlatte, Chairman; Harry J. Dworkin, Secretary; George
    Palda, Counsel

Portland (Oregon) Civil Liberties Committee, 1806 S. W. High St.
    David C. Epps, Chairman; Samuel Lockwood, Jr., Secretary

Pennsylvania

Pennsylvania Civil Liberties Committee, Box 863, Harrisburg
    Dr. Philip David Bockstaber, Chairman
Philadelphia Civil Liberties Committee, 215 S. Broad St.
    Edward Davis, Chairman
Pittsburgh Civil Liberties Union (a delegate and membership body).
    Permanent officers not yet elected
    Benjamin Sigal, Lawyer, Finance Bldg., Temporary Secretary

St. Louis Civil Liberties Committee, Paul Brown Bldg.
    Walter Diehm, Chairman; Victor Harris, Secretary
Seattle Civil Liberties Committee
    Irving M. Clark, Chairman; Bellevue, Wash.
Washington (D. C.) Civil Liberties Committee, 505a Insurance Bldg.
    John F. Finerty, Chairman; Gardner Jackson, Vice-Chairman; Frederick A.
        Ballard, Counsel; Elisabeth Higgins, Assistant Secretary
Wisconsin Civil Liberties Committee, 15 E. Dayton St., Madison
    Rev. George L. Collins, Chairman; Rev. W. R. Holloway, Secretary

The Union also co-operates with the following organizations not affiliated:
Kansas Civil Rights Commission, 121 West 6th Ave., Topeka
    George DeWitt Foos, Chairman
Conference for Protection of Civil Rights, 310 Hofmann Bldg., Detroit
    Rev. J. H. Bollens, Chairman; Hon. Patrick H. O'Brien, Counsel; Marit
        Hempel, Secretary
Professional League for Civil Rights, 910 Majestic Bldg., Detroit
    Frank E. Hartung, Chairman; Lillian Walerstein, Secretary
Ohio League for Constitutional Rights, Ohio State University, Columbus
    Judge Robert N. Wilkin, Chairman; Robert E. Mathews, Secretary
Portland (Maine) League for Peace and Freedom, 97 Exchange St.
    Rev. Vincent B. Silliman, Chairman; Mrs. Francis O'Brien, Secretary
Southern Committee for People's Rights, Box 665, Chapel Hill, N. C.
    Donald H. Stewart, Chairman; Olive Stone and Elizabeth Winston Malcombre,
    Secretaries

STATE CHAIRMEN

Alabama: Rev. Charles H. S. Houk, 932 Oxmoor Road, Birmingham
Arkansas: Kenneth Coffelt, New Donaghey Bldg., Little Rock
California: Clinton J. Taft, 624 American Bank Bldg., Los Angeles
Colorado: Rev. Edgar M. Wahlberg, Grace Community Church, 210 W. 13th Ave.,
    Denver
Connecticut: A. C. Worley, New Milford Times, New Milford
Delaware: Louis L. Redding, 1002 French Street, Wilmington
Georgia: Rev. Dr. P. D. McGeachy, 218 Sycamore St., Decatur
Idaho: Ray McKaig, 1922 N. 21st St., Boise
Illinois: Jessie F. Binford, 816 S. Halsted St., Chicago
Indiana: Rev. B. R. Johnson, 111 Downey Ave., Indianapolis
Iowa: Prof. Edward S. Allen, Iowa State College, Ames
Kansas: Prof. Seba Eldridge, University of Kansas, Lawrence
Kentucky: Byron Pumphrey, 316 Citizens Bank Bldg., Lexington
Louisiana: Isaac S. Heller, Canal Bank Bldg., New Orleans
Maine: Prof. Elbridge Sibley, Bowdoin College, Brunswick
Maryland: Elisabeth Gilman, 513 Park Ave., Baltimore
Massachusetts: A. Frank Reel, 20 Pemberton Square, Boston
Minnesota: George Leonard, Andrus Bldg., Minneapolis

Mississippi: Jo Drake Arrington, 411 Hewes Bldg., Gulfport
Missouri: Dale R. Johnson, 6925 Columbia Ave., University City
Montana: Daniel S. McCorkle, Conrad
Nebraska: Anson H. Bigelow, 1030 City National Bank Bldg., Omaha
Nevada: Martin J. Scanlan, 307 Lyon Bldg., Reno
New Hampshire: Prof. Philip M. Marston, University of New Hampshire, Durham
New Jersey: Prof. Edward A. Fuhlbruegge, 173 Park Ave., East Orange
New Mexico: Edward D. Tittmann, Hillsboro
North Carolina: Dean Elbert Russell, Duke University, Durham
North Dakota: Prof. Herbert C. Hanson, North Dakota Agricultural College, Fargo
Ohio: Prof. Lawrence A. Sears, Ohio Wesleyan University, Delaware
Oklahoma: Tupper Jones, Oakwood
Oregon: Ross W. Anderson, 3324 S. E. Woodward St., Portland
Pennsylvania: Dr. Philip D. Bookstaber, P. O. Box 863, Harrisburg
Rhode Island: Sigmund W. Fischer, Jr., 1002 Union Trust Bldg., Providence
South Carolina: Charlotte Stevenson, 1025 Pope St., Columbia
South Dakota: W. C. Rempfer, Parkston
Tennessee: Prof. William R. Amberson, University of Tennessee, Memphis
Texas: George Clifton Edwards, 502 N. Texas Bldg., Dallas
Utah: Alfred Sorenson, 435 E. 17th St., Salt Lake City
Vermont: Rev. Dayton T. Yoder, 164 Main St., Montpelier
Virginia: Virginius Dabney, Richmond Times-Dispatch, Richmond
Washington: Mrs. Charles Enoch Allen Bennett, 419 Boylston N., Seattle
West Virginia: Henry M. Russell, Register Bldg., Wheeling
Wisconsin: George L. Collins, 421 N. Park St., Madison
Wyoming: Rev. Roy Hills, Casper

COMMITTEES OF THE UNION

Committee on Academic Freedom
    Prof. E. C. Lindeman, Chairman
    Ellen K. Donohue, Secretary

Committee on Alien Civil Rights
    David M. Wainhouse, Chairman
    Lucille B. Milner, Secretary

Committee on Indian Civil Rights
    Prof. Jay B. Nash, Chairman
    Robert Gessner, Secretary

National Committee on Labor Injunctions
    Former U. S. Judge Charles F. Amidon, Chairman
    Alexander Fleisher, Secretary

National Council on Freedom from Censorship
    Prof. Hatcher Hughes, Chairman
    Clifton R. Read
    Mrs. Mildred Unger, Secretaries

Defense Agencies
(in which the Union participates)

Committee for the Defense of Civil Rights in Tampa, 112 E. 19th St.
> Norman Thomas, Chairman; Aron Gilmartin, Secretary

Joint Committee to Aid the Herndon Defense, 112 E. 19th St.
> Mary Fox, Secretary-Treasurer

Kentucky Miners' Defense Committee, 94 Fifth Avenue
> Herbert Mahler, Secretary-Treasurer

National Defense Committee for the Southern Tenant Farmers' Union, 112 E. 19th St.
> Aron Gilmartin, Secretary; Dr. Hubert Herring, Treasurer

Scottsboro Defense Committee, 112 E. 19th St.
> Rev. Allan Knight Chalmers, Chairman; Morris Shapiro, Secretary

You have noted the reports of progress of the American Civil Liberties Union. We are, therefore, giving you from the official bulletin of that organization, The Arbitrator, of January, 1937, the legislative program as outlined for the current session of Congress. The Legislative Committee of the Union, under the direction of Roger N. Baldwin, whose records you have previously noted, will attempt to pass the so-called liberalizations and thereby reduce the number of defense cases normally handled under existing laws.

"To Push Bills on Civil Rights

"A legislative program covering eight major proposals for Congress and seven state legislative campaigns has been announced by the Civil Liberties Union on the eve of the opening of Congress and forty-three state legislatures. Prospects for repeal of restrictive laws and enactments of other promoting freer exercise of civil liberties were considered more favorable than in years by Roger N. Baldwin, Union director.

"The Union's legislative proposals for Congress cover bills sponsored by the Union and support of bills promoted by other agencies. They are:

"1. Four bills to insure greater freedom on the radio.

"2. A bill to substitute for the present one-man Postoffice censor, a system of jury trials for excluded matter such as is now in successful operation in the Customs service concerning matter excluded from importation.

"3. A bill to re-establish the right of political asylum for bona fide refugees from foreign tyrannies.

"4. Support of the Department of Labor's bill granting wider discretion to prevent needless hardships in deportation cases.

"5. A bill to make military training in Federal-aided colleges purely optional.

"6. Support of the bill to provide for the Federal prosecution of lynchers where states fail to act.

"7. Repeal of the so-called red-rider adopted two years ago on the District of Columbia Appropriations bill prohibiting the 'teaching or advocacy of Communism.'

"8. A bill to provide a civil form of government for American Samoa, now under Navy rule.

"The Union's legislative proposals for state legislatures are:

"1.   Bills restricting the issuance of injunctions in labor disputes in industrial states still without that legislation.

"2.   Repeal of the laws in four states (Indiana, Arkansas, Tennessee and Delaware) denying the ballot to parties advocating certain proscribed doctrines. (These are the bills which exclude from the ballot any so-called political party which has as its aim the overthrow by force and violence of our form of government.)

"3.   Repeal of teachers' loyalty oath laws in the twenty-two states which now have them, and opposition to such legislation in other states.

"4.   Repeal of statutes in several states for compulsory flag-saluting of school children in violation of religious conscience.

"5.   Repeal of sedition and criminal syndicalism laws in such of the thirty-four states with this legislation in which vigorous campaigns can be organized.

"6.   Campaign for adoption of a model bill for the wider use of school buildings for public meetings in those states with unsatisfactory legislation.

"7.   Campaign for a model bill aimed at curtailing the practice of the third degree.

"In addition special legislation affecting civil rights will be considered in New York, Massachusetts, and possibly other states."

COMMUNIST AND UN-AMERICAN YOUTH ACTIVITIES

It is a recognized fact that the future of any nation depends upon the proper training of its youth. The Communists in the U. S. S. R. have realized this and have directed that a major portion of the Communist activity in the U. S. A. be among the youth. This chapter deals with the type of activities and propaganda now being carried on and spread among young people in this nation. The attention of the reader is particularly called to the emphasis placed upon the youth program in educational institutions.

"The Origin of the Young Communist International and the Young Communist League

From—"Young Communists in Action"—Compiled by Lewis Miller, Pages 33-38.

"The successful workers' revolution in Russia in November, 1917, led to the setting up of the all-Russian Young Communist League in October, 1918. At the same time numerous Communist youth groups were springing up throughout Europe. There was an urgent need for an international Communist youth organization. To set up such an organization, the International Youth Conference was held in Vienna on August 26, 1919. The Young Communist Leagues of Russia, Germany, Poland, Hungary, Italy, and Austria were represented. This Conference led to the meeting of the International Youth Congress in Berlin from November 20-26, 1919. The Congress had a much broader representation than the conference held earlier in the year. The International Youth Congress was attended by nineteen delegates representing fourteen countries which had 229,000 members in their Leagues. A final breach with the Second (Socialist) International took place, and the *Young Communist International* was established. The Young Communist International affiliated itself with the *Third (Communist) International* which had been set up in March, 1919.

"In the U. S., the struggle by the revolutionary workers in the Socialist Party against their reactionary leaders led to a final breach and the establishment of the Communist Party and the Communist Labor Party. Under the guidance of the Communist International, the Communist Party and the Communist Labor Party were united in May, 1921.

"The revolt that took place in the Socialist Party when the Militant workers came into conflict with the reactionary leaders was reflected among the youth, particularly in the Young People's Socialist League. Following the setting up of the Communist Party and the Communist Labor Party in 1919, the revolutionary youth broke with the Young Peoples' Socialist League, and formed the Independent Young People's Socialist League. The independent Young People's Socialist League affiliated to the *Young Communist International* in 1920.

"During the period 1919-1920 a wave of reaction swept the country. Attempts were made to crush any and all left-wing movements, and the Communist Party and Independent Young People's Socialist League were forced into illegality. After a period of underground work the revolutionary youth succeeded in regaining legality under the name of the *Young Workers' League of America*. The first convention of the Young Workers' League was held in May, 1922, and after a period of five months it had drawn into its ranks all the militant young revolutionists who were previously members of the Independent Young People's Socialist League and the Young People's Socialist League; established branches in fifty-one cities, and had a membership of 2,300. The Young Workers' League acted as the legal expression of the Young Communist League until 1924, when the Young Workers' League was abolished and the Young Communist League appeared as a legal youth revolutionary party.

"SUGGESTED READING FOR NEW COMRADES

"A. The following is a list of current Communist publications. New members should become acquainted with these as soon as possible, and become regular readers of the Communist press.

"1. Young Worker—weekly newspaper of the Young Communist League.

"2. International of Youth—official organ of the Executive Committee of the Young Communist International.

"3. Daily Worker—daily paper of the Communist Party.

"4. Western Worker—daily paper of the Communist Party.

"5. The Communist—monthly theoretical magazine of the Communist Party.

"6. Communist International—official organ of the Executive Committee of the Communist International.

"7. International Press Correspondence (Inprecorr)—news from the world revolutionary front.

"B. General pamphlets for the new comrade.

"1. The Program of the Young Communist International.

"2. The Program of the Communist International.

"3. A Program for American Youth—Seventh National Convention of the YCL.

"C. Pamphlets for further reading on subjects taken up in the Handbook.

"1. On 'What Does Capitalism Offer the Youth?'

"Youth in Industry by Grace Hutchins.

"What Is the New Deal? by Earl Browder.

"Youth Confronts the Blue Eagle by Gil Green.

"Twenty Years After by James Lerner.

"2. On 'What Is Communism?'

"Program of the YCI.

"Program of the CI.

"Why Communism? by M. Olgin (also see new membership classes on this pamphlet).

"3. On 'Why a Communist Party and a Young Communist League?'

"The Communist Party in Action by Alex Bittelman.

"Ten Years of the Comintern by I. Komor.

"4. On 'What Is the Character of the Young Communist League?'

"Program of the YCI.

"Who Are the Young Communists?

EDITOR'S NOTE: Photostat of front page of pamphlet entitled "Young Communist at Work," by Dora Zucker.

"Where to Begin—How to Build a Mass YCL by F. Fuernberg
"5. On 'The Work of the Young Communist League.'
"Young Workers in Action by Lloyd Brown.
"How to Organize and Conduct United Action for the Right to Live by
    Herbert Benjamin.
"Revolutionary Struggle Against War vs. Pacifism by Alex Bittelman.
"The Revolutionary Struggle Against War and the Tasks of the Commun-
    ists—Resolution of the Sixth World Congress.
"The Communist Position on the Negro Question.
"A Program for Negro Liberation by James S. Allen.
"Youth in the Happy Land.
"6. On 'Organization.'
"The Bolshevization of the Communist Parties by O. Piatnitsky.
"The Practice of Bolshevik Self-Criticism by S. Tsirul.
"Strike Strategy by William Z. Foster
"C. Biography.
"1. Days with Lenin by Maxim Gorky.
"2. Life of Stalin—a symposium.
"3. Lenin by Stalin.
"The pamphlets enumerated above cannot be swallowed in one gulp. New
Comrades should read them while taking part in practical work. In this way, the
material you read will find immediate application.
"Comrades who are interested in further theoretical study can use as a guide the
Home Study Courses issued by the League, or the *Marxist Study Courses* (on political
economy and the history of the working class).

"ABBREVIATIONS AND DEFINITIONS OF WORDS

"YCL	"Young Communist League
"YCI	Young Communist International
"CP	Communist Party
"CI	Communist International
"SC	Section Committee
"DC	District Committee
"NEC	National Executive Committee
"ECYCI	Executive Committee of the Young Communist International
"ECCI	Executive Committee of the Communist International
"TUUL	Trade Union Unity League—central organization of the left-wing trade unions
"MWIU	Marine Workers' Industrial Union (member of TUUL)
"SMWIU	Steel and Metal Workers' Industrial Union (member of TUUL)
"NTWIU	Needle Trade Workers' Industrial Union (member of TUUL) etc., etc.
"UC	Unemployed Council: left-wing organization of unemployed; affiliated to the TUUL
"A F of L	American Federation of Labor; craft unions under leadership of labor fakers famous for their betrayals and sell-outs of strikes
"LSU	Labor Sports Union

"IWO   International Workers' Order (has Youth Sections)
"FSU   Friends of the Soviet Union
"ILD   International Labor Defense
"WIR   Workers' International Relief (the Red Cross of the working-class)
"Agenda: List of things to be covered at a meeting.
"Agit-Prop: Agitation and propaganda
"Bourgeoisie: Capitalist class—bankers and bosses.
"Pettit-Bourgeoisie: Middle class, small merchants, etc.
"Deviation: Wavering or weakness that shows itself in attempts to leave the line of revolutionary struggle.
"Left Sectarianism: Isolation of the revolutionary movement from the masses of workers.
"Opportunism: Putting aside revolutionary objectives and searching for advantages that appear in the immediate situation.
"Plenum: Full meeting of any of the higher bodies (as District or National Committee.
"Proletariat: The workers; those who live by selling their labor power for wages.
"Radicalization: Trend of the working class towards the revolutionary movement.
"Renegade: A person expelled from the Communist Party or the Young Communist League for anti-revolutionary activity or failure to follow discipline.
"Social-Fascist: Covering fascist acts with socialist phrases—a common practice of the Socialist Party leaders.
"White Chauvinism: The theory of superiority of the white race over other races (particularly the black); developed and aided by the capitalists who use it as a weapon to divide the ranks of the workers.

DATES TO REMEMBER

"January 21st—*Three L Campaign*. We set aside the third week in January to commemorate the death of three great revolutionaries: *Lenin, Liebknecht*, and *Luxembourg*.

"May 1st—*May Day (International Labor Day)*. Originated in the struggle in the U. S. for the eight-hour day. At present, is a day of international one-day strikes and demonstrations of labor for better conditions.

"May 30th—*National Youth Day*. Main slogan on this day of anti-war demonstrations is 'Turn Memorial Day into Anti-War Day.'

"August 1st—*International Anti-War Day*. Anti-war demonstrations take place throughout the world, under the leadership of the Communist International.

"August 4th—On this day, in 1914, the World War broke out. It is used now as a day of anti-war demonstrations by the American League Against War and Fascism.

"September 1st to 8th—The week is one of international struggle of the youth against war. The high point is *International Youth Day* (September 1st), which originated during the World War as a day of demonstrations against the imperialist war.

"November 7th—Celebration of the Russian Revolution, which took place November 7, 1917.

"THE REVOLUTIONARY SONG OF THE WORKING CLASS

"THE INTERNATIONAL"

"Arise, ye prisoners of starvation,
Arise, ye wretched of the earth.
For justice thunders condemnation,
A better world's in birth.

"No more tradition's chain shall bind us,
No more, ye slaves, no more enthralled.
The earth shall rise on new foundations,
We have been nought, we shall be all.

"Tis the final conflict,
Let each stand in his place.
The International Soviet
Shall be the human race."

———

THE YOUNG COMMUNIST LEAGUE
Revolutionary Leader of the Youth
From: Young Communists in Action, compiled by Lewis Miller—a Handbook for Young Communists

"We Communists openly proclaim our aims. We tell the workers that under the leadership of the Communist Party and the Young Communist League capitalism will be overthrown and a government controlled by the workers and farmers put in its place.

"As a member of the Young Communist League it is your duty to study the Communist program. You must be able to explain to the satisfaction of any worker what are our aims and what we are doing in order to achieve these aims. Furthermore, in order to take your place in the revolutionary movement you must study our methods of work and put them into practice in everyday Communist activity." P. 1.

———

"Communists are not pacifists. We do not believe that war or capitalism can be gotten rid of by merely doing nothing about it. We fight the war danger through militant action—strikes, demonstrations, and finally, the overthrow of capitalism." P. 3.

"The organization of the working class under the leadership of the Communist Party and the Young Communist League will enable us to take over the factories, the banks, the railroads, the land, etc. The workers will then take charge of production." P. 5.

———

"Just as the Russian workers, with the leadership of the Russian Communist Party, were able to free themselves from the yoke of Tzarism and Capitalism, so will

To All Youth of Philadelphia

ATTEND THE

LIEBKNECHT - LUXEMBURG MEMORIAL
and SCOTTSBORO PROTEST MEETING

FRIDAY, FEBRUARY 1st, 1935, 8 P. M.

at Liberty Hall, 2109 Columbia Ave.

Karl Liebknecht founded and organized the first anti-militarist movement among the working class youth. He led the fight of the German workers against war, and after the war headed the movement which overthrew the Kaiser. An example of his courage and determination in the fight against the capitalist war makers was his stand in the German Reichstag. When all the so-called Socialists voted for the Kaiser's war measures, Liebknecht alone denounced and voted against these measures. For his part in leading the workers in this fight, Liebknecht was murdered by the capitalists' military agents.

Today, 16 years after Liebknecht's death, the war makers are again busy preparing a new world slaughter. The war budgets are twice as big as they were in 1914. The Roosevelt Government is spending over a billion dollars for new armaments. 300,000 young fellows are being trained by army officers in the C. C. C. Camps while they work at forced labor conditions for a dollar a day. The politicians talk peace but prepare for war. For the next summer the Navy is preparing the biggest war games in history to be held in the Pacific Ocean.

The United States, Japan, Great Britain and the other large capitalist powers prepare for war, and ignore the demands and needs of the working people.

In the Soviet Union, where there is the only workers government in the world, all the young workers have jobs. No one, young or old, suffers from unemployment. The workers' government takes care of them during illness. No flop houses, no homeless youth, no C. C. C. Camps but every opportunity to develope their minds and bodies. The sport, cultural and social facilities, which are the best in the world, are at the disposal of the Soviet youth. The youth of the Soviet Union enjoy a new life, because the working class carried out the ideas heroic Karl Liebknecht fought for in Germany.

The youth, just like all the workers, do not want war. We will not go in as easily as in 1917. The workers' organizations are stronger than they ever were before. In unity there is strength, and the capitalists realize this. They are introducing fascist measures in the United States because fascism is the most effective weapon of big capital in smashing workers' organizations and herding the workers into war. In order to most effectively break up the organizations they try to divide the workers. At present they are trying to divide the Negro and white workers. They are directing special oppression against the Negro people in order to make the white workers feel that the Negroes are inferior, and deserve to be treated worse. This is the meaning of the Scottsboro Case and of Angelo Herndon's sentence of 18 to 20 years on the Georgia chain gang because he fought for better conditions for the youth. The Young Communist League calls on every young worker to make the anniversary of the death of Karl Liebknecht a rallying point in the fight for which Liebknecht gave his life.

JOIN THE YOUNG COMMUNIST LEAGUE! FIGHT AGAINST WAR AND FASCISM!
FREE THE SCOTTSBORO BOYS AND ANGELO HERNDON!

GOOD PROGRAM—Main Speaker: **CLARENCE A. HATHAWAY,** Editor of "Daily Worker"

For news of the struggles of the working youth — Read the "YOUNG WORKER"
[Multigraphed] Young Communist League, 46 N. 8th St.

EDITOR'S NOTE: Reproduction of poster announcing a mass meeting in Philadelphia sponsored by the Young Communist League.

we in the United States, under the leadership of the Communist Party and the Young Communist League, overthrow capitalism and build a workers' and farmers' government—A SOVIET AMERICA!" P. 6.

"If it is necessary to destroy the capitalist government, why do we take part in elections?" you ask.

"The Communist Party and the YCL have a definite purpose in taking part in elections. To begin with, they afford us an opportunity to publicize our platform and the demands of the working class.

"Secondly, Communist candidates who are elected use their office in order to better carry on the fight to improve the conditions of the workers, and in order to expose the capitalist governments and show the necessity for setting up a workers' government. Lastly, the vote can be taken as a partial indication of the strength and support of the Communist Party, even though we know that many thousands of workers—Negroes, foreign born, 'paupers,' soldiers and sailors—are denied votes or cheated out of them. Young Communist League candidates in elections have the particular purpose of advancing demands for improvement in the conditions of the youth." P. 7.

"In its most general form the YCL is the *School of Communists*." P. 8.

"To train and prepare the working class for the final battles against capitalism." P. 10.

"We must fight against militarization of the youth in the schools, the CCC and transient camps. We call for the abolition of the Citizens Military Training Corps (CMTC), The Reserve Officers' Training Corps (ROTC), etc." P. 11.

" *'Every Factory a Communist Fortress'*

"To form unions and youth sections of unions in all industries, factories and farms. Through these unions we carry on the fight against discrimination toward the youth in industry (the apprenticeship system which means lower wages for young workers who do the same work as adults; the use of child labor; the intense exploitation of girl labor) and for the improvement of working conditions through shorter hours, higher wages, health and safety provisions, etc.

"The union is the fighting arm of the workers. To be most effective a union should take in all the workers of an industry. For this reason we Communists favor the formation of Industrial Unions—unions which are composed of all the workers of an industry. The left-wing unions in this country are organized into the *Trade Union Unity League* (TUUL). The unions belonging to the TUUL, such as the Marine Workers' Industrial Union (MWIU), the Steel and Metal Workers' Industrial Union (SMWIU), etc., are built on rank and file control, militant struggle for demands, and unity of all workers regardless of craft, race, color, religion, or political affiliation. We Communists support the TUUL and make every effort to build it and guide it along effective lines of struggle.

" *'Unemployment insurance at the expense of the federal and the bosses'*

"For the unemployed youth we demand immediate unemployment insurance at full wages to be paid by the employers and the government to all workers, including all youth without employment, regardless of age. We must rally the youth around the fight for passage of the Workers' Unemployment and Social Insurance Bill now before Congress (H. R. 7598).

"Until unemployment insurance is established we should lead the unemployed youth in the fight for relief, county work, free rent, light and water, and against evictions and forced labor camps (such as the SERA Transient Camps where the boys do a full day's work for 50 cents and their meals).

" *'Down with imperialistic War!'*

" *'All war funds to the unemployed!'*

" *'Defend the Soviet Union!'* "   P. 10-11.

"In this light we can understand how the Soviet peace policy is a revolutionary, international policy—and can see the significance of the slogan 'Defend the Soviet Union.' "   P. 12.

"The Young Communist League drill and defense squads have been formed." P. 12.

". . . and give our full support to building the American League Against War and Fascism."   P. 12.

"The Young Communist League endorses and supports the program of the National Student League."   P. 13.

"The question arises: 'How do we go about carrying on the fight for these demands?' Obviously, some form of organization must be set up. We cannot, in all cases, simply go to the youth and say, 'Join the YCL and we will help you improve

---

The World Young Communist League

YOUNG COMMUNIST INTERNATIONAL YCL	YCL (Germany	District Section Unit
	YCL (France)	District Section Unit
	YCL U. S. A.)	District Section Unit Section Unit Unit
	YCL (Great Britain)	District Section Unit
	Etc., etc., etc., etc.	

your conditions.' Many youth may not as yet be ready to join the YCL. Others may be interested primarily with their own problems, and are not particularly concerned with the other issues raised by the League. For this reason we set up what are known as *mass organizations*. A mass organization is built around some specific issue. It may be built around the simple issues of better wages and working conditions—that would be a trade union. It may be built around the struggle against war—such an organization is the Youth Section of the American League Against War and Fascism. Or around the issue of Negro Liberation, as the Young Liberator Clubs. All of these mass organizations draw their membership on the basis of some particular issue which concerns the youth." P. 15.

"What steps must we take to influence young workers and students who already belong to some form of organization, whether it be a trade union, a church group, the YMCA, or some sport and social club? We must do two things in order to influense them in our direction. One is to join these organizations, and through making friends and conducting educational work draw these organizations into the struggle around concrete issues . . ." P. 15.

"This diagram shows the set-up on a world scale. There is the Young Communist International, which is composed of all the Young Communist Leagues of the world (practically every country). The Young Communist International is also a member of the Communist International, the highest Communist body in the world.

"The Young Communist League of each country (as USA) is divided into districts. The district covers a certain territory. In the United States there are districts. District 13 covers California, Arizona and Nevada.

"Each district is in turn divided into sections, also based on territorial size. For instance, Southern California forms a Section of District 13. The sections may or may not be in turn divided into smaller territories, called sub-sections. With each section or sub-section there is a ceretain number of *units*.

"In order that decisions be formulated on a world, national, and local scale, and power given to carry out these decisions, certain principles of election are necessary. These are the principles of *democratic centralism.*

"*Democratic centralism* operates as follows:

"1. Election of all leading bodies at meetings of the League membership, at section, district, national, and international conventions.

"2. Decisions and programs of action are formulated and passed upon at conventions of the League (section, district, national, and international).

"Discussion on any particular issue or principle can take place up to the time a decision is made—by a convention, National Executive Committee of the League, or by the Executive Committee of the Young Communist or Communist International. After the passing of a decision by one of these leading bodies upon a particular question, the discussion must be ended and the decision carried out, even if the membership of the local organization is not unanimously in agreement with it. Discussion can again be opened at the next meeting of the body which made the decision.

"3. The different bodies of the League (unit, section, district or nation) are bound by the decisions of their elected leaders. The strictest League discipline and quick and complete carrying out of all decisions of the leading bodies is absolutely necessary. The leading bodies, in turn, must make regular reports of their activities to the membership.

"Democratic centralism insures two things—complete freedom in the choice of officers and carrying on of discussion before a decision is made; and, second, perfect unity of the League in carrying on its work.

"With this perspective in mind, let us take the case of a particular unit. There are several factories in the territory; a steel plant, a furniture shop, and a toy factory. The unit has only a certain number of members. What would be the best course of action? Should one comrade be assigned to do work around each factory, or should all the forces of the unit be thrown into work at the same place? A little consideration will show that the best course of action is to choose the most important plant and to plan our activity towards building a shop unit in that plant. In other words, we choose the most basic factory (in this case it would obviously be the steel plant) and *concentrate our work at that point*. Certain comrades will be assigned to take the license numbers of the automobiles and in that way contact the workers. Others will sell literature at the gate of the plant. When contacts are made in the plant a shop bulletin will be issued in the name of the *Young Communist League*. The bulletin will point out the poor conditions of work, and show how improvement can be obtained through organization. As soon as possible work will be done toward building a union in the plant—in this case it would be the Steel and Metal Workers' Industrial Union." P. 29.

"A good way in which to illustrate Young Communist League work as a whole is to compare it to a machine operating on the belt system. The YCL has numerous feeding belts connecting us to the masses of young workers and students—some of these belts connect us directly (as through our units); others, indirectly, through mass organizations. In turn, as a result of our mass work we recruit new members for the Young Communist League." P. 30.

"The prospect of successful Communist work is very good. Our analysis of capitalism and the way in which it creates the conditions which call for revolutionary action by the workers is correct. Karl Marx, the founder of scientific socialism, V. I. Lenin, the greatest modern revolutionary thinker and leader of the Russian Revolution, and Joseph Stalin, the present leader of the world Communist movement, have formulated the theory and tactics which will lead to the successful overthrow of capitalism and the creation of a Soviet World." P. 31.

"Your job is to win every young worker whom you personally know for the League. Don't abandon your friends even though they still go to church on Sunday." P. 32.

"We have a hard fight ahead of us—it is no simple job to overthrow capitalism and build a new society, a new life." P. 32.

A PEACE MOVE?

Taken from—"A Short History of the Young Communist League
of the Soviet Union," by A. Afonin.

"The Young Communist League is honourably keeping this pledge. Its patronage of the Red Navy and Air Force of the Soviet Union has been and still is of great importance in strengthening the military might of the proletarian state.

"At the time of the Ninth League Congress the Red Navy in which there was 55 per cent of workers had 45 per cent of Party and League members. By the Seventh Conference Party and League members constituted 68 per cent of the workers and 23 per cent of the collective farmers among the Red Sailors, 60 per cent of the junior commanders and 71 per cent of the senior commanders.

"The Ninth Congress (January 16-26, 1931) passed the following resolution on military work:

" 'The Congress considers that the scope and character of the military work in the Young Communist League does not correspond either to the present requirements for defence of the country or to the new technical equipment of the workers' and peasants' Red Army. It therefore demands immediate compulsory military training for all Young Communists, and that every Young Communist, while mastering a minimum of general military knowledge, must also master completely one branch of special, mainly technical, knowledge. There must be no room in the League for those who underestimate the need for military training and those who do not carry on military work from day to day.' " P. 55.

FACTS REGARDING Y. C. L. OF THE U. S. A.

The Young Communist League, U. S. A., Section Young Communist International, is subdivided into the same divisions as the Communist Party, U. S. A. (These divisions found on Pages 26-32), Section Communist International.

National Secretary: Gil Green—Member National Committee, Youth Section, American League Against War and Fascism.

Official Organ: "The Young Worker"—Published weekly by the National Executive Committee, Young Communist League, U. S. A., 35 E. 12th St., New York City. Mailing address: Box 28, Station D, New York City. Frank Carlson, Editor. Harry Hart, Managing Editor. Edward Corey, Business Manager.

"West Coast Supplement, Young Worker"—Official organ of the Young Communist League, District 13, U. S. A., 37 Grove St. (Same address as "Western Worker"), San Francisco, Calif.

The highest body of the Young Communist League of the United States is the National Executive Committee (NEC). This committee is elected at the National Convention, and is bound to carry out the plans and decisions formulated at the convention. The Seventh National Convention of the Young Communist League (U. S. A.) took place in June, 1934. At that time the work of the Y. C. L. as a whole was criticized and subjected to the most painstaking analysis. The good and bad points of its methods of work were brought out. Finally, after full and complete discussion, a program of action was decided upon and the National Executive Committee elected. The experience and thought of League comrades throughout the country went into the program of action by which the Y. C. L. will be guided for the period between the Seventh and Eighth Conventions (about two years).

"The Young Communist League—The Young Communist League is the big brother of the Young Pioneers. They help to organize and furnish leaders for the Young Pioneers, and when the latter become 16 years of age they join the Young Communist League. Both the Young Pioneers and the Young Communist League join in bitter attacks upon the Boy Scouts and Girl Scouts, and continually proclaim their desire to smash both organizations.

"The members of the Young Communist League are expected to join in all communist activities, such as parades, street demonstrations, and picketing.

"The Young Communist League is the American Section of the Young Communist International at Moscow, the central organization of the Revolutionary Youth of the World. In the United States the Young Communist League is bitterly hostile to and does everything it can to oppose and undermine military training in schools and colleges, civilian military training camps, the National Guard, and the Reserve Officers' Training Corps.

"The following are the 'Ten Commandments of a Young Communist':

" '1. The life of a young Communist is devoted to the fight for the emancipation of the working class from capitalist slavery. He must consider participation in this fight and the winning of new fellow fighters at his highest duty.

" '2. Every member of the Young Communist League must strive at all times to deepen his understanding of the political, economic, and social conditions and to broaden his knowledge of communism.

" '3. Every member must take part in all the activities of his unit and of the respective local bodies to which he belongs. Punctuality, attentiveness, and active participation in discussion is the duty of everyone. Every young communist must be a member of his trade-union and work everywhere for the organization of the unorganized young workers into fighting unions.

" '4. Every young communist must attentively read and study the Young Worker in order to be informed of all league tasks. Everyone must become a contributor to the league papers.

" '5. Every member must work to become an active functionary and to further the work of the league by his self-activity.

" '6. Every young communist must be an agitator wherever he meets young workers, especially in shops, trade-unions, the armed forces, and sports organizations.

" '7. It is the duty of every member to work for the building up of Young Communist League factory groups in the shops. Every member must belong to the Young Communist League fraction or form one in trade-unions, workers' sports clubs, schools, etc., to which he belongs.

" '8. A young communist must at once bring to the knowledge of the leading body of the organization any important social, economic, and political occurrences which he may observe.

" '9. The members of the Young Communist League must act as one in outside organizations and against the enemy. Criticism and differences within their own ranks must under no circumstances take place there.

" '10. In case of arrest a Young Communist League member must not give any testimony to the police which could be used against other comrades, even if the police tell him that other comrades have already testified. A young communist does not allow either police tricks or force to make him a traitor to his class comrades and his organization.' "

Taken from Report 2290, pages 27-31.

The Young Communist League celebrated its 13th anniversary on April 20th, 1935, with Communists Harry Gannes and Robert Minor as their New York City speakers. P. 1, D.W., 4/20/35.

The Young Communist League claims credit for training Jack Stachel, John Williamson, Sam Darcy, Harry Gannes, Sam Don, Harry Heywood, John Steuben, Tony Minerich, Pat Toohey, Leon Platt, Harry Yaris, Phil Bart, Carl Winters, Nat Kaplan and Gil Green for strong Communist Party leaders. P. 4, D. W., 4/20/35.

SPREAD OF INTERNATIONALISM

"Formation of the Young Communist International discussed at the First Congress was carried out one year later. The Central Committee of the Russian Young Communist League did considerable preparatory work for convening the Young Communist International Congress and established contact with revolutionary youth organizations abroad.

"The First Congress of the Young Communist International was held illegally in Berlin. There were nineteen delegates present representing 219,000 members of socialist and communist youth organizations.

"The Russian Young Communist League, which from the formation of the Young Communist International has been its leading section and an example for the international youth movement, is educating its members in the spirit of international solidarity and proletarian struggle. As its leading section, the Leninist Young Communist League has always carried on an active struggle to bolshevize the Young Communist International and takes the most active part in its work, giving Bolshevik guidance, calling upon the young proletarians of all countries to fight determinedly for communism and assisting in a Bolshevik manner the fight against all kinds of attempts to separate the struggle of the youth from that of the working class as a whole.

"Speaking at the Anniversary Plenum October 29, 1933, devoted to the fifteenth anniversary of the Leninist Young Communist League, Comrade Kaganovich said:

" 'In some countries the bourgeoisie is trying to imitate our methods of organizing the youth by setting up their own fascist youth leagues. The youth of the bourgeoisie are recruited into these leagues together with the bourgeois-landlord youth, and the backward and deceived strata of the petty-bourgeois and working youth.

" 'But inside these leagues, the class nature of the work is in irreconcilable contradiction with the composition of a considerable section of the misled youth.

" 'Consequently, these leagues are maintained by blinding the class consciousness of the youth, by preventing them from realizing their own power as a class. It is clear that there is no future for the youth in these leagues as they are based at present. The position in the Young Communist Leagues is diametrically opposed to this. Here the class nature and the class tasks to be undertaken fully coincide with the composition of the organization. Here the main task is to help the youth to discover themselves, to learn to understand themselves as a class. Our youth have the future before them, for the proletariat holds the future in its hands.'

In reply to questions put by the Komsomolskaya Pravda in 1925, Comrade Stalin said:

" Internationalism is the fundamental idea that permeates the activity of the Young Communist League. Therein lies its strength. Therein lies its might. The spirit of internationalism must always hover over the Young Communist League.'

"The Young Communist of the Soviet Union never forgets that the successes of the Leninist Young Communist League in all spheres of construction of the social-ist state, and the participation of broad strata of workers and young peasants in this work, are also the successes of the international Young Communist Leagues.

"Comrade Stalin has said that

" 'Our workers' state is the offspring of the international proletariat, it is the base for the development of the revolution in all countries, the final victory of our revolution is the business of the international proletariat.' " P. 63-64.

"FOR THE UNITY OF THE WORKING CLASS YOUTH

From Report to the Sixth World Congress of the Young Communist International—
"Youth Marches Towards Socialism," by Wolf Michal.

"The United Front is advancing! Communist and Socialist Youth Leagues are already working together in France, Spain, Austria, Italy, Poland, Switzerland, Bul-garia, Rumania, and Latvia." P. 27.

"The experience in France, Spain and Austria shows that a united front between the Socialist and Communist Youth Leagues can be set up on all questions which concern the vital interests of the youth, on the basis of a common platform." P. 27.

"ORGANIZATIONAL UNITY NEAR IN SPAIN

"The Communist and Socialist Youth Leagues of Spain are about to carry through organic unity. The best and most vivid example of this is the fact that not only delegates from the Young Communist Leagues participate in our Congress, but also an official delegation from the Young Socialist League of Spain." P. 28.

"There is a full possibility now of working out a common program with the Young Communist League of Spain for an amalgamation of both organizations, for the establishment of the unity of the young workers of Spain." P. 29.

"ORGANIZATIONAL UNITY IS POSSIBLE AT ONCE IN SOME COUNTRIES

"The Young Communist International considers its main task to be to help in the establishment of united Young Communist and Young Socialist Leagues in every country. In raising the banner of unity of the working class youth at our Congress today we tell the youth that it is also in its interest to establish one Youth Interna-tional. We are firmly determined to put all our forces at the service of amalgamating the revolutionary youth of the world and to fight for the setting up of one Youth International." P. 36.

"FOR THE ESTABLISHMENT OF ONE INTERNATIONAL
INDEPENDENT STUDENT MOVEMENT

"In the United States of America, the center of world imperialism, 184,000 stu-dents left their classrooms one day at a given hour, demonstrating the might of unity. What fear and horror came over the bourgeoisie and its press. American imperialism can no longer rely on its own students! Masses of students demonstrated their partisanship to the side of the anti-fascists and peace-loving people." P. 46.

"We must fight against existing economic, national, religious and racial discrimination and to open the doors to education and knowledge to all sections of the toiling youth. We know, and today a considerable section of the students the world over already know, that their future does not lie on the side of reaction, not on the side of fascism. Their future lies in the victorious struggle for peace, freedom and progress. It lies on the side of the working class and its youth, on the side of socialism." P. 47.

"FOR THE RIGHTS OF GIRLS

"It would, however, be absolutely wrong to assume that the young girls of our generation patiently accept all these insults. Many girls in the non-fascist organizations are beginning to take enthusiastic part in the general struggle against fascism. Members of the Young Women's Christian Association in the United States have displayed splendid militancy. They supported the fight against fascism, for peace and freedom, in scores of peace conferences and at many meetings.

"We must once and for all cease to underestimate the importance of work among the girls, and seriously fulfill our duties in this field. We must wage an energetic struggle for all the specific demands arising from the desperate position of the girls, for their social and economic requirements, their cultural demands and rights. Our Leagues must quickly change their policy of ignoring the question of developing strong cadres of girls in the leading bodies of the Young Communist League in every country. This is not a question of drawing girls formally into executive committees. We must give serious and comradely assistance to our girl comrades, to help them educate themselves and to study in order to be able to perform important work." P. 48-49.

RECRUITING MEMBERSHIP FOR THE YOUNG COMMUNIST LEAGUE

Taken from—"Party Organizer" issued by Central Committee, Communist Party, U. S. A.

"In the Jamaica section, we have a new young Negro comrade who has been in the League for approximately seven weeks and has already recruited four young people into the League. When commenting on her activity her answer was, 'Before I joined the League, the Y. C. L. conducted a series of militant actions in the neighborhood against Negro discrimination. Through this activity, I joined the League and continued similar struggles together with other comrades. I am now firmly convinced that the Y. C. L. is the only defender of Negro rights.'" P. 4.

"The great obstacle standing between us and the newly recruited comrades is the lack of a comradely approach to them. It is necessary for us to understand that each new comrade has a different background and therefore different and varied problems—problems which we must endeavor to solve. We must patiently explain over and over again why we participate on picket lines, why we sell the Champion of Youth, why we hold demonstrations, etc. Every small phase of our activity necessitates explanation to our new comrades, so that they can understand the correctness of this activity and on the basis of self-conviction participate in the work." P. 5.

COMMUNIST PARTY ORGANIZATION

Taken from—"Party Organizer," issued by Central Committee, Communist Party, U. S. A.

"From Baltimore comes a report this month that demonstrates once again that mass recruiting is not to be regarded as a phrase in a resolution but as a concrete and important possibility for our entire Party. All credit to Baltimore and may it continue to point the way to a mass Communist Party in America—and may it have many contestants for its leadership!—ED.

"The Section Committee of Baltimore accepted a quota of 100 new members to be recruited during the period of the election campaign, August 1 to November 3. On October 30, in checking our records, we found that we had already 107 recruits and so a new quota of 75 was set to be fulfilled by Lenin Memorial, January 21. For the Baltimore Party this represents an increase of approximately 67 per cent in three months. During the month of August 12 new members were recruited, 51 in September and 44 in October. The great majority of the new members were won over during September and October when the election campaign activities were at the highest.

"WHO ARE THE NEW MEMBERS?

"A checkup of the composition of the new recruits shows a broad representative group of the general population—largely from basic industry. Eighty of the total come from such industries as steel, marine, auto, textile, coal mining, harbor workers, drydock, railroad, needle trades and common labor, the balance are from offices, there are four farmers, some scattered building trades, some intellectuals, etc. Twenty-five of our recruits came from territory outside of Baltimore; twenty-four from Allegheny county in the western end of the state which includes Cumberland, second largest city of the state and a very important industrial center. In addition to the actual recruits the Party has established sympathetic friends in at least six other cities of the state.

"The outstanding weakness of the composition is the comparatively small number of Negroes. Not more than 9 per cent or ten new members are Negroes." P. 6-7.

"For example, 23 new members from western Maryland were won directly as a result of the national broadcasts. We received letters from that place in answer to the first broadcast as well as letters from a number of other sections of the state. These letters were given personal, individual answers, copies of literature were sent out and a regular correspondence established." P. 7.

"In Baltimore we are using the month of November for teaching the lessons of the nineteenth anniversary of the Soviet Union, the basic principles of the Party and its program. The Workers' School, now in preparation, will have special classes for new members on Principles of Communism and Party Organization." P. 8.

"An outstanding example of recruiting work that will bring results for the future is that of two of our comrades who, while soliciting signatures to put our candidates on the ballot, made personal friends of a number of people. They have made regular visits to them since, taking literature and explaining each pamphlet. As this is being written these comrades report that two needle trades workers will be recruited through this work tonight." P. 9.

AMERICAN YOUTH TO MOSCOW

From—Report on the Sixth World Congress of the Young Communist International "United We Stand for Peace and Socialism," by Gil Green.

"World-wide interest was aroused by the proceedings of the Sixth World Congress of the Young Communist International, which, in September, 1935, in Moscow, brought together hundreds of representatives from Young Communist Leagues of some fifty-seven different countries.

"More than five thousand young people crowded the St. Nicholas Arena in New York on November 15, 1935, to hear the first official report delivered in the country on the work of the Sixth World Congress of the Y. C. L. Among them were not only Young Communists, but numerous Young Socialists, members of trade unions, church youth organizations and unaffiliated youth.

"Gil Green, National Secretary of the Young Communist League of the U. S. A., headed the delegation from this country to the Congress. A member of the Executive Committee of the Communist International, he was also elected to the Secretariat of the Young Communist International at the Sixth World Congress." P. 5.

"ORGANIC UNITY WITH THE SOCIALIST YOUTH

"In the past period, we in the Young Communist League of the United States have energetically striven to establish comradely relations with the Socialist youth and their organization. These efforts have not been without success. At the Second American Youth Congress, the Socialist and Communist youth were united on nearly all questions and worked together in close harmony. Furthermore, on the student field we have worked closely together and are on the eve of the amalgamation of the two radical student organizations." P. 30.

"FOR UNITY OF THE WORKING CLASS YOUTH

"The Young Communist International will give the most practical help to bring about the formation of united Leagues of the toiling youth in any country. At the same time the Young Communist International announces its firm determination to fight for the unification of the revolutionary youth throughout the world, for the formation of a single Youth International." P. 55.

YOUNG COMMUNIST LEAGUE LEADERS

Listed below you will find the names of a few of the most highly advertised organizers of the Young Communist League:

Matt Pellman, Section Organizer, Young Communist League, Los Angeles, California. P. 3, W.W., 12/12/35.

Bob Goodwin, Organizer, East Bay Section, San Francisco, California. P. 2, W.W., 2/7/35.

John Marks, District Organizer, Chicago, Illinois. P. 4, D.W., 3/10/36.

Robert Cole, State Organizer, Indiana. P. 4, D.W., 10/23/36.

Joseph Roberts, District Organizer, Detroit, Michigan. P. 1, D.W., 9/9/35.

I. Wopsy, District Organizer, New York City. P. 3, D.W., 5/21/36.

Harry Winston, Organizational Secretary, New York. P. 6, D.W., 5/6/36.

Leo Turner, National Education Director, New York City. P. 6, D.W., 5/2/36.
Jack Kling, National Executive Committee. P. 2, D.W., 11/2/35.
Mary Himoff, District Organizer, New York City. P. 3, D.W., 5/2/36.
Gilbert Green, National Secretary. P. 3, D.W., 7/18/36.
Lloyd Brown, District Organizer, Pittsburgh, Pa. P. 3, D.W., 10/19/36.
Dave Doran, Organizer, Pittsburgh, Pa. P. 3, D.W., 5/20/35.
Ned Sparks, District Organizer, Pittsburgh, Pa. P 2, D.W., 6/25/36.
J. Herman, District Organizer, Ohio. P. 2, D.W., 7/25/35.
Dorothy Cannon, Local Leader, Toledo, Ohio. P. 3, D.W., 5/21/35.
David Morgan, Local Leader, Portland, Oregon. P. 3, D.W., 5/9/35.
George Alexander, Leader, Pittsburgh, Pa. P. 3, D.W., 9/3/35.

"Who Are the Young Communists?

Excerpts from the publication titled above. A Communist publication.

"The Young Communist League helps organize and build new militant unions of the Trade Union Unity League." P. 18.

"The Communist youth support and help build the Unemployed Councils who militantly fight for unemployment insurance from the government and against starvation." P. 19.

"The Young Communist League is the organization of young workers that leads their fight against the danger of another bosses' war and for the defense of the Soviet Union. The Young Communist League is not a pacifist organization. It organizes and mobilizes the young workers to fight against war before war has started. It also fights for the immediate needs of the soldiers and sailors, and calls upon these young workers in the armed forces to unite with the rest of the workers.

"The Young Communist League while fighting against war, realizes that wars are part of the present capitalist system, and cannot be abolished without the overthrow of capitalism. It teaches the young workers that when war is declared, they must turn their guns against their only enemy, the boss class." Pages 20-21.

"The Young Communist League joins hands with the Communist youth of all lands through affiliation in that mighty revolutionary youth organization, the Young Communist International." P. 22.

See report of Y. C. L. secretary at Moscow, 1935, on page 154.

Young Pioneers of America

The Young Pioneers is composed of boys and girls of grade-school age. Its programs are dedicated to hatred of American institutions and the American flag. Eighth-grade school children may form a nucleus of Young Pioneers, and these nuclei or groups have been organized in our public schools in various cities throughout the country, including New York, Boston, Philadelphia, Chicago, Detroit, Los Angeles, and other cities. They distribute communist publications such as the Young Spark, praising the red flag.

"WHO ARE THE YOUNG PIONEERS?"

Excerpts from the publication titled above—a Communist publication.

"Then why do we say the workers' children should join the PIONEERS of the NATURE FRIEND SCOUTS or the I. W. O. JUNIORS instead of the BOY SCOUTS? For this reason: You can use all knowledge either for the working class and against the boss class, or for the boss class and against the working class. And the Boy Scouts teach you to use your knowledge for the boss class. They teach you to be 'patriotic.'

"And what does the 'patriotism' of the Boy Scouts and the bosses mean? It means that when the bosses of this country want markets for their goods and decide to go to war to get the markets from other countries, YOU should put on a uniform and go to war for these bosses and their profits. It means that YOU might get killed, or have an arm or leg or a piece of your face shot off, that YOU will kill and injure workers of other countries who have been tricked into going to war for THEIR bosses. The rich people train the Boy Scouts so they can always count on them in time of war. Do you know that the Boy Scouts helped the last war a great deal? They sold Liberty Bonds and War Savings Stamps amounting to $200,000,000. That's a lot of money. Think how many families it would keep for a year! And it is very sad to think that each Liberty Bond sold meant that the war went on that much longer, and that more people were killed and injured.

"The 'patriotism' of the Boy Scouts and the bosses means defending the government and the property of rich and corrupt millionaires and their politicians, and preventing the workers from getting a living from their labor by fighting against strikers and the unemployed who demonstrate for relief. The Boy Scouts and the bosses call being willing to give your life or health, or killing workers of other countries or fighting workers of your own country. 'Love of Country.' " Pages 26 and 27.

THE PIONEER

Taken from: "A Short History of the Young Communist League of the Soviet Union" by A. Afonin.

"A special question discussed at the Ninth Congress was work among children. The Young Communist League had already done considerable work in organizing the children's communist movement. The Pioneer organization which had 4,000 members in 1922, had grown by 1933 into an army of 5,810,543 young Leninists, and 2,082,080 Octobrists.

"However, this growth had not been sufficiently guarded and strengthened by educational work. The decisions of the Ninth Congress emphasized that the League organizations should insure a real turn towards improving the communist education of children.

" 'This,' reads the resolution, 'should first of all take the line of drawing the Pioneers and all children into the general activities of the Young Communist League nuclei by means of suitable methods of work. This can only be done if the Pioneer movement is guaranteed the necessary cadres, further development of its activity, creative initiative, and a determined struggle against incorrect methods of leadership

WHO ARE THE
YOUNG PIONEERS?

Written by MARTHA CAMPION   **3c**   Illustrated by MARY MORROW

EDITOR'S NOTE: Photostat of front page of the pamphlet "Who Are the Young Pioneers?" by Martha Campion.

which convert the organization into one run for children instead of by the children themselves.' " P. 61 and 62.

"WHAT IS THE PIONEER PLEDGE?

"I stand ready for the cause of the working class in its struggle for freedom and pledge to observe the Pioneer (or the I. W. O., of the I. L. D.) rules at all times." P. 28.

"DO THE PIONEERS HAVE A MAGAZINE?

"Yes. The official organ of the Pioneer groups is the NEW PIONEER. This is the only magazine written especially for the children of the workers and farmers in the United States. It doesn't have stories about rich children with maids, or children who go to Europe for a vacation." P. 30.

"WHO SHOULD JOIN THE PIONEERS?

"Every worker's and poor farmer's child should join the Pioneers and help in the fight for a decent life and for all the good things in life for all workers." P. 32.

"And when we are strong enough we will help our parents and other brothers and sisters kick out the bosses, and then all the workers will share all the good things in America." P. 32.

The following poem taken from the April, 1935, issue of the "New Pioneer," one of the publications of the Young Communist, shows distinctly that an attempt is being made to build Lenin as the leader of all nations. P. 18.

All of the efforts of the Communist Party in directing their youth activities, through such groups as the New Pioneers, are to breed in the mind of the American boy and girl disrespect for God, for home, for parent, for Sunday School teacher and school teacher, and a thorough disrespect for the traditions of American statesmen and American founders.

"A REAL PROGRAM FOR SCOUTS—ACCORDING TO THE COMMUNIST PARTY

Taken from—"Scouting and the Boy Scout Jamboree," by Martha Millet and Sam Strong

"To you, the Scouts of America, we present a real program. Not like the program of Scouting, which separates itself from the misery and suffering of America's Youth. Not a program that asks you to be blindly patriotic to the present administration and the bankers and bosses who support it. Also, not a program that prepares you to die or be injured for life in another war, so the capitalists can make more money. No, not any of this stuff.

"We present you with a program in your interests, a program in the interests of the children and youth of America, in the interests of all labor, a program of peace, freedom and progress. P. 18.

"THE AMERICAN YOUTH CONGRESS

"On July 4, 5, 6, and 7, 1935, young men and women representing 1,300,000 youth and children met in Detroit, Michigan. The delegates to this Second American Youth Congress came from church groups, labor unions, Y's, settlement and community houses, student organizations and political organizations.

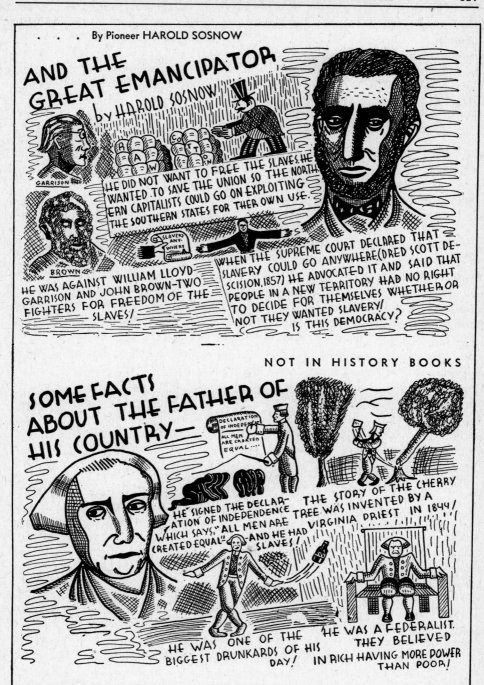

EDITOR'S NOTE: The above is reprinted from the February, 1935, issue of the "New Pioneer" magazine. This is a Communist Youth publication, published monthly at 98 4th Avenue, Brooklyn, New York. The editorial and executive offices of the publication are at Communist headquarters, 50 E. 13th Street, New York City.

"They arrive in Detroit eager to meet one another, eager to draw up together a program for American youth. And despite the different shades of opinion represented them—for there were religious youth and atheist youth, Democrats, Republicans, Socialists, Communists, college youth and factory workers, young people of many nationalities and backgrounds—the Congress mapped out a real program that they could all believe in and fight for." P. 18.

"And let me tell you, brother Scouts, you owe it to yourselves, to the millions of other young fellows and girls, to the people of America, to join up with the American Youth Congress.

"You owe it to the future of America to help make this country what it should be—a country of, by, and for the people!"

See page 157 for history of American Youth Congress.

" 'Do Your Part'

"Whether you are a Scout or not, we urge you to discuss all these questions in your organization and with your friends.

"We urge you to send a petition or resolution to . . . the National Executive Board of the Scouts demanding that they take up the problem of the needy children and use the war funds to provide for these children. Demand a stop to child labor. Demand a stop to military training and fascist teachings in the schools.

"Yes, demand the full program of the American Youth Congress, for it is this program that will lead the youth to a life of peace, freedom, and progress.

"Program of the Pioneer Movement

"The program of the Pioneers is a program in the interests of the American people and their children.

"First, the Pioneers fully endorse the program of the American Youth Congress. We participate in all the activities planned by the Youth Congress. We sent delegates to the Second Congress in Detroit this year.

"We believe the boys and girls in our organization should have a good time. Hiking, dramatics, sports, arts and crafts, etc., are a part of the life of every boy and girl. But Pioneers do more than that. They talk about important problems of the world today. They become educated to help the workers and farmers and their children. A Pioneer is 'Always Ready' to help improve the lives of America's boys and girls.

"Pioneers especially help organize the boys and girls in the schools they attend. They demand food, clothing, shoes for needy children. They organize to demand that military training be stopped in the schools. Pioneers demand more playgrounds, more schools, and more teachers for the schools. They demand a stop to child labor.

"Pioneers are helping to create an America in which the American people and their children will have Peace, Freedom and Plenty.

"This is a real program for the boys and girls! The Pioneers everywhere will be more than glad to have your troop co-operate with them for the carrying through of this program!" P. 19-20.

"Our Leader

"Lenin is leading the way,

"He won't let the capitalists lead us astray.

" 'Away with capitalism and the king!

" 'Lenin and Soviet Russia!' the cry will ring.

"Workers, stop your toil!

"Farmers, don't till the soil!

"We march today under the blood-stained red,

"We will fight to have our families fed.

"We march amid mothers' and fathers' applause;

"We will fight for a just cause.

"Lenin is our leader today,—

"Under Lenin we can't lose the way.

"We will destroy the capitalist;

"They won't be able to resist,

"Because we march under blood stained red,

"And we have Lenin at our head.

"Theodore Lerner, 10,
"Brooklyn, N. Y."

"The Boy Scout Jamboree[1]

"Next month about 30,000 Boy Scouts will be in Washington for their Jamboree to celebrate the 25th anniversary of the Boy Scout organization.

"Although led by militarists, by agents of the capitalist class, these youngsters are the sons of toiling America. They come in the main from the homes of workers, farmers and struggling lower middle class people. To win these children for the working class, to counteract the poison of jingoism to which these lads are subjected, is the solemn duty of all class-conscious workers.

"The New Pioneer, a magazine for working class children, is putting out a special issue for this Jamboree in 100,000 copies. Distribution of this issue will have a great effect in counteracting and exposing, at least partially, the war mobilization character of the Jamboree. But the support of all workers' mass organizations and all Party units is absolutely essential for this.

"The Daily Worker urges all organizations to order bundles of the Jamboree number of the New Pioneer. They are sold at 4 cents a copy in quantity. Orders should be placed with the New Pioneer, Box 28, Station D, New York City."

Communist Summer Schools

Many Young Pioneer summer camps, conducted by the Workers' International Relief, have sprung up in various sections of the United States since 1925, at which time there were 2 camps. In 1929 the number had increased to 20 located in 8 different states. New York State predominates, with 5 such camps, all teaching hatred of God, hatred of our form of government, and hatred for the American

---

[1]Editorial appearing on Page 6 of the Daily Worker, the official organ of the Communist Party, U. S. A., under date of July 22, 1935.

flag. In New York State alone over 15,000 young Communists are turned out each year from these camps, trained to promote class hatred and to urge the destruction of all American ideals and traditions. A large percentage of these Young Pioneers are either aliens or foreign-born, while others are the children of foreign-born parents, with perhaps not more than 15 per cent of native-born Americans. There are also a limited number of negroes, Japanese, and Chinese who attend these summer camps.

In the vicinity of New York City the Communist camps include a very high percentage of Jewish boys and girls. There is no Federal law prohibiting such camps teaching disloyalty and practically treason to thousands of healthy and bright young future Americans, and they are permitted to exist and continue to warp the minds of immature children whose parents have fled from countries where they were oppressed to a land of freedom and of equal opportunity.

During their attendance at these summer camps these children are educated in the principles and tenets of Communism; anti-patriotic and anti-religious instructions are stressed and they are taught hatred and contempt for the American Government, American institutions, and all religions. They render no respect or allegiance to the American flag—the Stars and Stripes—and it is never displayed. In fact they are taught not to salute the flag or to pledge allegiance to it or to the Government for which it stands. They are, however, taught to reverence the red flag of Communism and world revolution and to formally pledge allegiance to it. The red flag is displayed in the conduct of the daily camp programs.

Admission of children to these camps is not restricted to those whose parents are communists. An effort is made to draw into the camps children of working people, both white and negroes, who are non-Communists, with the hope of making them converts to the doctrines of Communism and through them influence other children and their parents.

The purpose of these camps is to prevent Communist children being drawn into and attending summer camps of the Boy Scouts, Girl Scouts, Young Men's Christian Association, and Young Women's Christian Association, and citizens' military training camps so that they will not become "tainted" with patriotism and loyalty to the United States or with becoming attached to the Christian religion.

Communist publications have during 1935 claimed that they were operating Communist Summer Camps in many states for 1935. At least 32 camps with the largest one at Rifton, N. Y., others at Old Fort, N. C., and still another large one in West Virginia very near Huntington. The official publication for these camps is "The Newspaper" of Pioneer Youth of America. Published at 219 W. 29th St., New York City. The editor is A. Sailer.

"HOMELESS YOUTH HOMES" REVEALED AS SCHOOLS FOR YOUNG COMMUNISTS

"An investigation conducted in Sacramento, California, revealed that the "Homeless Youth Homes" movement in the United States is nothing more than the establishment of recruiting centers for the Young Communist League. A dispatch appearing in the Sacramento Bee of Friday, May 12, states that three hundred young members of the Young Communist League were sent out eight months ago from the New York headquarters with complete instructions for the establishment of "Homeless Youth Homes" throughout the country. These organizers, according to Lawrence Langan, former leader of the Sacramento organization, who was recently sentenced to serve from one to ten years in prison on a statutory charge, are paid $40 a month by the New York headquarters of the communist group.

"Langen further confessed that the "Homeless Youth of America" idea was conceived and organized and directed by the Young Communist League of America to get new recruits for the organization. He stated that every move of the "Homes" was directed from the Young Communist League Headquarters in New York City.

"It can readily be seen that such a move, masquerading under the innocent name of "Homeless Youth of America" will receive wide support and city officials and civic groups can be easily duped into lending their sponsorship to these breeding places for the spread of communism."

Note: That the reader may more fully understand the background of these publications and revolutionary phraseology used, we set forth excerpts from each of them.

"COMMUNIST SPORTS INTERNATIONAL

"Another branch of the Communist International, closely connected with the Communist International of Youth, is the Communists' Sports International. The American branch of this organization was founded in New York on March 23, 1924. Its members have to do all they can to convert the youth to Communist doctrines. They have formed their own teams and leagues in various branches of sport, and issue a publication on workers' sports." P. 31—2290.

"A CHALLENGE[1]

"S-S-S-SH! Be more careful! The American Legion's anti-red "secret service" is right at your heels.

"And what discoveries? What an exposure?

"This time they really have us against the wall.

"They have discovered that Communists play baseball! That we hold picnics! That we go to summer camps! And, above all, that we are attracting the youth of the country!

"In short, after months of strenuous labor and hair-raising escapes, the Legion's "secret service" has discovered that Communists are *quite normal* human beings interested in the same sports and social activities as the masses generally.

"And they don't like it. They have decided to go in for baseball themselves to win the youth away from us.

[1] An editorial from the Communist Daily Worker, P. 6, 7/1/35.

"Good! We challenge them to a game—*the best team of Young Communists against the best of the Legion sponsored teams.* The Daily Worker will gladly sponsor the match.

"Young Communists! Get in trim for the great event!"

NATIONAL STUDENT LEAGUE

Many of the officers of the National Student League and some of the Communist supporters of this organization disclaim any Communist affiliation. We likewise realize that a huge percentage of the students who are active with the National Student League do not believe that they are lending their efforts to an organization that has not only the approval but the press support of the Communist Party. We nevertheless give the following history which is self explanatory.

After the suspension of a number of students from the College of the City of New York, a federation was formed known as the New York Student League, which immediately published the first number of "Student Review." Over night, this became a national organization. The first National Conference of the National Student League was called in March, 1932. The program adopted at the first National Conference is very similar to the one now followed. Donald Henderson immediately became the Executive Secretary of the new nation-wide organization, the National Student League.

Let us here review the activities of Donald Henderson as found in "The Red Network," written by Mrs. Elizabeth Dilling of Kenilworth, Illinois. Henderson is a radical who was ousted from the position of Professor of Economics at Columbia University in 1933. He served on the American Committee of the World Congress against war, is a contributor to the magazine entitled Student Review, Executive Director of the American Committee for Struggle Against War, The U. S. Congress Against War, The Student Congress Against War and was secretary of the American League Against War and Fascism in 1933. He served also on the National Committee of the Friends of the Soviet Union.

Y. C. L. ADMITS PART IN STUDENT STRIKE

Taken from—"Youth and Fascism," by O. Kuusinen—Pages 17 and 30.

"If the representatives of the Young Communist League of the United States had not known how to approach the student youth in a comradely fashion, it would have been impossible for them to have developed their great united front actions among the students, the most important of which was the big students' strike against war and fascism on April 12, 1935, in which 184,000 students took part.

"The American young comrades have also learned to overcome their former inflexibility in tactics and to apply elastic tactics."

"We also invite the pacifist youth organizations to join the united front. Nevertheless, we must continually remind the youth what Lenin taught us:

" 'You will be given a gun. Take it and learn well the art of war. This is necessary for the proletarians, not in order to shoot your brothers, the workers of other countries . . . but in order to fight against the bourgeoisie of your own country, in order to put an end to exploitation, poverty and war, not by means of good intentions, but by a victory over the bourgeoisie and by disarming them.' " P. 30.

The most definite tie-up between the National Student League and Communism is to be found in the booklet titled "Program for American Youth," published in August of 1934, at the National Headquarters of the Young Communist League. The book has a further introduction to its readers with the second title "Manifesto and Resolutions of the Seventh National Convention, Young Communist League of the U. S. A. (June 22-27, 1934)". On page 21 of the Young Communist League Report is this interesting paragraph giving the definite Communist working tie-up of the National Student League.

"The Young Communist League must work to build the National Student League into a broad mass organization. Every Section and District Committee must apply the principals of concentration and control tasks to the organization of the National Student League at the schools in its local city, especially in the high and evening schools where the students are in greater numbers, proletarian in origin. While intensifying the struggle against the R O T C, young Communist leaders must also work from within the R O T C to win the students for our Program. Young Communist League Student Units should be formed in colleges and high schools."

Further evidence of the affiliation of the National Student League with Communist activities in the United States is found in an article on page 7 of the January 22, 1935 issue of New Masses Magazine. This publication is a Communist propaganda sheet whose Business Manager is William Browder. Michael Gold, famous daily columnist in the Communist Daily paper The Daily Worker, is an associate editor and a further Communist associate editor is Granville Hicks, who was fired from Rensselaer Polytecnic Institute at Troy, New York, for his Communist activities there in 1935. In this article it is admitted that the leading element in the National Student League is composed of Communist students.

The official publication of the National Student League was "Student Review." This publication was published at 114 West 14th Street, New York City. Nine issues annually are made available to radical students and followers during the school year. Last year's editor was listed as Theodor Draper. In many parts of the country, high school sections of the National Student League publish their own local sheet, as is also the case in many Universities. In the University of Chicago, the National Student League publication is entitled "Up-Surge." A photostatic copy of it will be found in a group picture which is on page 113. In the University of California, the official publication is "The Student Out-Post." In the DePauw University, the official publication in 1934 was titled "The Bulletin." However, for the fall term 1935, we find the name has been changed to "The Student News." An editorial in the June issue of 1935 of the National Student League publication from DePauw University carried this editorial heading, "National Student League Overthrows Democratic Institutions." A heading in the September 26 issue of the Student Out-Post from the University of California says, "President Sprowl Drops

Liberal Cloak, Joins Re-actionary Patriots." An interesting little corner is set aside in the December issue of 1934 of "Up-Surge," which is the official publication of the National Student League of the University of Chicago, announcing that Karl Lockner will address the next regular meeting of the National Student League in one of the University Halls at 3:30 P. M. Karl Lockner ran for Mayor on the Communist ticket in Chicago last fall.

A meeting of the National Student League was called in 1934 at the University of Chicago in Social Science Hall, where the young radical students were addressed by Carl Haessler, editor of The Federated Press. He has taught classes at the Communist Workers' Schools in Chicago.

In all the Communist publications, the Communist press claim credit for having organized the Students Anti-War Strike of April 12, 1935. A great deal of propaganda and literature promoting this Students Anti-War Strike came out of Communist Headquarters.

On the front page of the Daily Worker of September 20, 1935, Central Organ of the Communist Party U. S. A. and a Section of the Communist International, we find a two-column article telling the story of the amalgamation of the National Student League and the Student League for Industrial Democracy, the latter organization claiming to be only Socialist in character. With the new combine of the Communist organized National Student League and the Socialist organized League for Industrial Democracy, a new radical youth united front is proclaimed. The name of the new organization is to be "The American Student Union."

AMERICAN STUDENT UNION

If you will turn to page 132, you will find the history of the National Student League. The story of its active organization and support by the Young Communist League is definite proof that the intended purpose of this radical minority student group was to form an organization through which the Communist Party could express itself officially on the campus of as many American universities and colleges as might tolerate the official existence of such a group.

If you will turn to page 165, you will find the history of the Socialist youth group, the Student League for Industrial Democracy.

A brief mention is made, along with the history of these two groups, of their combination into a new organization, the American Student Union. Delegates from the National Student League and the Student League for Industrial Democracy met in national convention at the Y. W. C. A. in Columbus, Ohio, December 28-29, 1935, to amalgamate and operate under a united front student program to be known thereafter as the American Student Union. Four hundred twenty-seven delegates were present, representing about seventy-six colleges and thirty-seven high schools. It was reported that twenty student councils were also represented as well as several campus groups.

At a convention session at Columbus, Ohio, the more than four hundred delegates took the Oxford Oath—pledging themselves that they would not bear arms in defense of the United States or assist the nation in any way, even if this country were to be invaded by a foreign enemy. They attacked the R. O. T. C. on the college

VEDUCATIONALRD VANGUARD

PUBLISHED BY THE TEACHERS COLLEGE AND COLUMBIA UNITS OF THE COMMUNIST PARTY • 415 LENOX AVE

VOLUME I. #3 • FORWARD TO A PROGRESSIVE, FREE, PROSPEROUS AND HAPPY AMERICA. VOTE COMMUNIST • JULY 23, 1936

WHO ARE THE T. C. COMMUNISTS?

The Communists at Teachers College are faculty members, staff, office, and service workers, and graduate students.

Contrary to the William Randolph Hearst stereotype, the Teachers College Communists are not "wild-eyed foreigners imported from Moscow"; nor are they "termites seeking to undermine our nation's schools." Ninety-five per cent of the membership of the Party at Teachers College are native born Americans from all sections of the United States, with the majority of them coming from the Middle West and South.

Zeal for adequate professional tools with which to deal with crucial educational problems brings thousands of students to Teachers College. Many of these forward-looking students are members of the Communist Party because they realize that progressive education includes a minimum of theory and is based on active participation, the working for better living conditions, and educational opportunities for ALL American children.

The Communist Party's positive stand on crucial issues in American life today makes teachers realize that Communism is the friend of education. Active championship of better education for ALL American children and not for just the privileged few; the vital alliance of

(continued on page 2)

Democracy or Fascism:
The Issue in 1936

Not since the Civil War have the American people faced such an important election as the one that will take place this November.

With a number of countries already in the grip of fascism, with fascism spreading its deadly poison over the U.S. through the medium of the Black Legion, the Ku Klux Klan and the American Liberty League, the main issue in the present campaign, as declared by Earl Browder in the recent convention of the Communist Party, is "Democracy or Fascism."

How do the various parties face this pressing issue? How do they propose to prevent the coming of fascism?

Republicans Chief Enemy

The Communist Party states without reservation that the Republican Party, backed by Hearst, Melon, Morgan, and other American fascists, represents the chief enemy of the liberties, peace, and prosperity of the American people.

Although the 1936 Republican platform contains certain "liberal" trimmings, a brief analysis reveals that it is a hollow sham, designed to intensify the misery of unemployment, starva-

(continued on page 3)

Dean Breaks Promise In Cafeteria Case

Dean William F. Russell has broken his promise to a committee of students and members of the faculty, headed by Prof. John L. Childs, to rehire four workers dismissed from the cafeteria for union activities.

A year ago, Manuel Romero, Costos Astraes, Valentino Juranoviton, and Henry Kolokithias, were discharged, after having worked in the cafeteria eight years or more.

Spirit of '76—A La Hearst

In one of the most scathing indictments yet levelled against the administration, the committee headed by Prof. Childs asserted unanimously that "the dismissal of these men constitutes a decided injustice and one that the administration should correct." The report said that "the four workers.... were discriminated against because of their union membership and activity."

Dean Admits Injustices

In a letter to Dr. Childs which appeared in the December 10, 1935, issue of the Teachers College News, the Dean admitted that "you have found certain injustices. I wish to correct these speedily and within the limits of administrative possibilities."

Then began prolonged deliberations. The Dean, despite his promise to right the "injustices" against the workers, and in the face of the Committee's report, refused to rehire the men at once. Instead he gave them $14 a week jobs on Dr. Irving Lorge's WPA educational project, making a gentleman's

(continued on page 4)

The above is a photostat of the regular publication of the Communist Party Unit at Teachers' College, Columbia University. Note the boastful manner in which our attention is called to the fact that faculty members, as well as other members of the staff and office force and graduate students, go to make up this Communist Party Unit in our University.

and high school campus and expressed themselves as opposed to the existing national defense system of the United States.

George Edwards was elected National Chairman of the Union; Joseph P. Lash, National Executive Secretary; Serril Gerber, Field Secretary; Molly Yard, Treasurer; Celeste Strack, National High School Secretary; and James Wechsler, in charge of publications.

The American Student Union Advisory Committee consists of the following persons, some of whom you will find affiliated with other activities mentioned in this book, such as, the League Against War and Fascism and the American Civil Liberties Union:

Alexander Meiklejohn	Lincoln Steffens
Julius Hochman	Waldo Frank
Reinhold Niebuhr	Mary Fox
Robert Morss Lovett	Louis Hacker
George Counts	Quincy Howe
Freda Kirchway	Norman Thomas
Francis Gorman	

The official publication of the American Student Union is "The Student Advocate," published monthly at 112 East 19th Street, New York City. J. A. Wechsler, Editor; Joseph P. Lash, Associate Editor; and Robert Rice, Business Manager.

Although some of the members of the American Student Union would have you believe that they are not affiliated with the Communist Party of the United States, it is interesting to note the type of advertising found in some of the issues of the above mentioned publication. The May, 1936, issue carries on page 22 advertisements for trips to the Soviet Union; an advertisement for the International Workers' Order, which is a Communist organization with the history given elsewhere in this publication; an advertisement for the Communist Theater School; another for the Communist Workers' Book Shops; and for an art exhibit sponsored by the American Youth Congress. The latter organization is closely affiliated with the Young Communist League.

The Daily Worker, official publication of the Communist Party of the United States, issue of December 30, 1935, has the following editorial in support of the American Student Union:

"STUDENTS POINT WAY FOR UNITED FRONT . . . .

"Hail the American Student Union!

"The achievement of student unity shows that the unification of any such movement can only be accomplished after and through the unity of the leading fighters. What significance this has at a time when the Communists are bending every effort to establish a firm, fighting united front with their Socialist comrades on every issue, small and large, which affects the American worker and farmer!

"The great victory of the Socialist, Communist and other progressive students should be an inspiration for working class united front and unity!"

A later issue of the Daily Worker, April 21, 1936, has the following article written by Celeste Strack, National High School Organizer for the A. S. U., and

EDITOR'S NOTE: Photostat of advertisement appearing in the Connecticut Teacher showing the 1935 proposed Moscow Summer School and the names of the American college professors serving as American advisors on that tour. Visitors touring Russia are not permitted to go on unguided tours. They are permitted to see only the good. The Friends of the Soviet Union then attempt to direct and control their speeches upon return to the United States.

Wilfred Mendelson. This article gives the definite tieup of the Young Communist League with the American Student Union.

"We turn now to the relation of the Communists to the Oxford Pledge. The Young Communist League has long been a leader in building organization in the schools for the struggle against imperialist war. It was the first advocate of the Oxford Pledge. It succeeded in having it adopted as a united front slogan at the National Student Congress Against War held in Chicago in December, 1932.

"The Communists have been persistent advocates of the Pledge because it has served as a rallying point for very effective anti-war actions among the American Student body.

"We Communists are never neutral in any war involving imperialist governments; in a war involving the Soviet Union we are a thousand times not neutral; we give our all for the victory of the Red Army."

From the above excerpt you have the definite admission of the National High School Organizer that she is a member of the Young Communist League and active with the Communist Party.

Miss Strack speaks again in the Daily Worker, issue of April 20, 1936, presenting the positive tieup of the American Student Union with the Communist Party. The following quotes are ample proof:

"Appraising the Activities of the American Student Union
By Celeste Strack and Wilfred Mendelson

"How do Communists approach the problem of winning the students for an alliance with the working class?

"First, we advocate the linking of student activity with the labor movement. We show the power of the labor forces in winning student demands for increased relief; in the fight for free education; in the fight against gag laws threatening academic freedom; in the fight against war preparations and the actual conduct of war; etc., etc.

Quotation from Joseph P. Lash:

" 'Is the YCL placing a damper upon ASU co-operation with labor? The ASU at Columbia contains many more YCLers than Yipsels, and the ASU at Columbia in the present elevator strike tied up the campus and brought unwilling service employees out on strike. There are no Yipsels at Dartmouth. There are Communists and the Dartmouth ASU has done splendid work in the Vermont quarry strike. In Chicago and Northwestern members of the YCL outnumber the YPSL, yet two busloads of students from those two universities went up to Milwaukee to picket alongside the American Newspaper Guild. In Akron the ASU was on the picket line in the Goodyear strike.'

"We Communists have proposed many times to make this politicalization more effective, through a united front within the schools of the YCL and the YPSL."

THEY CAN'T TAKE IT

The paragraph quoted below, taken from the Daily Worker, issue of May 15, 1936, is proof that the American Student Union is definitely in defense of the Communist Party in its program:

"Officers of the American Student Union promptly filed protests yesterday with

Governor Lehman upon news of the passage of the McNaboe resolution to investigate 'Communistic' activities in the schools."

The extensive quotation below from the Daily Worker of July 29, 1936, outlines the manner in which the Young Communist League attempts to strengthen and build the American Student Union into a stronger unit for the Communist cause:

"PROBLEMS OF ORGANIZATION AND GROWTH FACING THE STUDENT UNION

"Nearly five months have passed since the formation of the American Student Union. Its existence is assured. But the task of consolidation, both of its organizational structure and its perspectives, must now assume crucial importance if we are to explore the vast fields of expansion open to us.

"Communists have always fought for a mass student movement; one which would express the militance of an awakening student body, one which would organize its quest for peace and security, one which would, by carrying on these immediate struggles, lead the students to an understanding of the basic social forces involved. We are achieving such a movement. It was two years ago when the first student strike against war rallied only 25,000 students to its side. Last April nearly half a million demonstrated for peace. And it is clear that this demonstration, an embodiment of undergraduate unity in the struggle against war and the war-makers, was primarily the result of the unity achieved by the American Student Union.

"Socialists and Communists no longer present the student body with isolated groups, regarded with suspicion or contempt.

"In a sense they have fulfilled our belief, first expressed in the formation of the National Student League four years ago—such a movement is possible, necessary, potentially a vast force.

"We have too often placed the American Student Union in the hands of this impressive 'top committee,' composed of students unskilled in organizational work and often unaware of the necessity for an active, interested membership. The result? In many places the American Student Union is almost exclusively a committee; the membership appears only on days of spectacular actions like the strike.

"Certainly we should welcome this new, popular leadership; we should fear, however, the tendency of Young Communist League members to feel that 'the job is done' and their responsibility to the student movement ended. These new students need advice, guidance, and often pressure to keep the organization alive and vital.

"The Young Communist League has not fulfilled its role in this respect.

"But the American Student Union's achievements will be largely commensurate with the initiative and energy of the Young Communist League members within it. Let us not be afraid of a mass student movement born in struggles for academic freedom, for abolition of the ROTC, for economic relief."

The official publication of the American Student Union, the Student Advocate, issue of December 19, 1936, announced the call for the second annual convention of this organization to be held at Chicago, Illinois, December 28, 29 and 30, 1936. According to the Communist newspapers, this second national convention reiterated all of the previously adopted programs and presented an appeal for a strong student strike against war during April of 1937.

This organization, in co-operation with the Young Communist League, the

American Youth Congress and others, is responsible for the annual strikes on the campus of many universities and colleges during the month of April. This student strike against war, which is the brain-child of the Young Communist League and the Communist Party, is as much a misnomer and a racket as is the program of peace falsely presented by the American League Against War and Fascism.

We find the American Student Union in different parts of the country and its individual members, while purporting to stand for peace, appealing for money, clothing and arms for the united front (Socialist-Communist) government of Spain. This definitely disproves their interest in peace.

The office of the National Americanism Commission will provide the Legion Posts, upon application, with any additional information we have with reference to the number of American Student Union chapters and the campuses on which they are to be found.

STUDENT YOUTH GET CLOTHES FOR SPAIN

From the Daily Worker, Nov. 25, 1936—Page 2

"If the ship gets through, the clothes, collegiate cut of John Smith, '38, will cover the body of a brother student in far-off Spain this winter.

"In a drive sponsored by the American Student Union, colleges in New York State are conducting a collection of food, money and clothing for the relief of the Spanish people. After the Thanksgiving holiday which marks the peak of the collection campaign, the material will be sent to Spain.

"Columbia, New York University, Brooklyn and City College, aided by the student councils and under-graduates publications, are the leaders in the metropolitan area. At New York University Heights, a huge model ship placed on the campus is gradually being filled with supplies. At the other colleges, booths are situated about the campus grounds.

"Tomorrow an old-fashioned horse and buggy will draw up to the City College School of Business entrance, 23rd Street and Lexington Avenue, and student clothing for the aid of the fighters for the Spanish Government will be gathered.

"The American Student Union is to assist the loyalist forces and supporters."

AMERICAN LEAGUE AGAINST WAR AND FASCISM

A World Congress Against War convened in Amsterdam, Holland, August 27-29, 1932, as reported by the American Committee for Struggle Against War. Many nations were represented at this Congress. We find among those present were many leading Communists who assisted in directing the work of this Communist brain child, as well as the world-wide organization of its branches. Some of the leading American Communists who were elected to the International Committee of the Struggle Against War, at Amsterdam, were Ella Reeves, (Mother) Bloor, Michael Gold, and Harold Hickerson. Several well known supporters of Communist programs were likewise included on this committee—Ella Winters and Lincoln Steffens. Several nationally known Communists or Communist supporters who assisted in the early organization of the League Against War and Fascism were Henri Barbusse, of France, Maxim Gorky, of Russia, and Michael Karolyi, of Hungary.

Although some of the heads of the American League Against War and Fascism claim that it is not a Communist organization in their defense activities to unknowing Americans, we find that the 1933-34 report of the American Civil Liberties Union admits, on page 16, that the International Secretary of the League Against War and Fascism is Henri Barbusse, French Communist writer (now deceased). We find in addition to this, the following quotations taken from the book entitled, "Communism in the United States," written by Earl Browder, General Secretary of the Communist Party, U. S. A.:

"But the Socialist Party leaders put heavy pressure on them and threatened them with expulsion (and incidentally the loss of their jobs). Then these valiant 'left' leaders quickly found an excuse to withdraw and make another attempt to disrupt the united front against war and Fascism. They abandoned this program to which they had already pledged themselves. Already their names are signed to a new program issued by S. P. and liberal leaders which sees the war danger in the movements of the Red Army in Siberia.

"From the beginning of this movement, *the Communist Party safeguarded itself against all the lying accusations of its enemies by having a large majority of non-Communist individuals in every controlling committee of the movement. The Communists threw all their forces into support of the U. S. Congress Against War.* We welcomed every person and every organization that came into the movement, and agreed to support its declared objectives. The political and organizational platform of the American League was adopted unanimously at a Congress of 2,616 delegates, from 35 states, embracing a variety of organizations, ranging from churches and peace societies, Socialist Party branches, religious organizations, workers' cultural clubs, fraternal societies, revolutionary trade unions, A. F. of L. unions, independent unions, farmers' organizations, Negro organizations, youth organizations, the Muste groups (including even the Lovestoneites), and 130 delegates from various branches of the Communist Party. Was there ever a more promising beginning of the establishment of a united front movement against war and fascism in the United States? Since the Congress, a serious start has been made in spreading this united front throughout the country and among all strata of the population who were sincerely interested in fighting war and fascism. *It is true there was some lagging in this work because we Communists mistakenly refrained from pressing ourselves forward, hoping that our initiative would be taken up by the non-Communists. That was a weakness and mistake on our part.* It only encouraged every enemy of unity, every jackal of a renegade, to rally their forces for their latest attempt to disrupt the League. Again we have defeated the disrupters. The place of the deserting leaders is being taken by new recruits to this united front, non-Communists, whose influence reaches wider than that of the deserters. Into the front ranks must be drawn trade unionists, especially from the A. F. of L. We are calling upon all Communists and sympathizing organizations to boldly step forward in comradely co-operation with all other elements, to build the League in every locality to circulate its excellent monthly journal, Fight, and to prepare for the great second U. S. Congress Against War, which is being called for next October.

"We could recite a thousand local examples of the successful application of the united front tactic, initiated by the Communist Party." Pgs. 54-55.

"Another illuminating experience was our relations with the Socialist Party leaders in the U. S. Congress Against War, and in the American League Against War and Fascism that was set up there. The National Executive Committee of the Socialist Party voted to join this united front." Pg. 53.

"An outstanding feature of our united front efforts was the Second United States Congress Against War and Fascism, held in Chicago at the end of September. At this Congress were 3,332 delegates, from organizations with a total membership of 1,600,000. That represents an extension of the influence of our movement over about a million organized persons more than we have ever before had gathered around us." Pg. 198.

"Present indications are that the National Committee of the S. P. will try to obtain a temporary settlement of the conflicts on the united front by a decision to enter into the American League Against War and Fascism, with a series of conditions, such as the addition of a list of leading S. P. members to its leading committees, certain limitations upon criticism by the C. P. against the S. P. leaders and policies, etc. *Our policy is to facilitate so far as possible, without concession in principle, the entry of the S. P. into the League;* but at the same time to use this to raise even more sharply than before the question of direct negotiations between the two parties for a general united front on all the most burning questions of the class struggle, including the fight for the Workers' Unemployment and Social Insurance Bill, the Negro Rights Bill, Farmers' Relief, and the current strike movements." Pg. 201.

In the office of the National Americanism Commission, we have a photostatic copy of a letter written by Paul M. Reid, Executive Secretary of the American League Against War and Fascism, written from his office, November 20, 1935, to a man in Askov, Minnesota, in answer to questions asked by that individual. From that letter we have the following quotation:

"We have no apologies to make for the fact that Communists are active in the American League, and for the fact that the Communist Party is affiliated to the American League." (The American League, of course, here means the American League Against War and Fascism.)

In a following paragraph, we find one other very interesting line that is, we believe, self explanatory, as follows:

"One cannot be opposed to both Fascism and Communism." The Secretary of the League Against War and Fascism admits by its very title that it is opposed to Fascism. Then are we to interpret his sentence, that since you cannot be opposed to both of them that they favor Communism?

One of the earliest demonstrations of the American League Against War and Fascism was staged in New York City on Armistice Day, 1933. The following quotation from the "Daily Worker," of November 13, 1933, gives the picture of early activity:

"The militant challenge to the war danger was hurled Saturday when the organizations united in the Youth Committee of the American League Against

War and Fascism mobilized their membership at Columbus Circle and marched to the Soldiers' and Sailors' Monument, at 88th Street and Riverside Drive.

"Along Broadway, along Riverside Drive, through the heart of the 'silk stocking' district, the demonstrators paraded, carrying the banners of their organizations, shouting 'Down with Imperialist War, down with Fascism!'

"At the Monument speakers of the participating organizations addressed the workers and students, urging them to fight against the war preparations going on under the N. R. A. and the Civil Conservation Corps. The speakers emphasized the need for militantly protesting the war provocations against Soviet Russia, the workers' fatherland. They urged that the workers and students 'become traitors to the ruling class of their own country and refuse to fight to protect their profits.'

"The organizations participating were: National Student League, League of Struggle for Negro Rights, Young Communist League, Workers' Ex-Servicemen's League, War-Resisters' League, Conference for Progressive Labor Action, Labor Sports Union, I. W. O., Youth Section of T. U. U. C., and the I. L. D.' "

A continuous stream of European Communists and radicals has been permitted to flow into the United States since the first meetings of 1932 and 1933, to lecture before our schools and churches, in an effort to sell this Communist inspired League Against War and Fascism. In practically every meeting sponsored by the League Against War and Fascism, we find the following Communist publications on sale: Labor Defender, Soviet Russia Today, Moscow News, and the Daily Worker. The official publication of the League Against War and Fascism is "Fight." "Fight" is published monthly by the National Executive Committee of the American League Against War and Fascism, 112 East 19th Street, New York City. An analyzation of the Board controlling this publication shows that Harry F. Ward is Chairman. Doctor Ward is also affiliated with the Methodist Federation of Social Service in New York City, and is also present head of the A. C. L. U., as recorded on Page 99. The Vice-Chairmen of this publication are: Professor Robert Morss Lovett of the University of Chicago, Lincoln Steffens and Earl Browder. Earl Browder is the General Secretary of the Communist Party in the United States at the present time. His report on the growth of Communism in the United States, made during the Seventh International Congress of the Communists in Moscow, in August, reveals the true light of this Communist leader.

The following exact copy of the leaflet distributed by the Youth Section of the League Against War and Fascism clearly defines the tie-up of the Youth Section of the American League Against War and Fascism with Communism:

"WHAT DOES THE DECLARATION OF INDEPENDENCE MEAN TO

YOUNG WORKERS TODAY?

July 4, 1776	July 4, 1934
Toward the	Toward the United
United States of America	SOVIET States of America

"On July 4th, 1776, the American people approved the Declaration of Independence, which stated 'that all men are endowed with certain inalienable rights; that among these are life, liberty and the pursuit of happiness.' The signers of the Declaration gave us at the same time the wise advice that, 'Whenever any form of government becomes destructive of these rights, it is the right of the people to alter or abolish it, and to institute a new government.'

"DOES OUR GOVERNMENT GUARANTEE US LIFE, LIBERTY AND HAPPINESS?

"Obviously it does not. The Government has become the private property of a handful of rich financiers. These capitalists are not interested in the welfare of the working people—only in their own profits.

"And what do the capitalists and their Government offer us?

"1. In place of life they offer us war. Ten million young workers and students gave their lives in the last war so that the rich might profit. And now a new war endangers us—another war for capitalists' markets.

"2. In place of liberty they offer us Fascism. Fascism is the open, bloody, armed dictatorship of the capitalist class. It has as its object the destruction of all working class organizations and rights. It enslaves the people.

"3. In place of happiness they offer us hunger and misery. The thousands of youth who are graduating will take their places in the ranks of the unemployed millions. Those who are still employed have their wages cut, labor under bad working conditions, and are always in danger of losing their jobs.

"IS THERE A WAY OUT FOR THE YOUTH OF AMERICA?

"Yes, there is. By organizing the fight against wage cuts, against forced labor, for unemployment insurance, etc., we prepare ourselves to defeat hunger, war, and Fascism. *This means overthrowing the capitalist system.* After overthrowing the capitalist system, we shall be able to set up a workers' and farmers' government.

"CAN THIS ACTUALLY BE DONE?

"It has already been done in one-sixth of the world—the Soviet Union. There the masses of the people own the factories, the land, and everything else upon which life depends. There only those who work have the right to vote. They control the country through their councils, the SOVIETS. There unemployment, hunger, and insecurity of life do not exist.

"*We must follow the example of the Soviet Union.* We must overthrow the capitalist system and set up a government that will insure us life, liberty and happiness—*that will be a Soviet Government.* We, the youth of America, make our Declaration of Independence *TO FIGHT FOR A SOVIET AMERICA!*

"*Join the revolutionary leaders of the American working class youth. The Young Communist League, Room 410, 224 S. Spring St., Los Angeles.*

"*Support the July 4th outing arranged by the Youth Section of the American League Against War and Fascism, Vermont Canyon, Griffith Park.*"

The American League Against War and Fascism, co-operating with the National Student League and other radical youth groups, led the nation-wide so-called Student Strike Against War in colleges and universities on April 12, 1935. Press reports following the demonstration reveal the fact that in practically all of the demonstrations, banners were displayed, indicating that the Young Communist League was closely affiliated with the American League Against War and Fascism, and the youth groups sponsoring the movement.

In accordance with a leaflet distributed by the American League Against War and Fascism, entitled, "Manifesto and Program of the American League Against War and Fascism, Adopted at U. S. Congress Against War, New York City, September 29-October 1, 1933, their program is as follows:

"1. To work towards the stopping of the manufacture and transport of munitions and all other materials essential to the conduct of war, through mass demonstrations, picketing and strikes.

"2. To expose everywhere the extensive preparations for war being carried on under the guise of aiding National Recovery.

"3. To demand the transfer of all war funds to relief of the unemployed and the replacement of all such devices as the Civilian Conservation Camps, by a federal system of social insurance paid for by the government and employers.

"4. To oppose the policies of American Imperialism in the Far East, in Latin America, especially now in Cuba, and throughout the world; to support the struggles of all colonial peoples against the imperialist policies of exploitation and armed suppression.

"5. To support the peace policies of the Soviet Union, for total and universal disarmament, which today with the support of masses in all countries constitute the clearest and most effective opposition to war throughout the world; to oppose all attempts to weaken the Soviet Union, whether these take the form of misrepresentation and false propaganda, diplomatic maneuvering or intervention by imperialist governments.

"6. To oppose all developments leading to Fascism in this country and abroad, and especially in Germany; to oppose the increasingly widespread use of the armed forces against the workers, farmers and the special terrorizing and suppression of Negroes in their attempts to maintain a decent standard of living; to oppose the growing encroachments upon the civil liberties of these groups as a growing fascization of our so-called "democratic" government.

"7. To win the armed forces to the support of this program.

"8. To enlist for our program the women in industry and in the home; and to enlist the youth, especially those who, by the crisis, have been deprived of training in the industries and are therefore more susceptible to Fascist and war propaganda.

"9. To give effective international support to all workers and anti-war fighters against their own imperialist governments.

"10. To form committees of action against war and Fascism in every important center and industry, particularly in the basic war industries; to secure the support for this program of all organizations seeking to prevent war, paying special attention to labor, veteran, unemployed and farmer organizations.

"By virtue of the mandate granted by the thousands of delegates from all sections of this country and groups of the population which bear the burden of imperialist war who, though they differ in political opinions, trade union affiliations, religious beliefs, and the methods of carrying on the struggle against war, are bound together by their desire for peace, and on the strength of its unshakable conviction that the struggle against imperialist war is useful only to the extent to which it effectively interferes with and checkmates imperialist war plans, this Congress calls upon the working class, the ruined and exploited farmers, the oppressed Negro people, the sections of the middle class bankrupted by the crisis, the groups of intellectuals of all occupations, men, women and youth, together, to organize their invincible force in disciplined battalions for the decisive struggle to defeat imperialist war."

LEAGUE AGAINST WAR AND FASCISM PROMOTES WAR
"LEAGUE CALLS FOR BATTLE ON EMBARGO
"ANTI-WAR GROUP URGES PROTESTS AGAINST BAN ON SUPPLIES TO SPAIN

"The American League Against War and Fascism yesterday declared itself against any embargo upon the shipments of supplies from this country to the Government of Spain."

P. 1, Daily Worker, January 7, 1937.

"DR. WARD ASSAILS U. S. BAN AGAINST SPAIN
"EMBARGO AIDS FASCIST AIMS SAYS DR. WARD
"SAYS ADMINISTRATION DECEIVED CONGRESS; URGES RESCINDING

" 'It is time for the American nation to make its own policy, based solely upon the joint necessity of stopping Fascism and ending war. That joint objective requires the furnishing of supplies to democratic governments attacked by Fascist powers, in such ways as will not bring us into war, because that means Fascist control here, and the withholding of supplies from the Fascist powers. At present Germany and Italy are free to buy materials of war in this country.

" 'All Americans who are against war and Fascism should now demand of Congress that it rescind the joint resolution concerning Spain; that it order that no purchases of the Spanish government here shall be carried in American vessels; that no materials of war can be purchased here by Germany or Italy.' "

P. 2, Daily Worker, January 25, 1937.

The League Against War and Fascism, by this policy, gives proof that the organization is not against war when the safety of a (Socialist-Communist) Peoples' Front Government is at stake. Dr. Ward and Earl Browder want to arm their side and disarm the enemy. This is their neutrality policy.

The editors of this book attended the Third United States Congress Against War and Fascism, which actually means the Third National Convention of the American League Against War and Fascism. That Congress was held in the Public Auditorium in Cleveland, Ohio, January 3-5. Our attendance as delegates, under borrowed names, permitted us to have the true picture behind the scenes of the Communist control of this supposed American peace and anti-Fascist group. We found that the greatest ovations given to any speakers before the delegates at this Convention were given to Earl Browder, General Secretary of the Communist Party, at the Saturday night meeting, and to Clarence Hathaway, Editor of the official organ of the Communist Party, the Daily Worker, at his appearance before the Saturday morning business session of the Convention.

EDITOR'S NOTE: Photostat of a picture appearing in the Daily Worker, issue of Oct. 27, 1936. The American League Against War and Fascism claims to be "Against War" but here we find members knitting to help support the Spanish People's-Front (Socialist-Communist) part in the current war. Do you suppose they mean that they only favor REVOLUTIONS?

Report of H. L. Chaillaux on Third National Convention of L. A. W. and F.
Held in Cleveland, Ohio, January 3-5, 1936.

Friday morning we went down to the Municipal Auditorium in Cleveland to register and to obtain our official credentials. Long lines were in evidence before each of the registration windows. While standing in line, I noted that a very large percentage of those present were of foreign extraction. The fact that many could not speak good English made the process of registration a slow one. After completing this first detail of an interesting convention we hurried away to Hotel Hollenden, which was the official hotel, to attend the opening session of the Youth Section of the League Against War and Fascism. One of the first details of this Youth Session was the naming of a Program Committee. Several of the same persons who had been delegates to the national convention the prior week in Columbus, Ohio, attending the meeting of the American Student Union, which grew out of the amalgamation of the National Student League and the League for Industrial Democracy, were not only present at this second radical convention, but were given places of authority on the program or speaking committee.

Al Hamilton, who lost his case before the Supreme Court of the United States, where he had appealed for right of entry to the University of California at Los Angeles, without enrolling in the R. O. T. C., was a guest speaker. Hamilton received a great hand when he pledged his support to the Soviet Union and termed that government the outpost of the workers.

Robert Clemens, from the Union Theological Seminary in New York, spoke on the program, representing the inter-Seminary movement, at which time he claimed to represent thirty-two schools in the East. The most interesting part of his speech was that section in which he demanded that the youth go from the classroom to the picket line and fight for the striking masses.

Celeste Strack, long a leader of left-wing student groups, who was refused admission to Cuba, along with an American delegation of radicals, last year, and who was named high school organizer for the left-wing American Student Union, was honored at this session.

The real climax came when the four or five hundred delegates in this student conference were addressed by Angelo Herndon, admitted negro Communist from Atlanta, Georgia. Herndon received a great ovation for his customary revolutionary speech disguised to favor liberty and freedom.

All Friday afternoon sessions of the convention of the League were devoted to conferences on various subjects. The Trade Union and Women's Section were of particular interest. Professor Robert Morss Lovett, from the University of Chicago, has long associated himself with left-wing activities in the United States and is a National Vice-Chairman of the League. He appeared before the Women's Section and bitterly denounced the Boy Scouts of America.

The high spot of the three-day session was the mass meeting on Friday night, held in the main auditorium of the Municipal Building. Max Hayes, editor of the Cleveland Citizen, made a fiery speech in denunciation of William Green, President of the American Federation of Labor.

Caroline Hart, of Pittsburgh, Pa., representing the American Youth Congress, claimed that she was under a two-year prison sentence in her own state, the result of Capitalist-Fascist war maker's tactics.

Rabbi Barnett Brickner, of Cleveland, hid behind glowing gestures and magnetic curls in his attempt to make a speech that would be understood by at least ten per cent of Americans who were present. He finally closed by asking, "By what right does The American Legion condemn this convention?" For the Rabbi's information, The American Legion probably would not condemn the convention if its leaders were sound Americans, instead of Communists, and if it paid a tribute occasionally to the American flag instead of bitter denunciation of our form of government, and if its leaders occasionally paid respect to God.

Frank Palmer, late of the Federated Press, who not only admitted, but shouted to the world that, "he was a fool to win the World War alone for America," but that he would "never defend this country again," was the next speaker. Mr. Palmer gave the public copies of his masterpiece, "The People's Press," before the meeting. We later found that Palmer was just the mouthpiece for the collection plate which was next to be passed. The first large donations given in defense of this "red" convention, hiding behind the disguise of interest in peace and in opposition to Fascism, was the Communist Party, with a check for $100.00; the International Workers' Order, a Communist Fraternal and Insurance Group, $100.00; and "New Masses," the "red" monthly, $25.00. With all of this advance loyal support from the Communist Party, the League still pretends to be concerned only with peace. Peace is seldom maintained under the leadership of anarchists and revolutionists.

Bishop Edgar Blake, of the Methodist Episcopal Church, came down from Detroit, to add his admitted intellectual support to the mass program of theory, "red" strikes, and mass psychology. Although the Bishop claimed to know nothing about the white lights, when they were flashed on his face, he played the customary mass psychology program when he retorted, "Tinge your glare with a bit of red and I will like it." The Communist controlled government to which this psychology seemed to be appealing at the time, from the hand the Bishop received, would tinge the glare with plenty of red—his own blood—by terming him a counter-revolutionist in the U. S. S. R. for such a minor infraction of oratorical etiquette. Certainly the Bishop does not seek to promote Communism in the United States, but he is associating himself with lousy company on such occasions as this convention.

Seated near the Bishop on the platform for the honored guests, was Ella Reeves Bloor (Mother Bloor), seventy-two-year-old Communist, who just recently graduated from the House of Correction in Nebraska, where she found the revolutionary going a little tough. Although Mother Bloor loves publicity, she found that the picket lines of publicity hounds ahead of her on the stage never gave her an opportunity.

It was a great evening for Dr. Harry F. Ward, of the Union Theological Seminary at New York, Chairman of the American League Against War and Fascism, and as such, Chairman of all sessions during the convention. Dr. Ward is also head of the American Civil Liberties Union in the United States, better known as a "Communist Defense Group," which claims as its main objective the protection of civil liberties. Even though the "dear" Doctor, a teacher of young ministers, apparently forgets how to pray when flanked on the platform by such chief Communists as Earl Browder and the would-be Communist, Roger N. Baldwin, I never dreamed that he would treat an old "red" friend like Mother Bloor so dirty. In the future, remember Mother Bloor—no jail no publicity.

The thriller of this mass meeting came when Mrs. Victor Berger of Wisconsin was introduced as the "ace" Socialist, present as an observer at this Congress. She remained standing while Clarence Hathaway, Communist Editor of "The Daily Worker," was introduced, and Dr. Ward had them shake hands to show how the League was building a great United Front in America; but the Doctor failed to say, "A United Front against America." A great ovation was given the United Front handclasp of Socialism and Communism and it was especially interesting to find them joining hands under the guiding direction of a man who pretends to be a good Methodist—Dr. Ward.

Before the introduction of the principal speaker of the evening by Dr. Ward, he gave the program for the League in case of the necessity to defend this nation by war against any invader, by saying, "We must refuse to work at anything in case of a war—just fold your arms and stay put." He deplored, however, the possibility of invasion of the U. S. S. R. by the Fascist Government of Germany and left the impression that it was the duty of the League to fight for the defense of that supposed peaceful government of the Soviet.

This mass meeting was a financial success, with more than eight thousand paid admissions at twenty and twenty-five cents, and with donations and pledges of more than $2,100, all of which proves that Dr. Harry F. Ward, as Chairman of the Communists claimed League Against War and Fascism, is as good a collector for Communism or probably better than had he been speaking in one of his own churches.

The big guns of this convention were rushed up for the opening barrage of the Saturday morning business session. I almost fainted when a National Congress for Peace was opened by a minister—Dr. Ward—but with no prayer. It seemed bad enough to find no salute to the American flags which the Legion had placed near the stage, but which were never referred to with respect during the three days. Too bad, Dr. Ward, that you didn't have the nerve to put a red flag on the platform, so your associates could have saluted the flag they respect. Some of the interesting individuals named on the presiding committee at this opening session were Browder (communist), Bloor (communist), Hathaway (communist), and their very able left helpers Baldwin, Lovett and Chappell.

Charles Weber, of the Methodist Federation for Social Service, opened his remarks before the convention by saying, "The Methodist Federation for Social Service is a left-wing organization in the Methodist Church." Mr. Weber picked for himself a fancy sentence for his morning's masterpiece, when he said in closing, "The main objective of the Methodist Federation for Social Service is the abolition of the profit system." It isn't necessary for me to interpret for you the kind of company Weber has been keeping—Ward and his Communist pals.

Max Bedacht, representing the Communist Fraternal Society, the International Workers' Order, pledged the support of his 95,000 members to the United Front in their avowed program to disarm America, so that it could be gobbled up by the vultures like some of his companions on the National Executive Committee of the League.

Tom Wright, who apparently admitted that he got fat off the production of others and now heads the organization known as "New America," delivered a masterful one-sentence speech as follows, "Our organization is revolutionary in character, for we oppose the profit system." "Tubby," as he rightfully should be called, received a great welcome since he was speaking down the alley of the majority of this mob.

True, it is necessary to have the charming ladies admitted to the circle if it is to be a successful show. Ella Branon spoke next on the program and exposed the affiliation of the Women's International League for Peace and Freedom, with the Browder-Ward-Hathaway-Lovett-Baldwin combine. Ella was a rather clever lady. She appeared later in the role of the Chairman of the Resolutions Committee. Even though she misplaced two resolutions, she found them in time to keep herself in good grace.

The climax of the Saturday morning business session came when Dr. Ward presented our great hero, Clarence Hathaway, Chief Editor for the Communist Party in the United States. The twenty-five hundred in attendance gave this Communist a two-minute standing ovation before he was permitted to speak. I was surprised to find such a deep interest, at a supposed peace meeting, in a Communist like Hathaway, whose aim is the destruction of our constitutional form of government and the establishment of a Soviet America under a dictatorship similar to that in the U. S. S. R., where citizens are shot or exiled as counter-revolutionists if they seek to use freedom of speech or freedom of press in criticism of the existing form of government. Until I saw the approval on the face of Dr. Harry F. Ward, I did not realize that the entire convention, with the exception of we two, delegates by luck, favored the Communist control of the United States. A great smile of approval went over the faces in the entire audience when Hathaway pledged his continued support to the building of the League, and followed it by his pledge to defend the Soviet government against any outside invaders. I had understood that the aim of the League was for peace, but I here found that they were willing to fight, not for America, but for the Soviet Union. A roar of hearty approval went up when Hathaway assured the masses that he would help lend his support to the overthrow of the capitalist system of government in the United States, which Hathaway rather intimated, cramps the style of the "reds."

The last great thrill of the morning session was given the delegates with the second "masterful" introduction during two days of convention of Mrs. Victor Berger. Mrs. Berger was fortunate enough to take a trip to the Soviet Union this year as the guest of the Friends of the Soviet Union, she claimed. She boasts that the U. S. S. R. is a great government and the Soviet a great country, but when she wants to earn a dollar or have a comfortable home or have the rights of freedom of speech and the freedom of press and of religion, she returns to the United States where those things are possible. The dear lady admitted that as a pacifist she was embarrassed to find herself rubbing shoulder to shoulder with the great Red army of Russia everywhere she went, but said, "I learned to love that army because it is the strongest

army in the world today and is only there to keep peace." She failed to add, however, that she was here in the interest of abolishing the entire national defense system
of the United States, even though now only one-fortieth the size of the Red army
which she learned to admire. It was just a little bit embarrassing for me, while
seated in the third row from the front as an unsuspected delegate, to find Mrs.
Berger, in her address, referring to a meeting of the Law and Order League in her
home town, Milwaukee, a few weeks before. She admitted that 6,000 were in attendance and followed by saying that, "Many fools sat on the edge of their chairs to
hear a dirty Fascist from National Headquarters of the Legion, Chaillaux, pour out
his filth for an hour." She intimated that she was rather disgusted at the manner in
which I had denounced her "red" friends, who were now on the platform with her,
when I spoke in her home city.

Before leaving Indianapolis to go up to this convention, I did not dream that
my popularity with some of the staff to whom I had introduced myself under my
borrowed name, would win for me an invitation to sit in on the Saturday afternoon
discussion of "Fight," the national publication of the League. It was not at all en-
couraging when the Editor and Business Manager announced, during that session,
that "Fight" was a little more than $1,000.00 in debt. It likewise was a bit discour-
aging to find that they only have 178 agents and less than 30,000 circulation, while
Professor Robert Morss Lovett, as Chairman of the Credentials Committee, reported
that the 2,200 delegates present represented a total membership of 1,907,560 in the
affiliated groups. It seemed to me that that was very bad support from such a tremendous "reported" membership. I don't blame the Editor, Joseph Pass, for raising
the price of the publication and attempting to improve the issue beginning with
April, 1936. Mildred Rackley, Business Manager of the publication, was rather mild
in calling to their attention those branches of the League who are behind in their
obligations to the national organization.

The Saturday night session was advertised as a memorial meeting for the great
Communist—Henri Barbusse, the League founder. Dr. Ward led the Saturday
night's "entertainment" before a packed auditorium with a glowing tribute to the
dead Communist, Barbusse.

The second speaker on the Saturday night memorial program to be introduced
by Dr. Harry F. Ward was the well-known American Communist, Earl Browder.
The capacity audience gave Browder a rising ovation of two minutes length. Browder
told first of his many meetings with the French Communist, Henri Barbusse, and of
seeing him in Moscow a few days before his death. He later told how it was his
privilege to travel from Moscow to Paris with the body of the French Communist,
and boastfully expressed his pleasure at having been the only American Communist
who was permitted to speak at the grave of the deceased leader of the misnamed
Communist peace group. He attempted to be comical with reference to the charges
of Communism hurled at Dr. Ward from many angles, when he made the following
statement: "If there is a 'red' bogey man hanging around this Congress waiting to
seduce unsuspecting clergymen, it must be me." Unquestionably the seduction had
been an easy matter and had long previously taken place insofar as Dr. Ward is
concerned. Browder followed by saying, "We American Communists want to work
with you in loyalty with the hope that this League will expand and link up with us,

the workers, farmers, the intellectuals and the general circles of the middle class. Our role is to try to make this united front a great organization with 20,000,000, alongside that other country, the Soviet Union."

Ward next introduced Roger N. Baldwin, Director of the American Civil Liberties Union. Baldwin expressed his extreme pleasure at having been in Paris at the time of the funeral of the French Communist Barbusse, and only by coincidence did he claim to know of the funeral when he made this remark, "I picked up in Paris a Communist newspaper, as I pick them up in other places, and saw of the Barbusse funeral in Paris on that afternoon. In company with Earl Browder, I attended the funeral." Baldwin then told of the gold hammer and sickle designating Communist membership which was placed over the coffin of their deceased leader. Baldwin made a further interesting statement when he said, "Barbusse was the nearest to my idea of a saint of any person I have ever known." It was rather difficult to link the Communist version of abolition of religion up with Baldwin's choice of the French Communist as his only idea of a saint. Baldwin closed his speech with an expression of high respect for the police of France, when he referred to the long funeral procession through the streets of Paris made up of thousands of Communists, when he said, "The streets of Paris belong to the Workers and the police know it, hence not a Gendarme was in evidence."

The Sunday session of the convention was opened promptly at 10:30 a. m. I felt certain that Dr. Ward would open the Sunday meeting of the national convention with prayer, but I was astonished to find that no such procedure was to be permitted in the presence of all of Ward's "red" friends.

The Women's Report of the convention was the opening order of business, followed by the Educational Report. The most interesting phase of the Educational Report, which was given by Chairman LeRoy Bowman, was the demand that the schools sever all relations with the D. A. R., The American Legion, Veterans of Foreign Wars and the Liberty League. This was followed by the statement that teachers' oaths now existed in twenty-two states and that such oaths were in violation of all educational principles. Another resolution from the Educational Sub-Committee demanded the recognition by all school officials of the American Student Union, which is the new name for the Communist controlled National Student League.

The Youth Committee Report of the morning session was made by James Lerner, who discussed at length the American Student Union and the American Youth Congress, both of which were Communist inspired and Communist controlled. James Lerner next told how the youth on the previous night had given a "practical demonstration" of their willingness to go on the picket lines and to fight, if need be, for the overthrow of the present system of capitalist government, when some fifty of the youth delegates to the convention picketed the patriotic picture "Red Salute" on the previous night. He also told of the arrest of nineteen of these demonstrators who had been on the picket line and of the efforts now being made to get them out of jail without fines. A resolution of opposition to the Olympic Games being played in Germany was repeated by Lerner. He later boasted of the fact that the delegates who attended the Youth Sub-Committee meetings on the previous days had repeated in unison the Oxford Oath.

While this session of the convention was in progress, the National Executive Committee met backstage to decide some important issues. Since Dr. Ward was presiding over the convention itself, he sent Earl Browder, America's "Number One Communist," backstage to preside over the Executive Committee of the League.

The Farm Women's Report brought out one interesting demand in which the women of the League were asked to appeal to every Parent-Teachers' Association in farm communities in the United States to join this organization and also appealed to the P. T. A. to help get books and literature which call for the overthrow of the capitalist system into the libraries and into our schools.

The Children's Report to the convention was read by Mrs. Beaman, of New York, who was bitter in her denunciation of the Hearst Press and The American Legion. She denounced the program of Junior Birdmen, of Boy Scouts, and other youth organizations through which she claimed destructive programs were being taught early to American youth. She appealed to all of the delegates present to go home and contact school teachers and demand that they teach the meaning of "red" strikes and the meaning of "red" picket lines to American students and ask teachers to let the boys and the girls know the meaning of the organizations represented at the League Against War and Fascism convention so that they would know which picket lines to follow.

Harold Hickerson, well known because of the part that he played in bringing Communist organizers into the original bonus march, and better known because of the part he has played in directing the activity of the Veterans' Ex-Service Men's League, a Communist veteran group, reported for the Veterans' Section of the convention. His was not a healthy report, however, when he admitted that only sixteen veterans attended the Veterans' Sub-Committee meeting. He claimed that four of these were members of the Legion and that one was a Post Commander. Hickerson demanded that a delegate be sent to the National Executive Committee of The American Legion at its next meeting to ask the Legion to endorse the League Against War and Fascism, (O, Yeah!).

Dr. Ward immediately followed Hickerson with the following "brilliant" remark, "We must separate the rank and file of The American Legion from the Fascist and Big Business leadership of its officers." I am certain Ward will find that an "easy" detail to carry out.

Greetings were read from the 106th Infantry National Guard, of New York, in the form of a telegram. The impression intended was to show that the National Guard had gone "red" in New York. On the contrary, if the truth were known, it was either a fake telegram prepared at the desk of Waldo McNutt or Dr. Ward, or it was sent by one individual enlisted in that organization to carry on "the boring from within" tactics.

Roger N. Baldwin, in a special legislative report, demanded that the League help kill the Tydings-MacCormack Disaffection Bill, Kramer Sedition Bill, and all Teachers' Loyalty Oath Laws now presented before either Congress or State Legislatures.

A telegram of greetings was received from Wm. Z. Foster, perennial candidate for President of the United States on the Communist ticket.

Mrs. Ella Branon got her resolutions mixed up somewhat, and in her second appearance on resolutions presented orally the resolution to protect the U. S. S. R. against outside enemies; naturally this "peace" society agreed unanimously with this resolution.

The credentials report to the convention, presented by Professor Robert Morss Lovett, of the University of Chicago, disclosed 2,201 delegates in attendance, representing 1,907,560 American people. A hurried summary of organizations represented by delegates, outlined the fact that thirty-five delegates were present representing churches, seventy-five delegates representing educational organizations, 218 delegates reporting to represent the American Federation of Labor (William Green, President of the American Federation of Labor, denounced through the press the League Against War and Fascism because of its Communist affiliation and Communist control) and 209 youth organizations. Ohio led with 765 delegates; New York second, with 526; and Illinois third, with 246. Twenty-eight states sent delegates to the National Congress.

A brief financial outline disclosed the expense of the national convention to be set at $2,849.98 and the income at $3,017.88.

One of the closing orders of business was the election of the National Executive Committee members for 1936. It was interesting to note that the following Communist leaders in the United States were returned to the Executive Committee for next year: Earl Browder, Ella Reeves Bloor, Max Bedacht, Israel Amter, Gil Green, Clarence Hathaway, Roy Hudson, Harold Hickerson, James Ford, Paul Crosbie, and the following list of interesting helpers, some of whom pretend that they are not Communists, but affiliate and are active with the individual Communists and the Communist directed program: Dr. Harry F. Ward, Winifred Chappell, Roger N. Baldwin, Donald Henderson, Lincoln Steffen, Ella Winters, Ben Gold, James Lerner, Waldo McNutt, and many others.

The convention closed shortly after ten o'clock Sunday night as it had started and proceeded throughout three days, without a word of respect for the American government or the American flag and without prayer from even the professed Christian, Dr. Harry F. Ward.

This report on the Congress of the American League Against War and Fascism is being provided you because of the intensive program planned by the League for the coming year. In all probability the League will solicit financial and moral support from organizations and individuals in your state. In soliciting this support they will attempt to cover up the fact that the League is Communist controlled. They will emphasize as their main objective PEACE and, therefore, if the people of your state are not informed beforehand of the Communist affiliation they will unknowingly be drawn into this—another of the hundreds of affiliated and sympathetic groups who go to make up the United Front of the Communist Party.

The reader's attention is particularly called to the close resemblance of the program of the American League Against War and Fascism to that of the program of the Communist Party in America as revealed in this publication. Listed below is the present membership of the National Executive Committee of the American League against War and Fascism, taken from the official letterhead now being used by that organization. Note especially the following well known, active

Communists who are on the National Executive Committee—Browder, Amter, Bloor, Hathaway, Green, Hickerson, Hudson, as well as many borderline individuals.

ISRAEL AMTER, New York
Roger Baldwin, New York
Mrs. Helen Barr, Wisconsin
MAX BEDACHT, New York
Ruth Bennett, Ohio
Mrs. Victor L. Berger, Wisconsin
Joseph Bingel, New Jersey
Charles Blome, Missouri
MRS. ELLA REEVE BLOOR, Pennsylvania
LeRoy E. Bowman, New York
Eleanor Brannan, New York
Louise Bransten, New York
EARL BROWDER, New York
William Brown, Ohio
Clarence H. Carr, New York
Winifred Chappell, New York
Dr. George A. Coe, California
Prof. George S. Counts, New York
Margaret Cowl, New York
Malcolm Cowley, New York
PAUL CROSBIE, New York
Dorothy Detzer, District of Columbia
D. Mack Easton, Colorado
C. W. Fine, North Dakota
JAMES W. FORD, New York
Margaret Forsyth, New York
Sander Genis, Minnesota
Paul L. Goldman, New York
Corliss Lamont, New York
Harold Letts, New York
Rabbi Felix A. Levy, Illinois
Mrs. Edward Lewis, Maryland
E. C. Lindeman, New York
Arthur A. Link, North Dakota
Trent Longo, Ohio
Prof. Robert Morss Lovett, Illinois
Mrs. Chas. Lundquist, Minnesota
Dorothy McConnell, New York
J. E. McDonald, Illinois
Earl A. McHugh, Ohio
William P. Mangold, New York
Jacob Mirsky, New York
Jack C. Morgan, California
George A. Nelson, Wisconsin

Jessie Lloyd O'Connor, Pennsylvania
Frank Palmer, New York
Samuel C. Patterson, New York
Rev. A. Clayton Powell, Jr., New York
Reid Robinson, Montana
Prof. Paul Rogers, Ohio
Maurice N. Schaffer, Ohio
Henry Shepard, New York
Prof. Tredwell Smith, New York
S. R. Solomonick, New York
E. Spitzer, Ohio
Rev. William B. Spofford, New York
Rabbi Benjamin Goldstein, New York
Dr. Israel Goldstein, New York
Mrs. Annie E. Gray, Colorado
Lem Harris, Minnesota
CLARENCE HATHAWAY, New York
Max Hayes, Ohio
Harry Haywood, Illinois
A. A. Heller, New York
Donald Henderson, New York
HAROLD HICKERSON, New York
Helen Holman, New York
Rev. Wm. Lloyd Imes, New York
Clarence Irwin, Ohio
Manning Johnson, New York
Ernest Kornfeld, Pennsylvania
CHARLES KRUMBEIN, New York
Mike Stanowich, Pennsylvania
Maxwell S. Stewart, New York
Louise Thompson, New York
George Trepper, New York
Erich von Schroetter, Illinois
ALFRED WAGENKNECHT, Missouri
Dr. Harry F. Ward, New Jersey
Prof. Colston E. Warne, Mass.
Harry A. Warner, New York
Charles C. Webber, New York
James Wechsler, New York
Louis Weinstock, New York
Richard Babb Whitten, Arkansas
James Waterman Wise, New York
Tom Wright, Illinois

AMERICAN YOUTH CONGRESS

The organizational meeting of the American Youth Congress, a newly proposed mass student and youth group, was called at New York University, on August 15-17, 1934. The radical leaders claimed that delegates were present representing seventy-nine different organizations and representing 1,700,000 youths in sixteen states of the United States. The leadership in the American Youth Congress was immediately taken over by the left wing groups, which named Waldo McNutt as Vice-Chairman.

The following fifteen named persons and the organization which they purported to represent, were chosen as the Continuations Committee:

Alfred Bingham—Farmer-Labor, Political Federation
Albert Certner—C. C. C. Protective League
Manlio F. de Angelis—Student Christian Movement, Middle Atlantic States
Harold Draper—League for Industrial Democracy
Theodore Draper—National Student League
Gilbert Green—Youth Communist League
Jeannette Krutis—Y. W. C. A. Industrial Council
Aaron Levenstein—Young People's Socialist League
Harold Luxemburg—Ladies' Garment Shipping Clerks' Union
Waldo McNutt—Rocky Mountains Conference, Y. M. C. A.
Elizabeth Read—National Student Federation
Elizabeth Scott—St. James Presbyterian Church (Youth Council)
Wade Smith—National Municipal League
Alexander Taylor—Associated Office and Prof. Emergency Employees
Noah Walter—Young Negro Co-operative League

A group of conservative students attempted to maintain the safe and typical American leadership for the American Youth Congress, but found that the radicals were in the huge majority. Notations from the minutes of this first meeting disclose that the Young Communist League delegates presented a motion to invite Earl Browder, General Secretary of the Communist Party, to be one of the principal speakers on the program of the Congress, which resolution was passed.

The second nation-wide meeting of the American Youth Congress was called for January 5, 6, and 7, 1935, Washington, D. C., to be held in conjunction with the Communists called National Congress for Unemployment and Social Insurance. At this time, several Communist and radical leaders were again invited to appear on the program of the American Youth Congress. During the ensuing months, a series of sectional meetings were called by the American Youth Congress in different parts of the United States. Of particular interest were those meetings at Louisville, Kentucky, and San Francisco, California. Listed below are the names of the organizations which endorsed the call and agreed to send delegates to the American Youth Congress District Convention in San Francisco, California:

Alameda County Council, Epic Youth.
American League Against War and Fascism, Youth Section.
Association for Intellectual Liberty.
Baptist Memorial Church of Berkeley.

Bond Street Epic Club.

Epworth League of Oakland.

Golden Gate Scientific Association.

League of Struggle for Negro Rights, Youth Section.

National Association of Colored Girls.

National Student League.

Practical Idealists.

Students' League for Industrial Democracy.

Students' Rights Association.

University of California Young Communist League.

Young Communist League.

Young Epic League of Berkeley.

Y. W. C. A. of Berkeley.

Y. W. C. A. of Oakland.

On July 4 to July 7, 1935, the American Youth Congress assembled what was declared to be the second American Youth Congress, at Detroit, Michigan. Several hundred delegates were in attendance, with the claim by the Congress leaders of 1,205 official delegates from 853 organizations, representing 1,353,000 American youths. At the night session, on July 4, the principal speaker on the program was Angelo Herndon, Negro Communist, according to the A. C. L. U., from Atlanta, Georgia, who toured the United States on a speaking tour under the sponsorship of the International Labor Defense, Communist defense group. During his address before this Youth Congress, Angelo Herndon bitterly denounced the State Supreme Court of Georgia, and the United States Supreme Court, for upholding his sentence to the chain gang in Georgia. The "Young Worker," which is published monthly by the Young Communist League, carried many columns of publicity and front-page pictures outlining and supporting the Detroit Convention of the American Youth Congress, as did likewise the "Daily Worker," which is the official publication of the Communist Party, U. S. A. The Young Communist League claims that many of its members are active members and are directing the American Youth Congress.

In order that you may see the definite tie-up of Communism and the direction of the American Youth Congress program by the Young Communist League, the report of Gil Green, National Secretary of the Young Communist League, U. S. A., as presented before the Comintern Congress in Moscow at the Seventh World Congress of Communist International, is reproduced here.

The following reprint of page 5 of the Daily Worker of Saturday, September 28, 1935, is reproduced to show you the tie-up between the American Youth Congress and the Young Communist League, U. S. A. The underscoring is done by the editors.

"GROWTH OF THE UNITED FRONT AMONG THE YOUTH IN AMERICA DESCRIBED BY GIL GREEN AT THE COMINTERN CONGRESS

"One million youth are united in the American Youth Congress around an immediate program. Success achieved only as result of stubborn struggle against sectarianism in the ranks of the Young Communist League; proletarian, trade union base is broadened.

"NON-PROLETARIAN STRATA

"In building the broad people's movements, much attention will have to be devoted to developing a correct approach towards the non-proletarian strata, to the winning of the *Negro youth, farm youth and student youth. In the American Youth Congress we can see a living example of how unity between the proletarian and middle class youth is possible.* In the past years our Y. C. L. has radically broken with its previous sectarian approach towards the middle class youth, especially the student youth. *Only this has made possible the development of such powerful student action as the April 12 student strike against war and Fascism, on which day 184,000 students walked out of their classrooms at one given moment, in the greatest demonstration of youth solidarity ever witnessed in our country.*

"But much is still to be desired on this score. In many sections of our Y. C. L. we still accept student youth into our ranks as something of a necessary evil; and when drawing them into the united front we seem to get a great satisfaction out of emphasizing that their role is negligible and that by permitting them to join we are doing them a great favor. Can we hope to win these masses with such an approach? Can we effectively combat the Fascists who especially concentrate on these strata and heap flattery upon them, if we in turn treat them as undesirables, as second-class citizens? Of course not! Through united front struggle and life itself these youth will with our help learn to understand the leading role of the proletariat, but not through any sectarian mechanical approaches.

"TRADE UNIONS ATTRACTED

"We must, however, understand that the broader the unity with the middle class youth, *the deeper and firmer must be our roots among the proletarian youth,* especially the youth from industry. In the United States the working youth have played a most active part in the strike waves and in the unemployment struggles of the past three years and are also becoming more and more active within the trade unions. It is this industrial youth which must give backbone and firmness to our united front and by their activity guarantee the proletarian hegemony over this movement. This important question we have understood in the past months, *with the result that at the Second American Youth Congress, 150 trade unions participated and six important Central Trades and Labor Councils.*

"The point in the resolution which warns against tendencies to *"overestimate the degree of revolutionization of the masses"* has also great practical significance for our united front activity. While basing ourselves on the tremendous mass upsurge that is taking place in the United States, it would be fatal to also fail to see the special American characteristics of this radicalization, its uneven character, and its as yet low political level.

"The failure to learn to develop the broadest forms of activity, the widest educational work, will only result in creating a break between the politically advanced and the politically backward masses of youth. This must not take place. I would also like to place stress on what appear to us often as small trivial matters, but which take on great meaning to the non-Communist masses in the united front. Such matters as the habit of some of our comrades and lower organizations to exaggerate facts; tendencies on our part to take all the credit for united front actions; tendencies to ignore the views of other youth and to push these youth aside instead of drawing them into leadership, etc. Our experience teaches us that it is precisely such small sectarian errors which give credence to the charge of our opponents that the Communists want to dominate the united front and are not sincere in proposing united action."

" A BROAD APPROACH

"At the 2nd American Youth Congress the Y. C. L. delegation was faced with many complicated questions any one of which, if not handled in a broad way, could have resulted in a break in the united front. For example, the question of religion. Many religious youth were skeptical about uniting with Communists, although they were against Fascism, because they feared that this was a trap to force our atheist views upon them. This problem was solved by simply agreeing to permit all the religious youth in the congress to hold church services Sunday morning. This did not compromise the Communist youth and yet showed to the masses of religious youth that this was not a united front against religion but against political reaction.

"LEARN FROM THE MASSES

"The point that Comrade Dimitroff made that Communists must not alone teach the masses but also learn from them, our Y. C. L. began to understand only in the course of this united front movement. Before that we had the idea, and sections of our Y. C. L. still suffer from this, that whatever we say must be right, that we have nothing to learn from other people and the masses. To think we can seriously apply the tactics of the united front with such an outlook, is simply stupid. We Communists learned much from the masses of youth and we are going to learn a lot more. One thing we learned was to change much of our trite stereotyped language. And if the Declaration of Rights of American Youth, adopted at the Second American Youth Congress, speaks the language of youth, it is because we did all in our power to see to it that as many youth and their organizations as possible were drawn in to help formulate and finalize this document. By working in this manner we did not weaken the prestige of the Y. C. L. but strengthened it, we showed large numbers of youth that the Y. C. L. had no narrow interests but that its main conconcern was to broaden the Youth Congress and make it the most effective mass movement against reaction and for the immediate needs of the youth.

"In concluding, I want to remind this Congress of the words of Comrade Lenin to the Russian Bolsheviks in 1905. He wrote: "These are war times. *The youth decide the outcome of the struggle, first of all the working youth but also the student youth.*"

"Thirty years have passed since then, but I do not know of words which more fittingly express the burning need for winning the present young generation against the offensive of Fascism and for Socialism."

All emphasis shown by italics in quoted sections of the foregoing chapter is by the editors and is emphasized for the purpose of calling the special attention of the reader to those sections of the quotations.

YOUNG COMMUNIST INTERNATIONAL SUPPORTS THE AMERICAN YOUTH CONGRESS

From Page 21, Report on the Sixth World Congress of the Young Communist International —"United We Stand for Peace and Socialism," by Gil Green.

"We wish to make the youth conscious of the fact that at the head of all the toilers stands the working class to which all progressive forces must ally themselves in the interests not alone of the working class but of all toiling humanity.

"In the United States the beginning of such a front of the young generation is to be seen in the existence for the past year and a half of the American Youth Congress. The American Youth Congress unites in its ranks not only the organizations of working class youth, but also those of the youth of the middle classes. The Young Communist League will continue to support and help extend and broaden the American Youth Congress."

"THE AMERICAN YOUTH CONGRESS

From Page 39, Report to the Sixth World Congress of the Young Communist International —"Youth Marches Towards Socialism," by Wolf Michal.

"Thanks to the joint participation and work of the young American comrades with the Socialist and other non-fascist youth at the Youth Congress, originally called by a reactionary group desirous of fascist honors, our Young Communist League of the United States helped to bring about the unity of several non-fascist organizations with a membership of over a million. Jointly with these organizations our comrades energetically set to work and a second Youth Congress was called, the only one of its kind in the history of the American youth movement. Eight hundred and forty-six organizations with a membership of 1,350,000 were represented at this convention and co-operated in finding a path to be taken by the American youth to free itself from want and oppression. The bond of co-operation with all non-fascist youth organizations is becoming still stronger on account of that. This is the guarantee for further successes.

"The achievements of the Young Communist Leagues of France and of the United States, which, together with the Socialist youth and other groups have contributed to creating a broad front of non-fascist organizations in their countries, are not only due to their courage and initiative."

GROWTH OF AMERICAN YOUTH CONGRESS

Taken from—Youth Seeks Peace, Freedom and Progress—Report of William W. Hinckley, National Chairman of the American Youth Congress, to the Third American Youth Congress, July 3, 4, 5, 1936, Cleveland, Ohio.

"Only last week the Christian Youth Conference of North America pledged its support to free Herndon, to pass the American Youth Act, and took steps toward co-operation with the American Youth Congress.

"The National Industrial Council of the Young Women's Christian Association, as well as the Business and Professional Women's Council of this same organization, considered in their national assemblies the same problems we consider here, and voted affiliation to this body." P. 19.

"In the student field there was formed a unified progressive organization affiliated to our Congress, the American Student Union, and it plays a vital role in the

CONTINUATIONS COMMITTEE
AMERICAN YOUTH CONGRESS
112 East 19th Street

ALBERT CERTNER, *C.C.C. Protective League.*
MANLIO F. DEANGELIS, *Student Christian Movement, Middle Atlantic Region.*
HAROLD DRAPER, *League for Industrial Democracy.*
THEODORE DRAPER, *National Student League.*
GILBERT GREEN, *Young Communist League.*
JEANNETTE KRUTIS, *of the Industrial Council, Y.W.C.A., Elizabeth, N. J.*
WALDO MCNUTT, *Y.M.C.A., Rocky Mountain Region.*
MORRIS MILGRAM, *Ladies Garment Shipping Clerks Union.*
ELIZABETH READ, *National Student Federation of America.*
ELIZABETH SCOTT, *St. James Presbyterian Church Youth Council.*
ALEXANDER TAYLOR, *Associated Office and Professional Emergency Employees.*
AUGUST TYLER, *Young People's Socialist League.*
NOAH WALTER, *Young Negro Co-operative League.*
SELDON RODMAN, *New America.*

DELEGATE'S CREDENTIAL

Mail this promptly to
Continuations Committee
American Youth Congress
112 East 19th Street
New York City

Name of Delegate

Street and Number

City or Town   Age

Organization   Address

Number of Members   Indicate Round Table Preference

Secretary's Signature

A Registration Fee of 50 cents per delegate, payable on arrival, will be charged to help cover the expenses of the Congress.

TO BE KEPT BY DELEGATE

Name of Delegate

Street and Number

City or Town   Age

Organization   Address

Number of Members   Indicate Round Table Preference

Secretary's Signature

EDITOR'S NOTE: Photostat of Continuation Committee of the American Youth Congress as taken from their own official announcements.

American school system. The New England Division of the National Student Federation of America has affiliated to the American Youth Congress and we hope that the national body will soon follow the same course." P. 20.

The Third Annual American Youth Congress assembled in the Public Auditorium in Cleveland, July 3 to 5, 1936. The Congress was opened by Eleanor Ginsberg, Executive Secretary of the Cleveland Council of the American Youth Congress. After the usual welcome on the part of the host city official William W. Hinckley, National Chairman, proceeded to formally open the business sessions.

Some of the early speakers on the program were: Ben Fischer, National Secretary, Young Peoples' Socialist League; Elizabeth Scott, St. James Presbyterian Church, New York City; George Edwards, National Chairman, American Student Union; Rose Troiano, National Industrial Council, Y. W. C. A.; Gil Green, National Secretary, Young Communist League; H. Ross Bunce, Ohio Area Y. M. C. A.; Angelo Herndon, twenty-two-year-old Negro Communist from Atlanta, Georgia.

A subcommittee of the Resolutions Committee had as its chairman George Edwards, American Student Union. The other members were: Marie Henry, Detroit American Youth Congress; Rose Troiano, National Industrial Council, Y. W. C. A.; and Chester Witkowski, Amalgamated Association of Iron, Steel and Tin Workers.

Waldo McNutt assisted in the work of drafting bylaws, which he later read at the Convention.

The following interesting quotation taken from the Report of the American Youth Congress Convention shows the part the Communists played in drafting the program:

"Mac Weiss of the Young Communist League then moved that because of the shortage of time, the remainder of the Constitution be referred to the National Council for adoption, and that the whole Constitution be presented to affiliated organizations for a referendum vote."

Listed below is the number of representatives attending the Convention from each state. Also the names of the national officers and the names and addresses of several of the local American Youth Congress branches:

The final credentials report indicates that there were 1,323 official delegates and 116 official observers. Delegates represented 1,007 organizations, while observers represented 106. Approximately 1,650,000 young people were represented by delegates, while 2,300,000 were represented by observers. Delegates came from 29 states, Washington, D. C., Canada, Mexico, Cuba and China.

	Number of Organizations	Members
Anti-war, anti-fascist, civil rights	80	29,580
Church	57	44,115
Economic	16	267,130
Educational	42	12,485
Fraternal	106	83,030
Farm	5	35,100
Political	100	24,475
Settlement Houses	49	34,350
Social, Cultural, Sport, Etc.	151	23,200
Students	121	76,985

Trade Unions (AFL)	106	283,070
Trade Unions (Indep.)	32	37,165
Unemployed	26	137,890
Y's	74	143,380
Miscellaneous	44	405,540
	1,007	1,637,495

REPRESENTATION BY STATES

Alabama	1	Nebraska	1
Arizona	0	Nevada	0
Arkansas	1	New Hampshire	1
California	15	New Jersey	34
Colorado	0	New Mexico	0
Connecticut	13	New York	301
Delaware	0	North Carolina	0
D. C.	4	North Dakota	9
Florida	1	Ohio	355
Georgia	1	Oklahoma	0
Idaho	0	Oregon	1
Illinois	159	Pennsylvania	145
Indiana	25	Rhode Island	4
Iowa	1	South Carolina	0
Kansas	10	South Dakota	5
Kentucky	5	Tennessee	2
Louisiana	0	Texas	0
Maine	0	Utah	0
Maryland	22	Vermont	0
Massachusetts	12	Virginia	0
Michigan	139	Washington	7
Minnesota	32	West Virginia	2
Mississippi	0	Wisconsin	34
Missouri	23	Wyoming	0
Montana	0	Foreign	3

OFFICERS OF AMERICAN YOUTH CONGRESS

National Chairman	William W. Hinckley
Mid-West Vice-Chairman	Irma Garner
Executive Secretary	Joseph Cadden
Publicity Director	Roger Chase

A Southern and a Western Vice-Chairman, as well as a Treasurer and Field Secretaries are still to be elected.

LOCAL AMERICAN YOUTH CONGRESSES

California: Los Angeles—Jeff Kibre, 404 American Bank Building. Also San Francisco and Berkeley.

Colorado: Denver—Henry Gleed, 1837 Champa Street.

Connecticut: New Haven—William Post, 444 Dixwell Ave.

Florida: Miami—Ethel Marshall, 2328 S. W. 17th Street.

Illinois: Chicago—Minneola Ingersoll, 184 West Washington, Room 606.

Maryland: Baltimore—Morton Friedenberg, 1221 N. Charles Street.

Massachusetts: Boston—Grace Herbert, 16 Westland Avenue.

Michigan: Detroit—Marie Henry, 6553 Woodward Avenue, Room 311.

Minnesota: Minneapolis—John Thomas, Phyllis Wheatley Settlement, 809 Aldrich Avenue No. Also St. Paul.

Missouri: St. Louis—American Workers' Union, 1023 No. Grand Blvd. Also Kansas City.

New Jersey: Newark—Alfred Manning, State Chairman, 222 Market Street, Room 240. Also Elizabeth, Perth Amboy and Hackensack.

New York: New York City—Janet Feder, 55 W. 42nd Street, Room 753. Also Syracuse and Buffalo.

Ohio: Cleveland—Eleanor Ginsberg, 1317 Public Square Building. Also Cincinnati, Toledo and Youngstown.

Pennsylvania: Philadelphia—Benjamin Stahl, 538 Widener Building. Also Allentown, Pittsburgh and Wilkes-Barre.

Louisiana: New Orleans—William R. McHugh, Jr., 1320 St. Andrew Street.

Rhode Island: Pawtucket—Myrtle Korenbaum, 186 East Avenue.

Tennessee: Memphis—Edwin Mitchell, Box 5215.

Utah: Salt Lake City—Richard Rowland, Jr., 646 E. 17th So.

Washington: Seattle—Margaret Johnson, 512 University Building.

Wisconsin: Milwaukee—Mrs. S. G. Eisenscher, 749 No. 10th Street, Apt. 12. Also Kenosha, Madison and Racine.

THE STUDENT LEAGUE FOR INDUSTRIAL DEMOCRACY

The Student League for Industrial Democracy claims to be just a Socialist youth organization, through which students and some professors may spread their Socialist doctrines. The official publication of this League is the "Student Outlook," published monthly from October to May, by the Intercollegiate League for Industrial Democracy, 112 East 19th Street, New York City. This league publication places its stamp of approval on the programs of the League Against War and Fascism, and upon the programs of the National Student League. Even though only Socialist, the Student League for Industrial Democracy plays the program inspired and prepared by the Communists for the National Student League and the League Against War and Fascism. The L. I. D. is opposed to the R. O. T. C. and apparently favors the program of the American Civil Liberties Union. On page 3 of the "Student Outlook," the official publication of the Student League for Industrial Democracy, an editorial of the November-December, 1934, issue, gives this blunt statement:

"The National Student League is dominated by the Young Communist League. The young Communists in the National Student League know very well that they cannot get those of their members who are not Communists to support these" (T. U. U. L.) "unions. Consequently, unless there are severe abrogations of civil liberties during strikes of Communist unions, the National Student League lays low."

We now find that this same Student League for Industrial Democracy, which claims to be only Socialist, is shaking hands with the National Student League, which admits its Communist leadership, into a combined organization, now known as the *American Student Union*. This fact is reported in the September 20 issue of the Communist "Daily Worker."

The National Convention of the Student League for Industrial Democracy and the National Student League was jointly held in Columbus, Ohio, December 27-29, 1935. The purpose of this meeting was to form a united front between the Communist-controlled National Student League and the so-called Socialist League for Industrial Democracy. The detailed report of this Convention discloses that, even though between four and five hundred delegates present claimed to represent American Universities, many were graduate or former students and not actually students at the present time.

The same left wing control dominated the Convention as on former occasions. Celeste Strack was made high school organizer for the American Student Union for the coming year.

Many of the officials and delegates of the American Student Union, upon the completion of their three-day session at Columbus, Ohio, where they met in the Y. W. C. A., after they had been refused the use of the Ohio State University Auditorium, journeyed to Cleveland, Ohio, the following week end to attend the Convention of the League Against War and Fascism.

These facts are given to show you the united front tactics and to show you the manner in which the directors of all of the Communist-controlled groups interlock under Communist leadership.

BOOK SHOPS SPECIALIZING IN COMMUNIST LITERATURE

The following book shops are distributors for Communist books, pamphlets and magazines, according to the Workers Library Publishers' advertisement:

Aberdeen, Wash.: 115½ W. Heron St.
Akron: 365 South Main St.
Baltimore: 501A N. Eutaw St.
Boston: 216 Broadway
Buffalo: 61 W. Chippewa
Butte: 119 Hamilton St.
Cambridge: 6½ Holyoke St.
Camden: 304 Federal St.
Chicago:
    200 W. Van Buren
    2135 W. Division St.
    1326 E. 57th St.
Cincinnati: 540 Main St.
Cleveland: 1522 Prospect Ave.
Denver: 521 Exchange Bldg.
Detroit: 3537 Woodward Ave.
Duluth: 28 E. First St.
Grand Rapids: 336 Bond Ave.
Hollywood: 1116 N. Lillian Way
Houston: 503 Republic Bldg.
Los Angeles:
    230 S. Spring St.
    2411½ Brooklyn Ave.
    321 W. 2nd St.
Madison, Wis.: 312 W. Gorham
Milwaukee: 419 W. State St.
Minneapolis: 812 LaSalle Ave.
Newark: 33 Halsey St.
New Haven: 17 Broad St.
New Orleans: 130 Charles St.
New York:
    50 E. 13th St.
    140 Second Ave.
    218 E. 84th St.
    115 W. 135th St., Harlem
    2067 Jerome Ave., Bronx
    1001 Prospect Ave., Bronx
    4531 16th Ave., Brooklyn
    61 Willoughby St., Brooklyn

New York:
    369 Sutter Ave., Brooklyn
    Brighton Beach Boardwalk at 6th Street
    44-17 Queens Blvd., Sunnyside, L. I.
    2006 Mott Ave., Far Rockaway
Omaha: 311 Karbach Block
Oakland: 419 12th St.
Paterson: 201 Market St.
Philadelphia:
    104 S. Ninth St.
    118 W. Allegheny Ave.
    4023 Girard Ave.
    2404 Ridge Ave.
Pittsburgh: 607 Bigelow Blvd.
Portland, Ore.: 314 S. W. Madison St.
Providence: 335 Westminster St., Rm. 42
Racine: 205 State St.
Reading: 224 N. Ninth St.
Richmond, Va.: 205 N. 2nd St.
Sacramento: 1024 Sixth St.
St. Louis: 3520 Franklin Ave.
St. Paul: 600 Wabasha St.
Salt Lake City: 134 Regent St.
San Diego: 635 E St.
San Francisco:
    170 Golden Gate Ave.
    1609 O'Farrell St.
    121 Haight St.
San Pedro: 244 W. Sixth St.
Santa Barbara: 208 W. Canon Perdido
Schenectady: 204 Nott Terrace
Seattle: 713½ Pine St.
Spokane: 114 N. Bernard
Superior: 601 Tower Ave.
Tacoma: 1315 Tacoma Ave.
Toledo: 214 Michigan
Washington, D. C.: 513 F St., N. W.
Youngstown: 310 W. Federal St., 3d Fl.

The book stores listed above sell very few books or pamphlets or newspapers except those directed to the promotion of Communism in the United States. They also sell a few regular issues of Socialist papers. The Workers' Library Publishers have produced this outlet for their filthy revolutionary literature.

There are many cities in which their stores have not been able to survive and the cost of subsidy was too heavy on the finances of the Communist Party.

The following is the list of pamphlets and books on sale at Communist Book Stores, the addresses of which you will find on the preceding page.

THE WORKERS LIBRARY
Books and Pamphlets
1935
For Sale by
WORKERS BOOKSTORES
2135 West Division St.　　　　161 No. Franklin St.
1326 East 57th Street, Chicago, Ill.

ON THE CLASS STRUGGLE IN THE U. S. A.

Conditions of the Workers　　Price
Profits and Wages—Anna Rochester $0.10
Speeding Up the Workers—James Barnett .... .10
The Injunction Menace—Charlotte Todes .... .05
The Yellow Dog Contract—Elliot E. Cohen .... .05
Spying on Workers—Robert W. Dunn .... .10
The End of the Ford Myth—Robert Cruden .... .05
The Struggle of the Marine Workers—N. Sparks .. .10
Southern Cotton Mills and Labor—Myra Page .... .10
Dangerous Jobs—Grace Burnham .... .05
Your Dollar Under Roosevelt—Anna Rochester .... .02
The NRA from Within—Wm. O. Thompson, Mary
　Van Kleeck and Earl Browder .... .05
Tel and Tel—The Telephone and Telegraph
　Workers—Hy Kravif .... .05
Why a Workers' Daily Press?—C. A. Hathaway
　and Sam Don .... .03
What Is the I. L. D.? .... .03
The Eyes of the Movie—Harry Alan Potamkin .... .10
To American Intellectuals—Maxim Gorky .... .10
Red Sparks, No. 2—Jorge .... .05
Culture and the Crisis .... .05

Struggle of the Unemployed
Unemployment Insurance—The Burning Issue of
　the Day—Earl Browder .... .03
We Are For H. R. 2827—Report of the Committee
　on Labor to the United States Congress .... .02
Constitution and Regulations of the National Un-
　employment Countil of the U. S. .... .03
Why the Workers' Unemployment Insurance Bill,
　H. R. 7598—How It Can Be Won—I. Amter .... .02
Shall It Be Hunger Doles or Unemployment In-
　surance?—Revised Edition—Herbert Benjamin .... .02
Our Children Cry for Bread—Sadie Van Veen .... .01
The March Against Hunger—The Aims and
　Achievements of the National Hunger March—
　I. Amter .... .01

On all orders of 10¢ and less add 3¢ for postage.

Make the Democrats Keep Their Promises .... .02
The Jobless Negro—Elizabeth Lawson .... .01
Don't Take It Lying Down—Pen and Hammer.... .02
Industrial Slavery—Roosevelt's "New Deal"—
　I. Amter .... .01
Unemployment Insurance and the A. F. of L. .... .03
Unemployment—Grace M. Burnham .... .10
Social Insurance—Grace M. Burnham .... .10

Women
Women Who Work—Grace Hutchins .... .05
Women and Equality—Margaret Cowl .... .02

　　　　　　　　　　　　　　　　　　　Price
Women in Action—Sasha Small $0.02
What Every Working Woman Wants—Grace
　Hutchins .... .02
The Position of Negro Women—Eugene Gordon
　and Cyril Briggs .... .02
Women and Socialism—August Bebel .... .50

Youth
Youth in Industry—Grace Hutchins .... .10
The Highway of Hunger—Dave Doran .... .01
Schools and the Crisis—Rex David .... .10
It Happens Every Day—Phil Bard .... .05
Children Under Capitalism—Grace Hutchins .... .05
Youth Confronts the Blue Eagle—Gil Green .... .02
Young Communists at Work—Dora Zucker .... .02
From Young Socialists to Young Communists—
　George Smerkin and Sol Larks .... .03
Lenin, Liebknecht, Luxemburg—Al Steele .... .03
"In Flanders Field . . ."—Mac Weiss .... .03
Twenty Years After—Jim Lerner .... .02
Who Are the Young Pioneers? .... .03
Youth Against War and Fascism .... .02
Program of American Youth Congress .... .03
Youth in the Fight for Unemployment and Social
　Insurance—I. Amter .... .02
Youth in the World War—V. Motyleva .... .05

Struggle of the Farmers
The American Farmer—George Anstrom .... .10
Can You Hear Their Voices?—Whitaker Chambers .10
The Government Takes a Hand in the Cotton
　Patch—George Anstrom .... .02
Farm-Dollar Blight—The "New Deal" in Agri-
　culture—John Barnett .... .02
Farmers Unite Their Fight—Report to the Farm-
　ers' Second National Conference—November,
　1933 .... .15
Farmers' Call to Action—Issued by Farmers' Sec-
　ond National Conference .... .01
An American Farmer Sees the Soviet Union—
　Julius Walstad .... .05

Veterans' and Soldiers' Struggle
Veterans on the March—Jack Douglas 1.25
The Bonus March—Felix Morrow .... .10
Life in the U. S. Army—Walter Trumbull .... .10
The Veterans' Fight for Unity—H. E. Briggs .... .05

Graft and Corruption and Finance Capital
Wall Street—Anna Rochester .... .05
Graft and Gangsters—Harry Gannes .... .10
How Mellon Got Rich—Harvey O'Connor .... .05

"In a Soviet America" Series

Price

The Negroes in a Soviet America—James W.
Ford and James S. Allen..............................$0.05
Seamen and Longshoremen Under the Red Flag
—Hays Jones .... .05

Watch for announcements of further publications in
this series covering the position of steel workers, railroad
workers, miners, farmers, auto workers, youth, women,
professionals, white collar workers, unemployed, small
business men, and other sections of the toiling masses
in a Soviet America.

THE TRADE UNION MOVEMENT AND STRIKE STRUGGLES

The Great San Francisco General Strike—Wm. F.
Dunne .... .10
Permanent Counter-Revolution—The Role of the
Trotskyites in the Minneapolis Strikes—Wm.
F. Dunne and Morris Childs .... .10
The Communists in the Textile Strike—C. A.
Hathaway .... .02
Company Unions Under the New Deal—Robt.
W. Dunn .... .05
Printing Workers and the Printing Codes.............. .05
70,000 Silk Workers Strike—For Bread and Unity
—John J. Ballam .... .10
The Name Is Lewis, John L.—Tom Myerscough.... .03
Revolt in the Railroad Unions........................ .05

ON THE NEGRO QUESTION

Equality, Land and Freedom—Program of the
League of Struggle for Negro Rights.................. .05
On the Chain Gang—John L. Spivak..................... .05
Lynching—Harry Haywood and Milton Howard.... .05
Race Hatred on Trial—Proceedings of the Trial
of August Yokinen .... .10
Negro Liberation—James S. Allen...................... .10
The American Negro—James S. Allen.................... .10
The Communist Position on the Negro Question.... .10
Free Angelo Herndon—Charles White.................. .02
The Road to Negro Liberation—Report to the
Eighth Convention, C. P., U. S. A.—Harry
Haywood .... .10
"You Cannot Kill the Working Class"—Angelo
Herndon .... .05
The Communist Party and the Emancipation of
the Negro People—Earl Browder....................... .01
The Right to Revolution for the Negro People—
James W. Ford .... .01
Imperialism Destroys the People of America—
James W. Ford.. .01
World Problems of the Negro People—A Refuta-
tion of George Padmore—James W. Ford............ .02

THE STRUGGLE AGAINST IMPERIALISM, FASCISM AND WAR

War

War in Africa—Italian Fascism Prepares to En-
slave Ethiopia—James W. Ford and Harry
Gannes .... .05

Poison Gas and the Next War—   Price
Donald A. Cameron.................................$0.05
The Toilers Against War—Clara Zetkin................ .20
Revolutionary Struggle Against War vs. Pacifism
—Alex Bittelman .... .05
What War Means to the Workers—Robert W. Dunn   .02
From the First World War to the Second—Nemo....   .10
Who Wants War?—A. A. Heller........................ .03
Fighting to Live—Harry F. Ward...................... .05
Guns Are Ready—Seymour Waldman..................... .05
Why Fascism Leads to War—John Strachey.......... .05
National Defense for Whom —Harold Ward....... .05
Students Fight War.................................. .05

Fascist Movements in U. S. A.

The Truth About Father Coughlin—A. B. Magil.... .05
The Real Huey P. Long—Sender Garlin................ .05
How Can We Share the Wealth —The Communist
Way Versus Huey Long—Alex Bittelman........... .03
Hearst: Labor's Enemy No. 1—James Casey....... .03
Why Hearst Lies About Communism—Wm. F.
Dunn .... .05
Plotting America's Pogroms—John L. Spivak........ .25

Yankee Imperialism

Yankee Colonies—Harry Gannes...................... .10
Bananas—The Fruit Empire of Wall Street—Luis
Montes .... .05
Hawaii—Samuel Weinman .... .10
Who Fights for a Free Cuba —M. Kaye and L.
Perry .... .03
Hands Off Cuba—William Simons...................... .01

British Imperialism

The Class Struggle in Britain in the Epoch of
Imperialism—Ralph Fox. 2 vols. each .... .25
The Colonial Policy of British Imperialism—
Ralph Fox .... .75
The War for the Land in Ireland—Brian O'Neill ... .75
Ireland's Path to Freedom—Manifesto of the
Communist Party of Ireland.......................... .03
The Irish Case for Communism—Sean Murray.... .05
Ireland's Fight for Freedom and the Irish in the
U. S. A.—Sean Murray............................... .05
Marx, Engels, Lenin on the Irish Revolution—
Ralph Fox .... .10
Some Urgent Problems of the Labor Movement
in India—V. Basak.................................. .05

Germany

Dimitroff Accuses—Closing Speech at the Reichs-
tag Fire Trial....................................... .03
The Communist Party of Germany Lives and
Fights .... .05
The Fight for Communism in Germany................ .01
Who Burned the Reichstag .... .03
The Sonnenburg Torture Camp....................... .05
Ernst Thaelmann, The Leader of the German
Workers—R. Groetz .... .03
Do You Know Thaelmann —Henri Barbusse.......... .03
Fighting Fascism in the Factories—How the
Y. C. L. Works in the Factories to Overthrow
the Fascist Dictatorship.............................. .05

Austria

The February Struggle in Austria and Its Lessons
—Bela Kun .... .15

Social-Democracy—Stepping-Stone to   Price
Fascism—D. Z. Manuilsky..................$0.05

Spain

Soviets in Spain—The October Armed Uprising
Against Fascism—Harry Gannes.................. .10

China

The Fundamental Laws of the Chinese Soviet
Republic .... .20
Red China—President Mao Tse-Tung.................. .05
War in China—Ray Stewart .... .10
Soviet China—M. James and R. Roonping.......... .10
Chinese Toiling Women—How They Are Helping
the Chinese Soviets .... .05
An Eye-Witness in Manchuria—W. M. Holmes.. .15
War in the Far East—Henry Hall.................. .10

ON THE SOVIET UNION

The International Situation and the Soviet Union
—V. M. Molotov.................................. .03
The Soviet Union—Your Questions Answered—
Margaret Cowl .... .03
On Understanding Soviet Russia—Corliss Lamont.. .03
Dictatorship and Democracy in the Soviet Union
—Anna Louise Strong .... .05
Religion in the U. S. S. R.—E. Yaroslavsky...... .15
The Soviet Patent Law.................. .05
The Soviet Marriage Law.................. .05
Anti-Soviet Lies and the Five-Year Plan—Max
Bedacht .... .10

The Seventeenth Congress of the Communist Party

Stalin Reports—Report of Joseph Stalin on the
Work of the Central Committee.................. .10
Ready for Defense—K. E. Voroshilov.................. .05
The Task of the Second Five-Year Plan—V. M.
Molotov .... .10
The Organizational Problems of Party and Soviet
Construction—L. M. Kaganovich.................. .15
The Second Five-Year-Plan—V. V. Kuibyshev.... .10
Completion of the Reconstruction of the Entire
National Economy—S. Ordjonikidze.................. .10
The Revolutionary Crises Is Maturing—D. Z.
Manuilsky .... .10
Resolutions and Decisions, Including Party Rules .10

The Soviet Fight for Peace

The Soviets Fight for Disarmament—Introduction
by Boards—A. Lunacharsky .... .25
"Soviet Dumping" Fable—M. Litvinov.................. .02
The Red Army.................................. .03

The Trade Unions and Protection of Labor

Labor Protection in Soviet Russia—George M.
Price, M. D................................... .50
The Protection of Labor in the U. S. S. R.—
Z. Mokhov .... .10
The Trade Unions and Socialist Construction in
U. S. S. R.—K. Avdeyeva.................. .10
Soviet Trade Unions on Threshold of Second
Five-Year Plan .... .30
Interviews with Foreign Workers' Delegations—
J. Stalin .... .15

Socialist Planned Economy

The Results of the First Five-Year   Price
Plan—J. Stalin $0.10
The Success of the Five-Year Plan—V. M.
Molotov .... .10
Fulfillment of the First Five-Year Plan—V. M.
Molotov .... .15
Forward to the Second Five-Year Plan of Socialist
Construction—Resolution of the Seventeenth
Party Conference of the C. P. S. U.................. .05
Industrial Development Under the Second Five-
Year Plan—V. Kuibyshev.................. .10
Food for All—The Abolition of the Bread Card
System—V. M. Molotov.................. .03
Light Industry on the Border Line Between the
Two Five-Year Plans—A. Greishman.................. .10
Socialist Industry in the U. S. S. R. Victorious—
Issued by Supreme Council of National Econ-
omy—Edited by B. S. Bogushevsky.................. .10
Lyubertsy—A Cross Section of the Five-Year Plan
—Th. Neubauer .... .10
The Industrial Development of 1931 and the
Tasks of 1932—S. Ordjonikidze.................. .05
Socialist Reconstruction of Moscow and Other
Cities—L. M. Kaganovich.................. .15
The Construction of the Subway in Moscow—
L. M. Raganovich.................. .10
Socialist Planning in Soviet Russia—Corliss Lamont .05

The Victories and the Heroes of Soviet Labor

The Land of Inventors—J. Vasilevsky.................. .15
How the Workers Become Engineers in the U. S.
S. R.—V. Druzhinin.................. .10
The Fight for Steel—N. Michailov.................. .10
The Heroes of Grozny—T. Gonta.................. .10
Magnitogorsk—A. Malenky .... .10
Dnieprostroi—S. Zaslavsky.................. .10
The Bolsheviks Discover Siberia—S. Besborodov.... .10
An American Worker in a Moscow Factory—S.
Weinberg .... .08
Foreign Workers in a Soviet Tractor Plant—Fred
Beal .... .15
German Miners in the Donbas.................. .05
German Workers in the Soviet Union—German
Foundry Workers Tell Their Own Story.................. .05
German Workers in a Moscow Factory.................. .10
The Dzershinsky Tractor Plant.................. .05
Thomas Monger and J. Liebhardt—Heroes of So-
cialist Construction .... .10
Nefte-Chala—Short Stories of the Fight for Oil.... .10
From Stalingrad to Kuzbas—Anna Louise Strong .10
Kuznetskstroi—I. Bakhtamov .... .10
Soviet Sakhalin—V. Kantorovich.................. .15
Soviet Ukraine Today—P. P. Postyshev and S. V.
Kossior .... .10
New Points on the Map—A. Litvak.................. .05
Iron, Coal and Komsomol—F. Weiskopf.................. .10
The First Business Accounting Brigade.................. .10
100 Years in Ten—A. A. Heller.................. .10
Moscow of Tomorrow—A. Rodin.................. .10
Socialist Competition of the Masses—E. Mikulina,
with a preface by J. Stalin.................. .10
Development of Socialist Methods and Forms of
Labor—A. Aluf .... .10

Women and Youth

	Price
Women in the Soviet Union—F. Nurina	$0.15
Youth in the Happy Land—Lillian Andrews	.05
An American Boy in the Soviet Union—Harry Eisman	.10
Youth in the Soviet Union—V. Zaitzev	.10

Collective Farming

	Price
From Peasant to Collective Farmer—N. Buchwald and R. Bishop. Cloth, .75; Paper	.25
Kolkhozniki—Letters from Peasants on Collective Farms	.10
Collective Farm "Trud"—Told by Eudoxia Pazukhina	.10
One of 25,000—A. Isbach	.10
Workaday Heroics—Life and Work in Socialist Fields—Sketches and Stories by 12 Soviet Writers	.20
The Families of Lartsev and Pantushin—A. Alexandrov	.10
The Ferry—Sketches of the Struggle for Socialism in the Altai Mountains—Mark Egart	.25
On the Steppes of the Ukraine and the Caucasus —P. Vaillant-Couturier	.15
Free Soviet Tadjikistan—P. Vaillant-Couturier	.10
The Work in the Rural Districts—J. Stalin	.03
Collective Farming—1932—Y. A. Yakovlev	.10
J. Stalin: To the Collective Farm Shock-Brigade Workers	.05

Science and Technology

	Price
The Basis of the Technological Economic Plan of Reconstruction of the U. S. S. R.—G. M. Krizhizhanovsky	.05
Socialist Reconstruction and the Struggle for Technique—N. Bukharin	.05
Technical Institutes in the Factory	.05
The Natural Wealth of the Soviet Union and Its Exploitation—I. M. Gubkin	.10
Industrial and Technical Intelligentsia in the U. S. S. R.	.15

Anti-Soviet Sabotage

	Price
The Assassination of Kirov—M. Katz	.03
Anti-Soviet Sabotage Exposed—G. M. Krzhyshanovsky	.05
The Menshevik Trial—Text of the Indictment of the Counter-Revolutionary Menshevik Organization	.10
Vickers Wreckers Trial—Three Volumes, Each	.90
The Moscow Trial	.05
Safeguarding Public Socialist Property—N. Krylenko	.05

THE THEORY AND PRACTICE OF MARXISM-LENINISM

Marx and Engels

	Price
The Communist Manifesto—Karl Marx and Friedrich Engels	$0.10
Wage-Labor and Capital—Karl Marx	.10
Value, Price and Profit—Karl Marx	.15
Civil War in France—Karl Marx	.25
Critique of the Gotha Program—Karl Marx	.50
Germany: Revolution and Counter-Revolution— Friedrich Engels	.60

	Price
The Fourteenth of March, 1883—Friedrich Engels on the Death of Karl Marx	$0.10
Karl Marx—1883-1933—Max Bedacht, Sam Don and Earl Browder	.05
Karl Marx—L. Perchik	.10

Little Lenin Library

		Price
1.	The Teachings of Karl Marx	.15
2.	The War and the Second International	.20
3.	Socialism and War	.15
4.	What Is to Be Done	.50
5.	The Paris Commune	.20
6.	The Revolution of 1905	.20
7.	Religion	.15
8.	Letters From Afar	.15
9.	The Tasks of the Proletariat in Our Revolution	.15
10.	The April Conference	.20
11.	The Threatening Catastrophe and How to Fight It	.20
12.	Will the Bolsheviks Retain State Power?	.15
13.	On the Eve of October	.15
14.	State and Revolution	.30
15.	Imperialism, The Highest Stage of Capitalism	.30
16.	Lenin—Joseph Stalin	.10
17.	A Letter to American Workers	.05
18.	Foundations of Leninism—Joseph Stalin	.40
19.	Problems of Leninism—Joseph Stalin	.25
20.	"Left-Wing" Communism: An Infantile Disorder	.25
21.	The Proletarian Revolution and Renegade Kautsky	.30
22.	Two Tactics of Social-Democracy in the Democratic Revolution	.30
	The Foundation of the Communist International —V. I. Lenin	.10
	Lenin on the Jewish Question	.05
	Lenin on the Woman Question—Clara Zetkin	.05
	The Lenin Heritage—Joseph Stalin	.03
	Leninism—A. Bubnov	.05

Low-Priced Editions for Organizations

The following have been published in large editions at specially low prices for distribution in quantities to organizations.

	Price
Foundations of Leninism—Joseph Stalin	$0.10
State and Revolution—V. I. Lenin	.10
The Communist Manifesto—Karl Marx and Friedrich Engels	.05
A Letter to American Workers—V. I. Lenin	.03
Profits and Wages—Anna Rochester	.05
The American Farmer—George Anstrom	.05
The History of May Day—Alexander Trachtenberg	.03
Negro Liberation—James S. Allen	.05

I. Political Economy

		Price
1.	Marxist Theory of Value	.15
2.	Capital and Surplus Value	.15
3.	Capital and Surplus Value (Continued)	.15
4.	Wages and Accumulation of Capital	.15
5.	Wages and Accumulation of Capital (Part 2)	.15
6.	Distribution of Surplus Value	.15
7.	Distribution of Surplus Value (Continued)	.15
8.	Economic Crises	.15
9.	Economic Crises (Continued)	.15
10.	Imperialism	.15
10a.	Supplementary Material	.15
11.	Imperialism (Continued)	.15

II. History of the Working Class

	Price
1. The Great French Revolution	$0.15
2. The Industrial Revolution in England and Chartism	.15
3. The Revolution of 1878 in France and Germany	.15
4. The First International and the Paris Commune	.15

III. Political Education

1. The Two Worlds	.15
2. The Ultimate Aim	.15
3. The Communist Party	.15
Religion and Communism—Earl Browder	.03
Dialectical Materialism and Communism—L. Rudas	.20

ON THE COMMUNIST PARTY AND THE COMMUNIST INTERNATIONAL

Program of the Communist International—Together with Constitution and Statutes	.10
The Struggle Against Imperialist War and the Tasks of the Communists—Resolution of the Sixth World Congress of the Communist International	.05
The Revolutionary Movement in the Colonies—Resolution of the Sixth World Congress of the Communist International	.10
The Twenty-One Conditions of Admission Into the Communist International—O. Piatnitsky	.05

Thirteenth Plenum of the E. C. C. I.

Bound Volume of Theses, Reports and Speeches. Cloth	.65
Fascism, The Danger of War and the Tasks of the Communist Parties—Report by O. Kuusinen	.10
The Communist Parties in the Fight for the Masses—Speech by O. Piatnitsky	.10
We Are Fighting for a Soviet Germany—Report by William Pieck, Secretary of the Communist Party of Germany	.10
Revolutionary Crises, Fascism and War—Speech by D. Z. Manuilsky	.05
Fascism, Social-Democracy and the Communists—Speech by V. Knorin	.10
Revolutionary China Today—Speeches by Wan Ming and Kang Sin	.10
The Revolutionary Struggle of the Toiling Masses of Japan—Speech by Okano	.05
The Road to Woman's Freedom—K. Kirsanova	.03

Twelfth Plenum of the E. C. C. I.

Prepare for Power—The International Situation and the Tasks of the Sections of the Communist International—Report by O. Kuusinen	.15
The Soviet Union and the World Proletariat—Report by D. Z. Manuilsky	.10
The War in the Far East and the Tasks of the Communists in the Struggle Against Imperialist War and Military Intervention—Report by Okano	.05
The Next Step in Britain, America and Ireland—Speeches by Gusev, Pollitt, Troy and Pringle	.05
Guide to the Twelfth Plenum—Handbook for Propagandists	.15

	Price
Marxism Versus Liberalism—The Stalin-Wells Interview	$0.02
Tactical and Organizational Questions of the Communist Parties of India and Indo-China—Orgwald	.15
The Communist Party in Action—Alex Bittelman	.10
A Program for American Youth—Manifesto and Resolutions of Seventh National Convention Young Communist League of U. S. A.	.05
Why Communism?—Plain Talks on Vital Problems—M. J. Olgin	.05
An Open Letter to All Members of the Communist Party	.01
Trotskyism—Counter-Revolution in Disguise—M. J. Olgin. Paper .15; Cloth	.75
The Meaning of Social Fascism—Earl Browder	.05
Capitalism Defends Itself Through the Socialist Labor Party—Moissaye J. Olgin	.03
The Reds in Dixie—Who Are the Communists and What Do They Fight For in the South—Tom Johnson	.05
A Noon Hour Talk on the Communist Party—Harrison George	.02
Fifteen Years of the Communist Party—Alex Bittelman	.10
The Advance of the United Front—A Documentary Account—Introduction by Alex Bittelman	.05
Tasks of the American Communist Party in the Struggle for Social Insurance—S. I. Gusev and Earl Browder	.02
On the Road to Bolshevization	.10
Preparing for October—The Sixth Congress of the Bolshevik Party, August, 1917	.20
Shop Paper Manual	.10
Struggles Ahead—Thesis of the Seventh Convention of the Communist Party on the Economic and Political Situation	.10
The Most Burning Question—Unity of Action—Bela Kun	.10
Leninism—The Only Marxism Today—A Discussion of the Characteristics of Declining Capitalism—Alex Bittelman and V. J. Jerome	.15
How Do We Raise the Question of a Labor Party?—Earl Browder and Jack Stachel	.03
Short History of the Young Communist League of the Soviet Union—A. Alfonin	.10
We Are For the United Front—Chemadanov	.01
Let's Fight Together—Appeal of the Y. C. L.	.01
Young Communists and the Path to Soviet Power—Report to January, 1934, Plenum of the E. C., Y. C. I.—Chemadanov	.10
The Years of the Communist International—I. Komor	.10
Fifteen Years of the Communist International	.05

ON HISTORICAL STRUGGLES OF THE WORKERS

The History of May Day—Alexander Trachtenberg	.05
The Frame-Up System—Vern Smith	.10
The Paris Commune—In Historical Pictures	.05
The Paris Commune—A Story in Pictures	.05

"Bolshevik History" Library

	Price
Bolsheviks on Trial—S. Tchernomordik	$0.10
Book Publishing Under Tsarism—M. S. Kedrov	.10
Provocateurs I Have Known—C. Bobrovskaya	.10
The Strike of the Dredging Fleet, 1905—Peter Nikiforo v	.10
From the February Revolution to the October Revolution—A. F. Ilyin Genevsky	.15
Bolshevik Smugglers—S. Shaumyan	.10
Civil War in the Taiga—I. Strod	.25

BIOGRAPHY

Life and Teachings of V. I. Lenin—R. Palme Dutt	.50
Lenin in the October Revolution—Reminiscences of Participants	.10
The Architect of Socialist Society (Stalin)—Karl Radek	.10
Maxim Gorky—M. J. Olgin	.25
Life of Stalin—A. Symposium	.15
The Heritage of Gene Debs—Alexander Trachtenberg	.05
Steve Katovis—The Life and Death of a Worker—A. B. Magil and Joseph North	.10
J. Louis Engdahl—Revolutionary Working Class Leader—Harriet Silverman	.05
Mother Bloor—Ann Barton	.03
Ivan Babushkin—Lenin's Friend—C. Bobrovskaya	.10
Y. M. Sverdlov—First President of the Labor Republic—C. Bobrovskaya	.10
Natasha—A Bolshevik Woman Organizer—L, Katasheva	.10

FICTION AND SHORT STORIES

Tales of Modern China—Oskar Erdberg	.35
Six Seamen—Mike Pell	.15
Life in Review—And Other Soviet Sketches—Semyon Narinyani	.10
White Stone—M. Chumandrin	.10
Soviet Main Street—Myra Page	.15
Commissar of the Gold Express—V. Matveyev	.50

BOOKS FOR CHILDREN

Battle in the Barnyard—Stories and Pictures for Workers' Children—Helen Kay	.35
New Pioneer Story Book—Illustrated	.25
Twelve Plays for Boys and Girls—Illustrated by Wm. Siegel	.95
Our Lenin—Ruth Shaw and Harry Alan Potamkin. Pictures by Wm. Siegel	.95
Bows Against the Barons—Robin Hood for Boys and Girls—Geoffrey Trease	.85
Red Corner Book for Children	1.25

SONGS AND POETRY

Poems for Workers	.10
Pioneer Song Book—Words by Harry Alan Potamkin	.10
The Internationale—Sheet Music	.10

INTERNATIONAL BOOKS

	Price
5. Foundations of Leninism—Joseph Stalin	$1.00
6. The Economic Theory of the Leisure Class—Nikolai Bukharin	1.50
8. State and Revolution—V. I. Lenin	1.00
9. Civil War in France—Karl Marx	1.00
10. Two Tactics of Social-Democracy in the Democratic Revolution—V. I. Lenin	1.00
11. Critique of the Gotha Program—Karl Marx	1.00
12. Foundations of Christianity—Karl Kautsky	2.50
13. Germany: Revolution and Counter-Revolution—Friedrich Engels	1.50
14. What Is to Be Done?—V. I. Lenin	1.25
15. Ludwig Feuerbach—F. Engels	.75
16. "Left-Wing" Communism: An Infantile Disorder—V. I. Lenin	1.00
17. Letters to Kugelmann—Karl Marx, Introduction by V. I. Lenin	1.00
18. Anti-Duehring—F. Engels	1.00
20. Marx, Engels, and Marxism—V. I. Lenin	1.25
21. The October Revolution—J. Stalin	1.00
23. The Housing Question—Friedrich Engels	1.00
27. Brief History of Russia—M. N. Pokrovsky—Vol. I	2.00
28. Brief History of Russia—M. N. Pokrovsky—Vol. II	2.00
29. Correspondence of Marx and Engels	2.75
31. Lenin on Britain	2.00
32. Problems of Leninism—J. Stalin	1.00
33. The Peasant War in Germany—F. Engels	1.50
35. The Eighteenth Brumaire of Louis Bonaparte—K. Marx	1.50
37. Wage-Labor and Capital, and Value, Price and Profit—Karl Marx	1.00
Capital—Karl Marx	
Vol I. The Process of Capitalist Production	2.50
Vol II. The Process of Circulation of Capital	2.50
Vol III. The Process of Capitalist Production as a Whole	2.50
Critique of Political Economy—Karl Marx	1.25
Poverty of Philosophy—Karl Marx	1.25
Origin of the Family, Private Property and the State—Friedrich Engels	.60
Leninism—Joseph Stalin, Vol. I	1.90
Leninism—Joseph Stalin, Vol. II	2.50
Historical Materialism—Nikolai Bukharin	2.50
Dialectical Materialism—V. Adoratsky	.50
Fascism and Social Revolution—R. Palme Dutt	1.25
Political Economy—A. Leontiev	1.25
Are the Jews a Race?—Karl Kautsky. Regular $2.50; Popular	1.50
Toward Soviet America—William Z. Foster	1.25
Forced Labor in the United States—Walter Wilson. Cloth $1.50; Boards	1.00
Oil Imperialism—Louis Fischer	2.00
Whither China?—Scott Nearing. Cloth $1.75; Paper	.50
The Condition of the Working Class in Britain—Allen Hutt	2.00

The Collected Works of V. I. Lenin

The Iskra Period—In two volumes. Regular $4.00 each; popular, each	3.00
Materialism and Empirio-Criticism—V. I. Lenin. Regular $4.00; popular	2.50

The Revolution of 1917—In two volumes. Price
Regular $4.00 each; popular, each..................... $3.00
The Imperialist War. Regular $4.50; popular........ 3.50
Toward the Seizure of Power—In two volumes.
Regular $3.50 each; popular, each.................... 2.50

Special Lenin Set

The five volumes (eight books) listed above have
been issued as a special set which sells for a
limited time only at the special price of............. 8.00

Selected Works of V. I. Lenin

To comprise twelve volumes. The following are
now ready:
Vol. I. The Prerequisites of the First Russian
Revolution (1894-1899) 2.00
Vol. II. The Struggle for a Bolshevik Party
(1900-1901) 2.00
Vol. V. Imperialism and Imperialist War (1914-
1917) 2.00

Russia and the Russian Revolution

History of Russia—From the Earliest Times to the
Rise of Commercial Capitalism—Prof. M. N.
Pokrovsky. Regular $3.50; popular................. 2.50
Brief History of Russia—M. N. Pokrovsky, 2
volumes, each 2.00
The Bolsheviks in the Tsarist Duma—A. Badayev.
Regular $2.25; popular.................................... 1.00
Twenty Years in Underground Russia—C. Bobrov-
skaya .... .85
The Last Days of Tsar Nicholas—P. M. Bykov.... .50
From the February Revolution to the October
Revolution, 1917—A. F. Ilyin-Genevsky............. .75
Ten Days That Shook the World—John Reed........ 1.25
Illustrated History of the Russian Revolution.
Volume I, $2.75; Volume II............................. 4.00
The Soviet Union and Peace—With an Introduc-
tion by Henri Barbusse..................................... 1.75
The U. S. S. R.—The State of the Soviet Union
—Joseph Stalin .... .75
Outline History of the Communist Party of the
Soviet Union—N. Popov. Two volumes, each.... 2.00
The Soviets Fight for Disarmament—With an
Introduction by A. Lunacharsky, Soviet Dele-
gate to the Geneva Disarmament Conference.... .25
On Guard for the Soviet Union—Maxim Gorky.
Cloth $1.50; Boards... .75
American Policy Toward Russia Since 1917—
Frederick Lewis Schuman, Ph. D...................... 3.75
Education in Soviet Russia—Scott Nearing, Cloth.. 1.00
The National Policy of the Soviet Union—A.
Rysakoff .... .60
The Soviet Worker—Joseph Freeman.................... 1.50
The Five-Year Plan of the Soviet Union—A Politi-
cal Interpretation—G. T. Grinko, Commissar of
Finance, U. S. S. R. Regular $3.50; popular.... 2.00
Those Who Built Stalingrad—As Told by Them-
selves; Introduction by Maxim Gorky, Draw-
ings by Fred Ellis... 1.00
Men of Siberia—Hugo Huppert............................ 1.00
Socialism Victorious—Joseph Stalin and Others.... 1.50
Summary of the Fulfillment of the Five-Year
Plan—State Planning Commission...................... 1.25
From the First to the Second Five-Year Plan........ 1.50
Socialist Planned Economy in the Soviet Union—
V. V. Obolensky-Ossinsky and others. Regular
$1.50; popular .... .90

The Land Without Unemployment—Ernst   Price
Glaeser and F. C. Weiskopf.............................. $1.00
From Peasant to Collective Farmer—N. Buch-
wald and R. Bishop. Cloth .75; paper............... .25
Red Villages—The Five-Year Plan in Agriculture
—Y. A. Yakovlev, Commissar of Agriculture,
U. S. S. R. Illustrated. Cloth $1.50; paper.... .50
The Success of the Five-Year Plan—V. M. Molo-
tov, Chairman, Council of Commissars, U. S.
S. R. .... .75
Report of the American Delegation to the Soviet
Union 1.00
Dawn Over Samarkand—The Rebirth of Central
Asia—Joshua Kunitz 1.90

History

The Molly Maguires—Anthony Bimba. Regular
$1.50; popular 1.00
History of the American Working Class—A. Bimba 2.50
From Chartism to Laborism—Theodore Rothstein.. 2.50

Biography

Karl Marx—Man, Thinker, and Revolutionist—
A Symposium by Leading Marxists.................... 1.75
Karl Marx and Friedrich Engels—D. Ryazanov.
Regular $2.50; popular..................................... 1.50
The Life and Teachings of Karl Marx—Max Beer.. 1.50
Memories of Lenin—Nadezhda K. Krupskaya.
Vols. I and II. Each: Regular $1.50; popular.... .75
Days with Lenin—Maxim Gorky. Cloth, .75;
paper .... .25
Reminiscences of Lenin—Clara Zetkin. Cloth,
.75; popular .... .20
Thomas Moore and His Utopia—Karl Kautsky...... 2.25
Bill Haywood's Book—The Autobiography of Wil-
liam D. Haywood. Regular, $3.50; popular........ 1.50
The Life and Death of Sacco and Vanzetti—Eu-
gene Lyons. Regular, $1.50; popular................. 1.00
Memoirs of a Revolutionist—Vera Figner, Illus-
trated. Regular, $3.00; popular........................ 2.00
Memoirs of a Bolshevik—O. Piatnitsky. Cloth,
$2.00; Boards 1.00
Maxim Gorky—Writer and Revolutionist—Mois-
saye J. Olgin. Cloth .75; paper....................... .25
Dimitrov—Stella D. Blagoyeva............................ .75
Memoirs of a Barber—G. Germanetto.................. 1.25
Voices of Revolt—Each volume, bound in boards .50
1. Jean Paul Marat
2. Maximilien Robespierre
3. Ferdinand Lasalle
4. Karl Liebknecht
5. Georges Jacques Danton
6. August Bebel
7. Wilhelm Liebknecht
8. V. I. Lenin
9. Eugene V. Debs
10. C. E. Ruthenberg

Labor Research Books

Labor Fact Book—Prepared by the Labor Research
Association. Regular $2.00; popular.................. .85
Labor Fact Book II. Regular $2.00; popular........ .95
Women Who Work—Grace Hutchins. Regular
$2.00; popular 1.00
Labor and Coal—Anna Rochester. Regular $2.00;
popular 1.00

Labor and Textiles—Robert W. Dunn and Jack Hardy. Regular $2.00; popular..........Price $1.00

Labor and Lumber—Charlotte Todes. Regular $2.00; popular 1.00

Labor and Automobiles—Robert W. Dunn. Regular $2.00; popular...................... 1.00

Labor and Silk—Grace Hutchins. Regular $2.00; popular 1.00

Labor and Steel—Horace B. Davis. Regular $2.00; popular 1.00

The Americanization of Labor—Robert W. Dunn. Regular, $1.90; popular............. 1.00

The Woman Worker and the Trade Unions—Theresa Wolfson. Regular $1.25; popular.......... 1.00

Fiction

Conveyor—James Steele 1.25

Driving Axle—V. Ilyenkov. Regular $2.00; popular 1.00

Jews Without Money—Michael Gold.................. .75

Gathering Storm—Myra Page. Regular $2.50; popular .... .95

Barricades in Berlin—Klaus Neukranz. Cloth $1.50; Boards .... .75

Roar China—S. Tretyakov. Regular $1.00; popular .... .50

China's Red Army Marches—Agnes Smedley........ 1.60

Chapayev—D. Furmanov 1.50

The, Iron Flood—A. Serafimovich................. 1.00

I Love—A. Avdeyenko 1.00

Brusski—The Soil Redeemed—F. Panferov. Regular $2.50; popular 1.50

The Nineteen—A. Fadeyev. Regular $2.50; popular 1.50

Azure Cities—Stories of New Russia. Regular $2.50; popular 1.50

Cement—Feodor Gladkov. Regular $2.50; popular 1.50

120 Million—Michael Gold .... .95

Chains—Henri Barbusse, Two Volumes $4.00; One Vol. 3.00

Storm Over the Ruhr—Hans Marchwitza. Cloth, $1.50; boards .... .75

The Commissar of the Gold Express—V. Matveyev. Cloth $1.00; paper....................... .50

Armored Train 14-69—Vsevolod Ivanov. Cloth, $1.00; paper .... .25

The Cannery Boat, and Other Japanese Short Stories—Takiji Kobayashi and Others. Cloth, $1.50; boards .... .75

S. S. Utah—Mike Pell. Boards, $0.75; cloth........ 1.25

Art, Literature and Science

Literature of the Peoples of the U. S. S. R......... .50

Painting, Sculpture and Graphic Arts in the U. S. S. R. .... .50

Modern Russian Composers—Leonid Sabaneyeff.... 2.75

Russian Poetry—An Anthology — Chosen and Translated by Babette Deutsch and Avrahm Yarmolinsky 2.25

The Foundations of Aesthetics—C. K. Ogden, I. A. Richards and James Wood.................. 2.50

English for Workers—Eli B. Jacobson.................. 1.00

Elementary Russian—Edited by L. I. Basilevich.. 1.25

Psychology

Lectures on Conditioned Reflexes—Ivan P. Pavlov 6.50

General Principles of Human Reflexology—Vladimir M. Bechterov............................ 5.00

ITALIAN PAMPHLETS

	Price
Cosa Ogni Lavoratore Dovrebbe Sapere Intorno Alla N. R. A.—Earl Browder............................	$0.05
Perche Il Comunismo?—M. J. Olgin......................	.10
La Via D'Uscita—Una piattaforma per le masse lavoratrici d'America	.02
Il Comunismo-Spiegato Ai Lavoratori—Carlo Rappoport	.05

SPANISH PAMPHLETS

Lo Que Todo Obrero Debe Conocer Sobre El N. R. A.—Earl Browder... .05

La Union Sovietica—Respuesta a tus preguntas—Margaret Cowl .... .05

Por Que Le Comunismo?—M. J. Olgin.................... .10

Los Fundamentos Del Leninismo—Stalin............... .30

Marx, Maestro y Jefe Del Proletariado—Perchik.. .10

El Estado y la Revolucion—Lenin....................... .80

Precio, Salario y Beneficio—Marx........................ .20

Trabajo Asalariado y Capital—Marx.................... .20

Trabajo, Asalariado y Capital—Precio, Asalario y Beneficio—Marx .... .80

El Extremismo, Enfermedad Infantil Del Comunismo—Lenin .... .80

Dos Tacticas—La social democracia en la revolucion democratica—Lenin .... .30

La Comuna de Paris—Lenin....................... .30

El Socialismo y la Guerra—Lenin....................... .20

La Religion—Lenin .... .30

Quiero!—A. Avdeyenko .... .85

A SHORT SELECTION OF PAMPHLETS FOR BEGINNERS IN THE STUDY OF COMMUNISM

The Communist Manifesto—By Karl Marx and Friedrich Engels .... .05

State and Revolution—By V. I. Lenin.................... .10

A Letter to American Workers—By V. I. Lenin.... .03

Foundations of Leninism—By Joseph Stalin.......... .10

Marxism Versus Liberalism — The Stalin-Wells Interview .... .02

Program of the Communist International.................. .10

Why Communism? Plain Talks on Vital Problems—By M. J. Olgin....................... .05

The Truth About Father Coughlin—By A. B. Magil .... .05

The Real Huey P. Long—By Sender Garlin.......... .05

Unemployment Insurance—The Burning Issue of the Day—By Earl Browder....................... .03

The International Situation and the Soviet Union —By V. M. Molotov....................... .03

"Political Education" Series

1. The Two Worlds................................. .15

2. The Ultimate Aim................................. .15

3. The Communist Party................................. .15

BOOKS OF OTHER PUBLISHERS

Fiction	Price
Land of Plenty—Robert Cantwell	$2.50
The Disinherited—Jack Conroy	2.50
A World to Win—Jack Conroy	2.50
Those Who Perish—Edward Dahlberg	2.00
Mother—Maxim Gorki	2.00
The Executioner Waits—Josephine Herbst	2.50
Time Forward!—Valentine Kataev	.75
The Iron Heel—Jack London	1.00
To Make My Bread—Grace Lumpkin	2.00
You Can't Sleep Here—Edward Newhouse	2.00
Moscow Yankee—Myra Page	2.50
The Shadow Before—William Rollins, Jr.	2.50
Call It Sleep—Henry Roth	2.50

Drama

Black Pit—Albert Maltz	2.00
Waiting for Lefty and Till the Day I Die— Clifford Odets	1.25
Awake and Sing—Clifford Odets	1.25
Stevedore—Paul Peters and George Sklar	.50
Sailors of Cattaro—Friedrich Wolf	1.50
Floridsdorf—Friedrich Wolf	.60

Soviet Union	Price
Where the Ghetto Ends—Leon Dennen	$1.25
New Russia's Primer—V. Ilin	1.75
Red Medicine—John A. Kingsbury and Sir Arthur Newsholme	2.50
Changing Asia—Erwin Egon Kisch	3.00
In Place of Profit—Harry F. Ward	2.50
Red Virtue—Ella Winter	1.55

Miscellaneous

The Reichstag Fire Trial—Second Brown Book	2.50
Fatherland—Karl Billinger	1.90
Under Fire—Henri Barbusse	.90
Karl Marx's "Capital" in Lithographs — Hugo Gellert	3.00
The Great Tradition—Granville Hichs	2.50
Chinese Destinies—Agnes Smedley	3.00
The Coming Struggle for Power—John Strachey	1.75
The Nature of the Capitalist Crisis—John Strachey	3.00
Literature and Dialectical Materialism — John Strachey	1.00
I Change Worlds—Anna Louise Strong	3.00

BOOKS—TO BE PUBLISHED IN 1935

(From "1935 International Books" pamphlet)

Proletarian Literature in the United States—Editors: Granville Hicks, Michael Gold, Joseph Freeman, Isidor Schneider, Joseph North, and Paul Peters........8 vo. Regular $2.50; Popular $1.50

Selected Writings of Marx and Engels........8vo. In two volumes. Vol I, $2.00; Vol. II, $3.00

Dawn Over Samarkand—The Rebirth of Central Asia—By Joshua Kunitz........8vo. Popular Edition) $2.00

How Wall Street Rules—By Anna Rochester........8vo. Regular $2.50; Popular $1.50

Communism in the United States—By Earl Browder........12mo. Regular $1.50; Popular $0.75

Fascism—Make or Break?—By R. Braun........12mo. Regular $1.50; Popular $0.75

Fascism in Italy—By M. Bird........12mo. Regular $2.00; Popular $1.25

Marx on Trade Unionism—By A. Lozovcky........12mo. Regular $2.00; Popular $1.00

The Communist Handbook—Edited by Emile Burns........1,000 pages, $1.75

The Negro Question in the United States—By James S. Allen........12mo. Regular $2.00; Popular $1.00

China—As It Really Is—Introduction by Agnes Smedley........Quarto. Regular $2.50; Popular $1.50

The Clothing Workers—By Jack Hardy........12mo. Regular $2.00; Popular $1.00

Marxism and Literature—A Collection........8vo. Regular $2.50; Popular $1.50

Conveyor—By James Steele........12mo. Regular $1.75; Popular $1.25

The Soviet Writers' Congress—Maxim Gorky, Karl Radek and Nikolai Bukharin........12mo. $1.50

The Iron Flood—By A. Serafimovich........12mo. Regular $1.50; Popular $1.00

Clerks Under Capitalism—By A. Klinginder........12mo. $1.25

The Schools of the Soviet Union—By Rex David........12mo. $1.00

Comrades for the Charter—By Geoffrey Trease........12mo. $1.00

Martin's Annual—Edited by Joan Beauchamp........Quarto. $1.00

Eddie and the Gypsy—By Alex Wedding........12mo. $1.00

The Revenge of the Kabunauri—By Helena Bobinska and Kasimir Hertel........12mo. $1.00

The Second Five-Year Plan—By The State Planning Commission of the U. S. S. R.........12mo. Regular $2.00; Popular $1.25

The Seventh Soviet Congress........12mo. $1.75

British Imperialism in India—By Joan Beauchamp........12mo. Regular $1.75; Popular $1.25

Britain Prepares for War—By Andrew Rothstein........12mo. $2.00

New Guide Book to the Soviet Union........16mo. $3.50

Lenin on America—A Compilation........8vo. Regular $3.50; Popular $2.50

Capitalism and Agriculture in the United States—By V. I. Lenin........8vo. $1.00

War and Revolution—By V. I. Lenin........8vo. Regular $4.00; Popular $3.00

A Political Primer—By B. Volin........12mo. In two volumes. Regular $2.00 each; Popular $1.00 each

The Selected Works of V. I. Lenin, comprising 12 volumes—the first five volumes listed above. (Other volumes in preparation.)

The Prerequisites of the First Russian Revolution—By V. I. Lenin...............12mo. Regular $2.75; Popular $2.00
The Struggle for a Bolshevik Party—By V. I. Lenin...12mo. Regular $2.75; Popular $2.00
The Revolution of 1905-1907—By V. I. Lenin...12mo. Regular $2.75; Popular $2.00
The Years of Reaction and the Revival of the Movement—By V. I. Lenin........12mo. Regular $2.50; Popular $1.75
Imperialism and the Imperialist War—By V. I. Lenin.....................................12mo. Regular $2.50; Popular $1.75
The Communist Party of the Soviet Union—A Short History—V. Knorin, Editor..8vo. Regular $3.00; Popular $2.00
The Seizure of Power in Moscow—By O. A. Piatnitsky...12mo. $1.50
Ludwig Feuerbach—By Frederick Engels...8vo. Regular $1.00; Popular $0.75
Letters to Kugelmann—By Karl Marx, with an Introduction by V. I. Lenin......8vo. Regular $1.50; Popular $1.00
The Eighteenth Brumaire of Louis Bonaparte—By Karl Marx.....................................8vo. $1.50
The Civil War in France—By Karl Marx..8vo. $1.00
Germany: Revolution and Counter-Revolution—By Frederick Engels...................................8vo. $1.50
Critique of the Gotha Programme—By Karl Marx...8vo. $1.00
Introduction to Leninism...12mo. $0.75
The Theory of the Proletarian Revolution..12mo. $0.75
The National and Colonial Question...12mo. $0.75
The Agrarian and Peasant Question...12mo. $0.75
Militarism and Fascism in Japan—By O. Tanin and T. Yohan, with an
  introduction by Karl Radek..8vo. Regular $2.50; Popular $1.75
Outline History of the Communist Party of the Soviet
  Union—By N. Popoff.....................8vo. In two volumes. Regular $3.00 each; Popular $2.00 each
Marx, Engels, Marxism—By V. I. Lenin...8vo. Regular $1.75; Popular $1.25
Political Economy—By A. Leontiev...8vo. Regular $2.00; Popular $1.25
The Last Days of Tsar Nicholas—By P. M. Bykov...8vo. $1.00
Fascism and Social Revolution—By R. Palme Dutt....................................12mo. Regular $2.25; Popular $1.25
The Proletarian Revolution and Renegade Kautsky—By V. I. Lenin.................................8vo. $1.00
Two Tactics of Social-Democracy in the Democratic Revolution—By V. I. Lenin.................8vo. $1.00
Summary of the Fulfillment of the First Five-Year Plan...8vo. $1.25
Men of Siberia—By Hugo Huppert...12mo. Regular $1.50; Popular $1.00
I Love—By A. Avdeyenko...12mo. Regular $1.50; Popular $1.00
Chapayev—By D. Furmanov...12mo. Regular $2.00; Popular $1.50
Memoirs of a Barber—By Giovanni Germanetto...12mo. Regular $1.75; Popular $1.25
Socialism Victorious...12mo. $1.75
Those Who Built Stalingrad—Foreword by Maxim Gorky, Drawings by Fred Ellis.................12mo. $1.00
The Collected Works of V. I. Lenin, issued by International Publishers.
  The Revolution of 1917...................8vo. In two volumes. Regular $4.00 each; Popular $3.00 each
  Toward the Seizure of Power.........................8vo. In two volumes. Regular $3.50 each; Popular $2.50 each
  The Imperialist War...8vo. Regular $4.50; Popular $3.50
  The Iskra Period.......................8vo. In two volumes. Regular $4.00 each; Popular $3.00 each
  Materialism and Empirio-Criticism...8vo. Regular $4.00; Popular $2.50
  Anniversary Edition of Lenin's Works.
Imperialism, The Highest Stage of Capitalism—By V. I. Lenin..8vo. $1.00
State and Revolution—By V. I. Lenin...8vo. Regular $1.50; Popular $1.00
What Is to Be Done?—By V. I. Lenin..8vo. Regular $2.00; Popular $1.25
Lenin on Britain—A Compilation, with an Introduction by Harry Pollitt...........8vo. Regular $3.00; Popular $2.00
"Left-Wing" Communism: An Infantile Disorder—By V. I. Lenin.......................................8vo. $1.00
Life and Teachings of Lenin—By R. Palme Dutt... 12mo. $0.50
Memories of Lenin—By Nadezhda K. Krupskaya..12mo. In two volumes. Regular $1.50 each; Popular $0.75 each
Days With Lenin—By Maxim Gorky...12mo. $0.75
Our Lenin—Drawings by William Siegel, Edited by Ruth Shaw and
  Harry Alan Potamkin...Quarto. Regular $1.50; Popular $0.95
Reminiscences of Lenin—By Clara Zetkin...12mo. $0.75
Dimitrov—By Stella D. Blagoyeva...12mo. Regular $1.50; Popular $0.75
Bill Haywood's Book—The Autobiography of William D. Haywood....................8vo. Regular $3.50; Popular $2.00
Karl Marx and Frederick Engels—By D. Ryazanov.................................Large 12mo. Regular $2.50; Popular $1.50
The Life and Teachings of Karl Marx—By Max Beer...12mo. $1.50
Twenty Years in Underground Russia—By Cecelia Bobrovskaya.......................................12mo. $0.85
Memoirs of a Bolshevik—By O. Piatnitsky..8vo. Regular $2.00; Popular $1.00
Memoirs of a Revolutionist—By Vera Figner....................Illustrated. 8vo. Regular $3.00; Popular $2.00
Lectures on Conditioned Reflexes—By Prof. Ivan P. Pavlov.........................Illustrated. 8vo. $6.50
General Principles of Human Reflexology—An Introduction to the Objective Study of
  Personality—By Vladimir M. Bechterev...8vo. $5.00
The October Revolution—By Joseph Stalin..8vo. Regular $1.50; Popular $1.00
From the First to the Second Five-Year Plan—A Symposium..12mo. $1.50
The State of the Soviet Union—By Joseph Stalin...12mo. $0.75
The Soviet Worker—By Joseph Freeman...12mo. $1.50
On Guard for the Soviet Union—By Maxim Gorky, with an Introduction by Romain Rolland..................12mo. $1.50

American Policy Toward Russia Since 1917—By Frederick L. Schuman, Ph. D....................................8vo. $3.75
The History of the American Working Class—By Anthony Bimba..8vo. $2.50
The Molly Maguires—By Anthony Bimba...12mo. Regular $1.50; Popular $1.00
The War for the Land in Ireland—By Brian O'Neill, Introduction by Peader O'Donnell........................12mo. $1.50
The Colonial Policy of British Imperialism—By Ralph Fox......................................12mo. $0.75
The Peasant War in Germany—By Frederick Engels.......................................12mo. $1.50
History of the First International—By G. M. Steklov......................................8vo. $3.50
Ten Days That Shook the World—By John Reed......................................12mo. $1.50
A Brief History of Russia—By Prof. M. N. Pokrovsky......8vo. In two volumes. Regular $2.50 each; Popular $2.00
History of Russia—From the Earliest Times to the Rise of Commercial Capitalism
    —By Prof. N. M. Pokrovsky......................................8vo. Regular $3.50; Popular $2.50
The Bolsheviks in the Tsarist Duma—By A. Badayev......................12mo. Regular $2.25; Popular $1.00
From Chartism to Laborism—By Theodore Rothstein......................................8vo. $2.50
Foundations of Christianity—By Karl Kautsky......................................8vo. $3.50
Women Who Work—By Grace Hutchins   12mo. Regular $2.00; Popular $1.00
Labor Fact Book I—Prepared by the Labor Research Association...................12mo. Regular $2.00; Popular $0.85
Labor Fact Book II—By Labor Research Association...................12mo. Regular $2.00; Popular $0.95
Forced Labor in the United States—By Walter Wilson, with an introduction
    by Theodore Dreiser......................................12mo. Regular $1.50; Popular $1.00
The Americanization of Labor—By Robert W. Dunn......................12mo. Regular $1.90; Popular $1.00
Labor and Steel—By Horace B. Davis......................12mo. Regular $2.00; Popular $1.00
Labor and Coal—By Anna Rochester......................12mo. Regular $2.00; Popular $1.00
Labor and Textiles—By Robert W. Dunn and Jack Hardy......................12mo. Regular $2.00; Popular $1.00
Labor and Lumber—By Charlotte Todes......................12mo. Regular $2.00; Popular $1.00
Labor and Automobiles—By Robert W. Dunn......................12mo. Regular $2.00; Popular $1.00
Labor and Silk—By Grace Hutchins......................12mo. Regular $2.00; Popular $1.00
China's Red Army Marches—By Agnes Smedley......................................12mo. $1.60
Jews Without Money—By Michael Gold......................................12mo. $0.75
The Cannery Boat—Stories from Japan......................12mo. Regular $1.50; Popular $0.75
Driving Axle—By V. Ilyenkov......................12mo. Regular $2.00; Popular $1.00
Gathering Storm—By Dorothy Myra Page......................12mo. Regular $2.00; Popular $0.95
Bows Against the Barons—By Geoffrey Trease.................Illustrated, 12mo. Regular $1.25; Popular $0.85
120 Million—By Michael Gold......................................12mo. $0.95
Barricades in Berlin—By Klaus Neukranz......................12mo. Regular $1.50; Popular $0.75
Storm Over the Ruhr—By Hans Marchwitza......................12mo. Regular $1.50; Popular $0.75
Maxim Gorky—Writer and Revolutionist—By Mossaiye J. Olgin......................................12mo. $0.75
Armoured Train—By Vsevolod Ivanov......................................12mo. $0.75
Roar China—By S. Tretiakov......................12mo. Regular $1.00; Popular $0.50
Chains—By Henri Barbusse.........................12mo. Two Volumes $4.00; One Volume $3.00
S. S. Utah—By Mike Pell......................12mo. Regular $1.25; Popular $0.75
The Commissar of the Gold Express—By V. Matveyev, Illustrated by Ernst......................12mo. $1.00
The Nineteen—By A. Fadeyev......................................12mo. $2.50
Brusski—By F. Panferov......................8vo. Regular $2.50; Popular $1.50
Cement—By Feodor Gladkov......................12mo. Regular $2.50; Popular $1.50
Azure Cities—Stories of New Russia......................12mo. Regular $2.50; Popular $1.50
Russian Poetry—An Anthology—Chosen and translated by Babette Deutsch and Avrahm Yarmolinsky...12mo. $2.25
Modern Russian Composers—By Leonid Sabaneyeff......................................Large 12mo. $2.75
Russian Textbook (Popular first course in the Russian language)—Elementary Course 8vo. $1.25
The Soviet Union and Peace—A documentary history with an Introduction by Henri Barbusse......8vo. $1.75
The Five-Year Plan of the Soviet Union—By G. T. Grinko......................................8vo. $2.50
From Peasant to Collective Farmer—By N. Buchwald and R. Bishop......................12mo. $0.75
The National Policy of the Soviet Union—By A. Rysakoff......................12mo. $0.60
English for Workers—By Eli B. Jacobson......................12mo. $1.00
Oil Imperialism—By Louis Fischer......................................12mo. $2.00
Labor Protection in Soviet Russia—By Dr. George M. Price......................12mo. $1.00
From the February to the October Revolution, 1917—By A. F. Ilyin-Genevsky......................12mo. $0.75
The Woman Worker and the Trade Unions—By Theresa Wolfson......................12mo. $1.25
Whither China?—By Scott Nearing......................................12mo. $1.00
Education in Soviet Russia—By Scott Nearing......................................12mo. $1.00
Social Struggles in Antiquity—By Max Beer......................................12mo. $1.75
Social Struggles in the Middle Ages—By Max Beer......................................12mo. $1.75
The Civil War in the United States—By Karl Marx and Friederich Engels......................8vo. $2.50
The Jewish Question—By Karl Marx......................................8vo. $1.00
Marx on Religion—A Collection......................8vo. Regular $2.00; Popular $1.50
The Housing Question—By Friederich Engels......................8vo. Regular $1.25; Popular $0.75
Origin of the Family, Private Property and the State—By Friederich Engels......................8vo. $1.00
Engels on Capital......................................8vo. $1.00

Condition of the Working Class in England in 1844—By Friedrich Engels........8vo. Regular $2.50; Popular $1.75
The Poverty of Philosophy—By Karl Marx..8vo. Regular $2.00; Popular $1.50
Class Struggles in France—By Karl Marx..8vo. Regular $1.75; Popular $1.25
The Correspondence of Marx and Engels..8vo. Regular $3.75; Popular $2.75
Herr Duhring's Revolution in Science—By Friedrich Engels...........................8vo. Regular $2.50; Popular $1.90
Capital—The Process of Capitalist Production—By Karl Marx..Large 12mo. $3.00
Leninism—By Joseph Stalin..8vo. In two volumes. $2.50 each
Foundations of Leninism—By Joseph Stalin...:........8vo. Regular $1.50; Popular $1.00
Problems of Leninism—By Joseph Stalin..8vo. $1.00
Toward Soviet America—By William Z. Foster...12mo. $1.25
Fundamental Laws of the Chinese Soviet Republic—With an Introduction by Bela Kun...........................12mo. $0.75
The Condition of the Working Class in Britain—By Allen Hutt..12mo. $2.00
Dialectical Materialism—By V. Adoratsky...12mo. $0.50
Historical Materialism—By Nikolai Bukharin...8vo. Regular $3.25; Popular $2.50
Fundamental Problems of Marxism—By George Plekhanov.....................8vo. Regular $2.00; Popular $1.50
The Economic Theory of the Leisure Class—By Nikolai Bukharin.....................8vo. Regular $2.50; Popular $1.50
Imperialism and World Economy—By Nikolai Bukharin............................:.....8vo. Regular $2.00; Popular $1.50
Marxian Economic Handbook and Glossary—By W. H. Emmett...8vo. $2.75
Voices of Revolt..12mo. Each volume, bound in boards, $0.50

Magazines

International Literature (Central organ of the International Union of Revolutionary Writers)
    Published every month..35 cents a copy
International Theatre (Organ of the International Union of the Revolutionary Theatre)..................15 cents a copy
Soviet Culture Review (Monthly publication of the Soviet Union Society for
    Cultural Relations with Foreign Countries)..15 cents a copy

You will find many of the authors of the foregoing books and pamphlets appearing as speakers for the cause of Communism in American cities during the coming year. You will also find this long list of literature helpful for reference matter when you are called upon by your local libraries to approve new books suggested for public libraries.

In 1935 someone unfortunately and we assume unknowingly approved some of these books for use in the libraries of our Y. W. C. A. buildings. It is your duty to call such matters to the attention of your local organizations.

COMMUNIST WORKERS' SCHOOLS

ACCORDING TO Report 2290,, U. S. House of Representatives, 71st Congress, 3rd Session, there were dozens of Communist Workers' Schools located in different cities throughout the country as far back as 1930 and 1931. The main purpose of these schools is to teach the principles of Communism and to supply trained militant leaders for the growing Communist movement. These schools during the past four years have grown until there are now several score being operated throughout the country.

According to a Chicago newspaper these schools, which were operated in Chicago last year, openly taught revolutionary Communism to the pupils enrolled. All text books used in these schools are furnished by the Workers' Book Shops located in different cities throughout the country, and on the classroom walls are hung revolutionary banners which attempt to show the Workers' paradise which is now supposed to be in existence in Soviet Russia.

According to the official publication of the Communist Party, the "Daily Worker," the Communist Workers' Schools listed on page 76 were in operation during the past year in the United States.

MARXIST EDUCATION (DAILY WORKER EDITORIAL 1/10/35)

"Revolutionary practice gropes in the dark unless revolutionary theory throws a light on its path. But theory becomes the greatest force in the working class movement when it is inseparably linked with revolutionary practice; for it, and it alone, can give the movement confidence, guidance, and understanding of the inner links between events; it alone can enable those engaged in the practical struggle to understand the whence and the whither of the working class movement." (Stalin-Leninism, Volume I, page 94.)

"The teachings of Marx, Engels, Lenin, Stalin, etc., must become the property of the advanced sector of the working class, the toiling farmers as well as the radicalized section of the intellectuals.

"The Workers' Schools in New York, Chicago, Boston, Cleveland, San Francisco and other places base their work on the teachings of Marxism-Leninism. The Workers' Schools offer the opportunity of acquiring the theoretical knowledge for the understanding of the practical problems.

"WORKERS' SCHOOLS[1]

"The announcement that registration for the Fall Term is now in progress at the Workers' Schools throughout the country should receive wide response from labor unions, workers' organizations, Communist Party units and other mass organizations.

"It is with genuine pride that workers can look upon the increasing number of Workers' Schools throughout the country. The Central Workers' School in New

---

[1]Editorial, p. 6, D.W., 9/10/35.

York has been in existence for twelve years. It has grown at a truly phenomenal rate, until today it has become the largest labor school in the United States, and the largest workers' educational institution in any country outside of the Soviet Union. Beginning with the small group of students in 1923, the registration has mounted rapidly each successive year. Almost 10,000 students were registered for various courses during the 1934-1935 school year. In addition to four branch schools in New York, Workers' Schools have been established in Chicago, Cleveland, Detroit, San Francisco, Los Angeles, Boston, Pittsburgh, Youngstown, and other cities in various parts of the country.

"At the present time, more than ever before, it is necessary to make use of the theoretical training offered by the Workers' School. The Workers' School can serve as a real instrument for developing active workers for various phases of the labor movement and train leaders for the class struggle.

"In his recent book, 'Communism in the United States,' Earl Browder, General Secretary of the Communist Party, had occasion to speak of the special importance of Workers' Schools:

" 'Our schools are those places where we make available the knowledge that has been accumulated from the experience of the past struggles in order to solve the problems of present and coming struggles. Only in these struggles, by arming ourselves with the lessons of the past struggles, do we develop the theory, the knowledge and practice that makes up Marxism-Leninism.'

"Only a study of the theories upon which the revolutionary labor movement is based will equip workers, farmers, and intellectuals with that knowledge which is so essential in the present efforts of the working class to unify the ranks of all anti-Fascist fighters for the preservation of democratic rights and liberties and the fight against the growing danger of Fascism, and the menace of imperialist war.

"With special attention to the great need for an educational program of widest popular interest, the Workers' School curriculum includes a broad, extensive and varied course of study. According to all indications the coming season will be another banner year for the Workers' Schools."

Efforts have been made to build a new organization to be known as Friends of the Workers' School. The purpose of such an organization is to popularize the Workers' School among the masses of workers, students and professionals, to establish closer relations between the workers' organizations, to secure additional financial support and to assist in the establishing of additional Workers' Schools wherever possible.

Listed here are some of the subjects taught in the Workers' Schools: World News, Advanced Political Economy, Fascism and the World Trade Union Movement, History of Class Struggles in Europe, Historical Materialism, History of Class Struggles in Czarist Russia, History of the Soviet Union, Americanism and the Revolutionary Tradition, Fundamentals of Communism, "Americanism" and the Growth of Fascism, Capitalist Court Procedure, Theories of Social Reform, How to Build Workers' Organizations, Leninism, Labor Journalism, Elementary Russian and Youth in the Class Struggle.

COMMUNIST WORKERS' SCHOOLS

Below is a partial list of the Communist Workers' Schools in the United States of America:

New York—35 East 12th Street. (2,000 registered April 17.) D.W., P. 5, 6/13/35.

Chicago—161 North Franklin.

Baltimore—501 No. Eutaw St., Room 10. P. 4, D.W., 6/17/36.

Detroit—5969 14th Street. D.W., P. 5, 7/31/35.

Wilkes-Barre—325 East Market Street. D.W., P. 5, 7/31/35.

Milwaukee—113 East Wells Street. D.W., P. 5, 7/31/35.

Camp Elmwood Summer School, 1015 Third Avenue, Rockford, Ill. D.W., P. 5, 7/24/35.

District Agit-Prop for Chicago Workers' Schools. B. Shields, 208 North Wells Street. D.W., P. 5, 7/17/35.

Los Angeles—230 Spring Street. D.W., P. 5, 5/29/35.

Philadelphia—908 Chestnut Street. D.W., P. 5, 8/28/35.

New York (Harlem)—415 Lennox Avenue. D.W., P. 5, 8/28/35.

Pittsburgh, Pa.—6 Stevenson Street. D.W., P. 5, 9/4/35.

Toledo, Ohio—D.W., P. 5, 9/4/35.

Boston—919 Washington Street. D. W., P. 5, 5/15/35.

Brownsville, New York City, 1855 Pitkin Avenue. D.W., P. 5, 5/1/35.

Cleveland—1524 Prospect Avenue. D.W., P. 5, 4/3/35.

Newark, New Jersey—81 Academy Street. D.W., P. 5, 4/10/35.

Queens, Woodside, Long Island—5820 Roosevelt Avenue. D.W., P. 5, 3/27/35.

Paterson, New Jersey—201 Market Street. D.W., P. 5, 3/20/35.

Hudson County, New Jersey—71 Newark Avenue, Jersey City, New Jersey. D.W., P. 5, 3/13/35.

San Francisco—463 Hayes St.

Denver, Colo.—1450 Lawrence St. P. 5, D.W., 4/24/36.

In the pamphlet announcing the 1937 winter term of courses for the Communist Workers School, we find a very interesting page containing the courses of study, and the instructors' names, which will be used in the New York Workers School. On the next page we have reprinted this course of study. Your attention is particularly called to the fact that the majority of the subjects are either the principles of Communism or a study of Marxism and Leninism. Nowhere in the set-up will be found anything pertaining to the American way of doing things. This is definite proof that these so-called Workers Schools are for the purpose of building Communism.

WINTER TERM, 1937

Room	Course	Instructor	Room	Course	Instructor

MondayT7-8:30 P. M.

308—Principles of Communism 1	Gabriel Kent
207—Principles of Communism 2	Chas. Elstein
307—Principles of Communism 3	Martha Murray
203—Principles of Communism 4	Barbara Rand
305—Political Economy Ia	Edw. Smith
202—Political Economy Ib	Julius Low
309—Political Economy II	James Field
208—Introduction to Dialectical Materialism	Harry Martel
205—History of the Communist Party of the Soviet Union	Abraham Markoff
206—Negro America and the Struggle Against Reaction	Theo. Bassett
204—Marxism and Colonial Question	Alberto Moreau
306—Labor Journalism	Morris Colman
304—Elementary English	Ben Shaw
303—Intermediate English B	Jules Carter

Monday—8:40-10:10 P. M.

207—Principles of Communism 5	Chas. Elstein
203—Principles of Communism 6	Barbara Rand
206—Principles of Communism 7	Julius Low
308—Political Economy Ic	Gabriel Kent
205—Political Economy Id	Abraham Markoff
306—Political Economy II	Morris Colman
309—Advanced Political Economy	James Field
202—Marxism-Leninism I	Beatrice Blosser
208—Marxism-Leninism II	Harry Martel
307—Social and Political Forces in American History	Martha Murray
204—History of the Communist International	Alberto Moreau
303—Elementary Russian	Zachary Gisenkin
304—Intermediate English C	J. Edwards
305—Advanced English	Roy Norton

Tuesday—7-8:30 P. M.

309—Principles of Communism 8	Carl Brodsky
305—Principles of Communism 9	Arthur Carey
306—Principles of Communism 10	Frieda Ludwig
308—Political Economy Ic	Gabriel Kent
307—Political Economy If	Chas. Elstein

Tuesday—8:40-10:10 P. M.

309—Principles of Communism II	Harry Mann
307—Political Economy Ig	Chas. Elstein

Wednesday—7-8:30 P. M.

207—Principles of Communism 12	Timothy Holmes
205—Principles of Communism 13	Isidor Begun
305—Principles of Communism 14	Gilbert Douglass
307—Principles of Communism 15	Carl Wilson
208—Political Economy Ih	Geo. Lewis
306—Political Economy Ii	Steve Kingston
202—Political Economy II	Neil Brant
309—Advanced Political Economy	James Field
204—Marxism-Leninism I	Meyer Weise
308—Marxism-Leninism II	Art Stein
206—History of American Labor Movement	Charlotte Todes
203—Social and Political Forces in American History	Fred Day
304—Elementary English	Ben Shaw
303—Intermediate English A	Jo. Austin

Wednesday—8:40-10:10 P. M.

308—Principles of Communism 16	Art Stein
306—Principles of Communism 17	Steve Kingston
202—Principles of Communism 18	Neil Brant
204—Political Economy Ij	Meyer Weise
203—Political Economy Ik	Harry Mann
208—Political Economy II	Geo. Lewis
304—Marxism-Leninism I	Gilbert Douglass
307—Marxism-Leninism I	Carl Wilson
205—Fundamental Study of Marxian Classics	Milton Howard
309—Public Speaking	Joseph Arch
207—Theories of Literary Criticism	Angel Flores
303—Intermediate Russian	Zachary Gisenkin
305—Advanced English	Roy Norton

Thursday—7-8:30 P. M.

308—Principles of Communism 19	Gabriel Kent
306—Principles of Communism 20	Philip Cabot
207—Principles of Communism 21	Chas. Elstein
305—Principles of Communism 22	Fred Nelson
203—Political Economy IL	Eliz. Lawson
202—Political Economy Im	William Hart
304—Political Economy II	William Roberts
309—Advanced Political Economy	Alfred Goldstein
307—Marxism-Leninism I	Beatrice Blosser
205—Fascist Trends and Tendencies in the U. S.	A. B. Magil
204—Current Trade Union Problems	Alan Ross
208—Shop Paper and Leaflet Preparation	P. Culver-M. Pass
303—Intermediate English B	Jules Carter

Thursday—8:40-10:10 P. M.

306—Principles of Communism 23	Philip Cabot
307—Principles of Communism 24	Beatrice Blosser
202—Principles of Communism 25	William Hart
203—Political Economy In	Eliz. Lawson
206—Political Economy Io	F. H. Meyer
308—Political Economy II	Gabriel Kent
309—Advanced Political Economy	Alfred Goldstein
305—Social and Political Forces in American History	Fred Nelson
207—History of Class Struggle in Epoch of Industrial Captalism	Chas. Elstein
204—Trade Union Theory and Practice	Alan Ross
208—Shop Paper Leaflet Preparation	P. Culver-M. Pass
205—Organization Principles	Rina Epstein
303—Elementary Russian	Zachary Gisenkin
304—Intermediate English C	J. Edwards

Friday—7-8:30 P. M.

207—Principles of Communism 26	Chas. Elstein
305—Principles of Communism 27	Geo. Lewis
307—Political Economy Ip	Eliz. Lawson
306—Political Economy Iq	Leonard Mins
309—Marxism-Leninism I	Alfred Goldstein
208—Historical Materialism	I. Stamler
304—Trade Unionism: Theory and Practice	A. H. Hartfield
205—Critical Periods in American Trade Union History	Louis F. Budenz
202—Social Trends in Contemporary Literature	Angel Flores
308—History and Method of Science	James Leonard
203—A Marxian Survey of Psychology	R. Gley
206—Research Methods	L. R. A. Staff
204—Modern Economic Theories	E. C. Blake
303—Intermediate English A	Jo. Austin

Friday—8:40-10:10 P. M.

304—Principles of Communism 28	A. H. Hartfield
207—Principles of Communism 29	Chas. Elstein
306—Political Economy Ir	Bill Reich
307—Political Economy Is	Eliz. Lawson
309—Political Economy II	Alfred Goldstein
308—Science and Dialectical Materialism	James Leonard
205—Health and Hygiene	M. A. B.
303—Intermediate Russian	Zachary Gisenkin

COMMUNIST PRESS

THERE ARE hundreds of Communist publications[1] and leaflets now being circulated throughout the United States, the majority of which are transmitted through the United States mails. Practically all of these pieces of literature publicizes the major objective of the Communist Party—the overthrow of the American form of government. The compilers of this Handbook here name a part of these publications, and the information contained in this Chapter is as complete as it is possible to make it at this time.

"WHY A WORKERS' DAILY PRESS
By C. A. Hathaway and Sam Don
(Excerpts from the above titled Communist booklet)

"Alone among American daily newspapers, the Daily Worker, Central Organ of the Communist Party, U. S. A., carries on a day-to-day campaign against the lies and anti-working class propaganda of the capitalist press." P. 2.

"The Daily Worker is read today by workers in more than 1,500 American cities and towns. It is the American daily newspaper which militant working class organizations, the Unemployed Councils, the Trade Union Unity League, the Sharecroppers' Union in the South, the International Labor Defense, to mention only a few, rely upon for mobilizing the American masses for the defense of our revolutionary fellow-workers and farmers abroad, and for the united struggle here in America against hunger, Fascism and war." P. 3.

"Our paper, established by the workers, is their paper; it is the paper of the revolutionary working class movement, the central voice of the Communist Party." P. 5.

"Frankly, the Daily Worker is a revolutionary paper. It sets as its objective the overthrow of the existing capitalist system." P. 6.

"We aid in building the revolutionary trade unions of the Trade Union Unity League. We are the organizers of the Communist Party, the revolutionary vanguard of the workers' movement." P. 11.

COMMUNIST PUBLICITY CHANNELS

Every available channel of publicity is eagerly grasped by Communists and their sympathizers. It is estimated that their various publications have a paid circulation of well over 1,000,000. This total does not take into consideration the thousands of mimeographed and multigraphed shop publications, or the dodgers, which are distributed upon the campuses of educational institutions. The "Daily Worker," admittedly the central organ of the Communist Party, U. S. A., section of the Communist International, on Saturday, March 11, 1935, according to their own figures, had a press run of 66,000. This is a leading English-speaking Communist publication in the U. S. It has, however, many offsprings covering various sections of the U. S., such as the "Western Worker," the "Southern Worker," the "Young Worker" and "Masses."

---

[1]That the reader may more fully understand the background of these publications and revolutionary phraseology used, we set forth excerpts from each of them.

Who Is in Danger? — By JOHN STRACHEY

APRIL 28, 1936 15c

new Masses

American Courses in French Fascism

By ALFRED HIRSCH and ROGER BEAUCHAMP

Are Teachers Seditious?

By CONGRESSMAN BYRON N. SCOTT

How Wilson Fought Lenin

The U. S. State Dep't on American Intervention

By JOSEPH FREEMAN

Satevepost and Revolution by MICHAEL GOLD

This Way, Lawyer!
by S. M. BLINKEN

new Masses

APRIL 2, 1935

48-Page Quarterly Issue

I Escaped from Cub

By PABLO DE LA TORRIENTE-BRAU

Fight the Gag Bills!

By ROGER BALDWIN

Jailbreak—A SHORT STORY

By TOM JOHNSON

IN THIS ISSUE:

JAMES T. FARRELL   JOSEPHINE HERBST
GRANVILLE HICKS   WILLIAM GROPPER
LOUIS LOZOWICK   JOSHUA KUNITZ
JACOB BURCK   REGINALD MARSH

REVIEWED BY
MOISSAYE J. OLGIN

arkand"

JUNE 4, 1935   10c

sses

Granville Hicks Fired

First Major Victim of Big Business's Campaign to Gag the Colleges — Rensselaer Institute "Retrenches" by Discharging Its Most Distinguished Professor—Page 9

What Will the Middle Class Gain From the Revolution?

By EARL BROWDER

Margaret Wright Mather Reviews the Press

These photostats of the cover page of New Masses clearly show the part the Communist Party and its sympathizers play in attempting to bore into the education question and educational system within the United States.

Daily Worker
Central Organ Communist Party U. S. A.
(Section of Communist International)
Clarence Hathaway, Editor

Published daily except Sunday by the Comprodaily Publishing Co., Inc., 50 E. 13th Street, New York, New York. Washington Bureau: Room 954, National Press Building, 14th and F St., N. W., Washington, D. C. Midwest Bureau: 101 S. Wells Street, Room 705, Chicago, Illinois.

P. 3, D. W., 1/10/35: Bill Gebert, District Organizer of the Communist Party, today issued the following statement: "The building of Y. C. L. is one of the most burning and immediate problems of the Communist Party."

Free Press, Free Speech, Free Assembly, Zinoview and Kamenev are Banished: "Moscow, Jan. 17, 1935. Gregory Zinoview, Leo Kamenev and seventeen others charged with terrorist activities designed to overthrow the Soviet government were ordered banished by the Military Collegium of the Supreme Court tonight into exile for long terms." (The "D. W." 1/18/35, P. 1.)

Call for Congress of American Revolutionary Writers on May 1, 1935.

"The capitalist system crumbles so rapidly before our eyes that, whereas ten years ago scarcely more than a handful of writers were sufficiently far-sighted and courageous to take a stand for proletarian revolution, today hundreds of poets, novelists, dramatists, critics, short story writers and journalists recognize the necessity of personally helping to accelerate the destruction of capitalism and the establishment of a workers' government.

"Many revolutionary writers live virtually in isolation, lacking opportunities to discuss vital problems with their fellows. Others are so absorbed in the revolutionary cause that they have few opportunities for thorough examination and analysis. Never have the writers of the nation come together for fundamental discussion." (P. 5, D.W., 1/18/35.)

Communist—First American Writers' Congress

According to the Daily Worker of April 29, 1935, more than four hundred American revolutionary writers attended the first Communist called American Writers' Congress at Mecca Temple, New York City, April 26-27, 1935. Although we realize that many of these writers are not Communists, but have desired to throw their lot with left wing literature for the future and are thereby attaching themselves to what the Communists claim to be their Communist Writers' Congress.

A full list of the announced papers read during this two-day Congress were presented by the following:

Joseph Freeman, "The Tradition of American Revolutionary Literature;"
Kenneth Burke, "Revolutionary Symbolism in America;"
Harry F. Ward, "The Writers' Part in the Struggle Against War;"
Jack Conway: "The Worker as Writer;"
Edwin Seaver, "The Proletarian Novel;"
Isadore Schneider, "Proletarian Poetry;"
Edward Dahlberg, "Fascism and the Writer;"
Eugene Gordon, "Social and Political Problems of the Negro Writer;"

John Howard Lawson, "Technique in the Drama;"

Michael Blankfort and Nathan Buchwald, "Social Trend in the Modern Drama;"

Josephine Herbst, "Industrial and Agrarian Struggles and the Novel;"

Corliss Lamont, "The Writer and the Soviet Union;"

Meridel Le Sueur, "Proletarian Literature in the Middle West;"

James T. Farrell, "The Short Story;"

Matthew Josephine, "The Role of the Writer in the Soviet Union;"

Joshua Kunitz, "Literary Fellow-Travelers;"

Eugene Clay, "The Negro and Recent American Literature;"

Joseph North, "Reportage;"

Granville Hicks, "Dialectics in the Development of Marxist Criticism;"

M. J. Olgin, "The Soviet Writers' Congress;"

Malcolm Cowley, "What the Revolutionary Movement Can Give to the Writer;"

Albert Maltz, "The Working Class Theatre;"

Henry Hart, "Contemporary Publishing and the Revolutionary Writer;"

Alexander Trachtenberg, "Publishing for Workers." (P.1,2,D.W.,4/29/35.)

In the closing hours of the American Writers' Congress, a new organization was formed known as the League of American Writers—for revolutionary writers only. Waldo Frank was elected the first National Secretary.

The following members of the Executive Committee and the National Committee are listed in the "Daily Worker," of April 30, 1935. It is hoped that the non-Communist writers listed on these committees realize that the Communist press would like to have them believe that they are all Communists.

Executive Committee	*National Committee*
Kenneth Burke	Newton Arvin
Malcolm Cowley	Sterling Brown
Harold Clurman	Fielding Burke
Joseph Freeman	Erskine Caldwell
Michael Gold	Eugene Clay
Henry Hart	Jack Conroy
Josephine Herbst	James T. Farrell
Edward Dahlberg	Kenneth Fearing
Granville Hicks	Horace Gregory
Matthew Josephson	Langston Hughes
Alfred Krevmborg	Joshua Kunitz
John Howard Lawson	Tillie Lerner
Albert Maltz	Meridel Le Sueur
Isador Schneider	Grace Lumpkin
Edwin Seaver	Lewis Mumford
Genevieve Taggard	Clifford Odets
Alexander Trachtenberg	Paul Peters
	William Rollins
	Lincoln Steffens
	Richard Wright

EXCERPTS OR HEADLINES FROM THE COMMUNIST "DAILY WORKER"

"Red Army Celebrates Its 17th Anniversary; Garden Rally Tonight." D. W., p. 1, 2/25/35.

"Communists Propose United Labor Fight at Minneapolis Polls." D. W., p 2, 2/25/35.

"USSR Parley Hails Growth of Red Army." D. W., p. 1, 2/1/35.

"Behind U. S. S. R. Peace Policy Stands Mighty People's Red Army!" D. W., p. 6, 2/1/35.

"Soviet Congress Hails Gigantic Development of Red Army 'Its Revolutionary Might is Invincible,' Declares Tukhachevsky, Citing Gains." D.W., p. 3, Soviet Supplement, 2/4/35.

"Deportations—The wave of deportations is rising. Five workers, seized for their brave militancy in fighting for better conditions for all workers, now await deportation.

"John Ujich, Ray Carlson, Oscar Mannisto, Paul Kettunen, Christ Popoff are being held, with Ujich's case coming up today before the Court of Appeals.

"These workers are being sent back to fascist and semi-Fascist countries where who knows what fate awaits them.

"Delegates, carrying protests from 225 workers' organizations, will visit Perkins and Congressman Dickstein today demanding these workers' release.

"Every class-conscious worker has the immediate duty of standing behind this delegation.

"Wire at once to Perkins, Secretary of Labor; to Dickstein, Chairman of the House Committee on Immigration, and D. W. McCormack, Commissioner General of Immigration." D.W., p. 6, 2/4/35. (Editorial.)

"In the whole leadership of this vast strike movement, Communists played a leading role. *The San Francisco General Strike would not have taken place and spread had it not been for long, persistent previous preparation by the Communist Party* and the correct policy and leadership of our Party is helping the workers to launch this strike. . . .

"And it was the militant policy of the Communist which helped the workers, despite the treachery of the A. F. of L. bureaucracy, to gain important successes in this struggle." D. W., p. 5, 2/11/35.

"Sabotage! Cool and synical sabotage! . . .

"Think of it! Socialist and Communist workers are now fighting side by side in Alabama and Arkansas; militant Socialist leaders, Ward Rogers and R. L. Mitchell face terrorism and jail." D. W., p. 6, 2/11/35.

"C. P. Vote Increases 100% in East St. Louis." D. W., p. 4, 2/21/35.

"C. P. Expels Strike Dodger." D. W., p. 3, 2/22/35.

"Alex Bittleman Writes on Why Revolution is Inevitable in the U. S." D. W., p. 5, 2/18/35.

"Darcy Teaches Trial Judge Communism: The instructor was Sam Darcy, Communist leader, instructor at the San Francisco Workers' School and Communist candidate for governor of California in the last gubernatorial election." D.W., p. 1, 3/1/35.

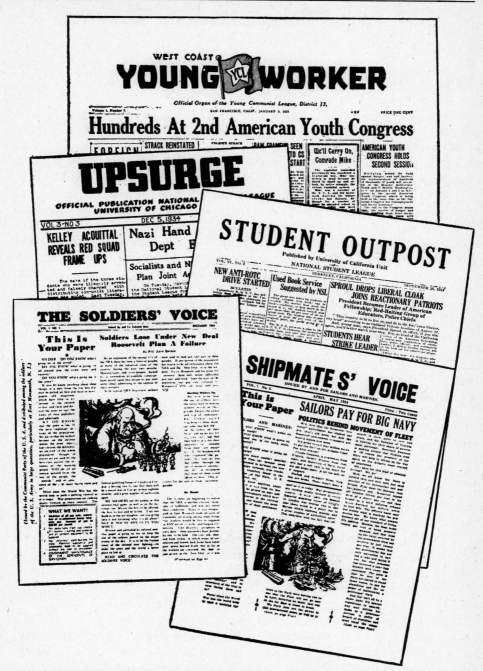

NOTE: Photostat copy of the young Communist paper, Young Worker; Upsurge and Student Outpost, both official papers of the Communist, aided National Student League of Chicago University and California University and the two publications which try to inject Communism into the soldiers and sailors.

"Dyers to Send Paterson Man on Soviet Tour.   Representative of 12,000 Workers to Spend May Day in Red Square."   D. W., p. 2, 2/16/35.

"Votes Against Recognition.   Brussels, Belgium, Feb. 8 (UP).—The Chamber of Deputies, by a vote of 87 to 73, rejected a proposal yesterday to resume diplomatic relations with the Soviet Union."   D. W., p. 3, 2/9/35.

"Disillusioned Intellectuals Must Be Won Over to the Side of the Revolutionary Working Class."   D. W., p. 5, 2/13/35.

"Chicago Revolutionary Theatre School Opens Second Term on Sunday." D. W., p. 5, 2/14/35.

"20,000 Hail Memory of Lenin at New York Meeting." D. W., p. 3, 1/23/35.

"Browder Inducts 2,000 Into Party; Kirov Pledge Made."   D. W., p. 3, 1/23/35.

"Demand Veto of Indiana Law.   Indianapolis, Ind., March 8.—A bill to bar the Communist Party from the ballot,[1] was passed today in the Indiana State Senate by a vote of 26 to 18.

"The Republican Party voted solidly for the bill, but the Democratic vote was split as a result of pressure exerted by labor and liberal organizations and the Communist and Socialist Parties.   While only Senator Vermillion of Anderson, Ind., spoke in favor of the measure, five senators spoke against it.   Among these was Allbright,[2] American Legion member, who stated he would throw in his Legion pin rather than vote for the bill.

"The Communist Party immediately issued a call to all organizations to flood the Governor's office with resolutions demanding the bill be vetoed."   D. W., p. 3, 3/11/35.

"Lenin Rallies in All Sections are Announced.   Preparations for Lenin Memorial meetings are being pushed in scores of cities and towns throughout the country.   Following is a partial list of the meetings so far scheduled:

"New York City—Madison Square Garden, January 20, at 8 P. M., Earl Browder and James W. Ford,[3] speakers.

"Chicago, Ill.—Coliseum Hall, Jan. 20, at 7:30 P. M., Bob Minor, speaker.

"Philadelphia, Pa.—Market Street Arena, 46th and Market Streets, Jan. 18, at 8 P. M.   Speakers, M. Olgin, M. Johnson and John Strachey.

"Baltimore, Md.—Jan. 25, place to be announced.   Speaker, M. Johnson.

"Wilkes-Barre, Pa.—Workers' Center, 325 E. Market Street, Jan. 20, at 8 P. M.   H. Benjamin, speaker.

"Boston, Mass.—Place to be announced.   Speakers, Mother Bloor and Mike Gold.

"Providence, R. I.—Swedish Workingmen's Hall, 59 Chestnut Street.   Margaret Cowl, speaker.

"Washington, D. C.—Place and date to be announced.   V. J. Jerome, speaker.

---

[1]Gov. Paul V. McNutt signed this bill March 15, 1935.

[2]Allbright is still a Legion member.

[3]Communist James W. Ford is a member of Col. Young Post, American Legion, in New York City for 1935.

"Buffalo, N. Y.—Labor Educational Hall, 760 Main Street, Jan. 20, at 8 P. M. Pat Toohey, speaker.

"Rochester, N. Y.—Place and date to be announced. George Siskind, speaker.

"Binghamton, N. Y.—Jan. 20. Place to be announced. Fred Biedenkapp, speaker.

"Pittsburgh, Pa.—Fifth Avenue High School, Jan. 28, at 8 P. M. Clarence Hathaway, speaker.

"Cleveland, O.—Public Auditorium Ball Room, E. 6th Street and Lakeside, Jan. 20, at 2 P. M. W. W. Weinstone, speaker.

"Detroit, Mich.—Arena Gardens, Woodward Ave. and Henry, Jan. 20, at 2:30 P. M. I. Amter, speaker.

"Minneapolis, Minn.—Eagles Hall, 117 Fourth St., S. E., Jan. 20, at 7 P. M. Morris Childs, speaker.

"St. Paul, Minn.—Odd Fellows Hall, Jan. 21, at 7 P. M. Morris Childs, speaker.

"Reading, Pa.—Knights of Friendship Hall, 113 N. Eighth St., Jan. 19, at 8 P. M.

"Lancaster, Pa.—Jan. 20. Place to be announced.

"Chester, Pa.—2524 West Second St., Jan. 22, at 8 P. M.

"Shamokin, Pa.—716 Shamokin St., Jan. 26, at 8 P. M.

"Newark, N. J.—Laurel Gardens, Jan. 20, at 2 P. M. Carl Reeve, speaker.

"Paterson, N. J.—Carpenters' Hall, Jan. 20, at 8 P. M. A. Markhoff, speaker.

"Passaic, N. J.—Russian National Home, Jan. 20, at 2:30 P. M.

"Elizabeth, N. J.—408 Court St., Jan. 20, at 2:30 P. M.

"Bayonne, N. J.—Labor Lyceum, Jan. 26.

"Union City, N. J.—Jan. 26.

"Cliffside, N. J.—Cliffside Workers' Center, Jan. 26.

"Jersey City, N. J.—New Polish Hall, Feb. 1.

"Stelton, N. J.—Jan. 20.

"Trenton, N. J.—Hungarian Workers' Home, Jan. 20.

"New Haven, Conn.—Jan. 19. Speaker, Margaret Cowl.

"Bridgeport, Conn.—Central High School, Jan. 20. Speaker, Harry Gannes.

"Hartford, Conn.—Jan. 20.

"Brookline, Conn.—Brookline Town Hall, Jan. 20, at 3 P. M. J. Milton, speaker.

"Waterbury, Conn.—Jan. 20, at 3 P. M. J. Milton, speaker.

"Milwaukee, Wis.—Milwaukee Auditorium, Jan. 20. Max Bedacht, speaker."
D. W., p. 3, 1/4/35.

WESTERN WORKERS

Western Organ of the Communist Party, U. S. A. Founded 1932. Published every Tuesday and Friday. Lawrence Ross is editor of the Western Worker. P. 1, W. W., 7/23/36. Editorial and business offices, 37 Grove Street, San Francisco, California; and Room 418, 224 S. Spring Street, Los Angeles, California. (Section of the Communist International.)

EXCERPTS OR HEADLINES FROM THE COMMUNIST "WESTERN WORKER"

"Bob Minor to Tour for Cal. Communist Election Campaign. Darcy Offers to Debate Dempster, Socialist Candidate." W. W., p. 1, 10/1/34.

"18 Indicted on 7 Syndicalism Counts in Sacramento.—Sacramento, Sept. 23. —Arraignments for the eighteen workers held in the county jail on reindictment on seven counts of 'criminal syndicalism' took place in court Friday, September 22.

"Leo Gallagher, International Labor Defense attorney, asked demurrers on all new counts." W. W., p. 1, 9/27/34.

"Otto Richter Wins Voluntary Departure. San Francisco, Feb. 17.—Otto Richter, young German anti-Fascist fighter was arrested here during the general strike and ordered deported to Nazi Germany. The International Labor Defense fought the case." W. W., p. 1, 2/18/35.

"7,000 Maritime Workers Out in Anti-Nazi Strike. San Francisco, March 4.— Approximately 7,000 maritime workers went on a half-hour strike here Saturday morning in protest against Hitler and the Nazi terror regime as the 'Karlsruhe,' Nazi training ship and 620 officers and men docked at Pier 37." W. W., p. 1, 3/7/35.

"2,000 Hear Strachey Expose New Deal, Denounce War, Fascism. San Francisco, Feb. 22.—An audience of 2,000 persons at the Filmarte Theatre here Wednesday night heard John Strachey, former British member of Parliament and revolutionary writer, rip the New Deal to shreds and point to the revolutionary road as the way out of the mire into which the capitalist system has plunged untold millions of workers." W. W., p. 1, 2/25/35.

"Protest Louise Todd Sentence! Another move was made last week by the representatives of the employing class of California in the drive to take the Communist Party off the ballot in the conviction and sentencing of Louise Todd for 'perjury.'

"Comrade Todd, one of the ablest working class fighters in California, was found guilty of the 'crime' of getting workers to sign a petition to place the Communist Party on the ballot at the last elections, and sentenced to three terms, of from one to fourteen years each, to run concurrently." W. W., p. 6, 2/14/35.

"Anna Louise Strong to Speak in S. F. on March 15. San Francisco, March 8.—Anna Louise Strong, American associate editor of the Moscow News, largest English-language newspaper in the Soviet Union, arrives in San Francisco on Wednesday to fill a speaking engagement for Friday the 15th at Scottish Rite Auditorium, on the subject: 'Dictatorship and Democracy in the Soviet Union.' The meeting has been arranged by the the American Russian Institute." W. W., p. 2, 3/11/35.

SOUTHERN WORKER

Official Organ of the Communist Party, U. S. A.
Jim Mallory, Editor, Box 572, Birmingham, Ala.

VOICE OF ACTION

Revolutionary Weekly of the Northwest
Published at Seattle, Washington
Lowell Wakefield is the editor. (D. W., p. 5, 5/11/35)

NOTE: Photostat of headlines during 1935 from the front pages of the Daily Worker and the Western Worker, both of which are official organs of the Communist Party, U. S. A. affiliated with The Communist International.

YOUNG WORKER
Official Organ Young Communist League, U. S. A.
(Section of the Young Communist International)

Published by the National Executive Committee of the Young Communist League, 35 E. 12th Street, New York City.

The "Young Worker" has a west coast supplement which is the official organ of the Young Communist League of District Thirteen and is published in San Francisco, California, 37 Grove Street.

VOICE OF YOUTH
Official organ of the Young Communist League, District 13

Published Semi-Monthly by the Young Communist League. Address: 37 Grove Street, San Francisco, California.

CHAMPION OF YOUTH

Young Communist League members and their helpers, according to the Communist press, saw the necessity of an additional monthly publication devoted to youth activities. The Champion of Youth was the outcome. It is published monthly by Champion of Youth Publishers, 2 East 23rd Street, Room 508, New York City. Subscription, $1.00 per year. Editor: Morrie Schnapper; Business Manager: Irvin Keith. Editorial Board: John Ames, Joseph Cohen, Dave Doran, Angelo Herndon, Roger Chase, Beryl Gilman, Sofie Juried, James Wechsler, Jane Whitbread.

NEW MASSES

An ultra-radical publication with headquarters at 31 E. 27th Street, New York City, featuring all the Communist programs. Editors: Michael Gold, Granville Hicks, Orrick Johns, Joshua Kunitz, Russell T. Limbach, Herman Michelson, Joseph North, Ashley Pettis, William Randorf. William Browder, Business Manager; Allan Taub, Mid-Western Representative.

Published weekly by the New Masses, Inc., at 31 East 27th Street, New York City. Copyright, 1935, New Masses, Inc., Reg. U. S. Patent Office. Drawings and text may not be reprinted without permission. Entered as second class matter, June 24, 1936, at the Post Office at New York, N. Y., under the act of March 3, 1879. (You should be particularly interested to note that Michael Gold, Communist specialty columnist for the "Daily Worker," is one of the editors.)

NEW PIONEER

A magazine for boys and girls, published monthly by New Pioneer Publishing Company, 98 4th Avenue, Brooklyn, New York. Editorial and executive offices, 50 E. 13th Street, New York City. Editor, Martha Campion; Art Editor, Mary Morrow; Business Manager, Anna Corblath; Editorial Board: Ben Blake, Eleanor Clayman, Bert Grant, Tillie Macklin, Martha Millet, Jack Parker, Rose Rogers, Vera Saunders, Sasha Small, Phil Wolfe.

LABOR DEFENDER

Official organ of the International Labor Defense. Editors, William L. Patterson, Sasha Small; Assoc. Editor, Louis Colman. Published monthly by the International Labor Defense, 80 East 11th Street, Room 430, New York. William L. Patterson, National Secretary. (See activity section of I. L. D.)

LABOR UNITY

Published monthly by the Trade Union Unity League. William Z. Foster, Secretary, 80 E. 11th Street, Room 326, New York, N. Y. Pat Toohey, Editor. (See activities, William Z. Foster.)

THE ARBITRATOR

Published 114 E. 31st Street, New York City. The official publication of the American Civil Liberties Union. Editor, Wm. Floyd. (See activities of A.C.L.U.)

PACIFIC WEEKLY

A Western Journal of Fact and Opinion, published every month at Carmel, California, P. O. Box 1300. W. K. Bassett, Editor and Publisher; Lincoln Steffen, Associate Editor; Ella Winters, Literary Editor.

ECONOMIC NOTES

Published monthly by Labor Research Association, 80 East 11th Street, New York City. This leaflet is sold by Communist Book Stores.

ILLINOIS LABOR NOTES

Published monthly by the National Research League, Chicago Chapter, Room 704, 184 West Washington Street, Chicago, Illinois. For sale at Communist Book Stores.

INTERNATIONAL OF YOUTH

Published by the Youth Publishers for the National Executive Committee of the Young Communist League, U. S. A. H. McDuff, Editor; Joel Remes, Managing Editor. From an article entitled "Problems of the United Front," by Max Weiss and Charles Wilson, on Pages 9, 10 and 11, Volume 2, Number 4, of International of Youth, we take the following quotes:

"1. We conduct our struggle for the united front in a country where the overwhelming majority of proletarian youth are not as yet organized in class organizations (trade unions, YCL, YPSI, etc.)."

"The fight for the proletarian united front proceeds parallel with the fight for a broad young people's front which is being carried on through the American Youth Congress. In this respect, the united front struggle of the youth in America proceeds differently than in France. In France, it was the proletarian united front between the Young Communist League and the Young People's Socialist League which was initiated first, and which made possible the initiation of the young people's front, the front of the young generation against war and Fascism— a movement which has many characteristics which are similar to the American Youth Congress. In the United States, on the other hand, the American Youth

Congress (which is developing along the lines of a young people's front) was initiated first before the consummation of the proletarian united front between the YCL and the YPSL.

"From this it is clear how incorrect it would be to place the American Youth Congress on one side as against the proletarian united front between the YCY and YPSL on the other side, or to look upon one as a substitute for the other. There is a live relationship between the two; each success of the American Youth Congress hastens the day on which it will be possible to achieve the united front of socialist and Communist youth. The achievement of such a proletarian united front will, in turn, immensely strengthen and solidify the young people's front in the American Youth Congress."

"As never before, we must work in the American Youth Congress in so broad a manner that the Young Communist League will become a model for united front relationships."

Novy Mir

This is a new Communist paper written in the Russian language for distribution and sale in the United States. P. 2, W. W., 9/26/35.

Working Women

Margaret Cowl is editor of this new radical publication, which seeks to gain the support of the American housewife to Communist activities. P. 1, D. W., 9/24/35. Published at 50 E. 13th St., New York City.

Labor Challenge

Published every two weeks by the National Unemployed Councils at 80 East 11th Street, Room 437, New York City. P. 3, W. W., 9/23/35.

Industrial Worker

Official organ of the I. W. W. Ralph Chaplin, Editor and Business Manager. Entered as second class mail matter in the Post Office at Chicago, Illinois.

The Militant

Official organ of the Communist League of America, with publishing address at 144 2nd Avenue, New York City.

The Communist

A magazine of the Theory and Practice of Marxism-Leninism. Published monthly by the Communist Party of the U. S. A. "The Communist," P. O. Box 148, Sta. D. (50 E. 13th St.), New York.

The Student Outlook
The Intercollegiate Socialist Review (Student Edition)

Published monthly from October to May by The Intercollegiate League for Industrial Democracy, 112 East 19th Street, New York City. Editor: Joseph P. Lash, Chairman; John Blair, Tulane; Roland Burdick, Syracuse; Lewis S. Feuer, Harvard; Howard Frisch, C. C. N. Y.; John Harrington, Wellesley; John Rockwell, University of California; Richard M. Scammon, University of Minnesota; Robert G. Spivack, University of Cincinnati; Aileen McGown, Goucher; Felix S. Cohen, Mary Fox, Lucy Kramer, Ruth E. Schechter, Monroe Sweetland.

INTERNATIONAL LITERATURE

Central organ of the International Union of the Revolutionary Writers, issued every two months in English, French, German, Russian and Chinese. Editor-in-chief: S. Dinamov. Assistant Editor: S. Ludkiewicz. Editor Russian Issue: S. Tretyakov. Editor French Issue: P. Vaillant-Couturier. Editor German Issue: Johannes R. Becher. Editor English Issue: S. Dinamov. Editor Chinese Issue: Emi Siao. International Advisory Board: M. Anderson-Nexo, Henri Barbusse, J. R. Becher, T. Dreiser, E. Glasser, Michael Gold, M. Gorky, Lu Sin, A. B. Magil, Go Ma-Jo, John Dos Passos, Ludwig Renn, R. Rolland, A. Serafimovich, Upton Sinclair, Tokunaga Naossi, Erich Weinert. Editorial Board: Anismov, Dietrich, Fadeyev, Germanetto, Hidas, Illes, Ludkiewicz, Mikitenko, Ognyov, Siao, Tretyakov, Valliant-Couturier, Volin. The State Literary Art Publishing House Moscow USSR. Printed in the Union of Soviet Socialist Republics.

ECONOMIC REVIEW OF THE SOVIET UNION

A monthly survey of the Soviet economical and cultural developments, foreign relations, and of trade between the United States and the Soviet Union. Published by the Amtorg Trading Corporation, Information Department, 261 Fifth Avenue, New York.

NEW THEATRE

Organ of the New Theatre League, National Film and Photo and Workers' Dance League. Published monthly by "New Theatre," 114 W. 14th Street, New York City. Editorial Board: Herbert Kline, Editor; Lionel Berman, Ben Blake, Charles Dibner, William Entin, Steve Foster, Leo T. Hurwitz, J. Leyda, Edno Ocko, Mollie Day Thatcher, David Crystal, Manfred Ettinger, R. Steck.

MOSCOW NEWS

Weekly edition of Moscow Daily News for English-speaking people in the Soviet Union and throughout the world. Editor-in-Chief: M. M. Borodin. Associate Editors: Anna Louise Strong, T. L. Axelrod.

SOVIET RUSSIA TODAY

Soviet Russia Today, Desk 4, 80 East 11th Street, New York, N. Y. Editorial Board: Edwin Seaver, Managing Editor; Myra Page, A. A. Heller, Hays Jones, Liston M. Oak, John Gilmore, Herbert Goldfrank. Published monthly by the F. S. U. Publications, Inc., 80 E. 11th Street, New York, N. Y.

THE NEW INTERNATIONAL

A monthly organ of Revolutionary Marxism. Published once a month by the New International Publishing Association, Station D, Post Office Box 119, New York, N. Y. Max Schachtman, Editor, Martin Abern, Business Manager.

THE FEDERATED PRESS

The Federated Press, with central bureau at 160 North LaSalle Street, Chicago, with Washington bureau at 1410 H Street, N. W., Washington, D. C., and an eastern bureau at 32 Union Square, New York City, sends out its daily sugar-coated press releases to all of the affiliated and sympathetic Communist publications. Carl Haessler has long been affiliated with the central bureau at Chicago, Illinois.

At the same office address and with the same Carl Haessler as Assistant Publisher, we find a new paper known as "People's Press," published weekly. It claims to be a purely socialist publication but is on sale at all the Communist book stores in the City of Chicago.

The following foreign language and English publications in the United States are reported to be either Communist or sympathetic to the Communist program or some of its affiliated groups.

This information is taken as an extract from Public Hearings before the Special Committee on un-American Activities, House of Representatives, 73rd Congress, 2nd session, at Washington, D. C., December 29, 1934, and is a part of the official report made to the House of Representatives by the Committee of that body.

REGULAR MAGAZINES AND NEWSPAPERS PUBLISHED AND CIRCULATED IN UNITED STATES—PUBLISHING CONCERNS, WRITERS, AND WIRE SERVICES (COMMUNIST)

Foreign Language

Western Workers (Hungarian)

El Martillo (Venezuelan)

Ukrania Prolitariai Writers & Correspondence Assn.

O'Brana (Czeck.)

Freheit (Jewish), circulation daily 46,400

Novy Mir (Russian)

Hungarian Proletarian Writers Assn.

Bunevestnik

Ronnost Ludu (Czeck.)

Saznanie (Bulgarian)

Ny Tid (Scandenavian)

La Jroduccion (Spanish)

Enpros (Greek)

Vilnis (Lithuanian)

Panvir (Armenian)

Vanguards (Portugese)

Russky Golos (Russian)

Pravda (Russian)

Signal (Jewish)

Tyomies (Finnish)

Eteenpain (Finnish)

Obrana (Bohemean)

Mundo Obrero

Korean Toiling Masses

Panvor

Lucha Obrera (Spanish)

Darbeninkio Balsas (Lithuanian)

Rodo Sinibo (Jap.)

Cultura Poletaria (Spanish)

Contempo

Soviet Telegraph Agency

Ujelore (Hungarian)

L'Unita Operaia (Ital.)

Laisve (Lithuanian)

Radnik (Jugoslav.)

Us Illm (Estonian)

Amerikos Zihna (Lettish)

Der Arbeiter (German)

Ukrain Daily News

Rodo Shinbum (Jap.)

Unita (Ital.)

Desteperes (Roumanian)

Vanguard (Chinese)

Tribuna Robstnicza (Polish)

Avanguarda (Portugese)

Toreri (Finnish)

Vida O'Brera (Spain)

Illavatore (Italian)

Nor Askor (Armenean)

Der Hammer (Spanish)

Nyagat (Hungarian)

Pienikki (Finnish)

Soveritar (Finnish)

L'Ouvrier (Canadian)

MAY, 1936

THE COMMUNIST

Review of the Month   A. B.

For a United Front May Day!
    Statement of the Central Committee of the Communist Party

Akron: A New Chapter in Labor History
                                    JOHN WILLIAMSON

Problems in Our Farmer-Labor Party Activities
                                    C. A. HATHAWAY

The Hand of God—and the Lack of Flood Control
                                    N. SPARKS

Japan, Outer Mongolia and the Chinese Liberation
    Movement   R. DOONPING

Political Highlights of the National Negro Congress
                                    JAMES W. FORD

Organizational Changes in the New York District of the
    Party   I. AMTER

Lenin on Birth Control

20
CENTS

NOTE: Photostat copy of the front page of The Communist, monthly magazine directed entirely to the Communist cause. Williamson is a Communist Party organizer. Hathaway is editor of the Communist Daily Worker. Ford was the Communist Party candidate for Vice-President in the last election. Amter is the New York District organizer for the Communist Party.

English

The Communist
Daily Worker (58,000 circulation 12/10/34)
Labor Defender (40,000 circulation)
Western Worker
Southern Worker
The United Farmer
Anti-Imperialist Review
The Liberator
Communist Review
Communist Int'l.
The Workers' Voice
Labor Unity
The Mesa Voice
The High School Out Post
China Today
The Workers Ex-Service Mens Nat'l
    News Bulletin
The Workers Defense
Young Fighter
Messengers Voice
Food Worker
Spark Plug
Harlem Worker
Workers School Bulletin
The Red Pen
The ABC Paper Worker
The Railroad Worker
The Tinplate Worker
The Illinois Steel Worker
The Fighting Miner
The Medicine Worker
Farmers Nat'l News
Int'l Union of Revolutionary Writers
    Bulletin
The Partisan
The Partisan Review
The West Front
Leftward
The Unemployed Teacher
The Furniture Worker
The Irish Workers Voice
The Black News
The United Action (N. Y.), Emanuel Levin,
    Editor
Action (Calif.), United Defense League
    Against Fascism
The Macy Worker
U. S. Worker
The Bloomingdale Worker
Namm Worker
Martin Events
Klein Workers Voice
Wanamaker Worker

The New Sports & Play
The Red Star Press
Labor Sports
The Left
N. Y. Metal Worker
Cooperatives
The Industrial Unionist
Int'l Literature
Art Front
Combate
The Barley Worker
The Packing House Workers Voice
The Monthly Literary Service
Auto Workers News
Imprecorr
The Int'l Theatre
Workers Age
Ford Body Worker
Fisher Body Worker
Dodge Worker
Party Organizer
Young Worker
Furniture Worker
Packard Worker
Moscow News (published in Russia in English;
    widely circulated in U. S. Edited by former
    employee of U. S. Dept. Labor)
Dynamo
Voice of Action
Students Book Service
The Workers Child
The Red Front
The Left Front
The Nat'l Textile Worker
Negro Champion
Labor Research Assn. (service to organizations
    and publications)
The Marine Workers Voice
The Workers Press Committee
Foresters Voice
The Red Int'l and Labor Union
Youth Publishers (official Communist publish-
    ers of youth publications, pamphlets & books)
The Partisan
The Young Spartacus
The Office Worker
Red Sports Clubs
The Steel & Metal Worker
College News
The Struggle Against War
The Medical Worker
Workers Theatre Magazine
The Michigan Worker

Title Worker
Wall St. Worker
The Word
The Gimbelites
Deering Worker
Int'l Harvester Worker
Rubber Worker
Painters
Mascots
Studebaker Worker
Young Comrades
Voice of Working Women
Hudson Worker
The Oil Worker
Spring Worker
Wright Propeller
Nativity
The Young Spark
The Rebel Guard
Int'l Publishers (official publishing house for
    millions of Communist pamphlets and books)
The Proletarian
Revolutionary Age
Workers Book Shops (one, two, or more in
    every important city in the U. S.)
New Masses, 28,000 circulation
The Proletpen
Int'l Youth
N. Y. Daily Worker
Int'l Book Stores (in all of the largest cities in
    U. S.)
Gary Steel Worker
Cleveland Unemployed Worker
Longshore Unity
Seamens Lookout
Minneapolis Worker
Pen & Hammer
Producers News
Fight (circulation, 28,000)
Rebel Poet
The Working Woman
Portland (Oreg.) Worker
Int'l Correspondence
Soviet Russia Today
The Veterans Rank & File
Unemployment Insurance Review
The Brooklyn Navy Yard Voice
The Packing House Worker
The Western Workers Bulletin
The SunnysideRed Rail
Los Angeles Workers School Bulletin
The Pulse
The Railroad Worker
The Left Review
Bremerton (Navy) Yard Workers

The Rank and File Federationist
The Queensboro Voice
The Tax Worker
The Militant
The Ford Worker (20,000 circulation)
New Pioneer
Negro Liberator
Revolt
Upsurge
The Young Communist
The New Int'l
The Auto Worker
New Theatre
The Soldiers Voice
The Navy Yard Worker
The Blast
The Industrial Workers Voice
The Unemployed Teachers
The West End Voice
The Negro Worker
The Partisan Review
The United Workers Press
The Hunger Fighter (N. Y. C.)
The Hunger Fighter (Wash., D. C.)
The Hunger Fighter (Chicago)
The Hunger Fighter (Los Angeles)
The Hunger Fighter (Portland, Oreg.)
The Messengers Voice
The New Order
The Needle Worker
The Young Fighter
The Coal Digger
The Veterans
Action
The Workers School Bulletin (anti-religious)
Red Express
Armour Young Worker
Red Motor
The Workers Defense
Needleworkers' Voice
The Anvil
The Nat'l Student League Bulletin
The Galley Wireless
The Ship Mates Voice
The Southern Textile Bulletin
The New Tide
The Scope
Workers Reference Bulletin
War & Fascism Bulletin
Nat'l Student Mirror
The Recreational Leader
The Hot Billet
The Live Wire
The Prophet
The Projectile

The Oven
The Red Pen
The Rank & File Coal Diggers
U. S. Veterans
The Black Diamond
The Red Dynamo
Workers Club Review
Unemployment Review
The Waterfront Worker
The Tannery

The Project News
The Monthly Review
New Order
The Recreational Leader
A. O. Pee News
A. O. Pee Projects
The News Letter
United Action
Solidarity

Workers Library Publishers, Inc. (publishers and distributors of Communist magazines, newspapers, pamphlets and books).

Vanguard Press (large publishers and distributors of Communism literature).

Rodo Simbo, published in San Francisco, Japanese language, bimonthly.

International Press Correspondence, published in Berlin, Germany, English language, weekly.

Pravda, published in Moscow, Russian language, daily.

Izvestia, published in Moscow, Russian language, daily.

PRESS AND PROPAGANDA AGENCIES

"Tass" is the official Soviet news agency. "Pravda" is the central organ of the Communist Party of the U. S. S. R. "Izvestia" is the organ of the Soviet Government. "Moscow News" is the weekly edition of the "Moscow Daily News;" the "Moscow News" is printed by the United Magazines and Newspapers in the Soviet Union and is circulated in English-speaking countries. M. M. Borodin is Editor-in-Chief; Assistant Editors: Victor Vacsov, T. L. Axelrod, Anna Louise Strong. Miss Strong is the daughter of Rev. Sidney Strong of Seattle, and contributes articles to "Unity" (700 Oakwood Blvd., Chicago, Ill.), of which John Haynes Holmes is Editor and with which her father is also identified. She was for some years Moscow correspondent of the Federated Press. She has also supplied articles on Soviet Russia which have been reproduced in "Soviet Russia Today," "Soviet Russia Pictorial," "Haldeman-Julius Monthly," etc. When she visited Los Angeles in 1930, she was featured by the American Civil Liberties Union. (By MK.)

While Communists and their allies demand unqualified freedom of expression in the United States and other nations, such freedom is not permitted by them nor tolerated in their fatherland, the U. S. S. R.

Maxim Gorky is advertised as the "senior proletarian writer," who was privileged to open the Congress of Soviet Writers in Moscow this past summer.

Communist Press Directs—

"WHAT TO DO WHEN ARRESTED IN DEPORTATION PROCEEDINGS

"In view of the present wave of deportation proceedings throughout the country, involving workers of every nationality, the International Labor Defense has issued the following instructions as to what to do when held for deportation or under arrest by immigration officials.

"Following these instructions may save you from being railroaded out of the country on a trumped-up charge.

"1.—Always remember that Immigration Inspectors have absolutely no power to compel you to answer any of their questions.

"2.—Refuse to answer all questions—anywhere—in jail, at home, in organization headquarters, on the street—except your name, until you have seen an attorney.

"3.—Notify the International Labor Defense.   (Number in phone book.)

"4.—Give no address, place of employment, the country you came from, when you arrived, whether or not you are a citizen. Don't give the name of the ship or the date when you came.

"5.—Don't sign anything. Don't be fooled into answering questions by an inspector who says he is trying to help you.

"6.—Deportation hearings are held in private. No workers are present. The only people in the room are commissioners, stenographers, the defendant and the lawyer. Everything you say is secret. Don't try to propagandize the officials at these hearings.

"7.—Always Remember—the Department of Labor must prove that you can be deported. They cannot get a visa to any country unless they prove you are a citizen of that country. Don't give them any free information. It will be used against you.

"8.—Always Remember—The Department of Labor still has not the right of arrest without warrant. If an inspector tells you to come along with him, demand that he show you his warrant. The same applies if he tries to search your home. He must have a warrant.

"Answer no questions. Don't sign anything.

"It is necessary to point out that in many recent cases, failure to follow these simple rules has made it impossible to put up a good legal fight against deportation, and has to a certain extent also undermined the possibilities of developing a mass campaign."—Page 4, W. W., April 22, 1935.

SPY SYSTEM OF THE U. S. S. R.

The following information setting forth the extent to which the spy system of the U. S. S. R. works in the United States, is taken from the report of Communist Propaganda in America, submitted to the State Department of the United States Government in January, 1935, by William Green, President of the American Federation of Labor:

"The authority of Moscow over Communists in the United States extends to trial and punishment for offenses against orders issued by the Moscow headquarters. The death penalty has been inflicted in the United States and has been passed upon others who have escaped execution by one device or another. That the O. G. P. U. is empowered to pass the death sentence and to execute it even in foreign lands is not disputed by Communist authorities. The death penalty has been inflicted in France and Italy as well as in the United States. This is a new and peculiar kind of extra-territoriality. The testimony of at least two witnesses that they, though living in the United States, were under Soviet sentence of death, is a matter of record. Early in August of 1931, Mr. George Djamgaroff occupied the witness stand in a Federal Court in Washington, D. C. He recalled that in September, 1930, he had testified at length before the Fish Committee regarding the activities in America of agents of the O. G. P. U. As a witness in a United States Federal Court, he testified that he was under sentence to be shot; that the sentence had been imposed by the secret tribunal of the O. G. P. U. in Moscow. There is likewise the case of Mr. Basil W. Delgass, who testified in 1930 with Mr. Djamgaroff. Both, incidentally, testified under oath. Mr. Delgass testified that for three and a half years he had been Vice-President of the Amtorg Trading Corporation and that at the time of his testimony he was under sentence by the O. G. P. U. to be shot. His offense was in refusing to return to Russia when ordered by the Soviet to do so. His resignation was for the double purpose of escaping the necessity of giving manufactured testimony and removing himself from an organization, the orders of which he could no longer obey. Though he was in New York, he was tried in Russia and sentenced to death.

"The Bessedovski case in Paris is too well known to need mention here. He was the Soviet Charge d'Affaires in Paris. His house was entered by would-be executioners; he escaped and lived to write an astounding account of O. G. P. U. intrigue.

"There is likewise the case of Voikov; tried by an O. G. P. U. Court; sentenced and shot in Poland, the country to which he had been ambassador.

"Eugene N. Levin, Secretary and Consul General of the Soviet Embassy in Rome, was tried in the embassy itself by O. G. P. U. agents sent there for the purpose; found guilty, and shot on the spot.

"As for additional assassinations; the drowning of a Russian named Chourgin, head of Amtorg, some four years ago, and of Sklianski, who had been but two days on American soil as a surreptitious arrival from Moscow, has never been explained. It has been assumed by many that Chourgin was the intended victim, Sklianski the intended executioner and the accidental co-victim.

"Again in New York City in 1932 the O. G. P. U. assassination went into action. Mrs. Tatiana Kouteynikeff, a white Russian refugee, was sitting before her dressing table in her sixth floor apartment at 68 Lennox Avenue. Her husband and son were sleeping in an adjoining room. 'Peter, look, I'm shot,' the woman cried, running to her husband and collapsing in death. A bullet had come through the window, striking her in the neck. Only from a building some 250 yards away could the shot have come. It must have been deliberate assassination. Her father had been Czarist Consul General at Constantinople. She had planned to leave New York City the following day. Whether she had knowledge that she was doomed has never been made known, nor have the assailants been captured.

"Arcady I. Pogdeff, a young Amtorg agent, was found dead under the window of his room in the Hotel Cartaret in April, 1930. It was reported that he had fallen or leaped to his death, but a friend, Gregory R. Bernadsky, went to the police and charged that Pogdeff had been slain by the O. G. P. U. for disobeying an order to return to Russia and that Pogdeff had expressed the fear that he would be killed in fulfillment of an O. G. P. U. death sentence passed upon him for disobedience.

"There are many other cases of executions and of attempted executions, including such noted cases as that of Gregory Sokolmkoff, first Soviet ambassador to the Court of St. James; twice ordered back to Moscow, he refused to obey the second order, whereupon a trio of intended executioners went to seek him in London. His cleverness undoubtedly saved his life.

"Paul Milyoukov, head of the Constituent Assembly, disbanded by Lenin, has declared that no less than eight Soviet ambassadors or agents have been either shot or imprisoned upon being recalled to Russia.

"O. G. P. U. Spies in American Factories

"That they have long been on duty in the United States, even as spies in American factories, is too well known to be disputed.

"The O. G. P. U.'s threatening finger came boldly into the trade union movement. Mr. Benjamin Schlesinger, late president of the International Ladies' Garment Workers, visited Russia in 1922. On his return, he was followed by an agent of the O. G. P. U. and in his own office in New York City he was told that unless he and his union deserted the American Federation of Labor immediately, Moscow agents would at once set up a rival union and exercise every effort to destroy Mr. Schlesinger, his fellow officers and the union. On the floor of an American Federation of Labor convention, Mr. Schlesinger confirmed these statements. The Moscow agent was ordered out of his office and from that day forward clearly defined Moscow-directed efforts to destroy the International Ladies' Garment Workers were in evidence.

"From a pamphlet written by George Agabekoff we take the following:

" 'One Chatzky was the G. P. U. first resident in America and lived there up to 1929. In 1929 he returned to Moscow and at the present time is in charge of the Anglo-American branch of the Foreign Department of the G. P. U.

" 'Inasmuch as there is not yet a Soviet legation in America, Chatzky went there as an Amtorg worker. His task in America was to familiarize himself with the attitude of the Government of the U. S. A. toward the U. S. S. R. and to endeavor to influence American public men and, if possible, members of the government, that is, to have them assent to the official recognition of the Soviet government.

" 'It is difficult for me to say whether Chatzky was successful or not in his endeavors, but on his arrival in Moscow he was much praised by those higher up.'

"We quote further:

" 'Reports of the English envoy to Washington as to the activities of the American Government were a permanent source of information to the G. P. U. It is necessary to say that, at the service of the foreign department of the G. P. U. there were reports of almost all the English representatives abroad (envoys accredited to foreign governments, and commissioners to the countries under British protectorates.) I was convinced of this many times. English diplomats, without their knowledge, rendered valuable service to the Soviet government through their detailed reports to the foreign office. . . . The reports of British diplomats accumulated in 1929 occupied a whole big closet in the G. P. U.'

"A special department exists in the Moscow headquarters of G. P. U. for the forging of passports and other credentials and documents. All witnesses agree that American passports are favored by this forgery machine.

"SUBTERRANEAN ORGANIZATION IN AMERICA

"It is a matter of official record, already cited, that the underground machine in America is never to be disbanded. The reason for this determination to carry on a subterranean organization, where identities are secret, becomes clearer as the role of G. P. U. is examined. G. P. U. likewise has its underground agents in America. These are unknown to the agents who come to do spy work in the guise of Amtorg agents. G. P. U. never lets its right hand know what its left is doing.

"Amtorg rises to the heights of indignation and rejects any implication of secret operations.

"In the records of the Fish Committee there is this colloquy:

" 'The Chairman—Do you know the business manager of the Amtorg, Mr. Ziavkin?

" 'Mr. Delgass—Yes, I met him once or twice. He is a recent importation, you know; before him we had Mr. Grafpen, office manager of Amtorg.

" 'The Chairman—Do you know anything about Mr. Ziavkin and any positions he held in Russia, or where he came from?

" 'Mr. Delgass—He came from Rostox on Don. He was there and was picked up there by Mr. Bogdanov who at that time was secretary of the Northern Caucasus Party Division. Whether he was a member of the Checka or not I cannot tell you exactly."

"But the evidence was forthcoming. Affidavits later were offered and are of record, sworn to by men who knew Ziavkin as the terror of the Don, local chief of the G. P. U. men who observed his operations there and to whom he boasted of his powers. He was identified by affidavit of persons in New York who knew his position and record in Russia; two of these affiants being parents of an employee of Amtorg. The parents of this employee made their affidavit as to the record of

Ziavkin at Quarantine, before they knew of their daughter's employment. Ziavkin was a high and unusually bloodthirsty G. P. U. executive in Russia and it is beside the point that he may be said to have been removed from his G. P .U. connections before coming to Amtorg. G. P. U. does not take men into its inner councils and then remove them.

"Grafpen, Ziavkin's predecessor, may or may not have been a Soviet G. P. U. spy, but he was one of the leading Communist propagandists and long a prolific writer in International Press Correspondence, one of the official Soviet outlets for propaganda in foreign lands. The probability is that Grafpen never was far from G. P. U. Lengthy quotations from Grafpen's authentic writings as an inner circle Communist are in the records of the American Federation of Labor, of the American State Department and of the Department of Justice. They have been available without recourse to any unusual effort at procurement. The so-called Whalen photostats were orders from Moscow to Grafpen for subversive work throughout the United States, with specific directions for local agents.

"Hendler, a former G. P. U. agent, now fugitive from Soviet authority, offered testimony to the effect that he had been asked to help establish secret channels between Amtorg and an arm of the Berlin branch of G. P. U. He asserts that he found the proper man, one Mikhail, who received his instructions and promptly proceeded to New York, landing illegally. He testifies further that he attended a meeting at which it was arranged to send to Amtorg three men who would pose as Amtorg employees in legitimate capacities, but would report to G. P. U. Other witnesses have identified three such men.

"Amtorg has its agents in every branch of the Communist movement, not excluding the Young Communists and the Young Pioneers, and from these, likewise, G. P. U. recruits assistants who perform services of value. It is an established fact that the purpose of G. P. U. is to leave no portion of the vast red machine uncovered, and it follows, almost as a matter of necessity, that G. P. U. agents are in America to spy on the work of the red leaders themselves, as well as to spy on and pervert, where possible, American institutions and operations."

THE UNITED FRONT

THE FOLLOWING listed organizations are reported to be either Communist or sympathetic to the Communist program or to some of its affiliated groups according to report 153, U. S. Congress. When any of them announce meetings in your city or community the office of the National Americanism Commission will be pleased to give you what information our files contain on their history. The harmless sounding names seldom do justice to their activities.

United Farmers' League
Workers' Ex-Servicemen's League
Share Croppers' Union in the South
League of Struggle for Negro Rights
*Young Communist League
*National Students' League
*American Youth Congress
*League for Industrial Democracy
*The Young Pioneers
*The Communist Students' League
*The League Against War and Fascism
*Friends of the Soviet Union
*Trade Union Unity League
Unemployed Councils
Revolutionary Policy Committee
C. W. A. Workers' Union
Relief Workers' Union
*International Workers' Order
*International Labor Defense
*American Civil Liberties Union
International Women's Congress
Communist League for Struggle
*Federated Press
*Garland Fund
*Amtorg Trading Corporation
Committee on Academic Freedom
Chicago Atheist Forum
Atheist Pioneers
Arcos Limited
American Russian Institute
Amalgamated Banks
New Dance Group
Scottsboro Committee of Action
Pen and Hammer Club
John Reed Clubs
Manumit School
Intourist
International Workers' Aid
Freiheit
Red Sports International
Vanguard Press
War Resisters' International
International Red Aid

Revolutionary Writers' Congress
International Committee for Political
 Prisoners
Industrial Workers of the World
Workers' Cultural Federation
Workers' International Relief
United Farmers' Protective Association
United Workers' Co-operative Association
National Council for Protection of Foreign
 Born Workers
Hungarian Proletarian Writers' Association
Emergency Committee for Southern Political
 Prisoners
Educational Workers' International
Amkino
Amkniga
Workers' Unemployment Insurance Bill
International Student Service
Farmer-Labor Political Federation
League for Independent Political Action
League of American Writers
Revolutionary Writers' Federation of America
Workers' Shortwave Clubs of U. S. A.
Labor Sports Union of U. S. A.
Finnish Workers' Pioneer
Nature Friends Scouts
Federation of Children's Organizations
Conference for Protection of Civil Rights
Southern Tenant Farmers' Union
American League of Ex-Servicemen
Highlander Folks School
Commonwealth Labor College
American Workers' Union
Workers' Dance League
Veterans' Rank and File Committee
League of Human Rights
Educational Workers' League
American Society for Cultural Relations with
 Russia
Communist League of America
League of Workers' Theatres
Workers' International Relief

RED FRONT

NO. 1   NEW YORK MAY 1933   2 CENTS

INTO THE STREETS ON MAY FIRST

Recriut Fighters For The Anti-Fascist Front!

EDITOR'S NOTE: Photostat of front page of circular used to promote a May Day parade in New York City. Do you like the flag?

ORGANIZATIONS OPERATING AMONG EMPLOYED AND UNEMPLOYED IN THE UNITED STATES OF AMERICA

Trade Union Unity League (national unions with many locals and cells)

Labor Sports Union (many leagues with many local teams)

Veterans National Rank and File

The Ex-Service Men's League (offices in 60 cities)

International of War Vets and War Victims

The Building Trades Industrial League

The Carpenters Section

The Bricklayers Section

Dairy Workers Industrial Union.

American Federation of Labor Rank and File.

Women's Council.

United Council of Working Class Women

The Red Front (military unit)

National Committee of Action

United Front Committees

United Election Front Committees

Trade Union Youth Committee

League of Struggle for Negro Rights

Red Builders

Anti-Mortgage Foreclosure Committee.

Anti-Eviction Committee.

Metal Workers Industrial Union.

Workers & Farmers Corporation Unity Alliance

Trade Union Educational League

Veterans National Liaison Committee

Pan-Pacific Trade Union Secretariat (operates in Latin and South America in conjunction with United States Communist branches)

The Cannery and Agricultural Workers Industrial Union

Chinese Anti-Imperialist Alliance

Trade Union Committee for Unemployment Insurance and Relief

American League Against War and Fascism

The Committee to Aid Victims of German Fascism

United Front Action Committee

Anti-Nazi Federation

Anti-Fascist League

The Committee for Protection of Foreign-Born Workers

Friends of the Chinese People

CULTURAL GROUPS AND MOVEMENTS IN THE UNITED STATES OF AMERICA

Blue Blouse Theatres

Workers Schools

The Society for Cultural Relations with Soviet Russia

Russian Educational Society

The National Training School

The Workers Music League

The Jno. Reed Club

The Jno. Reed Writers Club

Proletpen

Homeless Youth of America

National Student League

American League Against War and Fascism

Workers Forums

Workers Reading Clubs

United Farmers Educational League

Labor Research Association

United Workers Cooperative Colonies

Finnish Workers Cultural Federation

Midwest Workers Cultural Federation

Jno. Reed Writers Group

Jno. Reed Art League

Jewish Workers Clubs

Frederick Engels Club

Jno. Reed School of Art

New Masses Clubs

Workers Laboratory Theatre

United Council of Working Class Women

The International Book Stores (all large cities)

Workers Sick and Death Benefit Fund of United States of America

Jack London Clubs

The Workers Centers (1,500 or more cities in United States of America)

Working Mens Society Benevolent and Educational Federation

The Rebel Players

The League of Workers Theatres of United States of America

The First National Workers Theatre Council

ICOR

National Cultural Council

The Red Poet

Lithunanian Literary Society

The Marxian School

The Theatre Club

Natures Friends

The Workers Dance League

Workers camps (32 cities)

Workers Schools (178 cities)

International Workers order Schools (116 cities)

American Youth Federation

The Young Workers Dance League

The Workers Laboratory Theatre

Soviet Union Information Bureau
Russia Progress in Women Society
Lithuanian Literary and Dramatic Club
Revolutionary Writers Federation
Theatre Guild
Torgsen
International of Adult Education
Russian Cooperative Association
The Womens League
International Workers Order
Scandinavian Club
Labor Sports Union of America
League of Propsownel Group D
The Civic Club
The Mothers League
International Peasant Council
Red Sports Athletic Clubs
National Twiner Clubs
Little Theatre (shows Communist plays and pictures)
Workers Theatres
The Workers Book Shops
Proletarian Dramatic Society of America
American-Russian Chamber of Commerce
Drama League of America
Russian Godless Society
Summer Training Camps (under various names, "Nitgedaeget," "Unity")
League of Professional Groups (professors, writers, artists, etc.)
Tourist Bureaus (various names)
The Friends of the Soviet Union
The Workers Film and Photo League
The Finnish Cultural Federation
The Japanese Cultural Federation
The Workers Cultural Federation

The Industrial Union Party
The Workers Gymnastic and Sports Alliance
The Hoe and Hammer League
The Workers Dramatic League
Sport Aces Youth Clubs
Theatre of Workers Schools
Cleveland Workers Theatre Spartakaide.
The Theatre Collective
United Armenian Committee to Aid Soviet Armenia
The Workers Soccer League
The Workers School Forum
The Theatre of Action
The Save Our Schools Committee
Russian-Jewish Workers Clubs
Hospital Workers League
Central Pioneer Bureau
Artef (Jewish) Theatre
Prolet-Buhne (German) Theatre
The Lettish Club
Proletarian Camps
International Workers Theatre Olympiad
Russian Workers Dramatic Group
New York Workers Theatre Spartakaide
International Union of the Revolutionary Theatres
The Bronx Workers Club
Harlem Experimental Theatre
The Workers Sport Wave Club
The National Legion of Youth Against War
National Youth Committee Against War and Fascism
Revolutionary Writers Federation of America
Italian Drama Section Harlem
Hungarian Proletarian Writers League

COMMUNIST CO-OPERATION WITH PACIFISTS

IN EVERY instance the Communist Party and all of its affiliated and sympathetic groups co-operate and work openly with radical pacifist groups in their program to tear down an adequate system of National Defense for the United States of America. This fact has been shown in brief in the foregoing chapters of this publication, through opposition to the R. O. T. C. and the C. M. T. C.

Following will be found definite information concerning the inroads of Communist propaganda in the United States Army, United States Navy, United States Merchant Marine, Longshoremen's Union and other maritime groups. It is intensely interesting to note the pacifistic activities of the Communist group in this country, while their own publications have, time and again, pointed with pride to the continued enlargement of the Red army in the U. S. S. R.

Following is an exact copy of a dodger distributed by the Communist Party on the West Coast, which shows how they are working among the men of the United States Navy:

"SAY! SAILOR

"How About Getting Together on a Few Facts???

"Fellow Workers in Uniform, welcome back to the West Coast!

"You, too, are having much the same sort of ballyhoo shoveled out to you that the workers in civies receive.

"Roosevelt's government stands for a New Deal, for Economy and Peace. But why the expenditure of millions of bucks to move the fleet to the East Coast and back? Or is it worth that much to whoop up the War spirit for the rapidly approaching war?

"What else are maneuvers for?

"Who holds the cards after the New Deal? What do we see but hundreds of millions given to railroads, banks, etc. Hundreds of millions more poured into war equipment.

"What happens to the Workers? Under Roosevelt the unemployed have grown from 12 to 19 millions in less than two years. A huge army of Workers needing and wanting work, food and clothing. Then what happens? The government gives the order to plow under every third row of cotton when Workers freeze!! Destroys 6 million hogs when people are starving. This is 'Economy.'

"Then, to top it all off, a slick inflation scheme was added which boosted the cost of living 31% and wages only 9%. In other words, all of us have received a national pay cut of 22%. Many of the Workers in Uniform have relatives at home to whom they send money, helping to keep their families from literally starving in the (so-called) richest country in the world.

"All we are supposed to do is to sit quietly and take it. The question is 'Will We???'

"Next summer there will be maneuvers off the Aleutian Islands to demonstrate to the Japanese Imperialist Uncle's 'Preparedness.' That is, preparedness to make profits. Also the question arises how can the Workers profit from a war when 2%

More of the War Machine, the largest in the world, of the U. S. S. R. Top picture is taken from the Western Worker, p. 5, 12/7/36. Lower picture is from Soviet Russia Today, issue of December, 1936. Sailors seem to be looking for peaceful Spain to call them for more war supplies—a part of their stand for world peace?

of the people own the entire country? In other words, this 2% have the armed forces do their dirty work, while they sit back and say, as in the last war, 'We will fight to the bitter end.'

"Do you know that a stream of ships are leaving these shores loaded to the hatches with the most modern war equipment purchased here, and in case of war with Japan will be used against us? Japan has been taking the bulk of export scrap-iron. Cotton exports have been the greatest in the history of the U. S. Lead, steel, nickel, have run into hundreds of thousands of tons. The majority of sales have been in materials, but 3,000 airplane motors, machine guns and rifles as well as many small arms have been shipped. Still the papers tell us that Japan is an Enemy— but it seems *not to the capitalist class*, as they are the ones who profit. It matters little whether Japanese or American Workers are slaughtered, so long as they get new markets, or new territories. In the last war 64 leading (American?) corporations showed a net profit of $5,484,888,000 while the Workers showed a net loss of 32,000,000 casualties, with 20,000,000 dead and a debt of $350,000,000,000, which will never be paid. To sum it up:

"WARS ARE FOUGHT BY WAGE SLAVES FOR THE CAPITALIST CLASS

"District 13, Communist Party U. S. A.

"Get in touch with the Communist Party."

Another one of their publications used for the dissemination of propaganda among members of the United States Navy is one published in Washington, D. C., by the South-East unit of the Communist Party, U. S. A., entitled, "Navy Yard Worker."

The following Associated Press dispatch under date line of Indiantown Gap, Pennsylvania, August 25, 1935, clearly shows the methods used by the Communist leaders in planting their propaganda in the armed forces of this country:

"RADICAL LITERATURE DROPPED ON CAMP

"Indiantown Gap, Pa., Aug. 25.—(AP)—An unidentified airplane swooped low over the National Guard reservation here today and dropped literature which a high army official described as 'Communistic out and out.'

"The plane was painted the colors of an army plane but lacked the army insignia.

"HIGHER PAY URGED

"The eight-page pamphlets which it dropped over the 28th division camp were entitled 'The Soldiers' Voice, Special Maneuvers Edition,' and appealed to privates 'to organize and fight for your rights.'

"It urged that they demand $30 a month instead of $21; that they demand that the War Department not use them in domestic uprisings, and that they demand committees to run their own activities."

DEFENSE COMPARISON BETWEEN U.S.A. AND U.S.S.R.

In comparison to all of this effort on the part of Communist propaganda agencies to demoralize the National Defense of the United States, it is interesting to note that press dispatches from Moscow claim that by the close of 1935

DEFEND WHOM?

THE WAR OF 1914, FOR WHICH WE ARE STILL PAYING IN UNBEARABLE TAXES, WHOSE VET-ERANS ARE STILL DEMANDING THE BONUS, WHOSE CRIPPLES, WHOSE WIDOWS AND ORPHANS, STILL SEEK RELIEF, WAS PRESEDED BY SUCH PARADES AS THIS, AND BY SUCH A DEPRESSION AS THIS.

"DEFENSE" MEANS THAT YOU, WORKERS ARE GOING TO BE FORCED TO DEFEND WITH YOUR LIVES AND BODIES THE INVESTMENTS OF AMERICAN FINANCIERS IN FOREIGN COUNTRIES, TO KILL OTHER WORKERS AND TO BE KILLED BY THEM IN ORDER TO "SOLVE" THE CRISIS --- FOR THE BOSSES.

WAR IS BEING PREPARED !

MILLIONS OF DOLLARS OF "PUBLIC WORKS" MONEY IS GOING TO MUNITIONS MANUFACTUR-ERS FOR WAR SUPPLIES. CIVILIAN CONSERVATION AND REHABILITATION CAMPS UNDER ARMY SUPERVISION, ARE WAR TRAINING CAMPS. PARADES AND NEWSPAPERS WHIP UP PATRIOTIC FRENZY TO BLIND US TO OUR OWN WELFARE AS WORKERS.

IN THE LAST WAR WE WERE TOLD THAT IT WAS "A WAR TO END ALL WARS" AND "TO MAKE THE WORLD SAFE FOR DEMOCRACY" WE GOT --- NEW WAR PREPARATIONS, UNEMPLOYMENT AND HUNGER IN THE MIDST OF PLENTY. NOW ROOSEVELT'S NEW DEAL IS LEADING US INTO NEW WAR AND FASCISM.

THE BOSSES AND THEIR POLITICIANS WHO DROVE THE MASSES INTO WAR, MADE MILLIONS. U.S. STEEL MADE $338.00 FOR EVERY DOLLAR INVESTED IN THE LAST WORLD WAR. THEY HAVE NOT FORGOTTEN. THEY ARE GREEDY TO COIN OUR BLOOD INTO DOLLARS AGAIN.

LET US MAKE A STAND NOW !

LET US NOT ALLOW OURSELVES TO BE DRIVEN INTO A CAPITALIST WAR AGAINST OUR FELLOW WORKERS IN OTHER COUNTRIES, ESPECALLY IN THE SOVIET UNION. A WORKERS' SOCIETY WHERE THERE IS NO UNEMPLOYMENT, AND CONDITIONS OF WORKERS ARE IMPROVING FROM DAY TO DAY IS BEING BUILT THERE. IN THE LAST WAR THOSE WORKERS TURNED THEIR GUNS AGAINST THE ENEMY AT HOME, WHO HAD SENT THEM TO WAR, AND TOOK OVER INDUSTRY AND GOVERNMENT FOR A BETTER LIFE FOR THE MASSES OF PEOPLE. LET US DEFEND THEM AGAINST THREATENING CAPITALIST IMPERIALISM THAT FEARS THE EXAMPLE THEY ARE SETTING TO THE WORKERS OF THE WORLD.

THE FORCES RUNNING US INTO WAR ARE NOT TOO STRONG FOR US. ORGANIZED OPPOSITION TO IMPERIALIST WAR ON THE PART OF THE AMERICAN WORKERS CAN HALT IT! THE THREAT OF ORGANIZATION, DEMONSTRATIONS, AND CIVIL WAR CAN HALT WAR! REFUSAL TO MAKE AND TRANSPORT MUNITIONS CAN HALT WAR!

Organize And Fight Against American Imperialism And For The Withdrawal Of American Armed Forces From Cuba, China, And Other Subject Nations.
All War Funds For The Unemployed.
Fight The Enemy At Home--The Bosses Who Offer Us Bullets Instead Of Bread And Jobs.
Turn The Coming Imperialist War Into Civil War And Establish A Soviet America.
Workers Of All Countries Unite.

ISSUED BY: COMMUNIST PARTY U.S.A. LOS ANGELES SECTION
YOUNG COMMUNIST LEAGUE LOS ANGELES SECTION
ROOM 410, 224 SOUTH SPRING STREET

JOIN THE COMMUNIST PARTY !

Multigraphed

EDITOR'S NOTE: Photostat of literature distributed on the streets of Los Angeles during a pre-paredness parade. Of especial interest is the next to the last line from the bottom.

a standing army of at least 900,000, and with almost 17,000,000 trained men in reserve. While teaching disarmament in the United States, the U.S.S.R. boasts of an army and a reserve at least forty times the size of all the defense system of the United States.

Even though the Communist Party has the largest standing and reserve army of any nation in the world, they are constantly building up hatred for preparedness in other nations, sponsoring such organizations as, "The League Against War and Fascism;" joining with a few of our citizens to teach the youth of college age that he must never bear arms and that he should never permit compulsory training to be given him through the R.O.T.C. in college, yet it is compulsory for all able bodied men in Russia to serve in the Red Army. The following excerpts from Communist preparedness leaflets show the contrast between the huge defense system in the U.S.S.R. and their efforts to completely destroy the defense system of the U.S.A.:

THE RED ARMY
Excerpts from the publication titled above. A Communist leaflet.

"The first stage is pre-military training at the age of nineteen and twenty. The young men are trained for one month a year in their home districts. For the regular army recruits are called up at the age of twenty-one. Their period of service is two years in the land and air forces or three to four years in the navy, after which they are on the reserve list, training for one month each year, until they have completed five years in all. Territorials also begin their service at the age of twenty-one and terminate it at the age of twenty-five. Their training lasts eleven months in all—three months the first year, and two in each succeeding year. Reservists are divided into two categories. One includes ex-regulars up to the age of thirty-four, and the other ex-regulars from thirty-four to forty. Both categories may be called up for not more than three months' special training in all. In addition to these, all men eligible for service, but in excess of the numbers required for regulars and territorials, are trained for a period of six months in all, but not more than two months each year, in their own localities." P. 6-8.

"To illustrate the spirit of absolute unity that binds the soldier to his class, we may quote the solemn promise made by each recruit on entering the army— a promise that has been substituted for the old oath of allegiance to the Czar; 'I, the son of the toiling people, and a citizen of the Union of Soviet Socialist Republics, assume the duties of a fighter in the Workers' and Peasants' Army. Before the working class of the U.S.S.R. and of the whole world, I promise to bear this title with honor, conscientiously to study the profession of arms and to guard like the apple of my eye the national and military property from damage and theft. I promise to observe military discipline strictly and unswervingly and to carry out implicitly all orders given me by the commanders appointed by the workers' and peasants' government. I promise both to refrain myself and to restrain my comrades from any act unworthy of a citizen of the U.S.S.R., and to direct all my acts and all my thoughts towards the great goal of the liberation of all workers. I promise at the first call of the workers' and peasants' government to come forward in defense of the U.S.S.R. against every danger and against

COMMUNIST ACTIVITIES

Among Enlisted Men in the Army and Navy of the United States and Among Workers in Navy Yards

"THE SOLDIERS' VOICE", "Issued by and for enlisted men", a Communist "fraction" within the ranks, December, 1933, pictures Russian privates and officers together socially, "something you don't see in the United States Army", praises the Soviet Union as "a fine example to the workers of the rest of the world", as "giving a better life and doing away with misery and slavery imposed by the ruling class", and it indicates how "we soldiers can throw out our exploiters and oppressors, the capitalist class, and take things into our own hands".

This eight-page tabloid was distributed in large quantities among the soldiers, notably at Fort Monmouth, New Jersey, wtih a view to stirring up as many soldier grievances as possible. It wound up with the declaration that "the bosses of the United States plan to send us soldiers to destroy the Soviet Union"

"THE SHIPMATES' VOICE", "Issued by and for sailors and marines", a Communist "fraction", April-May, 1934 was found on shipboard in the Pacific Fleet. It is an eight-page paper in tabloid form, attacking the President of the United States and the Government itself, stressing the "slashing of pay", "cutting off of bonuses", "bad living conditions", "cost of upkeep of uniforms", etc., and upbraids Secretary Swanson for taking the Fleet to the ports of his own State, Virginia, "in the interest of local business". "The Shipmates' Voice" not only assails big business and capital but argues against re-enlisting and idealizes the Soviet Red Army, contrasting the "rigidly imposed discipline from on high which is the rule of capitalist armies with the self-imposed discipline of the Red Army". It pictures advantages to workers and farmers in the Russian Workers' Republic and states that "only by doing away with the capitalist class can we workers and sailors follow in the path of the successful working class of the Soviet Union".

It has been learned that "The Shipmates' Voice" will be distributed by young women offering it for sale to the men in the Navy when the Fleet arrives on the Atlantic Coast. This is the method of feminine appeal pursued in the Communist effort to penetrate the Army in Germany where attractive young girls were used to approach the officers and soldiers in cafés and elsewhere. The tactics are the same throughout the world.

"THE NAVY YARD WORKER", "Issued by the South East Unit of the Communist Party U. S. A., Washington, D. C." by an inside Communist "fraction", April, 1934, was distributed among the workers in the Navy Yard there.

It contains cartoon sketches demanding "full wages", attacking the N R A, cartooning President Roosevelt for "jingoism" in the "old Army game" and also the A. F. of L. "misleaders". It aims to create discontent in the Navy Yard by attacking "wage cuts, discontinuance of thirty days' leave", etc., advocates "mass action to win restoration of wage cuts and improve conditions", urges "building inside groups for a militant program" and "effective action to prevent the rich ruling class from driving us into another slaughter", It states: **"Only Through Getting Rid of This Parasitic Class and Setting Up a Government Run by and in the Interests of Labor Can We Get the Full Benefit of Our Labor".**

"THE YARD VOICE" was distributed among Brooklyn Navy Yard workers in February according to "The Daily Worker" which announced:

"Of course it will be the most important means for opening the eyes of the Navy Yard workers to class consciousness, and rally them for the final aim of the Communist Party—the overthrow of the capitalist system and **The Establishment of a Soviet America with All That Implies".**

Identical paragraphs are published in three of these papers in defense of the Soviet Union, indicating that they emanate from a single source.

New York, May 9, 1934.

EDITOR'S NOTE: Photostat of leaflet used to appeal to members of the U. S. branches of our National Defense to mutiny and disorder. How long do you think this could be practiced in the RED ARMY?

the attacks of all enemies. In the struggle of the U.S.S.R. for Socialism and for the brotherhood of all nations, I promise not to spare either my strength or my life itself. Should I of evil intent break this my solemn promise, may the general contempt of all be my lot and the heavy hand of revolutionary justice fall upon me'." P. 14.

THE STRUGGLE AGAINST IMPERIALIST WAR AND THE TASKS OF THE COMMUNISTS

Excerpts from the publication titled above. A Communist leaflet.

"The persecution and measures of suppression against the Communist Parties are being systematically intensified and the Comintern Sections in all imperialist countries are immediately confronted with the danger of being driven 'underground,' into complete illegality." P. 5.

"War is inseparable from capitalism. From this it follows that the 'abolition' of war is possible only through the 'abolition' of capitalism, i. e., through the overthrow of the bourgeois class of exploiters, through the proletarian dictatorship, the building of Socialism, and the elimination of classes." P. 9.

"But the overthrow of capitalism is impossible without force, without armed uprising and proletarian wars against the bourgeoisie." P. 10.

"The fight the Communists wage against imperialist war differs essentially from the 'fight against war' waged by pacifists of various shades. The Communists do not regard the struggle against such a war as being separate from the class struggle." P. 12.

" 'Radical' or 'revolutionary' pacifism, advocated by certain 'Left' Socialists who admit the danger of war, but strive to combat this danger frequently by meaningless phrases against war." P. 13.

"Semi-religious pacifism, which has its basis in the church movement. In the struggle against pacifism, however, the Communists must draw a distinction between the anti-war sentiments of large masses of the toilers—who are ready to fight against war, but do not as yet understand that the revolutionary way is the only proper way of combating war, and therefore, become a prey to pacifist swindlers —and the swindlers themselves, the pacifists of various shades.

"The masses must be patiently enlightened as to their error and urged to join the revolutionary united front in the struggle against war." PP. 13 and 14.

"Lenin was absolutely right when in 1922, on the basis of experience of the world war, he wrote: 'Boycott the war, is a stupid phase. The Communists must participate in every reactionary war.' " P. 24.

"In view of the fact that the 'enemy' in such a war is the Soviet Union, i. e., the fatherland of the international proletariat, the following changes must be made in tactics as compared with the tactics employed in 'purely' imperialist war:

(a) "The proletariat in the imperialist countries must not only fight for the defeat of their own governments in this war, but must actively strive to secure victory for the Soviet Union." P. 31.

"In the event of a war against the Soviet Union, the workers in capitalist

A Part of the War Machine of the (Peaceful!?) U. S. S. R., But They Tell Us How to Disarm

countries must not allow themselves to be scared from supporting the Red Army and from expressing this support by fighting against their own bourgeoise, by the charges of treason that the bourgeoisie may hurl against them." P. 31.

"Although the proletariat in imperialist countries is not bound by the duty of 'national defense,' in the land of the proletariat dictatorship, however, national defense is an unfailing revolutionary duty." P. 31.

"There is a glaring contradiction between the imperialists' policy of piling up armament and their hypocritical talk about peace. There is no such contradiction, however, between the Soviet Government's preparations for defense and for revolutionary war and a consistent peace policy. Revolutionary war of the proletarian dictatorship is but a continuation of revolutionary peace policy 'by other means'." P. 33.

"Nevertheless, the Chinese Communist Party committed a number of grave mistakes, from which the Communists of all oppressed nations have important lessons to learn. In this war, the duty of the Communist Party of China was to take full advantage of the revolutionary situation prevailing at the time to establish its own proletarian class army, and to extend the military organization and training of the workers and peasants in order to pave the way for the proletariat's struggle for the leadership of the revolution." P. 34.

"The tasks of the international proletariat in connection with wars of liberation of oppressed peoples, and with imperialist expeditions for the suppression of the national revolutionary movements and revolutions—with a few concrete exceptions —are the same as in imperialist wars against the Soviet Union." P. 37.

"No matter what their form of organization may be, armies are a constituent part of the bourgeois state apparatus, which the proletariat, in the course of its revolution, must not democratize, but break up.

"In the light of this task, the organizational difference between standing armies and militia, between conscript armies and volunteer armies, etc., disappears. The slogan: 'Not a man, not a penny for the army,' i. e., relentless struggle against bourgeois budgets, etc., holds good." PP. 40 and 41.

"Imperialism at the present time encounters serious obstacles in its ideological and organizational preparations for new imperialist counter-revolutionary wars, viz., the instinctive hostility to war aroused among the broad masses of the population, particularly among the workers, the peasants and the working women, since the last world war. For that reason, imperialism is compelled to make its preparations for war under the cloak of pacifism." P. 54.

"The Communist Parties must maintain permanent contact with the Communist organization and trade unions in the respective colonial countries. They must render every support, by means of mass action, to the revolutionary movements in the colonies.

"The Communist Parties of all countries must devote special attention to the setting up of non-party organizations like the League for the Struggle Against Imperialism." P. 63.

Soviet Russia says its Army, the largest of any nation in the world today, is intended only as a force for peace. Does this picture from page 5 of Soviet Russia Today, issue of February, 1936, look as though they intend to use peaceful means or force?

"AIR POWER OF USSR CALLED WORLD'S BEST

"AVIATION CHIEF SAYS AVIATION PRODUCTION HAS BEEN DOUBLED IN A YEAR—FASCISTS WILL REGRET ANY ATTACK, HE SAYS

(By cable to the Daily Worker)

"Moscow, Nov. 30.—Citing "just a few figures" to make his point, the assistant head of the administration of military and air forces, M. Khripin, today set the delegates at the Eighth All-Union Congress of Soviets into gales of applause and cheers with proof that Soviet aviation was superior to any other in the world.

"After a brief review of the strength in air armament of the capitalist countries as well as the Soviet Union's own past in this respect, Khripin said:

" 'During the first ten months of this year, production in our aviation plants practically doubled in comparison with the same period last year.

"AVIATION OUTPUT TREBLED

" 'We have increased production by 94.5 per cent. Engine plants in our industry increased 46 per cent over last year. Certain enterprises have even attained a higher figure of increase. For example, for the first ten months of this year, aviation construction plants increased their output by practically three times in comparison with last year.'

"Recalling that Marshall Tukhachevsky had told the Seventh Congress that the fighting strength of Soviet aviation had tripled in the previous four years, Khripin declared:

"AIR FORCE QUADRUPLED

" 'I must inform the Congress that during the past year we did not slacken our tempo. The number of our air force has increased even more and exceeds the number in 1931-2 by more than four times.

" 'The big role in the construction of the aviation fleet played by the Young Communist League gives Soviet aviation the best human material.' "

"In conclusion, Khripin put special emphasis on the fact that the successes of Soviet aviation were secured through the direct leadership of Comrade Stalin whom he called 'the best friend of the Red air fleet.'

"A stormy ovation followed Khripin's last words:

" 'If the clattering arms of the German fascists and the fascists of other countries threaten our Soviet Union, then woe to them if our Soviet country is obliged to set in action all our instruments and weapons of defense!' "

Page 2, Daily Worker, December 1, 1936.

U. S. S. R. BOASTS OF WORLD'S LARGEST ARMY

While the Communist Party appeals to such helpers as the American League Against War and Fascism, The American Student Union, The American Youth Congress and the Young Communist League to teach disloyalty to all defense forces of the United States and urges disarmament for this country they stand solidly behind the great War Machine of the U. S. S. R. The Daily Worker, official organ of the Communist Party, U. S. A., issue of January 13, 1937, boasts of the appropriation of 20,102,200,000 rubles for the 1937 defense forces for the Soviet. This is equivalent to more than FOUR BILLIONS of dollars. Just a peacetime army—Oh yeah!

U. S. S. R. CONSTITUTION SPEAKS ON MILITARY SERVICE

"Article 132: Universal military service is the law.

"Military service in the Workers' and Peasants' Red Army is an honorable duty of the citizens of the U. S. S. R.

"Article 133: To defend the fatherland is the sacred duty of every citizen of the U. S. S. R. Treason against the country—violation of the oath, desertion to the enemy, impairing the military power of the state, or espionage on behalf of a foreign state—is punishable with the full severity of the law as the most grievous offense."

This picture is taken from Soviet Russia Today, issue of December, 1936. If, as the U. S. S. R. Constitution says above, "Treason should be met with full severity" we wonder why we do not so treat those of the Communist Party who preach treason against our government.

COMMUNIST LABOR ACTIVITIES

THE PARENT organization of Communist labor groups and Communist labor unions is the Trade Union Unity League. T.U.U.L. has as its Secretary, William Z. Foster, who is the perennial Communist candidate for President of the United States, and who, along with Earl Browder, claims to be the head of Communism in the United States. William Z. Foster returned from Moscow on or about November 5, 1935, after having spent several weeks in the U.S.S.R., attending the Seventh World Congress of the Communist International, where he again told of the growth of Communism under his leadership in the United States. The official publication of the Trade Union Unity League is "Labor Unity," published monthly at 80 East Eleventh Street, Room 326, New York City. Pat Toohey is the editor.

Report No. 2290 gives a very complete history of the Trade Union Unity League from its inception as the Trade Union Educational League, as organized in 1922:

"The Trade Union Educational League, which was organized in February, 1922, by William Z. Foster, was the official American branch of the Red International of Labor Unions, with headquarters in Moscow and closely affiliated with the Communist International. Its object was to align the organized-labor movement in the United States with Moscow. The Trade Union Educational League did not make any real progress, due to the uncompromising position taken against it by Samuel Gompers, head of the American Federation of Labor, and other union-labor leaders in the United States.

"After failing to make any appreciable progress with their revolutionary aims in the organized labor unions in this country, the Trade Union Education League was abandoned and, on August 31, 1929, at Cleveland, the Trade Union Unity League (T.U.U.L.) was organized in its place. Foster was also the guiding spirit in this movement, following orders from Moscow.

"William Z. Foster was at one time an active organizer in the American Federation of Labor, particularly in connection with the steel strike, but when he was found out to be a Communist he was expelled. He is a member of the executive bureau of the Red International of Labor Unions, twice candidate of the Communist Party for President, and is now secretary general of the Trade Union Unity League.

"The purpose of the Trade Union Unity League was to create a revolutionary organization of workers to combat the American Federation of Labor and to broaden strike struggles and give them more of a class and political character in their fight against the capitalist state and against the employers. Its predecessor, the Trade Union Educational League, had placed its main stress on the organization of a revolutionary minority in the established trade unions, whereas the Trade Union Unity League has its main task in organizing workers into independent industrial unions opposed to the American Federation of Labor.

"Skeleton forms of affiliates have been set up, none of which appears to have a large local membership, comprising workers in many of the major industries in any locality. Certain of these craft organizations maintain small headquarters in

CANNERY & AGRICULTURAL WORKERS INDUSTRIAL UNION

DISTRICT OFFICE
P.O. BOX 646, SACRAMENTO, CALIFORNIA.

CREDENTIAL

June 6 1934.

TO WHOM IT MAY CONCERN:

This is to certify that_____is duly authorized by the District Executive Committee of the CANNERY & AGRICULTURAL WORKERS INDUSTRIAL UNION to:

1. Set up locals, Ranch, Shed and Cannery Committees of the Union.

2. Issue membership books and collect dues properly receipted by initiation and dues stamps.

3. To work with locals and sections.

4. To represent the C&AWIU at all times where an attempt is being made to organize the workers for the purpose of bettering their working and living conditions.

No. 424
To be renewed after three months.

Caroline Decker
District Secretary.

Pat Chambers
District Organizer.

NOTE: Workers are requested to immediately notify the above office if this delegate is not acting in the best interest of the workers and UNION.

EDITOR'S NOTE: Photostat of Credential forms used by Communist organizers in the vegetable and cotton strikes in California. The District Secretary, Caroline Decker, and the District Organizer, Pat Chambers, are now serving prison terms in California prisons for their Communist work. The Cannery & Agricultural Workers' Industrial Union is a Communist labor union.

New York, Chicago, and elsewhere, deriving their support from collections made and assessments imposed on its scattered membership.

"The Trade Union Unity League receives the co-operation of the Workers' International Relief and the International Labor Defense, whose local secretaries or representatives act as organizers in their respective localities.

"Most of these alleged unions, affiliated with the T.U.U.L., have adopted names which correspond closely with those of established labor organizations. As an example, the United Textile Workers is a veteran organization affiliated with the American Federation of Labor, and the name adopted by the Communists for a rival organization, affiliated with the Trade Union Unity League, is the National Textile Workers' Union. Wherever located, Communists almost invariably attempt to confuse the public and newspapers into believing that their organizations are a part of the legitimate trade-union movement.

"Imitative titles are used to take advantage of a natural tendency of a potential contributor to a fund to help strikers by confusing the bad with the good. It was asserted that the average person solicited remembers that there is an established and responsible textile union, with a name that seems like that used in Communist appeals, and it is assumed to be worthy. Appeals are made by the Workers' International Relief, and the International Labor Defense to 'help feed and clothe' the children of strikers 'who are fighting under the banner of the National Textile Workers' Union.' Such appeals do not explain or inform the person solicited that the alleged strike is conducted by Communists, whose movements and activities are directed by a committee in Moscow. None of the appeals submitted in evidence and made a part of the record states that Communist leaders have even won a major strike in the United States, nor do they admit that they deserted the workers after the strikes were lost.

"In a resolution adopted at the Sixth Session of the Red International of Labor Unions' central council, held in Moscow, on February 15, 1930, on 'tasks of the Trade Union Unity League,' the following is given with reference to the growth of the Trade Union Unity League since its organization:

" 'The economic depression in the United States of America, which precipitated the great stock exchange crash and which, in turn transformed the depression into a deep economic crisis, results—through wage cuts, speed up, unemployment, Government Fascist attacks, etc.—in accelerating the tempo of the radicalization of the masses and in giving it a more definitely revolutionary character. . . .

. . . " 'The new situation in the United States of America presents a highly favorable opportunity for the growth of the Trade Union Unity League and its affiliated unions. The great task of the Trade Union Unity League is to mobilize the masses of workers in order to smash the offensive of the capitalists. . . .' "

The T.U.U.L., according to the report of William Green, President of the American Federation of Labor, has no less than twenty-one subordinate divisions. The branches or divisions of the T.U.U.L. are:

Agricultural Workers' Union

Building Workers' Industrial Union

Cleaners and Dyers Laundry Workers' Industrial Union

A. F. OF L. TRADE UNIONISTS

Read This Message From the Communists It Will Help You Win Better Conditions

TO THE MEMBERSHIP OF THE A. F. OF L.

FELLOW WORKERS:

Your delegates to the San Francisco Labor Council June 22nd, adopted a resolution denouncing the Communist participation in the Waterfront strike, and calling for a drive against all members who have Communistic leanings. This resolution was introduced by the members of the Seamen's Unions, with Scharrenberg as the leading spirit. It had the full support of the old reactionary clique of the Labor Council.

Do you realize that this means the denying your membership the right to their own political beliefs? Why should you turn your union into an agent for the Republican, Democratic or any other capitalist party and deny your members the free right to support any political party they want? You should be especially interested in favor of their supporting a working-class party — the Communist Party. The Central Labor Council endorsed Rossi for Mayor—the same Rossi who sent the cops to shoot the waterfront strikers down. Naturally, they are against the Communists. For the same reasons they are against the strike. But you shouldn't be. You should not split your ranks. The Communists are the source, and have been the best mobilizer, of support for the strike.

What motives were behind this action? Was it that the bureaucrats were interested in strengthening the unions? Were they acting as friends of the longshoremen? What is their record as "friends?"

Scharrenberg fought to charter the "Blue Book" Company unions instead of the I. L. A.

O'Connell signed a decision of the Regional Labor Board endorsing the "Blue Book" as a bona fide union.

Casey has been the chief obstacle standing in the way of a strike vote of the Teamsters.

Vandeleur ruled out of order the motion of the I. L. A. delegates for discussion of a general strike vote in support of the longshoremen

These facts speak for themselves. Their only interest is to use the A. F. of L. membership as a weapon to feather their own nests by gaining political favors for themselves from capitalist politicians.

The action of such fakers must not go unchallenged. The rank and file of each union must immediately repudiate it. Introduce a resolution into your local, demanding the right of members to their own political opinions. You must fight against making your union a tool of the Republican and Democratic parties. These same capitalist parties have been responsible for every vicious attack against striking workers. Instruct your delegates to the Labor Council to rescind their action. Fight for rank and file control of your unions. Remove the fakers who try to split your ranks.

Don't be Drawn Into Police Activity Against Your Fellow Workers who are Communists!

The Communists Party is Your Party—it Fights for Workers in All Industries—it Fights for a Workers and Farmers Government!

VOTE COMMUNIST!   JOIN THE COMMUNIST PARTY!

COMMUNIST PARTY, U. S. A.
    37 Grove Street,
    San Francisco, California.
I Want to Become a Member of the Communist Party.

Name ....

Address ....

City ....

EDITOR'S NOTE: Photostat of leaflet used by the Communist Party in their appeal to members of the A. F. of L. to join the Communist Party, U. S. A. Such actions have resulted in the heads of the A. F. of L. using every effort to remove all known Communists from their ranks.

Packing House Industrial Workers' Union
National Food Workers' Union
Jewelry Workers' Industrial Union
National Metal Workers' Industrial Workers' League
Marine Workers' Industrial Union
National Railroad Workers' Industrial League
Needle Trades Workers' Industrial League
National Auto Workers' Industrial Union
Lumber Workers' Industrial Union
National Textile Workers' Union
Independent Shoe and Leather Workers' Union
National Miners' Union
Rubber Workers' Industrial Union
Painters' Industrial Union
Furniture Workers' Industrial Union
National Miners' Union
Smelters and Oil Workers' Industrial Union
Hotel and Waiters' Industrial Union
Medical Workers' Industrial Union
Office Workers' Industrial Union
Custom Tailors' Industrial Union
Drygoods Workers' Industrial Union
Youth Committee of the Trade Union Unity League

This does not complete the list of Communist labor organizations and subdivisions in the United States. From the Green report we continue with the enumeration of the official Communist organizations in the United States, although the list can never be known completely, outside the Communist headquarters, because of the rapid change of order and the continuous change of names.

C. P. STRESSES LABOR STRIFE

The Communist Party of the United States has attempted to strengthen on every front the part its leaders could play in destroying the unity of legitimate American labor organizations. Their continuous program of destruction is well expressed in a recent pamphlet put on sale in the Communist Book Stores, written by William Z. Foster, Chairman of the Central Committee of the Communist Party, U. S. A.:

"THE COMMUNIST PARTY
From—"Unionizing STEEL," by Wm. Z. Foster—P. 15.

"Last, but by no means least, the . . . organizers of today have a great advantage over the organizers of 1919 in the fact that today there is in existence a strong Communist Party to lend its active assistance. In 1919 the Communist Party was just being born and was in no position to give material aid. But now matters are vastly different. The Communist Party is well established and has a large following in steel as well as other industries. Its members are militant workers and fighters

EDITOR'S NOTE: Two pictures taken during the Communist inspired San Francisco General Strike which disprove the Communist Press stories of police brutality. The Central Bureau of the Federated Press (Communist Press Service) on February 11, 1935, reported that Col. D. W. McCormack, U. S. Commissioner of Immigration, reports there were 400 arrests, 118 of them aliens, and only one could be subject to deportation because of radical affiliation. The authorities claim there were 909 arrests in San Francisco alone, 262 of them aliens, and 33 radicals.

and they will use the last ounce of their energy, resources and courage to make the . . . drive a complete success."

AGRICULTURAL TROUBLES

Communist agitators have also given a goodly portion of their time and effort to stirring up trouble in agriculture. California has been the center of Communistic activities on the Pacific Coast, due to the fact that California is basically an agricultural state.

The Communist Party realizes this, hence their concentration on agriculture. In one year, the Communist Party fomented strikes in California agriculture that involved over 50,000 workers, and threatened for a time to tie up California's crops entirely. Therefore, the crippling of California agriculture would indirectly affect, by a raise in price, practically all of the people of the nation.

Nathaniel Honig, nationally known Communist leader and author, candidly admits that the Communist subsidiary organization, the Cannery and Agricultural Workers' Industrial Union, fomented, organized, financed and led strikes in California which involved over 50,000 people and indirectly resulted in the San Francisco general strike.

Caroline Decker, Albert Hougardy and Pat Chambers, executive heads of the Communist agricultural movement in California, issued a statement to the effect that they were working under direct orders from Moscow in the fomenting of agricultural disturbances, would continue to call strikes in order to promote discontent, suffering and starvation, and thus promote dissatisfaction and discontent, ripening the masses for revolution.

The California farm labor difficulties have involved not alone the Communist Party and the Cannery and Agricultural Workers' Industrial Union directly, but have been the focal point for the efforts of such Communist affiliates as the Red International Labor Defense, the American Civil Liberties Union, the Trade Union Unity League, the National Students' League, and dozens of similar organizations who flock to the scene of the trouble, either inciting crowds to violence, or playing the part of Good Samaritan and providing bail and defense—thus building up their party.

The "Daily Worker," official publication of the Communist Party, U.S.A., the "Western Worker," official publication of the Communist Party, District No. 13, the magazine "New Masses" and similar Communist controlled publications, have gleefully set forth in their columns that they have cost California agriculture millions upon millions of dollars and further, that they will continue to teach California agriculture and industry a lesson.

The Communist Party, U.S.A., advised headquarters of District No. 13 of the Communist Party, that they were sending into California trained "workers" from every state in the Union, in order that they have concentrated in California for the 1935 crop season their most experienced people. District No. 13 headquarters of the Communist Party was advised that these people would start with the first crop and follow the crop season through to its conclusion. (G. F.)

Attempts are continuously being made by Communists to bore from within industrial struggles in America. The Trade Union Unity League has released a

THE EMANCIPATION OF WOMEN—or that is what they call Hard Labor in Russia. This composite picture of women busy at Forced Labor is taken from the leaflet Women in the Soviet Union, by Nurina.

publication known as "Problems of Strike Strategy," wherein instructions are given to Communists as to their duties wherever and whenever industrial upheavals take place.

Following are quotations from the above mentioned publication:

"The problem of building the revolutionary unions of the T.U.U.L.—the American Section of the Red International of Labor Unions—as well as the problem of building a mass Communist Party in the United States is largely a question of a correct strike strategy. With this is bound up the problem of destroying the reformist illusions of the American Federation of Labor and the social fascists of its Muste wing whose program is that of the Socialist Party.

"Both of these problems are inseparable from the main problem of winning the majority of the decisive sections of the working class for Communism. Seen from this standpoint the importance of the question of working out and applying a correct strike strategy is brought clearly into the foreground—for our party, for the revolutionary trade unions and for our whole class." P. 5.

"The American working class will reap a rich harvest from the study of this pamphlet and in turn, by applying the lessons herein contained, will be able to add to its growing sum of achievements in the United States and give revolutionary proletarian aid to the millions of workers and colonial peoples who are marching forward under the revolutionary banners of that Communist International and the Red International of Labor Unions." P. 8.

"In order that the workers shall not be taken unawares, the trade union opposition and the independent revolutionary unions must carry on their work in the following manner:

"It is the duty of every revolutionary union and the trade union opposition (left wing) in every industry to organize the workers for future conflicts and struggles.

"At the first appearance of symptoms of growing dissatisfaction on the part of the workers, or aggressive intentions on the part of the employers, in a given industry, the question of an approaching conflict must be brought sharply before the masses.

"Preparatory agitational and organizational work must be carried on under the following slogans: 'Do not rely on the trade union bureaucrats!' 'Take the initiative in your own hands!' 'Set up your own organizational forms!' 'Prepare for the struggle, otherwise you will be defeated!' In this agitational work all concrete cases of treachery by the trade union bureauracy in recent economic struggles must be utilized.

"It is necessary during this preparatory period, through personal conversations and pressure at meetings to single out those elements among the non-party, reformist, anarcho-syndicalist or Catholic workers who may be drawn into the struggle against the employers on the basis of our independent tactics, i. e., not dependent on the trade union bureaucracy, and to participate together with the revolutionary workers in our independent instruments of struggle (shop committees, strike committees, committees of action, etc.—Ed.)." PP. 18-19.

"The revolutionary trade unions and the trade union opposition must carefully examine and constantly check up on the work of all its instruments, from the view-

More pictures of the FREEDOM OF LABOR for women of the Sovietland. What a future for girls after college and sorority days—if we tolerate the Communist way. Top picture from Moscow News of July, 1935. Lower picture from W.W., 11/30/36.

point of contact with the mass of workers in the various factories. Especially must all signs of red tape or bureaucracy hindering them from reacting quickly to any development among the workers be combatted.

"The revolutionary trade unions and the trade union opposition must carry on all of its preparatory work in such a manner that the need for creating militant instruments to lead the struggle should emanate from the rank and file workers. This question should become the subject of discussion in all factories and shops.

"At the approach of a lockout, it is necessary to issue slogans for the creation of militant committees of struggle against the lockout, elected in the factory by all the workers, regardless of their party and trade union affiliations, organized or unorganized.

"In case of favorable conditions for a strike, and with a militant mood prevailing among the masses, the creation of strike committees (this also holds true in those cases where the strike is led by revolutionary trade unions) elected by all workers should be undertaken. Workers of all beliefs and affiliations must participate in these elections, the organized, as well as the unorganized.

"At the same time, the sharpest agitation and propaganda must be carried on among the masses against the appointment of strike committees from the top (i. e., by the bureaucrats—Trans.) and against efforts of the trade union bureaucrats to transfer the leadership in these conflicts to such committees.

"Preparation of the working masses for the struggle must be carried on not only orally, but also in the press. In this regard the trade union and party press is taxed with a serious duty. It is necessary to issue special leaflets, special supplements of the press, shop papers, etc., dealing with the approaching conflict." PP. 19-20.

"Simultaneously with the withdrawal of the revolutionary minorities from a strike committee which has fallen under the influence of the reformists, the minority must appeal to the mass of workers and organize the election of a new strike committee in order to continue the struggle." P. 25.

"No official representation of reformist trade unions should be permitted on the strike committees. The adherents of the Profintern must counteract all the efforts of the representatives of the reformist trade unions to penetrate into the strike committee by putting forth the slogan that all members of the strike committee must be elected by all the workers, organized and unorganized as well." P. 28.

"The best and most militant workers of all beliefs—Communists, Social-democrats, Catholics, unorganized, etc.—must be included in all bodies which are elected." P. 29.

"It is necessary to allow non-party and reformist workers to carry various functions within the strike committee in order that they may be drawn into the immediate struggle." P. 29.

"It is particularly helpful during the strikes and lockouts to convene special broad conferences of organized and unorganized workers (men, women and young workers), in order to pick out and place the best and most energetic of them in posts of militant leadership." PP. 29-30.

"Absolutely all workers, no matter what their beliefs and affiliations, must

Picture from Working Woman in the Soviet Union by V. Sibiriak. Would those in the United States who associate with the Communist Party and its affiliated groups like to have this future for the American mother or daughter?

be drawn into the picket line, in such a manner as to have the experienced, militant comrades working together with the unorganized workers, the social-democrats, Catholics, etc.

"The leading pickets should be carefully chosen, utilizing not only the young workers, but also the older workers, men and women, and especially workers' wives.

"Special demonstrations of strikers' wives and children against the strikebreakers and the police force defending the strikebreakers, is very effective." P. 31.

"Especial attention should be given the fight against various police and private detective organizations (factory militia, detectives, shop spies, stool pigeons, fire brigades which are part of the police force, etc.)." P. 32.

"Because of the concentration of capital and the practice of the bourgeoisie and reformists to replace strikers by obligatory arbitration, every strike acquires political character. This does not mean that all the workers understand the political, i. e., the general class significance of the current economic struggles. In this situation, it is the task of the adherents of the Profintern to teach the masses politics on the basis of the everyday struggle. This means it is necessary to issue

Women either work or face the consequence in the Soviet Union. From the Moscow News of 11/18/36. Would you like to see this for your daughter? This is the future offered for the women of the U. S. S. R.

slogans at each stage of the struggle, on the basis of the demands, which will raise the fight to a higher level." PP. 41-42.

"The enthusiasm prevailing among the masses during strikes should be utilized for strengthening the campaign for the defense of the Soviet Union." P. 42.

"In conclusion, we wish to draw to the attention of all the adherents of the Profintern that the resolutions adopted at the IX plenum of the Executive Committee of the Communist International, the IV Congress of the Red International of Trade Unions and the VI Congress of the Communist International regarding the problems of working within the trade unions are still in force. Inasmuch as the economic struggle has become the center of attention for all Communist parties, revolutionary trade unions and revolutionary opposition, the Comintern and the Profintern will most carefully follow all economic conflicts." PP. 48-49.

"Only with such combined efforts of the Comintern, the Profintern, and their affiliated organizations, is it possible, with the maximum benefit to the international working class movement, to utilize the past economic conflicts and take the leadership of the masses out of the hands of international reformism." P. 49.

It is reasonable to assume that a certain amount of the trouble in recent years in textile mills throughout the country was due to Communist influence. C. A. Hathaway, editor of the "Daily Worker," the official Communist organ of the U.S.A., has prepared and distributed a booklet known as "Communists in the Textile Strike." On Pages 7 and 8 of this booklet, Hathaway sets forth eight purposes of the Communist Party in the Textile Strike. They read as follows:

"To insure victory for the textile workers, the Communist Party further proposes:

"1. Solidarity actions by all workers, employed and unemployed, Socialist, Communist and non-party, union and non-union, textile workers and non-textile workers—a solid united front of all workers against the textile bosses and their allies.

"2. Mass picketing to close, and to keep closed, every textile mill (cotton, wool, silk, rayon, etc.), until victory is assured.

"3. Unity of employed and unemployed to force the immediate payment of adequate relief to the textile strikers and to the unemployed.

"4. United struggle of all workers against deportations, against interference with the workers' right to picket, and for the maintenance of all the workers' civil rights (right to hold strike meetings, freedom of workers' press, etc.).

"5. Rank-and-file strike committee in every mill elected by the workers themselves; similarly elected rank-and-file committees in every textile center, representing all the mills, and with complete control of the strike in their hands.

"6. No settlement of the strike by arbitration, or otherwise, until all the demands of the workers are granted; until all the demands, as listed above, are unconditionally granted, the strike is to go on with the solid and active support of the entire working class.

"7. No final settlement of the strike, on any basis, until the proposed settlement has been submitted to the strikers, ample time given to the strikers for consideration of the proposals, and an affirmative vote has been taken by the strikers accepting the proposed settlement.

"8. No section of strikers to return to work until the demands of all strikers are granted, i. e., cotton, wool, silk, and rayon workers are all to stand solidly together until each group has won its demands.

"This is a clear statement of the Communist Party's 'own philosophy' so far as the immediate strike issues are concerned."

THE EMANCIPATION OF WOMEN

A well known world traveler, who spent some time in Russia just a year ago, had this to say of the highly advertised Emancipation of Women in Russia: "Russian women now have all of the privileges of men but none of the privileges of women."

The women of the U. S. S. R. have absolute equality with men politically, economically and legally. Positively no way are women protected or favored. They are given the same work and the same wages as men. They, therefore, must fight their own battles and they must struggle for life exactly as the men do. Half of the work in the mines, factories, machine shops, railroad construction and maintenance, and in the new industrial plants is done by the women. They build tanks, airplanes, and work in the railroad yards. They are brick masons, concrete mixers; they spread asphalt and run steam rollers. The women of Russia wear men's clothes; are as dirty, grimy and as hard as the men.

A survey of the schools of Russia shows that seventy-five per cent of the medical, dental and law students are women.

See pictures of women at work on pages 231, 233, 235 and 236.

FAMILY ABOLISHED

As a result of the forced labor activities of women in the U. S. S. R., the family life has been almost completely abolished. The mother works all day. Babies are cared for in government nurseries, and the children are in government controlled schools. The father works in a factory or elsewhere. In many instances the entire family is fed in a government kitchen. This means that the so-called home is one room allocated by the government.

There is no distinction between married and unmarried mothers. The marriage ceremony is not at all held as worth while. It takes on an average of sixty seconds to record a marriage, and less time in the adjoining room to report for divorce.

INTERLOCKING RED HELPERS

Examination of the list to follow discloses the fact that many of the organizations' names are made to interlock with the wide chain of non-Communist organizations through the inclusion of a minority of non-Communist directors, or directors who are sympathetic. The balance of the enemies of labor are named as follows: Taken from page 11, Report of William Green, President, American Federation of Labor.

Workers' International Relief
National Council for the Protection of Foreign Born Workers
American Negro Labor Congress, or the League of Struggle for Negro Rights
United Farmers' League
Friends of the Soviet Unions

Labor Sports Union which is a section of the Red International of Sports Union

John Reed Clubs

United Council of Working Class Housewives

United Council of Working Class Women

Workers' Library Publishers

International Publishers

Young Communist League of America

Young Pioneers of America

Russian Co-operative Association

National Committee for the Defense of Political Prisoners

Unemployed Councils

Workers Ex-Servicemen's League

International Workers' Order

Friends of the Chinese People and Friends of the Soviet Union

United Workers' Co-operative Association which conducts camps

Russian Mutual Aid Society

Hungarian Sick and Death Benefit Society

International Workers' Orders

Proletarian Dramatic Association of America

Soviet Union Information Bureau

Amkino, U. S. Branch of Sovkino promoter of Soviet motion pictures

Workers' Schools

International Labor Defense, section of the International Red Aid

Sacco and Vanzetti Branch, Mooney-Billings Branch, John Porter Branch (colored, Lenin Branch, Olgin Branch, Freiheit and other similarly named branches)

Emergency Committee for Southern Political Prisoners

Independent Workers' Order, which is the left wing organization within the Workmen's Circle.

THE TRADE UNION UNITY LEAGUE TODAY
(Excerpts)

"The great agricultural strikes in California led by the Cannery and Agricultural Workers' Industrial Union; the militant and victorious strikes led on Munson Line ships by the Marine Workers' Industrial Union." P. 5.

"The Trade Union Unity League has been organized in Cleveland, on August 31, 1929. It was a reorganization and expansion of the old Trade Union Educational League." P. 6.

"The Trade Union Unity League grew in struggles. The Needle Trades Workers' Industrial Union led struggle after struggle of the furriers, the dressmakers and other sections of the needle industry." P. 7.

"The Marine Workers' Industrial Union was formed in 1930." P. 8.

"The National Textile Workers' Union was formed, born in struggles like that of New Bedford in 1928, involving 15,000 and those of the Gastonia cotton mill workers and other southern strikes. Before it was many months old it was playing the leading part in a strike of 25,000 Lawrence woolen mill workers for better wages. Soon after it led a series of strikes in the Rhode Island silk mills, especially in Pawtucket and Central Falls." P. 8.

"The Steel and Metal Workers' Industrial Union soon joined the militant band of industrial unions." P. 8.

"As we have shown in the first chapter, the basic policy of the Trade Union Unity League is that of class struggle." P. 9.

"The T.U.U.L. is made up of the affiliation of the National Industrial Unions, and local industrial unions which as yet have no national affiliation." P. 11.

"The Trade Union Unity League fights militantly against the imperialist war plans, and pledges the utmost struggle in defense of the Soviet Union." P. 12.

"The Steel and Metal Workers' Industrial Union led the first major strike in the steel industry since the great 1919 steel workers." P. 20.

"The Marine Workers' Industrial Union, which concentrated on the Munson Line, led strikes on thirty ships of that company in a lightning series of struggles." P. 21.

"The Cannery and Agricultural Workers' Industrial Union, in the period since N.R.A. has led over 50,000 Pacific Coast workers in strikes against their starvation conditions. Six thousand grape pickers; several thousand lettuce pickers (in two strikes); and the brilliant strike of 15,000 cotton pickers in California and Arizona." P. 21.

"The Needle Trade Workers' Industrial Union led 15,000 dressmakers in the big strike of the early fall of 1933." P. 22.

"The Food Workers' Industrial Union led close to 3,000 Negro nut pickers on strike in St. Louis in the summer of 1933." P. 22.

"The Packing House Workers' Industrial Union led 2,000 strikers in the Pittsburgh packing houses." P. 22.

"The Furniture Workers' Industrial Union led strikes in New York, Boston, Baltimore, and other cities, in the upholstery, cabinet-making, frame-making and other branches of the industry. It has 8,000 members as a result." PP. 22 and 23.

WHAT! NO STRIKES?

There is no such thing as the right to strike on any job or in any factory in Soviet Russia. Bullets or exile to Siberia would be the fate of anyone who even thought of promoting a strike. Strikers in the U. S. S. R. would be counter-revolutionists and dealt with in the same manner as those who commit an act of treason. Murderous dictatorship denies all labor the right of collective bargaining. Yet we permit Communist labor unions to promote every kind of disorder imaginable in the United States!

"In New York alone, close to 60,000 workers struck, during the 1933 strike wave, under the leadership of the Trade Union Unity League." P. 23.

"The perspective of the Trade Union Unity League is for increasing strike struggles." P. 24.

"These policies will lead to a powerful revolutionary trade union movement." P. 24.

The Trade Union Unity League is the parent organization of all Communist labor unions in the U. S. Their booklet is on sale at all Communist book stores.

Unemployed Councils

While it is true that, during the nation-wide economic situation, there has been organized a number of legitimate American unemployed groups, yet a review of the activities of unemployed councils reveals the fact that the majority are either wholly controlled or dominated, to a certain extent, by Communist influence. In quite a large number of instances, the meeting places of these unemployed councils have been used as cells for the dissemination of Communist propaganda and as focal points for Communist demonstrations.

The National Unemployed Council, U. S. A., has as its National Organizer, Herbert Benjamin, a well known American Communist, and has as its National Secretary, Israel Amter, a well known writer for Communist causes in the United States.

The story of the Communist organized and controlled Unemployed Councils can best be told by the following quotation from "Communism in the United States," written by Earl Browder, General Secretary of the Communist Party:

"The Unemployment Council movement was only in its first beginnings in 1930. Four years of rich experience in local, state and national struggles and actions, the high points of which were the great March 6, 1930, Unemployment Day Demonstrations, the National Hunger Marches in 1931 and 1932, and the recent National Unemployment Congress in Washington in February, 1934, have crystallized real mass organizations on a nation-wide scale. In the Washington Conference, which brought together the Unemployment Councils, trade unions and all forms of mass organizations that support the struggle for the Workers Unemployment Insurance Bill, there was organized representation of about 500,-000 workers."

The above mentioned unemployed councils have now officially united with the Workers' Alliances.

PASS THE SALARY INCREMENT BILL

MANHATTAN'S

Municipal Employee

MANHATTAN'S
MUNICIPAL EMPLOYEE

published by

CIVIL SERVICE BRANCH *of*
COMMUNIST PARTY

Room 500—35 East 12th St., N. Y.

*The publication of this paper involves a serious
financial burden. We consequently appeal to you to
send us as much of a contribution as you can possibly spare. Won't you mail us some money* TODAY?

The above reproduction of the front and back pages of the monthly publication
of the Communist Party Branch of Municipal Employees of New York City will
give you an idea of the strength and growth of the Communist Party in one of our
cities. Yet we are told "It can't happen here"—it can't but does.

EXCERPTS FROM "A DOCTOR DIAGNOSES RUSSIA"

By Dr. L. M. Herrington

(Dr. Herrington toured Russia believing in Communism until he saw for himself. Now he is a bitter enemy of the U. S. S. R. His comments are timely.)

"The collective operates like a stock company and is a collective movement, as the name indicates, of a great number of the peasants, working their lands together, securing farm implements for common use, all supposed to be sharing equally. This was one of the very fine ideas promulgated by Lenin." P. 17.

"The communes practically have failed." P. 18.

"Now the Central Committee of the Soviet Union has announced that a new peasant policy will be enforced, intending by this, to stimulate grain production. But the government still executes Kulaks for paying more for grain that the government agents offer for it. This is another inconsistency." P. 19.

"Past experience shows that the Soviet cannot be trusted in any promises made." P. 19.

"The Commissar passes on the fertility of the land, assigns the use of the commons for pasturage, assesses the taxes, determines the amount of wood each peasant may take from the state forest, and distributes the funds raised for the support of the aged and indigent." P. 20.

"That his salary is only $32 a month." P. 20.

"The last man we visited had a wife and six children. They lived in the most abject poverty, without even a straw pallet to cover the boards upon which they slept." P. 21.

"When zero weather descended on the district, his family all crowded on top of the big brick stove for warmth, as they had little in the way of clothing and no bedding." PP. 21-22.

"It is difficult to hire help in Russia—not that there is not plenty of man power. . . . But if you live on another man's efforts in Russia, even if you pay him, you must pay the government a tax of twice the amount you receive from his labor. The same is true in some kinds of business there, if you earn a dollar in trade, you are taxed two dollars." P. 28.

"Industrial co-operation is unheard of in Russia." P. 32.

"Recently the Soviets have made an important gesture toward impressing American coal operators by sending a shipload of coal to the United States and selling it below the cost of mining it, to say nothing of the cost of transporting it here." P. 33.

"They point with pride to the fact that Russia delivered coal to Boston and sold it at $5.50 a ton." P. 33.

"But here are the facts. The Soviets admit they pay their miners $2.04 a day in Russia. But they do not say that much of the mining might be done by forced or convict labor." P. 33.

"In textile groups, some female workers received 23.8 rubles, equivalent in purchasing power to $6, a month." P. 34.

"More attention is given to the use of arms and the gas mask than any other activities.

"The Soviets are anxious to train the rising generation in the thorough knowledge of warfare, not only for the purpose of defense, but to hasten a world-wide revolution, aiming at the universal establishment of Communism. For this poverty-stricken government, without money, not able even to repair its own property, must rely upon outside contributions if it wants to add to its revenue." P. 35.

"Moscow is the Museum of the Revolution, in which is demonstrated every manner and form of the most rabid Socialistic propaganda. Pictures of Lenin and the scenes in which he took a leading part predominate." P. 43.

"A huge map shows the entire Eastern hemisphere to be Red with arrows of expectancy pointing toward North and South America." P. 43.

"The thinking persons wonder why the Soviet Government does not make needed improvements at home with what money it has, instead of using that money to proselyte in other countries. Communism would gain far more friends, if, in Russia, it was shown to have acted advantageously and to the benefit of the people." PP. 43 and 44.

"Divorce is easy to secure. One needs only to request it in writing by filling out a regular official form and showing proof of identity and paying a small fee. This fee first was 15 cents, but now is graduated according to the income of the person concerned and may be as high as 50 cents." P. 57.

"Either party can obtain the separation by mere application without the consent or even knowledge of the other. A card is sent to the other person stating that he or she no longer is united in the bonds of matrimony to the former wife or husband." PP. 57-58.

"We glanced into the birth registration room and we saw the first couple which had come in to be married registering the birth of their child—and this often happens." P. 59.

"Communists are forbidden to marry by a church ceremony." P. 59.

"The fact that hospitals and physicians are permitted and, many times, ordered by the government to perform abortions, especially for the student class and for the women who belong to the unions." P. 60.

"These abortions are permitted. If the husband and wife are not economically situated to care for children, or after the birth of a child, or after registering as students." P. 60.

"Unmarried women who prove that they are financially unable to support a child also may secure these permits." P. 60.

"The Russian child is given sex education early, but is cautioned against marriage. Insurmountable bans are placed against emigration, yet abortions and birth control are favored." P. 61.

"We have no guarantee that Sovietism over here would be any better than Sovietism there." P. 65.

"Although Atheism looms high in the system, and, I have heard, 20 per cent of the schools have been closed at one time because of physical and moral degeneration." P. 72.

"Compulsory education is impossible because of the lack of room. It is strange that Russia should be so poor when the leaders have confiscated so much wealth, but the explanation is that these leaders have no idea of economy or of sensible appropriations." P. 72.

"In Russia we found we dared not express ourselves openly, nor did anyone else so dare." P. 74.

"In Leningrad we talked to our taxi driver, a Jew. He said, very quietly, 'I would be the happiest man in the world if I could get out of Russia. It is abominable here.'" P. 75.

"Recently, October, 1930, 150 peasants were slain trying to leave Russia. Petty laws permit Soviet rule to make prisoners of the peasants and the bourgeoisie in any numbers to suit their needs for labor, so no wonder Russia can put up a bluff of cheap production. And tourists in Russia virtually are prisoners while there." P. 88.

"It is charged that a half million dollars of Communistic money poured into Western Pennsylvania during the last coal strike, and that the greater part of these funds was expended in Allegheny county." P. 106.

"No property is safe. Human life is cheap. No man's home is his castle. Nationalization extends even to the children. The family as a unit of civilization is doomed. Divorce is a mere formality. Human nature is taking on the ways of the wolf. The predatory instinct is paramount." P. 110.

"Starving, barefooted, ragged peasants do not care how much grain is to be raised in the future nor whether 20,000,000 pairs of shoes will be manufactured a year for 150,000,000 persons as was the case in 1929, the present is what the sufferers have in mind." P. 111.

"The 'Communist Program-Destruction,' tells of the itemized list which appeared in the Moscow, Pravada, the Communist paper in Russia, giving the number of political executions which took place under Soviet rule up to July, 1921. In this list of 1,250,000 souls, the largest single item was of 800,000 peasants." P. 115.

"The government taxes everything, oil, income, food, land, and hundreds of other things. Yet the Soviets cannot exist on the total, large as it is." P. 116.

"The Soviet regime does not deserve nor command the respect of other nations nor their confidence, because it does not recognize the sacredness of agreements, contracts nor treaties, and it attempts to overthrow every other government. Every Communist is favorable to a world revolution, and woe to the world if the Communists have their way." P. 118.

"Human experience teaches us that no nation can deny God and live. Russia is attempting to set up Atheism as its ethical system." P. 54.

"The young Communists are using every means at hand, backed by the Soviet regime, to destroy every vestige of religion." P. 54.

"The Communists sing ribald songs, put on sacreligious plays, and, upon Holy Days, install speakers on the streets and through these broadcast every possible vulgar, atheistic utterance." P. 54.

"From its first year in school the Russian child is taught 'Religion is the opiate of the people." P. 55.

"They offer nothing to replace Christian faith, but memories of Lenin." P. 56.

"No school teacher is permitted to attend church; he is disgraced and looses his job if he does." P. 56.

"There is neither free speech, free press, free religion nor even free thought in Russia." P. 74.

COMMUNISM VS. RELIGION
The Church and the U. S. S. R.

Sunday has been abolished. In fact, there is no designation of any day except by number. All holidays have been abolished to make certain that there can be no remaining memory of church holidays. A few churches remain, but they are now public museums of hatred for a belief in God. Displays of material things and a hatred for the spiritual replace the statuary and mosaics which originally lined the walls of the world renowned Cathedrals of Russia. Bolshevism has substituted Marx and Stalin for God and Lenin for Christ.

It is considered a counter-revolutionary act to possess a Bible. No member of the Communist Party can remain a member if he attends a religious ceremony or reports that he still believes in God.

Hatred for religion is taught as a part of the educational system in the schools of the U. S. S. R.

When one considers the history of Communism in Russia and the blunt admissions of Communist leaders in the United States, it seems incredible that some persons holding responsible positions of leadership in churches of this nation should, by word of mouth, by the written word, and by public actions, give aid and comfort to the efforts of the Soviet agents to Communize America—America, the nation which was founded upon the principles of the right of every citizen to worship God according to his own belief.

The history of Communism in Russia is one of absolute denial of the right of any citizen to worship God in any form—a denial that is enforced, if need be, by firing squads and the sharp end of bayonets. Religion has been driven from Russia, the churches have been seized and either destroyed or turned into club or business facilities; the Russian youth is being taught to believe that there is no God, and that religion was fostered solely for the purpose of crushing the so-called proletariat. We have published heretofore, and will publish hereafter, the sworn statements of Communist leaders in this country that this is the kind of system they propose to set up in America—if they can continue to win the support of the church leaders.

The American Legion does not believe for a minute that even a tithe of the splendid church men and women of this nation support such doctrines. To do so would be to admit that America is Communist, which it is not. We are generous enough to hope that the leaders who now give aid and comfort to Communist principles are themselves deceived. It is our duty, however, to bring before the American people the statements that have been published in various church periodicals and other media of publicity, confident in the belief that the vast body of church members in this nation will repudiate such actions and demand that they be discontinued. It is for this reason alone that we present the facts.

The following quotation was taken from "Soviet Russia and Religion," by Corliss Lamont.

"Today, of course, no church in Soviet Russia owns any land or building." P. 7.

NOTE: A reproduction of a poster used in Moscow.

"Contrary to the general impression, atheism is not an essential condition for entrance into the Communist Party of Russia (or of any other country).

"A great many churches have been closed in the Soviet Union since the Revolution and either demolished or put to such secular uses as serving as schools, recreation centers, or museums." P. 9.

"Whether country or city is concerned, the anti-religious campaign in the Soviet Union actively puts into practice the statement of Lenin that it is essential to give the masses of the people 'the greatest variety of atheist propaganda material— to acquaint them with facts from the most diversified forms of life. Every way of approach to them must be tried in order to interest them, to rouse them from their religious slumber, to shake them up by most varied ways and means.' The educational attack on religion in the U. S. S. R. follows out this counsel by utilizing every conceivable device that might help uproot the superstitions of the workers and peasants. Anti-religious books, magazines, newspapers, motion pictures, plays, lectures, and radio broadcasts sweep the country. In many of the higher educational institutions there are special anti-religious departments.

"Noteworthy in the larger cities are the anti-religious museums, several of which I inspected on my visit to the Soviet Union." P. 10-11.

SUNDAY ABOLISHED

"Both in order to increase productivity and at the same time to cut down on the length and strain of the working week the Soviet Government has drastically altered the religious basis of holidays in the U. S. S. R. In the urban centers it decreed a rest day for every sixth day, regardless of the exact day of the week. This, of course, has weakened greatly the influence of Sunday as a religious holiday." P. 11.

"The truth is that the social roots of religion are well on the way towards being totally abolished in Soviet Russia." P. 13.

"They are giving up the idea of immortality because they have the chance to lead happy and abundant lives on this earth. And they no longer require the moral sanctions of Christianity because the principles of Marxism are providing them with an all-inclusive and integrated code of life that unifies the country as a whole and also the individual personalities within it." P. 13.

"It now remains to be asked to what extent the anti-religious campaign has been successful. The most recent figures were announced at the meeting held in Moscow in February, 1936, to celebrate the tenth anniversary of the founding of the Union of Militant Atheists. The Union now boasts a membership of more than 5,000,000 with 50,000 active local organizations. There is also the youth section, the Young Militant Atheists, who number over 2,000,000. During its existence the Union has published more than 1,000 anti-religious titles, with the actual total of books and pamphlets issued running into several millions.

"Emelian Yaroslavsky, old Bolshevik and friend of Lenin's, who is President of the Union of Militant Atheists, claims that there are approximately 40,000,000 active atheists in the U. S. S. R. out of a population now close to 170,000,000." P. 18.

"The Red Army is one of the most active centers for the dissemination of

NOTE: A reproduction of a poster used in Moscow. No explanation is needed.

atheism. Its recruits are given systematic instruction in anti-religious theory just as they are in other Communist doctrines. And at least 75 per cent of the Red Army men declare themselves against religion before they are dismissed from service." P. 19.

"Religion Doomed in U. S. S. R.

"There is little reason to believe that Soviet Russia will in the course of time return to some species of religion, refined or otherwise." P. 23.

In making a study of this particular phase of Communist activities, we find in a book entitled, "Teachings of Marx for Boys and Girls," prepared by William Montgomery Brown, who was thrown out of the House of Bishops of the Episcopal Church in this country because of his Communist activities, the following quotations:

"Religion is a dangerous dope because it takes the people's minds off their misery and their poverty."

"Religion is dope like opium."

"Well, religion acts the same on the poor American as opium does on the Chinese Coolie."

"Now you will understand one of the most famous sayings of the great Karl Marx. He said, 'Religion is the opium of the people.' It makes them dream of a heaven in which they will be rewarded forever. if they suffer patiently the hell they have on earth.

"The preacher dopes them with his sermon. Then they go home dreaming about the beautiful heaven which is no more real than the beautiful palace of the Chinaman's opium dreams."

Going further with the research of Religion and Communism, we quote the following from a book, entitled "Religion and Communism," prepared by Earl Browder, General Secretary of the Communist Party, U.S.A., which is now being distributed by the Workers' Library Publishers of New York City:

"From this estimate of the social role of religion, it is quite clear that the Communist Party is the enemy of religion. We Communists try to do the opposite of what we hold religion does."

From the foregoing quotation, you can readily see that the leaders of the Communist Party in the United States are following in the footsteps of Karl Marx, in the teaching of Communism to their followers in this country. There are some church leaders in America today who claim that they are only liberals and are only interested in the social well-being of the unfortunate citizen of their congregation and community, yet we find them, either unfortunately or without the proper knowledge, co-operating with Communist leaders and Communist programs. This will be more convincing to you when you read the following quotations from the pen of Earl Browder, General Secretary of the Communist Party, U.S.A.:

[1]"You may be interested in knowing that we have preachers, preachers active in churches, who are members of the Communist Party. *There are churches in the United States where the preachers preach Communism from the pulpits;* in a very primitive form, of course. In one particular church service described to me, the

---

[1]This entire quotation is from the report of Browder on Communism in the U. S.—not a report from the U. S. S. R.

NOTE: A reproduction of a poster used in Moscow, which shows the industrialist week dumping Jesus Christ overboard.

substance of the sermon was that the Communists were the Angels of God that had been sent like Moses to lead the people from the wilderness, while the representatives of the devil were the capitalists and their agents. This, of course, is not an expression of the official Communist attitude on these questions, as you will understand; but we do not expel such persons from the Party."

As has just been stated, the compilers of this publication do not attempt in any way to classify or leave the impression that all church groups, whether co-operating or sympathizing in any way whatsoever with radical propaganda, are actual members of the Communist Party, yet they are using their publications for the dissemination of propaganda which is definitely in support of the Communist program.

Angelo Herndon, to whom the following editorial refers, *is an admitted Communist from Atlanta, Georgia,* which admission is even traced to the official report of the American Civil Liberties Union, which organization claims to be only interested in civil liberties, even while defending Communists and criminals, and an organization that has many prominent church people listed as its Directors. Herndon recently traveled throughout the country on a lecture tour, under the sponsorship and supervision of the much publicized International Labor Defense, another Communist defense group.

The following editorial is reprinted from the Christian Century magazine, which carries the slogan, "A Journal of Religion." The quotation is taken from the October 30, 1935, issue.

"ANGELO HERNDON MUST GO TO CHAIN GANG

"Last week's refusal by the Supreme Court to review the action of the Georgia courts in convicting and sentencing Angelo Herndon means that this young radical must go to the chain gang for from eighteen to twenty years unless Governor Talmadge intervenes with a pardon. Such a sentence, if carried into effect, is probably equivalent to a death sentence. It is impossible to believe that young Herndon—whose physique is anything but rugged—can survive a generation of such torture. Without attempting to go into all the details of the Herndon case, it can be said that it gives every promise of becoming even more famous in the history of radical movements than the case of Tom Mooney or of Sacco and Vanzetti. Herndon on the chain gang will be a perfect symbol for radicals of the brutality and injustice of the present American order. After all, it is possible for the conservative to argue that the conviction of Mooney or of Sacco and Vanzetti at the most represented only a mistake in the identification of culprits—a matter not necessarily connected with the class struggle. Scores of persons were killed in the San Francisco parade explosion, and the Massachusetts paymaster was undeniably murdered. In other words, Mooney, Sacco and Vanzetti were at least allegedly punished for actual crimes. But nothing happened to bring this savage punishment down on Herndon. Nothing was involved except a protest at a relief station in which nobody was hurt. But a society with nerves jumpy over an alleged red menace seized on this trifling incident to revive a forgotten law—passed to deal with a Negro uprising feared in 1866—as a means of inflicting a punishment which is nothing more or less than

THE NEW "STAR OF BETHLEHEM"

by Phil Bard

NOTE: The following reproduction of a cartoon is taken from the last page of "The Daily Worker," official publication of the Communist Party, U. S. A. It clearly displays the attitude of the Communist toward religion. P. 6, D.W., 12/25/35.

social sadism. The south should take the lead in asking Governor Talmadge to pardon Herndon."

In the chapter of this publication having to do with the Communist fight against the adequate defense of this country, it was clearly shown that their propaganda always seeks to tear down interest in R. O. T. C. and in military training of all kinds, likewise in the maintenance of an adequate system of internal national defense for the United States of America, but, at the same time, paints in glowing terms the fact that the U. S. S. R. maintains a vast army and the greatest organized reserve of any nation in the world. It is interesting, therefore, to note that a great number of our religious groups and their publications continuously fight to diminish or totally abolish the internal national defense of this country. In this connection, we quote an article from the Christian Century of June 12, 1935, and the reader's attention is especially directed to the fact that the Young Communist League was given a place among the sponsoring organizations.

"YOUTH GROUP ORGANIZES TO OPPOSE WAR

"The regional youth conference in Denver sponsored by the co-operating churches and national youth groups has resulted in the organization of a vigorous youth peace action group in Denver. Its personnel consists of delegates selected by the churches, Christian associations, and labor youth groups. Comprehensive programs and resolutions have been accepted by the group. They held a 'United Youth Day' program on Memorial day in the Denver Civic Center. An anti-war play was presented and addresses were given by Carle Whitehead, a prominent Socialist, and several of the young people. *The 'Young Communist League' was given a place among the sponsoring organizations."*

Going further in our review of the subject matter of religious publications, we find a publication, entitled "Unity," which has the slogan, "Freedom, Fellowship and Character in Religion." The editor of this publication, at a mass meeting in Union Square in New York City, made the following pronouncement:

"If war comes, I will not fight; if war comes, I will not enlist; if war comes, I will not be conscripted; if war comes, I will do nothing to support it; if war comes, I will do everything to oppose it, so help me God."

The following article taken from the September 16, 1935, issue of "Unity," has to do with Henri Barbusse, the French Communist, who was one of the organizers of the League Against War and Fascism:

"It was fitting that Henri Barbusse should have died in Moscow, for all his later years were devoted to Communism. But he will be remembered little for his political activities as compared with his literary achievements. He gained his fame and bade for immortality as the author of 'Le Feu,' published in 1916, at the very height of the War. There have been many war books since this first masterpiece. The latest of them all, 'Paths of Glory,' by Humphrey Cobb, is perhaps nearer to Barbusse's work in character and power than any of the others. But 'Le Feu' still holds, and we believe will ever hold, its primacy. As it was the first, so it remains the greatest, of all the imaginative studies of the Great War. The book was based, of course, upon reality—Barbusse's own experience as a soldier of France! But it

was shot through and through with such vision and beauty, such grandeur of con-
ception and idealism, that it took its place at once as one of the great epics of all
time. We think of it as we think of Dante's 'Divine Comedy,' as a work of almost
incredible range and splendor. Who that has read it can ever forget the closing
chapters describing the little group of French soldiers, lost in the sea of mud on the
western battlefront, discoursing of war and peace? It is not surprising that 'Le Feu'
made such a sensation. Not only was it a book of cosmic proportions and power,
but it was the first of all the revelations of what war is today in this modern machine
age. It was only when we had read Barbusse that we really understood the meaning
of front-line trenches, and 'no man's land' and 'going over the top,' and machine
guns, and barrages, and Flanders mud, and disease, and death, and horror. Of
course, France and the Allies had to suppress the book, but it lived, and will ever
live. It was inevitable, after the War, and Barbusse should become a leader in the
anti-war movement. His 'Clarte' was a powerful propaganda treatise for peace, but
it was not literature, and never took rank with 'Le Feu.' To the end Barbusse's
passion was for a war-less world. This was his appeal on his visit to this country
a year or so ago, when we saw and met him.. A great spirit has found its rest!"

To further show to the readers of this publication the fact that the Communist
Party and its affiliated and sympathetic groups in America are not only attempting
to build a hatred of God and all forms of religion, but are also blasphemous in their
work in this connection, we re-print here a little play which was produced in Los
Angeles, California, Sunday evening June 13, 1931, at the American Civil Liberties
Forum, Music-Art Hall, 233 South Broadway, to a packed house, at which Reverend
Clinton J. Taft, Executive Secretary and Editor of the Los Angeles Branch of the
A. C. L. U., acted as Chairman, Leader, Director, Announcer and Manager.

"Rev. Taft, as per custom, first introduced Prof. Briggs, who gave the usual
cynical, sneering, and subversive talk on 'Current Events.'

"Rev. Taft then introduced the famous Communist leader and platform speaker,
'Mother' Bloor, who gave, and very cleverly and with much virility for her 60 odd
years, her denunciatory and inflammatory and impassioned philippic against the
U. S. Government and for the Workers' Government.

"Rev. Taft then announced that 'nobody must leave, the meeting is not by any
means through; we are now about to have presented to us a one-act play by The
'Rebel Players,' entitled 'Mr. God Is Not In.'

"THE BLASPHEMY

"Now, with the above setting, get the play:

"The stage is a modern business office, with a large office desk in the center,
and a stenographer-secretary's desk on the right.

" 'God' walks onto the stage. Our Heavenly Father is portrayed by a cocky,
slangy, cigar-smoking young man of 25 or so, dressed in ordinary business clothes.

" 'St. Peter,' his confidential secretary, dressed in a short hospital gown to
represent a white robe, but with his golf knickers loudly evident below, follows
'God' on, and taking his cigar from his mouth rushes over as 'God' seats himself,
and affixes a brass wire halo, which he ostentatiously brushes off, to the back of
'God's' chair.

"A young widow in distress forces her way in past some angel-clerks in the outer office, and says she has been directed by her pastor to 'take her troubles to "God".' 'God,' palpably vexed, bawls out 'St. Peter' for letting her bother him on this, 'my busy day'; but upon her insistence he directs 'St. Peter' to 'Give her blank form No. 58 to fill out.' 'Peter' gives her a blank, and a push toward the outer office.

"Two 'gentlemen' enter: One is a respectable attorney in cutaway, who is introduced as a 'very proper person,' by the gentleman with him, who then introduces himself as the 'Very Reverend Doctor Such and Such, A.M., D.D., Ph.D., and ————' (an obscene word spelled out). This man is of course dressed in clerical garb; and, most interestingly to all members of the Masonic fraternity, the frock coat he wore was a uniform dress coat of the Knights Templar!

"Much business of affable and chummy handshaking and backslapping. 'Come again, gents, glad to see you any time,' says 'God.'

"HIGH PRESSURE SALESMEN

"Then are introduced two young egotistical, cock-sure, cigar-chewing advertising salesmen. These two young blades, one with a derby and the other with a fancy straw hat, worn at intervals as they sit on the corners of 'God's' desk, proceed to high-pressure 'God' into signing a contract for a half million dollar advertising campaign for the purpose of cutting into the more prosperous resort business which Heaven's chief competitor, Hell, is enjoying.

" 'God,' after these two go-getters have had him in a close literal huddle at his desk, finally signs on th dotted line. The salesmen slap him on the back, give him a cigar, which 'St. Peter' promptly lights for him with a cigar lighter. Magnanimously, in parting, these two salesmen say, 'God,' old man, since this is a highly religious enterprise, we'll do this job for only 15% commission instead of our customary 20%!'

"The troubled widow again breaks into the office, just at the moment that 'God' and 'St. Peter' are preparing to go out to the golf links. 'St. Peter' angrily upbraids her for crashing in, and grabs the blank form from her hands. He scans it, and then gives her a cruel scolding because she has failed to state her politics in the space provided!

"Another woman suppliant, ineffectually retarded by angel clerks, comes in and says she has been sent to 'God' for advice. The first woman, in a revulsion of hate and despair, breaks into sardonic bitter laughter and screams to the other woman:

" 'You fool! You are a fool! I was such a fool as you, but I'm not any longer!'

"The woman said:

" 'But I must have help to live!' The first woman replies, shrieking:

" 'Help? Help from "God?" The only place you will find help is where I am now going: onto the street!'

"The women leave by one exit, 'God' and 'St. Peter' by the other. Curtain.

"Profanity was frequent, and came from the mouths of the Salesmen, 'St. Peter,' and 'God' himself. But in all instances, in place of the name of the Deity, the actors said 'by yourself,' and 'God' swore by saying 'by myself.'

"Allusions to the Christ were such as:

" 'The youngster,' 'how has he been since he got back?' etc.

"And the Rev. Clinton J. Taft, pleased at the limit audience which very evidently greatly enjoyed this play, announced an early forthcoming play of similar character to be given by these same 'Rebel Players.'

"And the Rev. Clinton J. Taft urged his hearers to interest themselves in the displayed Communist, Atheist and Anarchist papers, magazines, books, pamphlets and hand-bills of forthcoming events under the auspices of these afore-named groups and those of the Civil Liberties Union." (M. K.)

IS SABOTAGE THE CHRISTIAN WAY TO PEACE?

The following article, entitled, "A Decision Must Be Made!" written by Winifred L. Chappell, Secretary of the Methodist Federation for Social Service, appeared in the March 3, 1934, issue of the Epworth Herald; it is self-explanatory:

"Young church fellows of draft age must decide something when war breaks out. I say when rather than if, for though the pending war could even yet be stopped if enough people did the necessary thing about it, the fact is that today the peace forces are doing almost nothing, while the war makers are as busy as bees and the forces that make for war are running forward headlong.

"In general these youth have four choices instead of two as most of them think. First they can conform, yield to the draft, play the game of the war makers, be cannon fodder, get shot or gassed or blinded or delegged or dearmed—but, if possible, beat 'the enemy' to it and shoot, gas, blind, dearm the fellows on the other side first.

"In the second place, they can be conscientious objectors and go to prison. A few score did that during the World War; a few hundred or thousand will do it next time. That takes even more courage than to go over the top. It takes just as much physical courage—the C.O.'s (Conscientious Objectors) in some prisons during the World War were subjected to extremely cruel treatment. And, in addition, it takes moral courage of a type and degree impossible in peace time to measure or comprehend. When the country is suddenly set toward war—when moved by persuasive picture and radio by persuasive voice, when the press, the pulpit, the schoolroom, the conversation of all the people, the enticements of the blonde or the brunette beauty, are for 'patriotism,' for defense of one's country, for bayoneting the enemy, what unspeakably clear thinking and brave doing it takes to be a C. O.! them held traitors offsets the help it gives. His preacher must be with him. If you will be a C. O., insist that your pastor stand back of you. Our church has spoken.

"If the fellow's parents are with him it helps some—unless the burden of having Just now, while peace is still here, the tide in the church is running pretty strongly in the direction of refusal to bear arms. Also in the schools that point of view is getting something more than a hearing. Several Methodist youth at this very hour are forfeiting their greatly desired college courses, because they refuse preparation to participate in the war game. In at least one or two of our universities some

students and faculty members are preparing to see to it that the resources of the
public speaking, the literature, the chemical, and technological departments are not
used for war, not, at least, without the public knowing all about it. In Great Britain
the famous Oxford Union has publicly stated that it will not, in the event of war,
defend king and country.

"But now a third choice, hardly so much as even heard of during the World
War, appears in this possibility: Stay out of jail—why thus separate yourself from
the masses? Why thus let yourself be put out of the game? *Accept the draft, take
the drill, go into the camps and onto the battlefield, or into the munitions factories
and transportation work—but sabotage war preparations and war. Be agitators for
sabotage.* Down tools when the order is to make and load munitions. Spoil war
materials and machinery.

"If, thinking realistically of this third way, you shrink violently back because
you see that it means deceit, lies, by word and deed, the answer is that if you choose
the first way, the 'honorable' way of patriotism, then also will you have to lie and
deceive—that's part of war. Nor will you wholly escape these ungodly practices
if you make the second choice. Very likely, for instance, you will be called on to
give evidence against other C. O.'s. Will you do it or will you lie in their behalf?

"*The fourth choice* is really a further development of the third. *It calls for
sabotage but with the deliberate, conscious, informed intent to get rid of the present
economic system, of which war is a part, and to build a new world to the existence
of which peace is a necessity.*

"*If you will make this choice, make it now and begin to meet, before war breaks,
with others of like purpose and of iron will to carry out the purpose.* This means
knowing what selfish capitalism is like, not just in general, but in particular—not
flinching even from knowing by name and specific deed the big profit takers who
have betrayed the people—how they have profited from the starvation of children;
how they have called upon police and militia, club and gas bomb and machine gun
to put down the workers when they have cried for bread.

"And it is not enough to know about capitalism. Also you must know with
mind and emotion and will to achieve, the kind of new society you want. Those
who would build the new world must look with wide, appraising eyes at the good
earth's resources and at man's brilliant achievements in converting the resources
into usable and beautiful forms, and at man's organizational power and knowledge
to transport the things garnered and made to meet the needs of the remotest peoples.
They must want desperately that all the peoples of the world should be set free
forever from poverty and given a chance at culture, beauty and spirituality.

"Youth in the Christian church must wake up, or they are not going to be the
leaders in the programs here described. *We church folk are getting little or no teaching or training in the hard matter of turning the war situation, when it is here, into
a deliberate program for a new social order.* It is well, then, for the fellows who are
earmarked for cannon fodder and for aiming their targets (targets being a soft word
for the most diabolical equipment for killing that an age of science and technology
can devise) at the boys in the enemy camp, to begin to make contact with others with

the same ideals, and begin to study these possibilities—and others you may think of —in the light of Christian teachings.

"High ideals will give zest to the task—but it is a grim way. Perhaps church boys (and though I write of boys, the girls have almost precisely the same choices to make) are right in thinking that for them there are but two choices—war or jail."

In 1935, The American Legion, along with other American patriotic groups, sponsored various types of legislation in the State Legislatures and in the Congress of the United States, which, if enacted into law, would have gone far toward the goal of dispersing the organized programs of Communism and other types of un-American activities from this country. Again we find the Social Service section of the Epworth Herald joining hands with Communists and their affiliated and sympathetic groups in a battle to defeat all such types of legislation. In support of this statement, we quote you from the Epworth Herald of April 20, 1935.

"Bills are now 'in committee' which, if passed, will seriously threaten the rights of free speech. The proposed laws in this 'patriotic legislation' include:

"1. A Federal sedition law to punish advocacy of the violent overthrow of Government, or membership in any organization which teaches such a doctrine.

"2. An act excluding from the mails all matter which advocates overthrowing the Government by force and violence, assaulting or killing Federal officers, or unlawful destruction of property, and sabotage.

"3. An act penalizing any attempt to incite disaffection or insubordination in the armed forces of the United States.

"4. The creation of a special agency in the Department of Justice to investigate subversive activities.

"*Write to the Methodist Federation of Social Service, 150 Fifth Avenue, New York City, and enclose a stamp for a copy of 'The Social Question Bulletin' for January, 1935, which explains these issues and tells why the bills should be killed by the committees now considering them and how you may help to prevent their being passed by writing to senators and congressmen. Watch the actions of your state legislatures, for such bills are being presented in nearly every state in the Union, and be prepared to protest to your state representatives and senators, too.*"

During the month of September, 1935, under the auspices of the Methodist Federation for Social Service, a two-day retreat was held in Pittsburgh, Pa. A number of ministers, who were either officers, members, or worked with the Methodist Federation for Social Service, discussed activities having to do with the defense of the radical element within the Church. A portion of the discussion which took place is set forth in a mimeographed bulletin mailed under date of October 15, 1935, by the committee which was composed of the following:

Lee H. Ball, Catskill, New York
George Lackland, New Haven, Connecticut
Herbert N. Shenton, New York City
Ralph B. Urmy, Westfield, New Jersey
William B. Waltmire, Chicago, Illinois
Loyd S. Worley, New Haven, Connecticut.

From a copy of this mimeographed bulletin, which was mailed to many ministers throughout the United States and which Bishop Francis J. McConnell accepts as a fair and accurate account of the discussion at the conference, we have taken the following excerpts:

"First, we are impressed by the utter necessity of a united front among Methodist liberals and radicals. There is the action of our Chicago laymen, the attack of the Hearst press against Methodist "reds," the new anti-red drive of the American Legion and the American Federation of Labor and the Catholic church—all of which point to a rising tory mood within our own churches. The lay and clerical reactionaries in the Methodist church are going to bring all the pressure they can muster (which is considerable) against Methodist liberals at the General Conference next May. And our MFSS will be the spearhead which will have to bear the brunt of this tory reaction. . . . Methodist liberals and radicals must present a united front next May, or separately be overwhelmed."

"But in the Methodist church some of us are again going to have to raise the proposition that Methodists have always stood for political freedom. That is to say, any Methodist, if he sees fit, has the right to be a member of the Communist Party and remain a member (or minister) of the Methodist church, in good standing, without being subject to any criticism or official octracism. . . . No Methodist should be called upon to explain why he is a Socialist or Communist. . . ."

All emphasis shown by italics in quoted sections of the foregoing chapter is by the editors and is emphasized for the purpose of calling the special attention of the reader to those sections of the quotations.

SOVIET PROPAGANDA IN CHURCH PUBLICATION

In the January 20, 1937, issue of The Christian Century, a "so-called" journal of religion which has often carried different types of Soviet propaganda, we find an article entitled "The Soviets Face a Warring World," written by Anna Louise Strong. The contents of the article are purely Communist propaganda, telling in glowing terms of the much talked of workers' Eutopia in the U. S. S. R.

As stated, the article speaks for itself as far as Communist propaganda is concerned, but of further significance is the fact that it was written by Anna Louise Strong, who is Associate Editor of the Moscow News and who is now touring the United States (February, 1937), filling speaking engagements under the sponsorship of the Friends of the Soviet Union. She is also a contributing editor to "Soviet Russia Today," another Communist propaganda sheet, and a correspondent for the Federated Press, a Communist supporting press service in the United States of America. Miss Strong is the daughter of Reverend Sidney D. Strong, a well-known writer of pamphlets of different kinds.

The article referred to is reprinted here to show the type of Soviet propaganda being used in The Christian Century, a "so-called" journal of religion:

"Two events during the past year absorbed the attention of all Soviet citizens: the adoption of the new Soviet constitution and the civil war in Spain. Two chief moods, similarly, dominate their outlook as they face the future: confident pride in the achievements of their socialist state mingled with apprehension lest swift war engulf the world.

"When The Christian Century asked me to tell what the 'thoughtful Soviet citizen' sees as he faces the world's future, I had a threefold reaction. 'Why ask me? Why not ask instead some Soviet citizen?' . . . Then I remembered how a Soviet leader had told me: 'The mind of our people is changing so fast under the conditions of socialism that we find it increasingly difficult to speak to the rest of the world. When H. G. Wells was here, he hardly understood a word we said to him.' Yes, it is difficult, and every year makes it harder for men whose minds were formed by capitalism to understand the men who live in the U. S. S. R. Soviet citizens would not know how to tell you; so I, who commute between Moscow and New York, must attempt the task.

I

"Why not quote the latest speech of Stalin or Litvinoff? Are they not 'thoughtful Soviet citizens'? Such was my next thought. Indeed, it is their thoughtfulness which makes them noted among Soviet citizens, who prize them for the depth of their analysis of world affairs. Not five per cent of the people in the U. S. S. R. today would disagree with Stalin's analysis. But I realize that Americans do not expect political leaders or foreign ministers to express 'the mind of a country,' nor have most Americans the patience and intellectual seriousness to read through one of those reports of Stalin's which millions of Soviet citizens avidly study.

"Who is the thoughtful Soviet citizen? This was my next reaction. In America one implies by this word some doctor, professor, lawyer, one of those 'intellectuals' who make a profession of thought. Added to these a small percentage of progressive business men and intelligent workers. But truly I would ask a Soviet cotton-picker about the world and expect to get much the same reaction as if I asked a professor. A much larger percentage of Soviet folk are thinking seriously about the world and its future than in any other country. The cotton-picker would put his thoughts more crudely and perhaps more picturesquely. But the basic reaction would be the same.

" 'There are no more officer-kulak-pigs on the Don! The old unequal, exploiting life is over! We Cossacks got eighty million bushels more grain this year than last! Our combine operators hold the all-Union record, harvesting 12,500 acres this season on a single combine!' This is the way the Cossack farmers expressed it, bringing their greeting to the constitutional congress. They added: 'The people of our villages sent us here to tell you that we are heart and soul with the Spanish people in their fight against fascism, and ready any moment to go and help them.'

"Liubchenko, head of the government of the Ukraine, is a much more seasoned speaker, with a much wider vision than these Cossack farmers. But his outlook is the same, expressed not in terms of a few farms but of a country the size of Poland. In a masterly speech he compared what has happened to Poland since the World War with what has happened to the Ukraine. Both were pieces of former tsarist Russia, roughly equal in size, population and industries. He noted 250,000 unemployed in Poland. 'We have forgotten what unemployment is like in the Ukraine. Polish industry decays, her schools close. But the Ukraine is a flourishing land of wheat and sugar, of coal and steel and chemicals, well able to defend itself and its

socialist fatherland. If it had not been for Soviet power, the Ukraine today would be·
like Poland, ruined and drained of its wealth by foreign imperialists.'

"Pride in socialist achievement, on the scale of a single farm, a factory or a
whole country. This is the note you hear most often in Russia. Indeed, the Soviets
have something to be proud of. During the past twelve years while the rest of the
world went backward Soviet industry increased sevenfold, her farm production rose
fifty per cent, her total national wealth rose fourfold. Best of all, every citizen knows
that all this increasing wealth is the property of the whole people; it is his, for his
children's children. His to hold, to enjoy, to increase, to defend. 'The land, its
natural resources, waters, forests, mills, factories, mines, railroads, water and air
transport, banks, means of communication, large scale farm enterprises, as well as
the essential housing facilities in city and industrial localities are state property, that
is, the property of the whole state.' Thus run the words of the new constitution.

"The greatest political event in the U. S. S. R. the past year has been the
nation-wide discussion of this constitution. Published in preliminary draft in June,
it went out to the people for consideration. Sixty million copies were circulated in
a short time in pamphlet form, besides thirty-seven million copies in the newspapers. No document in the world's history ever had a publication approaching
this. It was discussed in 527,000 meetings attended by thirty-six million people.
These people turned in 154,000 proposed amendments and additions, all of which
were printed and considered, though the number that actually went into the constitution numbered forty-three. But everyone cheers the constitution and is glad to
have had a hand in making suggestions, even if they weren't all adopted.

II

" 'With golden letters our constitution is written in the history of mankind,'
said a blacksmith-delegate to the constitutional congress. 'We were lifted to a great
height and saw the whole path of our future,' a Leningrad mechanic wrote to his
wife of Stalin's report. What is it that Soviet citizens see in their constitution which
makes them study it for months and grow rapturous over its import. They see in it
the dividing line between two world epochs, the epoch of capitalism and the epoch
of socialism. They believe they have made an unparalleled contribution to mankind, that future generations will look back at them as the originators of a new era.

"Many Americans are so little 'thoughtful citizens' that they think a new era
can be created by simply voting a good man into power. Soviet citizens are more
sophisticated. They know that a long, painful struggle is needed. First to seize and
hold the basic economic power for the people, the power that inheres in ownership
of the means of production and of life. Next to develop these publicly owned resources honestly, fighting down the attempts of private interests to take or corrupt
them, building up slowly in the population new habits of conscientious industry and
care for the public properties. To this task the U. S. S. R. has devoted itself for
nearly two decades. Now, in the words of Stalin, they consider 'socialism, the first
and lower stage of communism,' achieved.

"The constitution is the seal on their achievement. It is the first expression in
basic law of the world's first socialist state. It announces confidently and for the
first time the new 'rights of man' under socialism. The right to work is guaranteed

to every citizen; unemployment has ceased since 1931 and Soviet citizens are confident that under socialism it need never reappear. With this goes the right to leisure, insured by the seven-hour day and annual vacations with pay. The right to education is insured not only by free tuition up through the university but by stipends for student support which last year totaled three per cent of the entire government budget.

"The right to maintenance in sickness, disability and old age is another constitutional right of the citizens of a socialist state. Last year the U. S. S. R. spent one-tenth of its national income on its social insurance. The funds are not yet large enough to give full support to everyone who is thus pensioned. But for the first time in history a government dares assume the responsibility for maintenance of its citizens during work, while preparing for work and when no longer able to work.

"This is only the beginning of the rights of man under socialism, which Soviet citizens believe marks a new epoch. Absolute equality for women and for all races 'in economic, governmental, cultural, social and political rights' is another announcement in the constitution; in this also the U. S. S. R. leads the world. For this and for similar reasons, Soviet citizens believe they have the honor of leading mankind into the next stage of human progress.

"But if this proud consciousness forms half the world outlook of the Soviet citizen as he faces 1937, the other half of his outlook is full of apprehension for the future. For he looks beyond his borders and sees a capitalist world in which war grows apace. The Soviets themselves have felt compelled to curtail the extent of their possible production of peacetime commodities in the interests of adequate military preparation against the threat that advances against both their borders.

III

"Since the World War no year has passed in which wars, of greater or less importance, were not being waged in the world. Today war flames in Spain, in China and Manchuria; it has not yet died out in Abyssinia; tomorrow it may burn more widely through Europe. The Soviet citizen believes that the world is in a more or less continuous state of war which may last for years, even for decades. History may not say that the World War ended in 1918. Only its first acute phase ended; it was followed by a chronic war condition which will last as long as capitalism survives. This chronic war condition may perhaps be damped down and somewhat kept from flaming till the forces of capitalism itself are worn out. Or, what seems today more likely, war may flame out in an acute form which might set back for decades the productive forces and the civilization of the world.

"The Soviet citizen holds that wars are the inevitable outgrowth of capitalist competition for world markets. Nonetheless every particular war has a particular cause, and these causes may be sought out and dealt with and that particular war prevented. The whole Soviet attitude towards foreign politics today is to seek out these causes and try to overcome them, to stop war, to put it off, to damp it down, to lessen it. For though world war would in the Soviet opinion, bring world revolution, it might so destroy the world that the present generation could never know a good life. But if peace can be maintained, capitalism will nonetheless destroy itself, more slowly perhaps, but just as inevitably and with much less suffering.

"Fascism, in the opinion of the Soviet citizen, is the great war menace today. Not because Italians and Germans are worse than the rest of us, but because capitalism of those lands is more hard pressed, and at its death grapple. Hence it assumes brutally dictatorial forms in order to survive. It presses beyond its borders, sending armed intervention into Spain. If fascism is imposed on Spain by foreign intervention, no country will be safe. In Czechoslovakia Hitler will subsidize a revolt of the German minority; in France he will back the Croix de Feu. One country after another in Europe may enter the fascist condition of internal suppression and outward belligerence, till Europe goes down in war.

IV

"As the Soviet citizen looks on the world outside his borders, what does he see? He sees democracy retreating in most of the capitalist countries. Of twenty-six countries in Europe sixteen, or two-thirds of Europe, are fascist or semi-fascist; in only ten do the democratic forms survive. Even in those ten democracy is under attack; the protagonists of armed suppression of democracy find hearers even in France and England. Moreover, when the Spanish democracy is attacked by a handful of generals aided by the armed might of Italy and Germany, the democracies of the world are afraid to act. They retreat before the fascists; in their fear of entanglement they forget international law that has been sanctioned for generations. Even in the most democratic capitalist countries, the powers of big business side with the armed fascist suppression of the Spanish people.

"The democratic forces of the world demand for human beings the 'right to life, liberty and the pursuit of happiness,' even if this means that capitalism must go. If capitalism cannot furnish these, if capitalism is bankrupt, human life, the people, can go on without capitalism. The democratic forces of the world have not perhaps made up their mind yet that they cannot improve capitalism. But they are on their way. And in the final struggle their choice is fixed, for human beings against property.

"Against them stand the dark forces which declare that the ancient property forms must survive, at whatever cost in human life. That, basically, is the characistic of fascism. Whatever it may cost in suppression, whatever it may cost in war, the privileges of property must remain.

"Between these two groups the struggle is for life and death. The Soviet Union in this struggle is naturally on the side of the democratic forces. The feeling of the Soviet people for the Spanish democracy is so deep that they raised twelve million dollars in contributions for the women and children of Spain. Every lecturer on Spain who goes to the Soviet factories is asked: 'When are we going to be properly helping Spain?'

"The Soviet citizen has no antipathy toward any nation as such. He distinguishes always between the people and their rulers. 'We have no other sentiments toward the great German people except those of friendship and sincerity,' said Premier Molotov amid stormy applause of the constitutional congress. He added: 'But the fascist gentlemen had best be classed as belonging to a special nation of cannibals, that is, maneaters.'

"Although the fascist states drive toward war and organize for war, the Soviet citizen nonetheless does not believe in forming an international bloc against the fascist states. He believes in forming collective agreements against war, agreements of mutual protection against invasion, but he believes in leaving these agreements open to the fascist countries to enter also. He would not set up one military alliance against another. He would set up as wide a collective agreement as possible through the League of Nations, and invite others to join.

"For the nineteen years of its existence, the Soviet has struggled for peace. It is still struggling. By world-wide publicity, by appeals to the conscience of nations, by pacts of mutual assistance, and by announcing the might of its own defense. 'I am proud,' said Litvinoff when he appeared before the Soviet government to receive the Order of Lenin, 'in the consciousness that in endeavoring to give all the services in my power to our great socialist fatherland, I am at the same time serving all peoples, all humanity. Soviet diplomacy is a struggle for peace and peace is necessary for mankind. We want peace not only for ourselves but for all nations.'

V

"The Soviet citizen knows that the chances of war loom dark ahead. But in spite of this he feels confident, not only for his own country but for the future of the world. For his own country he says in the words of Litvinoff: 'Our Soviet Union is strong. It is strong in the unity, fitting together and working order of all its parts. It is strong in the aspirations of all the peoples inhabiting it and the unity of the aim inspiring them. It is strong in its true democracy. It is strong in the great sympathy and love felt for it by millions of toiling folk beyond its borders.'

" 'Our country was once the most oppressed in the world,' said a Russian official to me. 'And now it is the happiest. And the luckiest—oh, incredibly the luckiest. Now when all the world slips further and further toward chaos and fierce struggle, we know that our children are safe. . . . Oh, there will be battles in plenty as the old system struggles with its doom. In every other land there will yet be great strife and deeds of horror. But we have made our revolution and our land is unified and strong. Our border cities may suffer. But the heart of our land is safe. Our farms will expand and our children go to school in peace, through all the coming decades of great wars. . . .'

" 'We shall continue to struggle for peace, to mitigate as far as we may the horrors of the difficult change the world will yet pass through. But if the worst comes to the worst, we known our socialist state will survive all shocks, and will preserve and carry forward the forms of life and society that are needed to rebuild the world.' "

FASCISM IN THE UNITED STATES

Fascism has been defined in the American press in the following manner:

"Fascism aims at a totalitarian state—i. e., a highly centralized government under control of a political group which allows no representation to other political parties. The individual is subordinated to the good of the state.

"The Fascist program has always resulted in a dictatorship.

"Mussolini founded the Fascist movement in 1919 and it seized power in 1922, following the famed 'March on Rome.' Germany, under Hitler, is the second outstanding example of a Fascist state."

Members of The American Legion and other American citizens are not concerned over the form of government adopted by the two nations referred to in the definition of Fascism. It is none of our business what form of government foreign nations see fit to adopt. Our concern enters the picture only when or if the agency of government or citizens of one or more of those foreign powers attempt to spread propaganda in the United States designed to forceably change our form of government.

It has been charged that the National Americanism Commission devoted entirely too much space in its book "ISMS" to Communism as compared to the mention of Fascism. We have accepted this challenge and have sought authentic information from every conceivable source in order to provide factual data for you on Fascist activities under foreign control in this country. In dealing with the subject of Fascism, the compilers of this publication will only use information which is absolutely authentic and which has been substantiated by evidence in the files of the National Americanism Commission. In treating the subject of Communism in the foregoing chapters of this book nothing but authentic facts were used. The same is true of this chapter.

Every organization or individual suggesting a broader expose of Fascism to the office of the National Americanism Commission has been contacted immediately for authentic information. In the majority of cases we found they were unable to produce anything other than hearsay. In the cases of other organizations such as the American Civil Liberties Union and the American League Against War and Fascism, both of which groups have been mentioned at length in the earlier sections of this book, we find an entirely different definition of Fascism. When such organizations as these two refer to Fascism, they apparently mean to refer to every individual or group in the United States opposed to their individual programs; particularly those who oppose Communism. For example, the following letter from Roger N. Baldwin, Director of the American Civil Liberties Union, whose written statement on page — is indeed interesting, defines Fascism in the following manner:

> "In reply to yours of December 2nd, we will get together the material you request and send it as promptly as possible.
>
> "What we cover is not only the activity of Fascist organizations inspired from abroad, but corresponding movements among Americans, either definitely committed to Fascist tactics or objectives, or so operating that in effect they head in that direction.

"As you will doubtless agree, the measure of Fascism in any country is the extent to which labor and radical movements are suppressed by force and are thus denied their democratic rights."

The Executive Secretary of the American League Against War and Fascism in his definition of Fascism, given from the following letter, also shows that he is not referring to the foreign dictatorship but concerned primarily with the affairs of organizations in the United States which oppose his group:

"Dr. Ward has asked me to reply to your letter of December 2nd requesting material and information regarding Fascist activities in the United States.

"Under separate cover we are sending you several of our publications that deal with this issue. Please note that we put more stress on Fascist tendencies that are developing indigenously than upon those coming from the outside. On the latter point we enclose list of organizations and materials for further information.

"I trust you are aware of the large amount of material in the report of the Dickstein Committee. Likewise, you will find a pamphlet published by the American Civil Liberties Union entitled 'Shirts' to be a valuable source of information. It was written by Travis Hope and published in June, 1934.

"I trust that this information will be useful to you."

This difference of opinion and definition of Fascism in the United States clearly shows the reason for our demands for actual information and proof. We are not willing, as other people have done, to call every person a Fascist who is opposed to Communism. Neither are we willing to apply the term of "Fascist" to all of those persons who oppose our viewpoint. We are concerned only with any efforts which might be carried on within the United States by friends of a foreign government which seeks to establish a Fascist dictatorship in the United States by means of propaganda or force to replace our constitutional form of government.

The following excerpt on Fascist activities in the United States is taken from Report No. 153 of the McCormack un-American Activities Investigating Committee which reported to the House of Representatives its findings, in February, 1935.

"There have been isolated cases of activity by organizations which seemed to be guided by the fascisti principle, which the committee investigated and found that they had made no progress.

"However, in the latter part of December evidence was received from sources worthy of credence that would justify an investigation, if time and funds permitted, tending to show Fascist activity by an Italian vice-consul at Detroit, Mich.

"This evidence was submitted in affidavit form, the originals of which have been sent to the State Department. The evidence submitted warranted and justified an investigation, which the termination of the committee (Jan. 3, 1935) did not permit. The chairman of the committee (Mr. McCormack) has conferred with the State Department in relation to the evidence submitted, and has been assured that an 'energetic investigation is being made.'

"The committee has recently received evidence which justifies an inquiry showing interference by a consul of the Mexican Government assigned to San Bernardino, Calif., with the religious practices and religious freedom of some of our people.

"This evidence has been submitted to the State Department and assurances have been given that an immediate inquiry will be made.

———

"This committee asserts that any efforts based on lines as suggested in the foregoing and leading off to the extreme right, are just as bad as efforts which would lead to the extreme left.

"Armed forces for the purpose of establishing a dictatorship by means of Fascism or a dictatorship through the instrumentality of the proletariat, or a dictatorship predicated in part on racial and religious hatreds, have no place in this country."

NAZI-ISM IN THE UNITED STATES

Since we have classified the existing government of Germany as a Fascist dictatorship, we must in fairness present this complete text of the report of the McCormack un-American Activities Investigating Committee, made to the House of Representatives, in February, 1935, of that committee's findings on the spread of Nazi propaganda within the limits of the United States.

"We would not be fully responsive to our duty if we failed to compliment the twenty-odd million Americans of German birth or descent who have refused to participate in the Nazi movement and propaganda in this country, which the evidence plainly shows have been founded, in the main, on racial and religious prejudices.

"This committee has had evidence to show the strenuous efforts made to enlist these twenty-odd million persons. This committee has evidence to show the wiles and blandishments that were employed, and when these failed, the scurrilous attacks that were utilized, in an effort to bring them into the Nazi program.

"Again, this committee compliments in the highest terms those people who have adhered to the American principles and American ideals, because they have made this country their homeland and because they believe in the rights of equality granted under our form of government.

"This committee has unearthed evidence showing that an effort to spread the theory of the National Socialist German Labor Party, commonly referred to as the Nazi philosophy, had been under way in the United States for several years.

"In order to simplify matters, we shall divide the Nazi activities into two periods, the first covering all of the time prior to the designation of Adolph Hitler as Chancellor of Germany, and the second, covering the period after Adolph Hitler became Chancellor and to the present time. By way of explanation, it should be stated that up until the time that Adolph Hitler became Chancellor, the National Socialist German Labor Party was a minority political party in Germany.

"The first real representative of the National Socialist German Labor Party of which this committee has definite knowledge, was one Kurt Georg Wilhelm Luedecke, who admitted under oath before this committee that he utilized his position of traveling representative for a German commercial house as a smoke-screen behind which to disseminate his propaganda in the United States, in an effort to gain adherents and financial support for the Nazi movement.

"Luedecke, on his own admission, stated that while he was here acting as a propagandist for a minor political party in Germany, he gained access not only to the press galleries of the Congress, but also to press gatherings in the White House.

"During this time, Luedecke established in Brookline, Mass., what was known as the 'Swasticka Press,' in one issue of which he said:

" 'We repudiate the doctrine of popular sovereignty. Believing in the authority of leadership, in the value of personality, we advocate a state of truly sovereign authority, which dominates all the forces of the Nation, co-ordinating them, solidifying them, and directing them towards the higher ends of national life; an authority which is at the same time in constant touch with the masses, guiding and educating them, and looking after their interest.'

"Luedecke characterized himself as No. 7 in the Nazi Party, designating Adolph Hitler as No. 1. He boasted of this friendship with all the heads of the various branches of the Nazi Party and the Nazi Government of Germany (pp. 96-138, N. Y. 12.)

"During this first period, as we have characterized it, efforts were inaugurated by individuals and groups who believed in the policies of the National Socialist German Labor Party to establish them here. This committee has evidence of such efforts, particularly in the cities of New York and vicinity, Chicago and Los Angeles. They sought diligently to bind together in this country people of German birth and German descent into a political group that was and was to be directed from abroad, in distinct violation of every known American principle.

"These individuals organized a group which became known as 'Teutonia,' and which, through various stages, finally became known, after the advent of Adolph Hitler as Chancellor, as 'The Friends of New Germany,' which brings us to the second period of activity.

"Early in the history of 'The Friends of New Germany' the leadership was usurped by one Heinz Spanknoebel, an alien, who entered this country claiming to be a clergyman.

"One of his first activities was to take over, by intimidation and without compensation, a small newspaper in New York published by the German Legion, which paper he largely financed by subsidies under the guise of advertisements granted him by the German steamship lines as well as the German railways (pp. 229-245, D. C. 4).

"Documentary evidence before the committee obtained from the companies shows that this subsidy was ordered from Germany and amounted, in the case of the steamship lines, to $600 per month and in the case of the railways to $200 per month without regard to the amount of space used. The evidence established that Spanknoebel ordered another American-German paper in New York City to discontinue its publication, which order, while resented, was complied with. The evidence also shows that he undertook to determine and supervise the news and editorial policy of certain other American newspapers, and that in at least one case his orders were refused and his efforts resisted (pp. 17-37, N. Y. 7).

"He also became very active in and obtained control of the Stahlhelm, a German veterans' organization, causing those members who were opposed to his policies to withdraw, and utilized the remainder of the membership and this organization in the Nazi movement (pp. 308-331, D. C. 4).

"Through devious methods he gained control of the United German Societies of New York, a body in that city composed of delegates from many American-German organizations, causing a breach among the members which has not yet been healed. As a result of such efforts Spanknoebel exerted tremendous influence on the various organizations, most of which had been in existence for decades in the United States.

"Successful efforts were made to establish locals or units of 'The Friends of New Germany' in many other American cities, the membership consisting in the main of aliens. The evidence clearly shows that the movement received the direct and indirect aid of certain accredited German representatives to this country (D. C. 4 and N. Y. 7).

"In the fall of 1933 a Federal grand jury in New York City indicted Spanknoe-bel for failing to register as the agent of a foreign country, and he is now a fugitive from justice.

"His successor, Fritz Gissibl, one of the original founders of the 'Teutonia,' also an alien, then became the leader of the Nazi group in this country and carried on the same general activities (pp. 71-145, D. C. 4).

"Later Gissibl was succeeded by one Reinhold Walter, who is a citizen of this country. This was done in an effort to give the organization the appearance of being 'American' in character, although Walter admitted to the committee that Gissibl remained the real head of the movement and continued to dominate its policies, although he, Walter, desired to divorce the organization from its German connections. Mr. Walter was succeeded in July, 1934, by Huber Schnuch, a naturalized citizen and college graduate, who was chosen for the position by Gissibl and continued Gissibl's policies. He is the present party leader (pp. 37-62, N. Y. 7).

"Although started seven or eight years ago, its self-appointed leaders did not seek to charter their organization until the fall of 1934. Recently Justice Edward J. McGoldrick of the Supreme Court, New York County, N. Y., refused to grant them a charter.

"However, lack of a charter, lack of a constitution or bylaws or any of the steps usually taken by American organizations did not hinder these leaders from functioning.

"The evidence plainly shows that they took orders not only from the National Socialist German Labor Party, but from some members of the Cabinet of that country.

"This committee found indisputable evidence to show that certain German consuls in this country, with all the appurtenances of diplomatic immunity, violated the pledge and properties of diplomatic status and engaged in vicious and un-American propaganda activities, paying for it in cash, in the hope that it could not be traced (pp. 14-32, D. C. 4; pp. 87-110, N. Y. 7; pp. 3-14, D. C. 4).

"One of the transactions in question, which can be found in the evidence taken by this committee, goes to the German Embassy itself, and until recently no effort was made to stop such practices (pp. 14-32, D. C. 4; pp. 703-727, D. C. 6 II).

"Several American firms and American citizens as individuals sold their services for express propaganda purposes, making their contracts with and accepting compensation from foreign business firms. The firms in question were Carl Byoir & Associates and Ivy Lee-T. J. Ross. The owner of the Ivy Lee-T. J. Ross firm admitted to the committee that the reports he furnished to the I. G. Farben Industrie, his ostensible employer, dealt with public and political questions rather than trade promotion, and that they were intended to be relayed to the German Government. For this service he received $25,000, all payments of which were in cash, and an effort was made to secrete the connections. Mr. Lee also admitted that he had never made such a contract before (p. 192, N. Y. 7).

"Carl Dickey, junior partner of Carl Byoir & Associates, testified that his firm handled the contract with the German Tourist Bureau with the fee for services set at $6,000 per month. He testified that the contract was secured with the help of George Sylvester Viereck, who received $1,750 per month with free office space and secretary as his share of the $6,000. The committee finds that the services rendered by Carl Byoir & Associates were largely of a propaganda nature (pp. 33-67, D. C. 4).

"Viereck admitted that he discussed the Byoir contract with a German Cabinet officer before it was entered into. He further testified that he had also been paid the sum of $500 monthly 'for 4 or 5 months' by Dr. Kiep, former German Consul-General in New York City, which was paid in cash for advice of a propaganda nature (pp. 87-111, N. Y. 7).

"The first payment on the contract, amounting to $4,000, was made by Dr. Kiep, German Consul-General in New York City, in cash.

"The National Socialist German Labor Party, through its various agencies, furnished tons of propaganda literature, which in most cases was smuggled into this country. Some of it, however, came through our Customs, because there is no law against it.

"With the advent of Adolph Hitler as Chancellor, efforts to obtain supporters for the Nazi movement were redoubled in the United States. Campaigns were conducted, gigantic mass meetings held, literature of the vilest kind was disseminated and the short-wave radio was added to the effort.

"Orders were issued in Germany and transmitted to the United States ordering certain lines of conduct in connection with this movement. Evidence shows, in one case, that when German officials ordered certain people in the United States to give up their membership in the Nazi Party of Germany or to resign from The Friends of New Germany, the head of the latter organization made a trip abroad at its expense to protest, which protest was made to party officials in Germany (pp. 71-145, D. C. 4).

"There is ample evidence showing a dual allegiance to this country and to Germany on the part of those interested in this movement.

"German steamship lines not only brought over propaganda, but transported back and forth certain American citizens without cost, for the purpose of having them write and speak favorably of the German Nation. A German steamship company's records show that some of these persons received free transportation at the request of the German Ambassador 'in the interest of the State.' Members of the crews of these ships carried messages between party officials in Germany and leaders of the Nazi groups here (pp. 17-37, N. Y. 7).

"It was quite a common occurrence for steamship companies to invite residents in this country to attend social parties on board ships while they were in port and persons attending these parties were addressed by representatives from Nazi organizations abroad on the subject of Nazi-ism and the philosophies of the National Socialist German Labor Party.

"It is also important to note that the conditions of membership in 'The Friends of New Germany' were the same as membership in the National Socialist German Labor Party; that its principles were the same; that it permitted only those of so-called 'Aryan blood,' born in Germany or of German descent, to join, and that it was fashioned entirely along the lines of the Nazi Party of Germany; that it was receiving and recognized orders from Germany; that it was for all practical purposes, if not in fact, the American section of the Nazi movement of Germany, designed to influence, if necessary and possible, our governmental policies. The evidence conclusively shows that this movement in the United States is inconsistent with our principles of government (D. C. 4).

"The membership lists of 'The Friends of New Germany' showed a large number of aliens who, although they have resided in this country for a number of years, had never made an effort to obtain their first papers to become citizens. Yet, these self-same aliens sought to dictate to American citizens and to find fault with the American philosophy of government.

"The following table of the membership of 'The Friends of New Germany' in Chicago taken from sworn testimony given by the secretary of the organization shows clearly the preponderance of aliens in the organization:

Alien:		Naturalized:	
Germans	146	German birth	84
Austrian	2	Austrian birth	2
Swiss	1		
	—	Total	86
Total	149	Unknown, German birth	2
United States citizens, native born	2	Grand total	239

(Pp. 648-654, D. C. 6 II.)

"Others who became naturalized evidently felt that this conferred upon them a dual citizenship. Some employees of the steamship lines, who are naturalized American citizens, went so far as to maintain a permanent residence abroad, to pay taxes abroad, and to have their families live abroad continuously (pp. 163-214, D. C. 6).

"The organization known as 'The Friends of New Germany,' through a subsidiary organization, in July, 1934, conducted so-called 'youth summer camps' at different localities, at which camps nothing of American history or of American principles of government were taught, even to the children of American citizens of German extraction, to say nothing of the children of aliens.

"On the contrary, the children were taught to recognize Chancellor Hitler as their leader, to salute him on all occasions, and to believe that the principles of government taught by him were superior to the principles of our Government.

"At these camps the official language was German, the swastika flag was prominently displayed at the headquarters tent, and at morning and evening exercises the flag was saluted in Nazi style, and the director of the camp, in charge of these children, was an alien who displayed unusual ignorance of many of the principles of the United States Government, and whose personal allegiance was solely to the German Government and its present ruler (pp. 75-95, N. Y. 12).

"An instance showing the close connection between the Nazi movement in this country and the Nazi Party in Germany, and of the close connection between the Nazi Party in Germany and the Government of that country, is the case of Ernest Berkenhoff. This man was a Nazi storm troop leader (captain) residing at Asslar, Germany. In September, 1934, he applied to the foreign bureau of the Nazi Party for a 60-day leave of absence for the purpose of visiting the United States on business.

"Documents in his possession showed that he was first instructed by the Nazi

Party officers in Germany to report to the 'local' of the party in New York City and the address given him in Germany at which to report was that of 'The Friends of New Germany' in New York City. Subsequently, the party authorities in Germany wrote him that they found the party in Germany had no 'local' in New York City and directed him to 'report' to the consul-general of Germany at New York City (pp. 41-67, N. Y. 12).

"During the past two years this country has been flooded with propaganda material dealing with the Treaty of Versailles and also extensively devoted to defamatory statements, the purpose of which was to create racial and religious intolerance in the United States. The author and publisher of such propaganda was Dr. Otto H. F. Vollbehr, a citizen of Germany, who in recent years sold to our Government certain rare books and other incunabula for which he received the sum of $1,500,000.

"Dr. Vollbehr testified before a subcommittee in New York City that he had paid many thousands of dollars of his own funds to circularize these various 'memoranda.' He also admitted furnishing Americans with material for lectures and articles to present a pro-Nazi point of view.

"In the course of his testimony Dr. Vollbehr stated that he had been warned by Dr. Hans Luther, German Ambassador to the United States, not to 'mix in American politics.'

"He further testified, under oath, that he did not intend to return to Germany for some time, that he would desist in his propaganda activities and that the bulk of his funds were in Germany.

"Investigators of the committee have found, however, that he left for Germany despite his testimony, within ten days, and that while Vollbehr was in Germany, in January, 1935, another 'memoranda' of similar character, was circulated in the United States from his address at Los Angeles.

"Within recent weeks Vollbehr has again entered this country. He has been coming here for 35 years and although for the past several years he has had an immigration visa, he has never seen fit to take out his first citizenship papers, and as a German citizen continues his propaganda efforts while in this country (pp. 703-727, D. C. 6 II).

"The testimony also shows that the 'Friends of New Germany' had a select committee, known as the 'Uschla,' appointed by the party leaders to hear all complaints against members for violations of the rules, regulations, and orders of the movement in the United States, and that some of the recommendations of such committee were forwarded to the proper officials in Germany for final action (pp. 10-41, N. Y. 12).

"This report can only touch upon the highlights contained in thousands of pages of testimony.

"From the evidence taken by this committee in its investigation of Nazi-ism in the United States it develops that all kinds of efforts and influence, short of violence and force, were used to obtain its desired objective, which was to consolidate persons of German birth or descent, if possible, into one group, subject to dictation from abroad.

"When this committee was appointed the Nazi movement had made considerable headway, greater in its influence than its actual membership would indicate.

Its efforts and activity, particularly with reference to its intolerance features, were disturbing.

"The disclosures made by the committee not only have stopped their progress and caused the activities of certain German accredited representatives to this country to cease, but a disintegration of the movement has and is taking place. Efforts are still being made by the leaders of the movement but without the success that they heretofore enjoyed.

"This committee condemns the establishment and the propaganda of the Nazi principles in this country. We are unalterably opposed to any individual or any group of individuals seeking to bring about discord among the people of this country, either as a reprisal or as a means of changing our form of government."

NAZI DRILLS TROOPS IN UNITED STATES

The following interesting testimony is taken from public hearings held before a special committee, House of Representatives, on un-American activities held in New York City, October 16, 1934. This testimony discloses information to substantiate the fact that leaders of foreign governments made definite attempts to set up a defense in the United States for their form of government:

"Statement of Frederich Karl Kruppa

"(The witness had previously been sworn.)

"The Chairman: The committee will come to order. Congressman Dickstein.

"Mr. Dickstein: Getting back to the boats for a question or two. Since the organization or the creation of the National Socialist Party under the direction of the Hitler government, the German boats are under the control of the National Socialist Party That is, the North German Lloyd and Hamburg American Lines?

"Mr. Kruppa: Yes.

"Mr. Dickstein: Then they have a number of what we call "tramp steamers," that go to the southern part of the United States, tramp steamers that bring in material?

"Mr. Kruppa: Yes, I understand.

"Mr. Dickstein: In these big ships they have what they call a leader on each boat?

"Mr. Kruppa: Also on the small ones.

"Mr. Dickstein: On the small ones, too?

"Mr. Kruppa: Yes.

"Mr. Dickstein: That leader is looked upon, is he not, as the "big boss" of the boat?

"Mr. Kruppa: Correct.

"Mr. Dickstein: He is bigger than the captain of the boat?

"Mr. Kruppa: To some extent.

"Mr. Dickstein: Then he creates groups or cells, as you have answered the question?

"Mr. Kruppa: Yes.

"Mr. Dickstein: And then this leader delivers a certain number of instructions once or twice a day to the so-called "seamen" who are on the boats, how, when they get to the United States, and get their shore leave, they should conduct themselves with regard to spreading this movement among the people they come in contact with. Am I correct in saying that?

"Mr. Kruppa: Yes; to some extent.

"Mr. Dickstein: To some extent?

"Mr. Kruppa: Yes.

"Mr. Dickstein: To what extent; do you know?

"Mr. Kruppa: For instance, the troopers that appeared at meetings within the Friends of New Germany in the early beginning appeared or tried to connect each other with the German element in the United States.

"Mr. Dickstein: How many seamen has the Bremen?

"Mr. Kruppa: I think approximately 800.

"Mr. Dickstein: About 800?

"Mr. Kruppa: Yes, sir.

"Mr. Dickstein: They all get a shore leave of how many days?

"Mr. Kruppa: It is a shore leave according to the time and hours they have; but being in the harbor, it means they are working 8 hours, and the rest of the day belongs to them.

"Mr. Dickstein: They get a shore leave and are permitted to go—

"Mr. Kruppa: Anywhere.

"Mr. Dickstein: Anywhere they want to go?

"Mr. Kruppa: Yes.

"Mr. Dickstein: When they get that leave of absence, it is at that time that that stuff is being taken off or smuggled off?

"Mr. Kruppa: Correct.

"Mr. Dickstein: Is it at that time that they wrap themselves around with these loose sheets, books, and so forth, and distribute them among the Friends of New Germany or the American people?

"Mr. Kruppa: Yes.

"Mr. Dickstein: Do they have any drills on these boats insofar as propaganda is concerned with regard to the seamen?

"Mr. Kruppa: I am not informed on that.

"Mr. Dickstein: You are not? All right, then.

"The committee's attention has been called to the next most important point—that is, that these so-called "alien troopers" drill every week or twice a week out in the fields of Long Island, Jersey, and Irvington. Can you give us something about that?

"Mr. Kruppa: Yes. The way they are drilled, the commands are given by certain wehrsporttafel. It means "defenseport table." This table is brought from Germany, and it instructs the boys how to form formations and what are the commands, and how to work in different groups or in defense or attack, and so forth. I have a copy of this with me. This is officially acknowledged with the leader.

"Mr. Dickstein: That is a document that is brought from Germany?

"Mr. Kruppa: Yes.

"Mr. Dickstein: That is the official program with regard to the storm troops?

"Mr. Kruppa: Yes.

"Mr. Dickstein: That is the direction as to how they shall drill and in what manner they should drill in the United States?

"Mr. Kruppa: Of course.

"Mr. Dickstein: These drills that take place in the early morning are on the same style, are they, as the drilling in Germany today?

"Mr. Kruppa: Exactly.

"Mr. Dickstein: What is their purpose? What are they playing, soldier boy, or what? Why do they have to get up early in the morning to march in the fields and parade? And some of them have guns, and some have wooden guns. What is the purpose of it? What are they going to accomplish by it, if you know?

"Mr. Kruppa: I know. Their purpose is to keep up a certain spirit of showing a union. That is why they have the same uniforms and march and develop themselves physically. But this side is rather the stupid side of it, as I might call it. The more successful part of it is getting into politics and bringing their members into the police force as well.

"The Chairman: Mr. Dickstein asked you about storm troops.

"Mr. Kruppa: That is just an exercising for them.

"The Chairman: Is that a part of the general plan to further the movement in this country?

"Mr. Kruppa: Yes.

"The Chairman: The theory being to bring about an obedience of mind to the state, and make the individual a server of the state rather than the state a server of the individual?

"Mr. Kruppa: You might reframe it, Mr. Chairman?

"The Chairman: The storm troops, these drills and everything, that is a part of the Nazi movement?

"Mr. Kruppa: Yes.

"The Chairman: The same thing is carried on in the Nazi Party in Germany?

"Mr. Kruppa: Yes.

"The Chairman: The storm troopers are in a sense one of the bulwarks of the party; is that right?

"Mr. Kruppa: Correct.

"Mr. Dickstein: If the purpose of this group, the storm troops in the United States, is physical training, why is it necessary in the early mornings to carry the big swastika flag? Are those the orders also from Germany, that the flag be kept during the parade?

"Mr. Kruppa: There is no direct order to that extent.

"Mr. Dickstein: But they do carry the swastika flag?

"Mr. Kruppa: Of course.

"Mr. Dickstein: And they salute the swastika flag?

"Mr. Kruppa: Of course.

"Mr. Dickstein: There is no American flag carried during this particular drill and particular parade, is there, so far as you know?

"Mr. Kruppa: Sometimes they carry a flag.

"Mr. Dickstein: Sometimes, you mean, when it is late in the afternoon? but I am talking about the early mornings.

"Mr. Kruppa: I do not know this.

"Mr. Dickstein: You do not know that. Where do they get the uniforms— the German uniforms?

"Mr. Kruppa: The original uniforms brought from Germany and the uniforms of the so-called "storm troopers," the pants are made by a tailor and the boots are bought, I suppose, in a shoe shop.

"Mr. Dickstein: The boots are brought from Germany or bought here?

"Mr. Kruppa: Bought here.

"Mr. Dickstein: What is brought in from Germany?

"Mr. Kruppa: The steel helmets uniforms and the old storm troopers' uniforms.

"Mr. Dickstein: Are they smuggled in, or do they openly bring them in and pay duty on them?

"Mr. Kruppa: I do not know that.

"Mr. Dickstein: You have seen these uniforms in the United States, have you?

"Mr. Kruppa: Yes.

"Mr. Dickstein: By the hundreds?

"Mr. Kruppa: I could not give any number.

"Mr. Dickstein: Did you see any of their parades?

"Mr. Kruppa: With the Friends of New Germany; yes.

"Mr. Dickstein: They have another leader at the head of that parade. Are these people citizens of the United States?

"Mr. Kruppa: No; very few.

"Mr. Dickstein: Were you down to the German consul? Do you know a Father Gross? Did you ever hear of him?

"Mr. Kruppa: Yes; I know him.

"Mr. Dickstein: This is the Father Gross that appeared before this committee. Were you ever down to the consul's office when Father Gross was there?

"Mr. Kruppa: No. I met him the first time in Colonel Emerson's office.

"Mr. Dickstein: Emerson is also a man that has been connected with this movement in this country?

"Mr. Kruppa: To some extent; yes.

"Mr. Dickstein: Emerson was the man who originally formed the Friends of Germany?

"Mr. Kruppa: Yes.

"Mr. Dickstein: Then, when the Friends of New Germany came along, that organization was absorbed by the Friends of New Germany?

"Mr. Kruppa: No.

"Mr. Dickstein: Emerson, however, has an office right near the consul's office?

"Mr. Kruppa: He had one.

"Mr. Dickstein: He had one?

"Mr. Kruppa: Yes.

"Mr. Dickstein: Emerson was the "contact man," so-called, the American contact man for the Friends of New Germany movement in this country?

"Mr. Kruppa: I would rather say he was the testing point. He communicated the state of mind in the United States.

"Mr. Dickstein: Was that the same Emerson that was a spy during the war?

"Mr. Kruppa: I heard about it. He is the same man.

"The Chairman: A German spy?

"Mr. Dickstein: A German spy?

"Mr. Kruppa: I just know that he was allowed as the only American to be in the general staff of the German Army during the war.

"Mr. Dickstein: During the war?

"Mr. Kruppa: Yes.

"Mr. Dickstein: That is the same Emerson that was the person who made speeches in the groups of the Friends of New Germany?

"Mr. Kruppa: Yes; the same man.

"Mr. Dickstein: The same person?

"Mr. Kruppa: Absolutely.

"Mr. Dickstein: And the same person that was conducting certain public meetings in which he tried to entice Americans to come there and listen to him on Hitler?

"Mr. Kruppa: Yes.

"Mr. Dickstein: That is the same Emerson that had to a certain degree helped spread certain propaganda in this country on the Hitler philosophy?

"Mr. Kruppa: Yes.

"Mr. Dickstein: You agree then that the Hitler philosophy or the Hitler atmosphere in this country is absolutely un-American?

"Mr. Kruppa: Yes; I agree.

"Mr. Dickstein: It has no place here?

"Ms. Kruppa: Not within the structure of the United States.

"Mr. Dickstein: You promise this committee to keep off it?

"Mr. Kruppa: Yes.

"Mr. Dickstein: All right.

"The Chairman: Senator Hardwick, have you any questions to ask?

"Mr. Hardwick: Just one or two, Mr. Chairman. I think you gentlemen have covered the field so well that I will not repeat, but there are just one or two questions I want to clear up a little.

"I recall you said that Spanknoebel was kidnaped, according to your information, by a man named Feldman.

"Mr. Kruppa: Feldman.

"Mr. Hardwick: F-e-l-d-m-a-n?

"Mr. Kruppa: Yes.

"Mr. Hardwick: Who was an agent of the German Government or the German National Socialist Party, which?

"Mr. Kruppa: Both.

"Mr. Hardwick: Of both. And he was kidnaped from the home of Dr. Griebl?

"Mr. Kruppa: Yes.

"Mr. Hardwick: On October 27, 1933, and put on the steamer Europa that carried Lund, the secret-service agent of the German Government and party on that boat?

"Mr. Kruppa: Yes.

"Mr. Hardwick: Do you know why he was kidnaped?

"Mr. Kruppa: Yes. He disobeyed orders from abroad. He had received a telegram to withdraw from the movement, but for some possible human reason he continued.

"Mr. Hardwick: The night he was kidnaped was just the night before the indictment against him was returned to the United States court, was it not?

"Mr. Kruppa: I think the subpena was given, if I am not mistaken, October 27, and the same night Spanknoebel was kidnaped, and the 28th or 29th, the same month—

"Mr. Hardwick: I am talking about the indictment.

"Mr. Dickstein: Not the subpena.

"Mr. Kruppa: Did it come on—

Mr. Hardwick: The next day.

"Mr. Dickstein: That is right.

"Mr. Hardwick: The next day the indictment was returned in court as a true bill.

"You say this Feldman was an agent of the German Government who took him away from this country?

"Mr. Kruppa: Yes.

"Mr. Hardwick: They secreted him on this boat?

"Mr. Kruppa: Yes.

"Mr. Hardwick: And took him back to Germany. You mentioned the name of a place in Germany where he is located now.

"Mr. Kruppa: Yes.

"Mr. Hardwick: That name is what?

"Mr. Kruppa: Wuerzburg.

"Mr. Hardwick: What is he doing at that place; do you know?

"Mr. Kruppa: Yes.

"Mr. Hardwick: What?

"Mr. Kruppa: He is the business manager of the Division Franconia East and West.

"Mr. Hardwick: What is that? I do not understand.

"Mr. Kruppa: Franconia is like a province. We would say Maine and Dixie. And he is also the political leader of Division East, Franconia.

"Mr. Hardwick: In whose employ is he now?

"Mr. Kruppa: Julius Streicher is the head of that.

"Mr. Hardwick: Is that a Government agency?

"Mr. Kruppa: They are synonymous. Government and party.

"Mr. Hardwick: He is an agent either of the Government or the party in Germany now?

"Mr. Kruppa: Yes.

"Mr. Hardwick: Of this place you mentioned?

"Mr. Kruppa: Yes.

"Mr. Hardwick: He is stationed there?

"Mr. Kruppa: Yes.

"Mr. Hardwick: All right. How do you know this?

"Mr. Kruppa: I have received publications of Spanknoebel on that account, and they were received in America, and I have seen it myself.

"The Chairman: How recently?

"Mr. Kruppa: As early as in April.

"The Chairman: As long ago as in April? And how recently since then in time?

"Mr. Kruppa: I had connections up as late as in early August this year.

"Mr. Hardwick: As late as August, this year, he was at that place and in the employ of the German National Socialist Party?

"Mr. Kruppa: Socialist government; yes.

"Mr. Hardwick: In the capacity you have named. Have you heard of him changing, going any place else? Have you heard of him since then?

"Mr. Kruppa: No.

"Mr. Hardwick: You have not heard of him since August. Now, I recall, you stated that individuals in this country were put in fear of their lives after the commission of deeds for the organization here, or were threatened if they did not perform certain tasks that had been assigned to them they would be punished, and that these threats are not only to those here but to relatives in Germany. Is that right?

"Mr. Kruppa: Yes.

"Mr. Hardwick: Do I get it right?

"Mr. Kruppa: Yes.

"Mr. Hardwick: I understood you to say that something like that had been done in your own case. Am I right about that?

"Mr. Kruppa: Yes.

"Mr. Hardwick: What happened to you? Let us get down to the facts.

"Mr. Kruppa: While I was publishing the Jungsturm, a small weekly paper, I received an order from Gissibl and a certain Eberhard von Nasse, and also some other men, to discontinue. I saw no reason in it. Later on letters were published and sent to people and business men here in New York discrediting me and telling them that they were advised not to advertise any more in my paper.

"Mr. Hardwick: All right, we understand that. Now, did they do anything to your people in Germany about it?

"Mr. Kruppa: No.

"Mr. Hardwick: You do know of instances, however, where they have taken it out on relatives in Germany of people here who have not obeyed orders?

"Mr. Kruppa: Of course, it is an official order.

"Mr. Hardwick: What do they do to these relatives?

"Mr. Kruppa: They are immediately put in a concentration camp, if there are no reasons found, and they are investigated.

"Mr. Hardwick: They are put on suspicion, and sometimes put in concentration camps?

"Mr. Kruppa: Yes.

"Mr. Hardwick: Because some relative of theirs over in this country does not obey orders; is that correct?

"Mr. Kruppa: Yes.

"Mr. Hardwick: You know that to be true?

"Mr. Kruppa: Absolutely.

"Mr. Hardwick: Just one other question, then, I think, as far as I am concerned, the examination is complete. I understood the general tenor of your testimony to be that while this organization called the Friends of New Germany was camouflaged as an American organization, really its leaders were selected and its policies were dictated by the foreign division of the National Socialist Party of Germany in Germany. Is that right or not?

"Mr. Kruppa: Yes.

"Mr. Hardwick: That is all I care to ask him.

"The Chairman: Just one or two questions. You said in response to Senator Hardwick's questions that Spanknoebel now occupied a prominent position in the party in Germany.

"Mr. Kruppa: Yes.

"The Chairman: If he was forced to go back because they wanted him back in Germany, rather than have him compromise the party by disclosures—

"Mr. Kruppa: Yes.

"The Chairman: When he was forced last October, why is it that now he occupies a prominent position in the party over there?

"Mr. Kruppa: Because Spanknoebel, in the beginning, had personal fear on account of his disobedience, and reports have been going from America to Germany constantly discrediting Spanknoebel, such as already Spanknoebel discredited other leaders, for instance like Ludecke, and Ludecke, Hanfstaengl, and Hanfstaengl put Ludecke in jail, of couse, because either one wanted to be the leader. Hanfstaengl wanted to be the leader of the Friends of New Germany. Ludecke wanted to be the leader. Gissibl wanted to be the leader. Kappe wanted to be the leader. And by constantly discrediting each other, Spanknoebel had the natural fear of returning to Germany. And the conditions for Spanknoebel have been very bad in Germany until we cleared Spanknoebel of all suspicions through our Uschla meetings.

"The Chairman: Spanknoebel was discredited in Germany?

"Mr. Kruppa: Yes.

"The Chairman: Then, this Uschla meeting which cleared him over here was the meeting of January 23, 1934, that you have testified to?

"Mr. Kruppa: Yes.

"The Chairman: Was that the meeting that the Spanknoebel situation in this country was taken up by the Uschla meeting?

"Mr. Kruppa: Yes.

"The Chairman: The Uschla committee; and the report that was sent over there related to Spanknoebel?

"Mr. Kruppa: Yes.

"The Chairman: Your Uschla committee over here cleared him?

"Mr. Kruppa: Yes.

"The Chairman: You say that this contains the instructions to the storm troops?

"Mr. Kruppa: Yes.

"The Chairman: Where did that come from?

"Mr. Kruppa: From Germany.

"The Chairman: How did you get in?

"Mr. Kruppa: I got in through the storm troopers, and it comes over on the boat.

"The Chairman: Are those the instructions issued to the storm troopers of the United States?

"Mr. Kruppa: Yes.

"The Chairman: We will put that in as an exhibit. What does that say, starting out, Mr. Interpreter?

"Mr. Mueller: It is a list of commands to be given to the storm-troop formations, but it seems to be a general card and not particularly for any particular country.

"Mr. Hardwick: You can prepare a translation of that in English, can you not, to accompany the exhibit?

"The Chairman: Read it out loud.

"Mr. Kruppa: Shall I translate it? This is on page 6. It means arm movements. This arm movements, it means, are used instead of a commander when the noise of battle, and so forth, does not allow any verbal information. Therefore, a strong swinging of the hand and arm in front of the body means clearing the machine guns. So far that is one particular outline.

"The Chairman: That contains the instructions to storm troopers?

"Mr. Mueller: Under the general heading "Signs with your arms," "Signals with your arms."

"The Chairman: That will be introduced as an exhibit.

"*(The document was marked 'Exhibit 1.')*

"The Chairman: There was no change of conditions of leadership or breaks between the time of this alleged convention in the Friends of New Germany and the National Socialist Party, no orders came down for them to stop this movement in this country, as far as you know?

"Mr. Kruppa: As far as I know, later on, after the investigation was on, even previous, I should say, it was sent through Dr. Griebl to start within the German-American conference a so-called "cultural committee," in order to cultivate through means of enlightenment, not to say propaganda, educated people, so naturally, being just a stepping stone to success—

"The Chairman: What Mr. Dickstein means, as I understand it, the instructions are still being sent over from Germany. Is that right?

"Mr. Kruppa: Yes.

"Mr. Dickstein: The relationship between Germany and the Friends of New Germany and the alien sympathizers in this country is just the same as it was before?

"Mr. Kruppa: Absolutely.

"Mr. Dickstein: They were not told to stop?

"Mr. Kruppa: No.

"Mr. Dickstein: In my examining you, you have given me a number of exhibits. Will you contact the clerk before you leave and file the other exhibits that you referred to?

"Mr. Kruppa: Yes.

"Mr. Dickstein: As documents of this committee?

"Mr. Kruppa: I want to state, has this one document been filed?

"Mr. Dickstein: We will find it. I have it somewhere. But you contact Mr. Randolph, the clerk of this committee, and give him all your documents, which, I believe, we have checked and find that the testimony is pretty accurate.

"The Chairman: All right, Mr. Kruppa. Thank you.

"(Witness excused.)"

SUGGESTIONS FOR COMBATING UN-AMERICANISM

THE RED MOVEMENT must be met and overcome, but that cannot best be done by "viewing with alarm," "red-baiting," riding professional martyrs on a rail, and vainglorious "flag-waving." When an emergency calls for militant action in dealing with the Reds, the function properly belongs to constituted authority, which can always draw on the loyal citizenship of the country to carry out its mandate.

The greatest weapon with which to successfully combat Communism, and its kindred diseases, is education. Focus patriotic educational activities upon the foreign colonies in America. See that the boys and girls of this country are given a thorough understanding of the slowly developed and soundly tested principles on which the American government is founded so that they may be able to judge rightly between these and the airy ideas of the radicals.

Properly train the youth of this land and you not only accomplish a passing hurt to Communism, but you throw a safeguard around the next generation. Take an active, friendly interest in the boys of this country—teach them leadership and loyalty through such media as the school, Boy Scouting, R. O. T. C., C. M. T. C., and clean sports, and there can be no doubt as to their reaction to the approach of the economic fiction from the Communist and Fascist tongue and pen.

Many things in America need changing; things that served well in the past are outworn. With the growth of this country new needs have come. We are faced with heavy tasks and problems in going ahead with the development of America. The Communist and the Fascist move with a desire to blast away the fruits of the labor, toil and sacrifices of the generations which have gone before. Upon the wreckage and ruin, they would attempt to create a Fairyland or Utopia.

There is no short-cut to a better America. The path is confused by difficult, many-sided problems. The way does not lie over the ruins of the things that have made America great, but rather by continuous study and strong-hearted labor, building patiently on the work of those who have preceded us, where the work is sound, and replacing it where found faulty; replacement to be by methods provided by the Constitution. To do this, constant effort must be made to arouse the citizens of the country to a point where a greater percentage of them will interest themselves in government, take part in the councils of their party and go to the polls thoroughly informed on the issues at stake. In many places Legion Posts have established open forums to promote public discussion, for in this way may be solved the problems that confront the progress of the country.

Slowly but surely the people of the United States are beginning to realize the priceless value of the Constitution of the United States and the danger of carelessly departing from its spirit and purpose. The study of it in our schools, clubs, civic and commercial associations, forums and churches is worthy of consideration by every person living under the American Flag and on American soil.

Professional martyrs, who would weaken our National character and destroy our National ideals, want the field of discussion to themselves. Whenever a loyal American citizen or a patriotic group moves forward in the teaching of American ideals; arousing interest and love of country; pointing out the need of an adequate national defense; or striving to inculcate in the individual mind a patriotic sense of responsibility, to community, state and nation, the professional martyr and certain groups of self-styled intelligentia throw up their hands and shout aloud "super-patriot!"

This is the same group that would use the right of free speech as a screen to pollute the minds of our young, incite to crime, corrupt public morals and overthrow our government.

It is a fundamental principle that the freedom of speech which is secured by the Constitution of the United States does not confer an absolute right to speak without responsibility, whatever one may choose, or an unrestricted and unbridled license that gives immunity for every possible use of language and prevents the punishment of those who abuse this freedom. Freedom of speech does not protect disturbances to the public peace or the attempt to subvert the government. It does not protect publications or teachings which tend to subvert or imperil the government. In short, this freedom of speech does not deprive a State of the primary and essential right of self-preservation, which, so long as human governments endure, they cannot be denied.

The American Legion can never watch unconcerned the abuse of freedom of speech. Freedom of any kind to be a benefit rather than a curse must be used with intelligence, decency and a regard for the rights of others. If not, it will become discredited, refuted by the people, restricted by law and destroyed. The right of the entire nation to free speech may be endangered by the flagrant abuse of the right by a few. Already other liberties have been restricted because of their abuse. We, of the Legion, take our citizenship seriously. We do so because it came to us as a heritage from our fathers with privileges and opportunities known to the citizenship of no other nation in the history of the world and was earned for this generation by hard work and great sacrifice and sanctified by the blood of our comrades. We would be derelict in our duty if we would merely dig in and attempt to hold the ground that has been gained.

The Legion is ever working to keep America a place where there is political and economic justice for all; to keep it a country where occupation and industry offer opportunity to all its people, and where social conditions are such as to add to the pleasure and happiness of life.

In order that you may have a better understanding of the present conditions of government, of the deprivations of freedom as we know it, and of the hardships which form a daily part of the citizens of the Soviet Union, we would suggest that you read the following books:

"The Tragedy of Russia"
    By Will Durant
"The Terror in Europe"
    By Ziltman
"The Russian Crucifixion"
    By Mackenzie

"Stalin, The Career of a Fanatic"
    By Essad-By
"Kapoot"
    By Carveth Wells
"The Communist Shakes His Fist"
    By Bruce Reynolds

CONCLUSION

A number of individuals and organizations have been helpful to the National Americanism Commission in the compilation of this book, and it is the sincere desire of the compilers to give due recognition to them. Our thanks and appreciation is extended to the following:

The American Coalition
The American Federation of Labor
Associated Farmers of California
Elizabeth Dilling
Guernsey Frazer
Hon. Hamilton Fish, Jr.
The Fish Report on Un-American Activities
Hon. B. W. Gearhart
Louis Greenbaum
Nelson Hewitt
Dr. L. M. Herrington
The Lusk Report on Un-American Activities
Leon Lewis
The McCormack Report on Un-American Activities
Walter Reynolds
Walter Steele

Also to the many hundreds of Legionnaires who have kept the office of the National Americanism Commission in close touch with the activities of un-American groups in their communities. Many members of the American Legion Auxiliary and of the Forty and Eight have likewise presented evidence of value.

21330

INDEX

	Page
Affiliated and Sympathetic Groups	77
American Civil Liberties Union	90
America's Creed	1
American Fund for Public Service	77
American Student Union	134
American Writers' Congress	186
American Youth Congress	157
Amtorg Trading Corporation	84
Baldwin, Roger N.	90
Books and Literature	168
Book Shops	167
Browder Testimony	17
Champion of Youth	194
Church Publications	260
Communist, The	196
Communist Membership Book	41-43
Communist Party Districts	35
Communist Party Election Errors	46
Communist Party at the Polls	42
Communist Party's Stand on Violence	44
Communist Press	184
Communism vs. Religion	246
Communist Summer Schools	129
Communist Workers' Schools	180
Conclusion	286
Conditions of Admission to Communist Party	31
Constitution of Communist International	26
Co-operation with Pacifists	212
Daily Worker	186
Doctor Diagnoses Russia	243
Emancipation of Women	238
Fascism in the United States	266
Fifteen Years of Communist International	52
Ford Testimony	24
Foreign Language Publications	198
Foreword	5
Formation of Communist Party, U. S. A.	29
Foster, Wm. Z.—on Labor Unions	228
Freedom of Speech	8
Friends of the Soviet Union	87
History of the Communist Party	16
International Labor Defense	87
Labor Activities	224
League Against War and Fascism	140
League for Industrial Democracy	165

	Page
Legion Convention Mandates	11
Membership National Americanism Commission	10
Moscow's Subordinate Branches	15
Moscow Summer School	137
Municipal Employee, C. P. Branch	242
National Student League	132
Nazi-ism in the United States	269
New Masses	194
New Pioneer	194
Origin of the Young Communist League	105
Party Dues and Membership Requirements	40
Petition of Fellowship of Reconciliation	56
Program of Communist International	49
Recognition of Russia	55
Report of League Against War and Fascism Convention	148
Sabotage—The Way Out	257
Seventh World Congress Report by Browder	64
Southern Worker	192
Soviet Aviation	222
Soviet Constitution on Defense	223
Soviet Position on Strikes	240
Soviet Russia Today	197
Soviet Spy System in U. S. A.	204
Soviet Union Helps Spain	74
Strack, Celeste	138
Suggestions for Combating Un-Americanism	284
Sunday Abolished	248
Trade Relations with U. S. S. R.	56
Trade Union Unity League	239
Unemployed Councils	241
United Front	208
U. S. S. R. on National Defense	216
Ward, Dr. Harry F.	146
Western Worker	191
Why Communism?	50
Young Communist League	110
Young Communist League Organizers	122
Young Communist League Student Tieup	119
Young Pioneers	123
Young Worker	194
Youth Activity of Communists	105

Date Due

OCR 24 '67			
NOV '79			
MN 21 78			
	PRINTED	IN U. S. A.	